7 Day

LAW OF COMMONS AND OF TOWN AND VILLAGE GREENS

LAW OF COMMONS AND OF TOWN AND VILLAGE GREENS

Navjit Ubhi

Barry Denyer-Green

JORDANS

2004

Published by
Jordan Publishing Limited
21 St Thomas Street
Bristol BS1 6JS

British Library Cataloguing-in-Publication Data
A catalogue record for this book is available from the British Library.

ISBN 0 85308 821 7

Typeset by Jordan Publishing Limited
Printed in Great Britain by The Cromwell Press Ltd, Trowbridge, Wiltshire

PREFACE

The last few years have seen an increasing number of people develop an interest in the law relating to common land, and town or village greens. Some, such as lawyers, surveyors, local authorities and land agents, will have a professional interest; others, such as landowners and commoners, will have a practical interest. Therefore, although this book is aimed primarily at lawyers, we have tried to ensure that it remains accessible to the non-property specialist. Although we have tried to state the law as at 10 December 2003, we have nevertheless been able to take into account the recent case of *Oxfordshire County Council v Oxford City Council* [2004] EWHC 12 (CH) which has resulted in a substantial revision of Chapters 8 and 9.

Navjit Ubhi
Barry Denyer-Green
December 2003

CONTENTS

		Page
Preface		v
Table of cases		xvii
Table of statutes		xxiii
Table of statutory instruments and guidance		xxvii
Glossary		xxix

Chapter 1   BACKGROUND — 1

1.1   INTRODUCTION — 1
1.2   WHAT IS COMMON LAND? — 1
1.3   WHAT ARE RIGHTS OF COMMON? — 2
1.4   WHAT ARE TOWN AND VILLAGE GREENS? — 3
1.5   FACTUAL BACKGROUND — 4
1.6   HISTORICAL BACKGROUND — 4
1.7   COMMONS REGISTRATION ACT 1965 — 5
1.8   FUTURE DEVELOPMENTS — 7
    1.8.1   Rights of common — 7
    1.8.2   Fencing and other works — 7
    1.8.3   Town and village greens — 8
        (a)   Parking — 8
        (b)   Private rights of vehicular access — 9

Chapter 2   HISTORICAL DEVELOPMENT — 11

2.1   INTRODUCTION — 11
2.2   PRE-1066 — 11
    2.2.1   The importance of agricultural practices — 11
        (a)   The rural economy — 12
        (b)   The open-field systems — 13
        (c)   Royal Commission Report on Common Land — 13
    2.2.2   The Celts — 14
    2.2.3   Anglo-Saxon period — 15
2.3   NORMAN CONQUEST — 17
    2.3.1   Manorial courts — 19
    2.3.2   Approvement — 20
2.4   INCLOSURE MOVEMENTS — 21
    2.4.1   Changes in agricultural practices — 21
2.5   LEISURE AND RECREATION — 22

Chapter 3   **CLASSIFICATION OF COMMON LANDS**   25

3.1   INTRODUCTION   25
3.2   MANORIAL WASTE   25
3.3   COMMONABLE LANDS AND SIMILAR RIGHTS   27
    3.3.1   Commonable lands   27
    3.3.2   Lammas lands or half-year lands   27
    3.3.3   Shack   29
    3.3.4   Stinted pastures   29
    3.3.5   Regulated pastures   30
    3.3.6   Commons Registration Act 1965   30
3.4   THE OLD ROYAL FORESTS   31

Chapter 4   **CLASSIFICATION OF RIGHTS OF COMMON**   33

4.1   INTRODUCTION   33
    4.1.1   Effect of the Commons Registration Act 1965   33
4.2   CLASSIFICATION OF RIGHTS OF COMMON   34
    4.2.1   The forms of landownership and rights of common   35
    4.2.2   Rights of common as legal interests   35
    4.2.3   Rights of common classified by legal form   36
        (a)   Rights of common appendant   37
        (b)   Rights of common appurtenant   38
        (c)   Right of common in gross   38
        (d)   Rights of common by reason of vicinage   39
4.3   RIGHTS OF COMMON OF PASTURE   40
    4.3.1   Rights of common of pasture appendant   41
        (a)   Registration   41
        (b)   Origin and creation   41
        (c)   Limitation on numbers of animals   42
        (d)   Type of animals   42
        (e)   Miscellaneous characteristics   43
    4.3.2   Rights of common of pasture appurtenant   43
        (a)   Customary freeholds and copyholds   44
        (b)   Registration   44
    4.3.3   Right of common *pur cause de vicinage*   44
    4.3.4   Common of pasture in gross   45
    4.3.5   Right of foldcourse   45

4.4	COMMON OF TURBARY	45
4.5	COMMON OF ESTOVERS	46
4.6	COMMON OF PISCARY	46
4.7	COMMON IN THE SOIL	47
4.8	COMMON IN PANNAGE	47
4.9	RIGHTS OF SOLE	48
	4.9.1 General meaning	48
	4.9.2 Vesture	48
	4.9.3 Herbage	49
	4.9.4 Pasture	49
	4.9.5 Other sole rights	49
	4.9.6 Commons Registration Act 1965	49

Chapter 5 OWNERSHIP OF COMMON LAND 51

5.1	INTRODUCTION	51
5.2	LORD OF THE MANOR	51
5.3	OWNERSHIP OF THE SOIL OF COMMON LAND	53
	5.3.1 Powers of leasing	54
	5.3.2 Right to grant grazing rights	54
	5.3.3 Grazing for the owner's animals	54
	5.3.4 Trees, timber and woodland	55
	5.3.5 Rights to game	55
	5.3.6 Warrens	55
	5.3.7 Rights to minerals	56
	5.3.8 Right to drive	56
	5.3.9 Prescription or custom	56
	5.3.10 Right of approvement	56
	5.3.11 Wayleaves and easements	57
5.4	COMMONABLE LANDS	57
5.5	EASEMENTS OVER COMMON LAND	58

Chapter 6 CREATION AND TRANSFER OF RIGHTS OF COMMON 61

6.1	INTRODUCTION	61
6.2	CREATION	62
	6.2.1 Custom	62
	(a) Custom and copyholders	62
	(b) Custom and the common law	64
	6.2.2 Express grant	64
	(a) Formal requirements	64
	(b) Competence of the grantor	65
	(c) Exclusive right of grazing	65
	6.2.3 Reservation	65
	6.2.4 Prescription	66
	(a) Prescription at common law	67

		(b) Lost modern grant	67
		(c) The Prescription Act 1832	68
6. 3		THE COMMONS REGISTRATION ACT 1965	68
	6.3.1	Express grant of rights of common over registered commons	69
	6.3.2	Grant of new rights over land not registered as common land	70
	6.3.3	Acquisition of rights by prescription and the Commons Registration Act 1965	70
		(a) Registered commons	70
		(b) Rights acquired by prescription over land not registered as common land	71
6.4		TRANSFER	71
6.5		STATUTE	72
6.6		PROTECTION OF RIGHTS OF COMMON	72
	6.6.1	Extent of rights of common	73
	6.6.2	Liability for damage to the soil	73
	6.6.3	Legal remedies for interference with rights of common	73
		(a) The scope of likely interference	73
		(b) Overstocking by other commoners	74
		(c) Physical obstruction	74
	6.6.4	Self-help abatement	74
	6.6.5	Statutory remedies	75

Chapter 7   INCLOSURE AND EXTINGUISHMENT OF RIGHTS OF COMMON   77

7.1		INTRODUCTION	77
7.2		EXTINGUISHMENT WITHIN THE CONTROL OF THE PARTIES	77
	7.2.1	Unity of ownership	77
	7.2.2	Abandonment and non-use	78
	7.2.3	Express release	79
7.3		BY STATUTE	79
	7.3.1	Generally	79
	7.3.2	Commons Registration Act 1965	80
7.4		INCLOSURE	80
	7.4.1	Inclosure before 1845	80
	7.4.2	Inclosure post-1845	81
		(a) Inclosure Act 1845	81
		(b) Commons Act 1876	83
		(c) Inclosure today	83

Chapter 8 **REGISTRATION OF COMMON LAND AND RIGHTS OF COMMON** 85

8.1 INTRODUCTION 85
8.2 REGISTRATION: COMMONS 86
    8.2.1 Registration 86
    8.2.2 Meaning of common land and rights of common 86
        (a) Common land 86
        (b) Rights of common 87
    8.2.3 Land subject to rights of common 88
    8.2.4 Waste land of the manor not subject to rights of common 88
8.3 REGISTRATION: TOWN OR VILLAGE GREENS 91
8.4 REGISTRATION PROCESS 92
    8.4.1 The registration authorities 92
    8.4.2 The Registers 93
    8.4.3 Original application and provisional registration 93
    8.4.4 Notification and objections to registration 94
    8.4.5 Exemptions 94
    8.4.6 Quantification of grazing rights 95
    8.4.7 Subsequent registration under the Land Registration Acts 95
8.5 EFFECT OF REGISTRATION 95
    8.5.1 Effect of provisional registration 95
    8.5.2 Effect of final registration 96
8.6 EFFECT OF FAILURE TO REGISTER 97
    8.6.1 Unregistered rights no longer exercisable 97
        (a) Rights of common 97
        (b) Town and village greens 99
    8.6.2 Unclaimed land: town or village green 99
    8.6.3 Unclaimed land: common land 100
8.7 AMENDMENTS, RECTIFICATIONS AND NEW COMMONS 100
    8.7.1 The amendment of registers 100
    8.7.2 Creation of rights of common after 31 July 1970 101
    8.7.3 Town or village greens 103
    8.7.4 New common land and land registration 103
    8.7.5 Applications to register new commons and greens 104

	8.7.6	Land ceasing to be common land and alterations to rights of common	106
	8.7.7	Rectification	107
	8.7.8	Dwelling-houses and rectification	107
8.8	COMMONS COMMISSIONERS AND APPEALS		108

Chapter 9   TOWN AND VILLAGE GREENS   111

9.1	INTRODUCTION		111
9.2	REGISTRATION OF GREENS UNDER THE COMMONS REGISTRATION ACT 1965		113
	9.2.1	Registration	113
	9.2.2	Effect of non-registration	115
	9.2.3	New greens	115
9.3	CLASS A: ALLOTTED LAND		116
9.4	CLASS B: CUSTOMARY RIGHTS TO INDULGE IN LAWFUL SPORTS AND PASTIMES		117
	9.4.1	Local inhabitants	118
	9.4.2	Ancient, certain, reasonable and continuous	120
	9.4.3	Nature of the activities	121
	9.4.4	Conclusions	121
9.5	CLASS C: USE OF LAND FOR LAWFUL SPORTS AND PASTIMES AS OF RIGHT FOR 20 YEARS		122
	9.5.1	Deficiencies in requirements for customary rights	122
	9.5.2	Significant number of inhabitants	122
	9.5.3	Any locality or neighbourhood within a locality	123
	9.5.4	As of right	123
	9.5.5	20-year period and lack of continuity	125
	9.5.6	Lawful sports and pastimes	126
	9.5.7	Effect of registration of green based on 20 years of public use	127
9.6	REGULATION AND PROTECTION		127
	9.6.1	Ownership	127
	9.6.2	Effect of rights of common	128
	9.6.3	Management powers and duties	129
		(a) Metropolitan Commons Acts 1866 – 1878	129
		(b) Commons Act 1899	129
		(c) Open Spaces Act 1906	130
		(d) Criminal offences: nuisance and inclosure	130

| | 9.6.4 | Buildings and other works on town or village greens | 131 |
| | 9.6.5 | Driving on greens | 132 |

Chapter 10 PUBLIC ACCESS TO COMMONS 133

10.1	INTRODUCTION		133
10.2	COMMON LAW RIGHTS OF ACCESS TO COMMONS		134
	10.2.1	Easement of recreation	134
	10.2.2	Customary rights	135
10.3	COUNTRYSIDE AND RIGHTS OF WAY ACT 2000 (CROW ACT 2000)		136
	10.3.1	Rights of access	137
	10.3.2	Exceptions	138
	10.3.3	Restrictions	139
	10.3.4	Additional land open to access	141
	10.3.5	By-laws	141
	10.3.6	Mapping of open country	141
	10.3.7	Representations against maps	142
	10.3.8	Consultations	143
	10.3.9	Confirmation of maps	144
	10.3.10	Appeals	144
	10.3.11	Maps in conclusive form	145
10.4	SECTION 193 OF LAW OF PROPERTY ACT 1925		145
	10.4.1	Definition of a common under s 193	146
	10.4.2	Metropolitan commons	147
	10.4.3	Borough or urban commons	147
	10.4.4	Rural common subject to dedication	148
	10.4.5	Extent of rights of public access	148
	10.4.6	Effect of subsequent legislation	149
10.5	ADDITIONAL STATUTORY RIGHTS OF ACCESS		150
	10.5.1	Commons Act 1876	150
	10.5.2	Commons Act 1899	150
	10.5.3	National Parks and Access to the Countryside Act 1949	151
10.6	LOCAL ACTS		151

Chapter 11 REGULATION AND MANAGEMENT OF COMMON LANDS 153

11.1	INTRODUCTION	153
11.2	MANAGEMENT BY THE OWNER OF THE SOIL	153
11.3	REGULATION OF NON-METROPOLITAN COMMONS	154
11.4	REGULATION OF METROPOLITAN COMMONS	155

11.5 REGULATION OF COMMONS UNDER THE
COMMONS ACT 1899 156
    11.5.1 Commons Act 1908 156
11.6 LOCAL REGULATION OF COMMONS 157
11.7 NATURE RESERVES AND SITES OF SPECIAL
SCIENTIFIC INTEREST 157
    11.7.1 Notification 157
    11.7.2 Special orders 158
    11.7.3 Effect of sites of special scientific
interest 158
    11.7.4 Future developments 159
11.8 THE COUNTRYSIDE AND RIGHTS OF WAY ACT
2000 (CROW ACT 2000) 160
11.9 FENCES ON COMMONS 161
    11.9.1 Duty to fence 161
    11.9.2 Right to erect fences 161
11.10 DRIVING VEHICLES OVER COMMON LAND 162
11.11 NATIONAL TRUST COMMON LAND 163

**Chapter 12 COMPULSORY ACQUISITION AND COMMON
LANDS** 165

12.1 INTRODUCTION 165
12.2 COMPULSORY ACQUISITION OF LAND 166
    12.2.1 Certificate excluding special
Parliamentary procedure 166
    12.2.2 Exchange land 168
    12.2.3 Special Parliamentary procedure 168
12.3 ACQUISITION OF RIGHTS OVER COMMONS 169
12.4 COMPENSATION FOR THE FREEHOLD 170
    12.4.1 Value of land taken 170
    12.4.2 Injurious affection and severance
compensation 172
    12.4.3 Payment of compensation and
conveyance 172
12.5 COMPENSATION FOR THE COMMONERS 173
    12.5.1 Meeting of commoners 173
    12.5.2 Exchange land 174
    12.5.3 Valuation of rights of common 174
    12.5.4 Disputes 175
    12.5.5 Effect of payment of compensation 175

Appendix　**LEGISLATION**　　　　　　　　　　**177**

COMMONS REGISTRATION ACT 1965　　　　　179
LAW OF PROPERTY ACT 1925, ss 193–194　　192
INCLOSURE ACT 1857, s 12　　　　　　　　195
COMMONS ACT 1876, s 29　　　　　　　　196
COUNTRYSIDE AND RIGHTS OF WAY ACT 2000,
　　ss 1–46, 68, and Schs 1–4　　　　　　197
COMMONS REGULATION (GENERAL)
　　REGULATIONS 1966, SI 1966/1471　　　241
COMMONS REGULATION (NEW LAND)
　　REGULATIONS 1969, SI 1969/1843　　　260
VEHICULAR ACCESS ACROSS COMMON AND
　　OTHER LAND (ENGLAND) REGULATIONS
　　2002, SI 2002/ 1711　　　　　　　　293

INDEX　　　　　　　　　　　　　　　　301

TABLE OF CASES

References are to paragraph numbers

A-G v Hanmer (1858) 27 LJ Ch 837, 31 LTOS 379, 22 JP 543   5.3.1, 8.2.4, 10.4.1
A-G v Reynolds [1911] 2 KB 888, 80 LJKB 1073, 104 LT 852   4.5
A-G for British Colombia v A-G for Canada [1914] AC 153, 83 LJPC 169,
     30 TLR 144, PC   4.6
Addington v Clode (1775) 2 Wm Bl 989, 19 Digest (Repl) 66   6.2.4(a)
Anderson v Bostock [1976] 1 Ch 312, [1976] 3 WLR 590,
     [1976] 1 All ER 560   6.2.2(c)
Arlett v Ellis (1827) 7 B&C 346, 9 Dow & Ry KB 897,
     5 LJOSKB 301   5.3.2, 5.3.3, 5.3.10, 6.6.4, 7.4.1
Atkinson v Teesdale (1772) 2 Wm BL 817, 3 Wils 278   5.3

Bakewell Management Ltd v Brandwood [2003] EWCA Civ 23,
     [2003] 1 WLR 1429, [2003] 09 EG 198; *sub nom* Brandwood v
     Bakewell Management Ltd [2003] 1 P&CR 424, CA   5.5, 6.2.4(b)
Baring v Abbingdon (1892) 2 Ch 374, 62 LJ Ch 105, 8 TLR 576, CA   4.3.1(e)
Baten's Case (1610) 9 Co Rep 54b, 36 Digest (Repl) 302   6.6.4
Baylis v Tyssen-Amhurst (1877) 6 ChD 500, 46 LJ Ch 718, 37 LT 493   3.3.2
Benn v Hardinge (1992) 66 P&CR 246, [1992] NPC 129, (1992) *The Times*,
     October 13, CA   7.2.2
Bennett v Reeve (1740) Willes 227, 4 Vin Abr 583 pl 6   6.4
Benson v Chester (1799) 8 Term Rep 396, [1775-1802] All ER Rep 601   7.2.3
Besley v John [2003] All ER D 481 (Oct), (2003) SJ October 29   4.3
Bettison v Langton; *sub nom* Bettison v Penton [2001] UKHL 24,
     [2002] 1 AC 27, [2001] 2 WLR 1605, [2001] 3 All ER 417, HL   4.2.3(c), 4.3.2, 11.7.3
Betts v Thompson (1871) 6 Ch App 732, 25 LT 363, 19 WR 1100   5.3.10
Bourke v Davis (1889) 44 ChD 110, 38 WR 167, 62 LT 34   9.4.1
Box Parish Council v Lacey [1980] Ch 109, [1979] 2 WLR 177, [1979] 1 All ER 113,
     CA   8.2.4
Brandwood v Bakewell Management Ltd. See Bakewell Management Ltd v
     Brandwood
Britford Common, Re [1977] 1 WLR 39, [1977] 1 All ER 532,
     (1976) 33 P&CR 377   8.2.4
Bryant v Foot (1868) LR 3 QB 497, 37 LJQB 217, 32 JP 516, Ex Ch   6.2.4(a)
Bunn v Channen (1813) 5 Taunt 244   4.2.3(c), 6.4
Burton v Winters [1993] 1 WLR 1077, [1993] 3 All ER 847, CA   6.6.4

Carr v Lambert (1866) LR 1 Ex Ch 168, 35 LJ Ex 121, 30 JP 181, Ex Ch   4.3.1(b), 7.2.2
Central Electricity Generating Board v Clwyd County Council
     [1976] 1 WLR 151, [1976] 1 All ER 251, (1975) 31 P&CR 238   8.6.1, 10.4.6
Cheesman v Hardham (1818) 1 B & Ald 706   3.3.3
Chesterfield (Lord) v Harris [1908] 2 Ch 397, 77 LJ Ch 688, 24 TLR 763, CA   4.6
Chewton Common, Christchurch, Re; Borough of Christchurch v Milligan
     [1977] 1 WLR 1242, [1977] 3 All ER 509, (1977) 35 P&CR 220   8.2.4
Chilton v Corporation of London (1878) 7 Ch D 562, 47 LJ Ch 433, 26 WR 627   4.8
Clarkson v Woodhouse (1782) 5 Term Rep 412n, 101 ER 231   4.3.2(a), 4.4

Clayton v Corby (1843) 5 QB 415, 14 LJQB 364, 8 Jur 212   4.6
Coaker v Willcocks [1911] 1 KB 649; *aff'd* [1911] 2 KB 124, 80 LJKB 1026,
    27 TLR 357, CA   11.9.1
Commissioners of Sewers v Glasse (1874) LR 19 Eq 134, 44 LJ Ch 129,
    31 LT 495   4.2.3(d)
Cooper v Marshall (1757) 1 Burr 259, 2 Keny 1, [1558-1774] All ER Rep 300   6.6.4
Co-operative Wholesale Society v British Railway Board [1995] NPC 200,
    (1995) *The Times*, December 20, CA   6.6.4
Corbet's Case (1585) 7 Co Rep 5a, 77 ER 417   3.3.3
Corpus Christi College, Oxford v Gloucestershire County Council
    [1983] QB 360, [1982] 3 WLR 849, [1982] 3 All ER 995, CA   8.5.2, 8.6.1, 8.7.5
Cowlam v Slack (1812) 15 East 108, [1803-13] All ER Rep 583   6.2.4(b)
Cox v Glue (1848) 5 CB 533, 12 Jur 185, 136 ER 987   4.9.4
Cresstock Investments Ltd v Commons Commissioner [1992] 1 WLR 1088,
    [1993] 1 All ER 213, [1992] NPC 70   8.7.7
Crow v Wood [1971] 1 QB 77, [1970] 3 WLR 516, [1970] 3 All ER 425, CA   11.9.1

Duncan v Louch (1845) 6 QB 904, 14 LJQB 185, 9 Jur 346   10.2.1
Dunraven (Earl) v Llewellyn (1850) 15 QB 791, 19 LJQB 388,
    15 LTOS 543, Ex Ch   4.2.3(a)
Dynevor (Lord) v Richardson [1995] Ch 173, [1994] 3 WLR 1091,
    [1995] 1 All ER 109, ChD   6.2.4(b), 6.3.3(a), 8.6.1

Earl de la Warr v Miles (1881) 17 Ch D 535, 50 LJ Ch 754, [1881-5] All ER Rep 252,
    CA   4.5, 4.9.3, 6.2.4(b), 6.2.4(c)
Earl Pembroke's Case Case (1636) Clay 47   4.5
Edwards v Jenkins [1896] 1 Ch 308, 65 LJ Ch 222, 60 JP 167   9.4.1
Egerton v Harding [1975] QB 62, [1974] 3 WLR 437, [1974] 3 All ER 689, CA   11.9.1
Ellenborough Park, Re; Davies decd, Re; Powell v Maddison [1956] 1 Ch 131,
    [1955] 3 WLR 892, [1955] 3 All ER 667, CA   10.2.1
Ewart v Graham (1859) 7 HL Cas 331, 29 LJ Ex 88, 23 JP 483, HL   5.3, 5.3.5, 5.5

Farmor v Hunt (1611) Yelv 201, Cro Jac 271; *sub nom* Farmer v Hunt
    80 ER 132   6.6.2
Fitch v Fitch (1797) 2 Esp 543   9.6.2
Fitch v Rawling (1795) 2 H Bl 393, [1775-1802] All ER Rep 571   9.4.1, 9.4.3
Fitzgerald v Firbank [1897] 2 Ch 96, 66 LJ Ch 529,
    [1895-9] All ER Rep 445, CA   6.6.3(c)
Fitzhardinge (Lord) v Percell [1908] 2 Ch 139, 77 LJ Ch 529, 99 LT 154   5.3.6
Freeman v Middlesex County Council (1965) 16 P&CR 253   12.5.2

Gateward's Case (1607) 6 Co Rep 59b, [1558-1774] All ER Rep 48; *sub nom* Smith
    v Gatewood Cro Jac 152   4.7
Greenwich London Borough Council v Secretary of State for the Environment
    [1993] Env LR 344   12.2.1
Gressill v Hoddesden (1608) Yelv 143, 80 ER 96   5.3.6
Gullet v Lopes (1811) 13 East 348, 104 ER 404   4.3.3

Hall v Byron (1877) 4 Ch D 667, 46 LJ Ch 297, 36 LT 367   4.3.2(a)
Hall v Nottingham (1875) 1 Ex D 1, 45 LJQB 50, 33 LT 697   9.4, 9.4.3
Hammerton v Honey (1876) 24 WR 603, 17 Digest
    (Reissue) 5   6.2.1(b), 6.2.4, 9.4.1, 9.4.2

Hampshire County Council v Milburn [1991] 1 AC 325, [1990] 2 WLR 1240,
    [1990] 2 All ER 257, HL   3.2, 4.2, 8.2.4, 10.4.1
Hanning v Top Deck Travel Group Ltd (1993) 68 P&CR 14, [1993] EGCS 84,
    [1993] NPC 73, CA   5.5, 6.2.4(b)
Heath v Deane [1905] 2 Ch 86, 74 LJ Ch 466, 92 LT 643   4.7
Hope v Osborne [1913] 2 Ch 349, 82 LJ Ch 457, 109 LT 41   5.3.4, 6.6.4
Hoskins v Robins (1671) 2 Wms Saund 324, 85 ER 1123   4.9.1

Jackson v Mulvaney. *See* Mulvaney v Gough
Jones v Robin (1847) 10 QB 620, 17 LJQB 121, 116 ER 235, Ex Ch   4.2.3(d)

King v Brown, Durant & Co [1913] 2 Ch 416, 82 LJ Ch 548, 29 TLR 691   6.6.3(c)
Kirby v Sadgrove (1797) 1 Bos & P 13, 3 Anst 892, 145 ER 1073   6.6.4

Land at Freshfields, Re (1993) 66 P&CR 9, 91 LGR 502, [1993] NPC 15   8.7.7
Lay v Norfolk County Council [1997] 37 RVR 9, Lands Tribunal   12.5.2
Leicester Forest Case (1607) Cro Jac 155   3.4
Lemmon v Webb [1894] 3 Ch 1, 58 JP 716, 63 LJ Ch 570, CA   6.6.4
Lewis v Mid Glamorgan County Council [1995] 1 WLR 313, [1995]
    1 All ER 760, 93 LGR 179, HL   7.3.1, 8.2.4, 12.5.5
Lewis v Mid Glamorgan County Council. *See* Mid Glamorgan County Council v
    Ogwr Borough Council
Lockwood v Wood (1844) 6 QB 64   10.2.2
Lonsdale (Earl) v Rigg. *See* Rigg v Earl of Lonsdale
Luttrel's Case (1601) 4 Co Rep 84b   4.5

Mason v Clarke [1955] AC 778, [1955] 2 WLR 853, [1955] 1 All ER 914, HL   6.2.2(a)
Maxwell v Martin (1830) 6 Bing 522, 8 LJOSCP 174, 130 ER 1382   4.4
McKay v The City of London Corporation (1966) 17 P&CR 264, [1966] JPL 652,
    199 EG 358, Lands Tribunal   12.5.2
Mellor v Spateman (1669) 1 Saund 339; *sub nom* Mellor v Staples 1 Mod Rep 6;
    sub nom Miller v Spateman 2 Keb 527, 550, 570   4.3.4, 5.3
Mellor v Staples. *See* Mellor v Spateman
Mercer v Denne [1904] 2 Ch 534, 74 LJ Ch 71, [1904-7] All ER Rep 71; *aff'd*
    [1905] 2 Ch 538, 74 LJ Ch 723, [1904-7] All ER Rep 74   3.2, 6.2.4, 9.4, 9.4.3
Mid Glamorgan County Council v Ogwr Borough Council; *sub nom*
    Lewis v Mid Glamorgan County Council [1995] 1 WLR 313,
    [1995] 1 All ER 760, 93 LGR 179, HL   7.3.1, 8.2.4
Miles v Etteridge (1692) 1 Show 349   7.2.3
Mill v New Forest Commissioners (1856) 18 CB 60, 25 LJCP 212, 20 JP 375   6.2.4(b)
Miller v Spateman. *See* Mellor v Spateman
Ministry of Defence v Wiltshire County Council [1995] 4 All ER 931,
    [1995] NPC 78, ChD   9.4.1, 9.5.1, 9.5.3, 9.5.5, 10.2.2
Moffett v Brewer (1848) Iowa 1 Greene 348   6.6.4
Moore v Rawson (1824) 3 B&C 332, 5 Dow & Ry KB 234, 3 LJOSKB 32   7.2.2
Mulvaney v Gough; *sub nom* Mulvaney v Jackson; Jackson v Mulvaney [2002]
    EWCA Civ 1078, [2002] 3 EGLR 72, [2002] 44 EG 175, (2002) 99(38)
    LSG 34, CA   10.2.1
Mulvaney v Jackson. *See* Mulvaney v Gough
Musgrove v Inclosure Commissioners (1874) LR 9 QB 162, 43 LJQB 80,
    30 LT 160   4.3.1(e)

Neaverson v Peterborough RDC [1902] 1 Ch 557, 71 LJ Ch 378,
    86 LT 738, CA   6.2.4(b)
New Windsor Corporation v Mellor [1974] 2 All ER 510, *aff'd* [1975] 1 Ch 380, [1975]
    3 WLR 25, [1975] 3 All ER 44, CA   8.5.2, 8.7.3, 9.1, 9.4.1, 9.4.2, 9.4.3, 9.5.1,
                                                                       9.5.7, 10.2.2

Newman v Bennett [1981] QB 726, [1981] 2 WLR 132, [1980]
    3 All ER 449, DC   4.2.3(d), 4.3.3

Owen v Blathwayt [2002] EWHC 2231, [2003] 1 P&CR 28, [2002] NPC 137,
    [2002] PLSCS 234, ChD   11.7.3

Oxfordshire County Council v Oxford City Council [2004] EWHC 12 (CH), [2004]
    PLSCS 16   8.3, 8.5.2, 8.6.1, 8.7.3, 8.7.5, 8.7.7, 9.19.2.1, 9.2.3,
                                                             9.5.5, 9.5.6, 9.6.3

Paine & Co Ltd v St Neots Gas & Coke Co Ltd [1939] 3 All ER 812,
    161 LT 186, 55 TLR 1062, CA   6.2.2(b)
Perry v Fitzhowe (1845) 8 QB 775   6.6.4
Potter v North (Sir Henry) 1 Ventr 383, 1 Saund 346, 86 ER 245   3.2

R v Ashby Folville Inhabitants (1866) LR 1 QB 213, 7 B & S 277,
    35 LJMC 154   6.2.4(a)
R v Joliff (1823) 2 B&C 54, 1 LJOSKB 232,
    [1814-23] All ER Rep 20   6.2.4(a)
R v Norfolk County Council, ex parte Perry (1996) 74 P&CR 1, QBD   8.5.2
R v Oxfordshire County Council, ex parte Sunningwell Parish Council [2000] AC
    335, [1999] 3 WLR 160, [1999] 3 All ER 385, [1999] 2 EGLR 94, HL   1.4, 9.1, 9.2.1,
                                                 9.4, 9.5.3, 9.5.4, 9.5.6, 10.2.2
R v Secretary of State for the Environment, Transport and the Regions ex parte
    Billson [1999] QB 374, [1998] 3 WLR 1240, [1998] 2 All ER 587, [1998] JPL 883,
    QBD   10.4.5
R v Suffolk County Council ex parte Steed (1995) 70 P&CR 487,
    [1997] 1 EGLR 131   8.7.6, 8.8, 9.2.1, 9.4, 9.5.4, 9.5.6, 10.2.2
R v Sunderland City Council ex parte Beresford. *See* R (Beresford) v Sunderland
    City Council
R v Whixley Inhabitants (1786) 1 Term Rep 137, 2 Bott 85   3.3.4
R (Alfred McAlpine Homes Ltd) v Staffordshire County Council
    [2002] EWHC 76, [2002] ACD 63, [2002] NPC 26, [2002] 2 PLR 1, QBD   9.5.2
R (Beresford) v Sunderland City Council; *sub nom* R v Sunderland City
    Council ex parte Beresford [2004] 1 All ER 160, [2003] 3 WLR 1306, HL *on appeal
    from* [2001] EWCA Civ 1218, [2002] QB 874, [2002] 2 WLR 693, [2001] 4 All ER
    565, [2001] 3 PLR 120, CA   9.5.2, 9.5.4
R (Cheltenham Builders Ltd) v South Gloucestershire District Council [2003]
    EWHC 2803 (Admin)   8.7.4, 8.7.6, 8.8, 9.2.1, 9.2.3, 9.4.1, 9.5.3, 9.5.4, 9.5.5
R (Laing Homes Ltd) v Buckinghamshire County Council and Secretary
    of State for the Environment, Food and Rural Affairs [2003] EWHC
    1578 (Admin), (2003) 29 EG 119 (CS), [2003] 3 PLR 60 8.5.2, 8.7.3, 9.1, 9.5.4, 9.5.6,
                                                                       9.5.7, 10.2.2
R (Whitney) v Commons Commissioners (unreported) 29 November 2003   8.8
Rabett v Poole (unreported), Cty Ct   9.6.3(d), 9.6.5, 11.9.2
Ratcliffe v Jowers, Barnes Common Case (1891) 8 TLR 6   9.6.2

Rigg v Earl of Lonsdale (1856) 11 Ex 654, 156 ER 992   4.9.1
Rigg v Earl of Lonsdale (1857) 1 H&N 923, 28 LTOS 372; 156 ER 1475 *sub nom*
   Lonsdale (Earl) v Rigg 26 LJ Ex 196, Ex Ch   3.3.4
Roberts v Rose (1865) LR 1 Exch 82, 4 H & C 103, 35 LJ Ex 62   6.6.4
Robertson v Hartopp (1889) 43 ChD 484, 59 LJ Ch 553, 62 LT 585,
   CA   3.3.3, 4.3.1(c), 4.3.2(a), 7.4.1
Robinson v Duleep Singh (1878) 11 Ch D 798, 39 LT 313, 27 WR 21, CA   4.3.5, 5.3.7
Rogers v Brenton (1847) 10 QB 26, 17 LJQB 34, 9 LTOS 352   4.7
Rotherham v Green (1597) Cro Eliz 593, (1597) 2 And 89, Noy 67   7.2.3
Rumsey v Rawson (1669) 1 Vent 18, T Raym 171, 2 Keb 410; 86 ER 13, *sub nom*
   Rumsey v Rawson 2 Keb 504, 84 ER 316   4.3.1(d)

St Edmundsbury & Ipswich Diocesan Board of Finance v Clark (No 2)
   [1975] 1 WLR 468, [1975] 1 All ER 772, (1974) 29 P&CR 336, CA   6.2.3
Sacheverell v Porter (1637) W Jo 396, Cro Car 482   4.3.2(a)
Sandgrove v Kirby (1797) 1 Bos & P 13, 3 Anst 892, 145 ER 1073   5.3.4
Scholes v Hargreaves (1792) 5 Term Rep 46   4.3.1(c)
Scrutton v Stone (1893) 9 TLR 478; *aff'd* (1893) 10 TLR 157, CA   4.3.1(b)
Secretary of State for Health v Birmingham City Council (unreported)
   20 July 1995   8.7.6
Simpson v Wells (1872) LR 7 QB 214, 36 JP 774, 26 LT 163   10.2.2
Smith v Earl Brownlow (1870) LR 9 Eq 241, 21 LT 739, 34 JP 293   4.5
Smith v Fetherwell. *See* Smith v Feverell
Smith v Feverell (1675) 2 Mod Rep 6, 86 ER 909; *sub nom* Smith v Fetherwell
   (1675) Freem KB 190   5.3.2, 5.5
Smith v Gatewood. *See* Gateward's Case
Southern Water Authority v The Nature Conservancy Council [1992]
   1 WLR 775, [1992] 3 All ER 481, (1992) 65 P&CR 55, HL   11.7.3
Storey v Commons Commissioner (1993) 66 P&CR 206, [1993] EGCS 33   8.7.7
Sutherland (Duke) v Heathcote [1892] 1 Ch 475, 61 LJ Ch 248, 66 LT 210   4.2.2

Tehidy Minerals Ltd v Norman [1971] 2 QB 528, [1971] 2 WLR 711, [1971]
   2 All ER 475, CA   6.2.4(b)
Tenants of Owning, Re (1587) 4 Leon 43, 74 ER 718   4.9.2
Thames Water Utilities Ltd v Oxford City Council [1999] 1 EGLR 167,
   [1998] EGCS 133, (1999) 77 P&CR D16, ChD   7.3.1
Thomas v Nicholls (1681) 3 Lev 40   5.3.8
Tickle v Brown (1836) 4 Ad & El 369, 1 Har & W 769, 5 LJKB 119   6.2.4(c)
Turnworth Down, Dorset, Re [1978] Ch 251, [1977] 3 WLR 370,
   [1977] 2 All ER 105   8.6.1
Tyrringham's Case (1584) 4 Co Rep 36b   4.2.3(c), 4.3.1(b), 6.1
Tyson v Smith (1838) 9 Ad & El 406, 3 JP 65, [1835-42] All ER Rep 95, Ex Ch   6.2.4

Valentine v Penny (1605) Noy 145, 74 ER 1107   4.4

Waltham Forest District Council v Secretary of State for the Environment and
   Secretary of State for Transport [1993] NPC 31, [1993] EGCS 34   12.2.2
Ward v Cresswell (1741) Willes 265   4.6
Ward v Ward (1852) 7 Ex Ch 838, 21 LJ Ex 334   7.2.2
Welcome v Upton (1840) 6 M&W 536, [1835-42] All ER Rep 314, 151 ER 524   4.9.4
White v Taylor (No 2) [1969] 1 Ch 160, [1968] 2 WLR 1402,
   [1968] 1 All ER 1015   6.2.2(a), 6.2.4, 6.4

White v Williams [1922] 1 KB 727, 91 LJKB 721, 127 LT 231, CA   6.4
Wickham v Hawker (1840) 7 M&W 63, 10 LJ Ex 153, [1835-42]
    All ER Rep 1   5.3.5, 5.5
Willingdale v Maitland (1866) LR 3 Eq 103, 36 LJ Ch 64, 31 JP 296   3.4
Wolstanton Ltd v Newcastle-under-Lyme Corporation
    [1940] AC 860, [1940] 3 All ER 101, 109 LJ Ch 319, HL   5.3.9, 9.4.2

Yateley Common, Hampshire, Re; Arnold v Dodd [1977] 1 WLR 840,
    [1977] 1 All ER 505, (1976) 33 P&CR 388   7.2.2

TABLE OF STATUTES

References are to paragraph numbers

Acquisition of Land Act 1981   8.7.2
   s 19(1)   6.5, 12.2
       (a)   12.2.1
       (aa)   12.2.1
       (b)   12.2.1
       (2)   8.7.5, 12.2.1
       (2A)   12.2.2
       (4)   12.2.1
   Sch 3, para 6(1)   12.3
         (a)   12.3
         (aa)   12.3
         (b), (c)   12.3
         (2)   12.3
Acquisition of Land (Authorisation Procedure) Act 1946
   Sch 1, para 11   8.7.2
Ancient Monuments and Archaeological Areas Act 1979
   s 19   10.3.4
Ashdown Forest Act 1974   10.6, 11.6

Channel Tunnel Railway Act 1996   12.1
Common Land (Rectification of Registers) Act 1989   8.7.7
   s 1(1), (2)   8.7.7
       (4)   8.7.7
Commonable Compensation Rights Act 1882   12.5.4
   s 2   12.5.1
Commonhold and Leasehold Reform Act 2000
   s 2   1.3
Commons Act 1236   5.3.10, 7.4.1
Commons Act 1285   2.3.2, 5.3.10, 7.4.1
Commons Act 1876   7.4.2, 7.4.2(b), 7.4.2(c), 9.6.4, 10.5.1, 11.3
   ss 4, 5   11.3
   s 7   7.4.2(b), 10.5.1, 10.5.2
   s 29   1.8.3(b), 9.6.4
   s 35   11.4
Commons (Expenses) Act 1878   11.3
Commons Act 1879   11.3

Commons Act 1899   8.6.2, 9.6.1, 9.6.3(b), 10.5.2, 11.3, 11.5
   Pt I   9.6.1, 10.3.4
   s 1   9.6.3(b), 10.5.2, 11.5
   s 2   11.5
   s 6   11.5
   s 10   11.5
   s 15   9.6.3(b)
Commons Act 1908   11.5.1
   s 1   11.5.1
Commons Registration Act 1965   1.1, 1.2, 1.6, 1.7, 2.5, 4.1.1, 4.2.3, 4.3.3, 4.9.5, 4.9.6, 6.1, 6.2.4(b), 6.3, 6.3.1, 8.1, 8.2.2(b), 8.2.3, 8.2.4, 8.4.5, 8.4.7, 8.7.1, 8.7.3, 8.7.7, 9.1, 9.2.2, 9.4.3, 9.5.7, 9.6.1, 10.3.1, 10.3.7, 10.3.10, 11.7.3, 11.7.4, 12.4.1
   s 1   4.3.1(a), 4.3.2(b), 6.1, 6.3.2, 6.3.3(b), 8.2.1
     (1)   1.4, 4.1.1, 8.3, 9.2.1
       (a)   1.4, 8.3, 9.6.1
       (b)   4.9.6
       (c)   9.6.1
     (2)   6.3.1, 8.6.1, 10.4.6
       (a)   6.3.3(a), 9.2.2
       (b)   4.1.1, 4.2.3, **4.3.1(a)**, 4.3.2(b), 6.1, 6.2.1(a), 6.2.4(b), 6.3.3(a), 7.3.2, 8.2.1, 8.6.1, 8.7.2, 10.4.6
   s 2   8.4.1
     (2)   8.4.1
   s 3   8.4.2, 9.2.1
     (1A)   9.2.1
     (1B)   9.2.1
     (2)   8.4.2
   s 4   6.4, 8.4.3, 8.4.4, 8.7.2
     (1)   8.3, 8.4.3, 9.6.2
     (2)(a), (b)   8.4.3
   s 5   8.4.4, 8.5.1
   s 6   8.5.1, 8.5.2
   s 7   8.4.3
     (1)   8.5.2
   s 8   8.6.2

Commons Registration Act 1965 –
cont
  s 8(1), (2)   8.6.2
        (3)   8.6.2, 9.6.1
        (4)   8.6.2
        (5)   8.6.2
          (a)–(c)   9.6.1
  s 9   8.6.3
  s 10   8.5.2
  s 11   8.4.5, 11.3
  s 12   8.4.7
  s 13   6.1, 6.3.1, 7.1, 8.2.1, 8.7.4,
    8.7.5, 8.7.6, 8.8, 9.2.3, 9.5.4, 11.7.4
  s 14   8.7.4, 8.7.6, 9.2.3
        (b)   8.7.3
  s 15   4.1.1, 4.3.1(a), 4.3.2(b), 6.6.1
        (1)–(3)   8.4.6
  s 21(1)   10.4.6
  s 22   8.2.4
       (1) 1.2, 1.7, 3.2, 3.3.6, 4.9.6, 5.3,
   6.1, 6.4, 8.2.2(a), 8.3, 8.7.5, 9.2.1,
                     9.3, 9.6.2, 10.4.1
         (a)   8.2.2(a)
         (b)   8.2.2(a), 8.2.4
         (1A)   8.3, 8.5.2, 9.2.1
         (1B)   9.2.1
Commons Registration (East
  Sussex) Act 1994   8.4.2
Communable Rights Compensation
  Act 1882   11.3
Compulsory Purchase Act 1965
  s 5   8.2.4
  s 7   12.4.2
  Sch 4   7.3.1, 8.2.4, 12.5, 12.5.5
          para 1(1)   12.4.3
          para 2(1)–(3)   12.4.3
          para 3   12.5
          para 4   12.5.1
              (5)   12.5.1
          para 5(1)–(4)   12.5.1
          para 6   12.5.1
Countryside Act 1968
  s 15   11.7.1
Countryside and Rights of Way
  Act 2000   1.2, 1.6, 2.5, 8.2.3, 8.5.2,
   9.5.1, 9.5.5, 10.1, 10.3, 10.3.3,
  10.3.4, 10.3.5, 10.3.7, 10.4, 10.4.4,
                    11.8, 12.4.1
  s 1   10.3.1
      (1)–(4)   10.3.1
  s 2(1)   10.3.1, 11.8
  s 4   10.3.6

  s 4(4), (5)   10.3.6
  s 5   10.3.6, 10.3.9
  s 6   10.3.10, 10.3.11
      (1)–(4)   10.3.10
  ss 7, 8   10.3.10
  s 9   10.3.11
  s 10   10.3.11
  s 15(1)   10.3.1
  s 16   10.3.1
  ss 17–19   10.3.5
  s 20   10.3.2
  s 21(3)   11.8
  s 22   10.3.3, 11.8
  s 23   10.3.3
  s 24   10.3.3
       (1)   11.8
  ss 25, 26   10.3.3
  s 68   1.8.3(b), 5.5
       (1)   5.5
  s 98   1.8.3, 9.2.1
  Sch 1   10.3.2

Dartmoor Commons Act 1985   10.6,
                              11.6
  s 8   4.2.3(c), 6.4

Epping Forest Act 1878   10.6, 11.6
Epping Forest Act 1880   11.6

Highways Act 1980   12.1, 12.3

Inclosure Act 1773
  s 15   5.3.1
Inclosure Act 1845   2.5, 3.3.5, 7.4.2,
         7.4.2(b), 7.4.2(c), 9.3, 9.6.1,
                 10.4.2, 11.3, 11.4
  s 11   7.4.2(a)
  ss 13, 14   7.4.2(a)
  s 15   7.4.2(a), 9.3
  s 31   9.3
  s 73   9.3
  s 106   9.3, 11.3
  ss 113, 114   11.3
  s 116   11.3
  ss 147, 148   8.7.2, 8.7.5
Inclosure Acts 1845-1882   12.2.1
Inclosure Act 1848
  s 10   9.6.4

Inclosure Act 1852
  s 22   12.5.1
Inclosure Acts 1852–1854   12.5.4

Inclosure Act 1857
　s 12　　　　1.8.3(b), 9.6.3(d), 9.6.4

Land Compensation Act 1961　12.4.1
　s 5(2)　　　　　　　　12.4.1
　ss 14–18　　　　　　　12.4.1
Land Registration Act 1925　　6.1,
　　6.3.1, 8.2.1, 8.4.7, 8.6.1, 8.6.2,
　　　　　　8.6.3, 8.7.4, 9.6.1
　s 70(1)　　　　　　　　8.7.4
Land Registration Acts 1925–1966
　　　　　　　　　　　8.7.4
Land Registration Act 1936　　6.1,
　　6.3.1, 8.2.1, 8.4.7, 8.6.1, 8.6.2,
　　　　　　　8.6.3, 9.6.1
Land Registration Act 2002　8.2.1,
　　8.4.7, 8.6.1, 8.6.2, 8.6.3, 8.7.4
　s 27(2)(d)　　　　　　8.7.4
Law of Property Act 1922　1.6, 4.2.1,
　　　　　　　　　　6.2.1(a)
　Sch 12　　　　　　　6.2.1(b)
Law of Commons Amendment
　Act 1893　　　　　　　7.4.1
Law of Property Act 1925
　s 1　　　　　　　　　1.3
　　(1)　　　　　　　　5.3
　　(2)　　　　　　　　4.2.2
　　　(a)　　　　　　　6.2.2(a)
　　(3)　　　　　　　6.2.2(a)
　s 13　　　　　　　　6.4
　s 40　　　　　　　　6.2.2(a)
　s 51　　　　　　　　6.4
　s 52(1)　　　　　　6.2.2(a)
　s 62　　　　　　　　6.4
　　(1)　　　　　　　6.4
　　(3)　　　　　　　5.2
　s 65　　　　　　　　6.2.3
　s 94　　　　　　　　9.6.4
　s 193　　　1.2, 9.6.5, 10.3.4, 10.4,
　　10.4.1, 10.4.4, 10.4.5, 10.4.6,
　　　　10.5.3, 11.10, 12.4.1
　　(1)　　　　　　　10.4.1
　　　(b)　　　　　　10.4.5
　　　(d)　　　　　　10.4.1
　　(2)　　　　　　　10.4.4
　　(4)　　　5.5, 9.6.5, 10.4.5
　s 194　　　1.8.2, 1.8.3, 5.5, 11.9.2
　　(1)　　　　　　　11.9.2
　　(3), (4)　　　　　11.9.2
Law of Property (Miscellaneous
　Provisions) Act 1989
　s 2　　　　　　　　6.2.2(a)

Local Government Act 1972
　s 122　　　　　　　　7.3.1

Metropolitan Commons Acts
　1866–1878　　　　　　9.6.3(a)
　ss 3, 4　　　　　　　9.6.3(a)
Metropolitan Commons Acts
　1866–1898　　　　　　10.4
Metropolitan Commons Act
　1866　　　　　　10.5.1, 11.4
　s 3　　　　　　　10.4.2, 11.4
　s 4　　　　　　10.4.2, 10.5.1
　s 5　　　　　　　　　11.4
　s 6　　　　　　9.6.3(a), 11.4
　s 11　　　　　　　　10.4.2
Metropolitan Commons Act
　1869　　　　　　　　10.5.1
　s 2　　　　　　　　10.4.2
Metropolitan Commons Act
　1887　　　　　　　　11.4
Metropolitan Commons Act
　1898　　　　　　　　11.4
Metropolitan Commons
　Amendment Act 1869　　11.4
Metropolitan Police Act 1829
　s 4　　　　　　　　10.4.2
　s 34　　　　　　　　10.4.2
Metropolitan Police Act 1839
　s 2　　　　　　　　10.4.2
Military Lands Act 1892　　10.3.2
Military Lands Act 1900　　10.3.2

National Parks and Access to the
　Countryside Act 1949　　10.5.3
　Pt V　　　　　　　10.3.4
　ss 59–65　　　　　　10.5.3
　s 60　　　　　　　　11.7.1
　s 64　　　　　　　　11.2
　Sch 2　　　　　　　10.5.3
National Trust Act 1971
　s 23　　　　　　　　11.11
　s 29　　　　　　　　11.11
New Forest Acts 1877–1970　11.6

Occupiers Liability Act 1957　10.3
　s 13(1), (2)　　　　　10.3
Open Spaces Act 1906　5.5, 9.6.3(c)
　ss 1–7　　　　　　　9.6.3(c)
　s 9　　　　　　　　9.6.3(c)
　s 10　　　5.5, 8.6.2, 9.6.3(c)
　s 15　　　　　8.6.2, 9.6.3(c)

Open Spaces Act 1906 – *cont*
  s 20   9.6.3(c)

Prescription Act 1832   5.5, 6.2.4,
         6.2.4(c), 6.3.3(a), 9.5.1
  s 1   6.2.4(c)
  s 4   6.2.4(c)

Quia Emptors 1290   4.2.3(a), 4.3.1(b)

Road Traffic Acts   5.5
Road Traffic Act 1972
  s 36   9.6.5
Road Traffic Act 1988   11.10

Statute of Merton 1235–1236
  c4   2.3.2, 4.2.3(a)
Statutory Orders (Special
  Procedures) Act 1945   12.2.3
  s 2(1)   12.2.3
  ss 3–5   12.2.3

  s 6(1), (2)   12.2.3
Town and Country Planning Act
  1990
  ss 226–227   7.3.1
  s 232(1), (2)   7.3.1
  s 237   7.3.1
Transport and Works Act 1992   12.1

Wild Creatures and Forest Laws
  Act 1971   3.4
Wildlife and Countryside Act 1981
             11.7.3, 11.7.4
  s 28   11.7, 11.7.4
    (4)   11.7
    (5)(a)   11.7.1
    (6)   11.7.1
  s 29   11.7.2
    (6)   11.7.2
Wimbledon and Putney Common
  Act 1871   10.6

TABLE OF STATUTORY INSTRUMENTS AND GUIDANCE

References are to paragraph numbers

Access to the Countryside (Correction of Provisional and Conclusive Maps)
(England) Regulations 2003, SI 2003/1591   10.3.6, 10.3.9
Access to the Countryside (Exclusions and Restrictions) (England) Regulations
2003, SI 2003/2713   10.3.3, 11.8
Access to the Countryside (Exclusions and Restrictions) (Wales) Regulations 2003,
SI 2003/142   10.3.3, 11.8
Access to the Countryside (Maps in Draft Form) (England) Regulations 2001,
SI 2001/3301
     reg 2(1)   10.3.7
     reg 4   10.3.8
     reg 5   10.3.7
     reg 12(1)–(3)   10.3.7
     Sch   10.3.8

Commons Registration (Exempted Land) Regulations 1965,
SI 1965/2001   8.4.5, 11.3
Commons Registration (General) Regulations 1966, SI 1966/1471   8.7.5, 9.2.3
     regs 27, 28   8.7.5
     reg 29   8.7.5
         (1)   6.4
Commons Registration (General) (Amendment) Regulations 1968, SI 1968/658   6.4
Commons Registration (New Land) Regulations 1969,
SI 1969/1843   4.1.1, 4.3.2(b), 6.1, 8.7.2, 8.7.4, 9.2.3
     reg 3   6.3.3(a), 6.3.3(b), 8.7.2
         (1)   8.7.2
         (2)   6.3.1, 8.7.2
         (3)   8.7.4
     regs 5–7   8.7.4
Commons (Schemes) Regulations 1982, SI 1982/209   10.5.2, 11.5
Commons (Schemes) (Welsh Forms) Regulations 1982, SI 1982/667   10.5.2

Good Practice Guide on Managing the Use of Common Land (DETR 1998)   11.7.4

Land Registration Rules 1925, SR & O 1925/1093   8.7.4

MAFF Guidelines for Joint ESA Agreements with Commoners   11.7.4

Vehicular Access across Common and Other Land (England) Regulations 2002,
SI 2002/1711   5.5
     reg 6(2)   5.5
     regs 7, 8   5.5
     regs 14, 15   5.5

GLOSSARY

Abatement
A self-help remedy enabling commoners to remove obstructions to the exercise of their rights, the abatement of a nuisance.

Amerciaments
A punishment by which the offender stood in the court of his lord and was at his mercy.

Appendant rights
Rights that were attached to land by operation of law such as rights of common of pasture attached to arable land that was granted by the lord of the manor before 1290 (or possibly 1189).

Approvement
The lord of the manor or owner of the soil had the right to inclose the land not required for the commoners.

Appurtenant
Rights attached to land by express deed of grant or by prescription not being rights attached by operation of law.

Award
The formal document made under an Act of Inclosure setting out the terms of inclosure of land or the regulation of the common lands.

Beastgates
A right to graze a fixed number of animals. See Stint.

Bookland
An Anglo-Saxon form of land ownership of ecclesiastical origin.

Bote
A Saxon word for the products of the soil in the form of wood or timber.

Bridle path
A public highway over which the public have rights to pass on horse, cycle or foot.

Bylaws
Local laws made under delegated law-making powers.

Cart-bote
Wood required for making and repairing agricultural implements.

Cattlegates
See Stint.

Chief rents
Rents payable in respect of land held from the lord of the manor.

Common fen
Fens and marshes in eastern England were often subject to rights of common.

Common land
Has various meanings according to the statutory context but generally means land subject to rights of common.

Common of shack	Right to put animals in common in a common field after harvest to pick up the fallen ears of corn.
Common fields	Originally large fields, strips of which were separately owned, but over the whole of which the several owners had rights in common to graze animals after the removal of arable crops.
Commonable lands	Has various meanings but confined in this work to land divided into separate strips over which all the several owners have rights of common grazing after harvest or in fallow years.
Commoners	Persons having rights of common over common land.
Cone-burrow	See Coney-burrow.
Coney-burrow	A type of warren where rabbits are bred.
Copyhold	A form of land ownership by which the owner held title to land within a manor and according to its customs subject to the will of the lord: abolished in 1922.
Court Baron	Manorial court dealing with the rights of copyholders.
Court Leet	Manorial court of criminal jurisdiction.
Cowgrasses	See Stint.
Cow-leaze	See Stint.
Curtilage	The immediate court yard or land surrounding a dwelling.
Custom	A right, obligation, or privilege having the force of law.
Customary Court	One of the manorial courts.
Customary freeholders	A form of copyhold by which the owner held title according to the custom of the manor and not at the will of the lord.
Customary rights	See Custom.
Damages	In litigation a sum awarded for compensation from a wrongdoer.
Deed	Document satisfying certain formalities and which is used for the creation and transfer of land and interests in land, amongst other matters.
Deed of dedication	A formal undertaking by the maker having legal consequences, such as the dedication of land for public access under section 193 of the Law of Property Act 1925.

DEFRA	The Government Department for Environment, Food and Rural Affairs.
Demesne	Land within a manor owned and occupied by the lord for his own purposes.
Demise	The grant of a lease.
Depasture	To bring to an end the rights of pasture.
Dominant tenement	Land having the benefit of rights, such as the rights of common.
Driving the common	The rounding up of animals on a common to remove strays and those in excess of individual rights.
Easement	A right attached to land exercisable over other land in a different ownership, such as a right of way.
Enclosure	See Inclosure.
Enfeoff	To make a person the owner of land by means of a feoffment. See Feoffment.
Equitable right	An interest in land enforceable under the rules of equity and generally only, against persons having notice of the same.
Estate	An interest in land. Since 1925 the only legal estates are the fee simple absolute in possession (freehold) or the term of years absolute (leasehold).
Estovers	Produce of the land in the form of wood or timber.
Express grant	The grant of an interest in land by way of an actual deed of grant.
Extinguishment	The bringing to an end of a right or interest in land.
Fallow land	Land resting between arable crops and usually down to grass.
Fee simple absolute	One of the two estates in land. See Estate.
Fen	Marshy tracks of land in east England.
Fence month	Period during which a royal forest was closed for the protection of deer.
Feoffment	Originally a public ceremony by which a person acquired an interest in land.
Feudal system	The form of society under which the manor was the principal unit, the lord of the manor providing protection for his serfs and his tenants and they in turn owing him service or payments.
Foldage	The right of the lord of the manor to require his tenants to put their sheep on his demesne.

Folkland	Anglo-Saxon land ownership where the owners cultivated land under a open or common field system.
Footpath	A public highway over which the public have the right to pass on foot.
Franchises	A liberty or privilege, such as the right to hold a market, existing at common law or as a custom as an interest in land.
Frankpledge	The means of preserving the peace by which men where pledged in groups of ten with each member providing surety for the others.
Free warren	Right to keep and kill hares and rabbits within a specified area.
Freehold	One of two legal estates in land amounting, in effect, to absolute ownership. See Estate.
Furzes	Small bushes cut for fodder or bedding.
Gated pasture	See Beastgate.
Glebe	Land belonging to the parish priest.
Grant	As in the grant of some right or interest in land to another, usually by deed.
Grantee	The person to whom a grant is made.
Grantor	The person making the grant.
Half year land	Land cultivated by its several owners for half a year and subject to grazing in common for the remainder. See also Lammas land.
Hay-bote	A right to take wood or timber to repair fences.
Herbage	The produce of land that can be cut or grazed by animals.
Hereditament	Interest in land capable of passing, originally to an heir; corporeal hereditaments are tangible objects such as land and buildings and incorporeal hereditaments are intangible objects such as *profits à prendre*.
Heriots	In relation to copyhold the customary right of the lord of the manor to take the best beast of a tenant upon the latter's death.
House-bote	The right to take wood or timber to repair buildings.
Husbandry	The activity of farming.
Implied grant	In relation to a *profit à prendre*, arising by implication from long user ('prescription') rather then by express grant.

In gross	A *profit à prendre* existing independently of the ownership of any land.
Inclosure	The process of extinguishing rights of common and converting common land to land free of such rights.
Inclosure award	See inclosure and award.
Incorporeal hereditament	See hereditament.
Injurious affection	In relation to compulsory purchase compensation, the diminution in value caused by public works to land retained by a claimant.
Intercommoning	In relation to common fields, the rights of the owners of the field strips to graze the whole in common after the removal of the arable crops.
Lammas Day	1 August (New Calendar), land opened on Lammas Day for grazing in common, usually land used for hay crops.
Lammas land	See Lammas Day.
Laneland or Lænland	Anglo-Saxon form of ownership having commercial basis.
Leasehold	One of two legal estates in land by which a tenant holds land for a defined period. See Estate.
Legal memory	The Coronation of Richard I 1189.
Levant **and** *couchant*	A qualification of the extent of rights of common of pasture limited to the number of animals that can 'get up and lie down' on the dominant tenement during winter.
Licence	Permission or consent to be on land not amounting to a legal interest.
Licensee	The person to whom a licence is given.
Licensor	The person who grants a licence.
Limitation	A statutory bar on bringing legal proceedings after a specified period of time.
Lord of the manor	The person owning the Norman unit of land ownership known as the manor, the manor remaining a property right the owner of which retains this descriptive title.
Lost modern grant	A legal fiction arising where an easement or *profit à prendre* is claimed by prescription; the law assumes that the legal interest was granted by deed, and the deed has been lost.

Lot meadow	Commonable land owned in severalty usually used as hay meadows where owners draw lots to determine the individual strips to be cut for hay by each owner.
Manor	See Lord of the manor.
Manorial court	See Courts Baron, Leet and Customary.
Manorial waste	See waste land of a manor.
Meadow land	Land down to grass and usually used for grazing and hay.
Memorandum	A clause or document noting the particulars of some transaction or matter.
Mean high water mark	The average of the high tide water levels; below which the land is owned by the Crown
Metes	Measurement
Metes and bounds	By measurements and boundaries.
Metropolitan commons	Usually a common within the metropolitan police district on the 10 August 1866.
National parks	Areas of land identified for special scenic protection under the National Parks and Access to the Countryside Act 1949.
Nuisance	A tort or legal wrong.
Open field system	An agricultural practice by which a large field was held in strips by separate owners who together grazed their animals over the whole after the removal of the arable crops.
Pannage	A right to put swine to woodlands to forage for acorns and beech mast.
Part performance	A legal doctrine by which a lack of formality can be overcome where one party partly performs his legal obligations.
Pasturage	A right of pasturage is a right to use land for grazing.
Piscary	A right to take fish.
Prescription	Legal doctrine by which easements and *profits à prendre* can be acquired by long user.
Profit à prendre	A legal interest in land consisting of a right to take the produce or part of the soil of another, such as rights of common.
Pur cause de vicinage	The right to inter-common as between adjoining commons; actually a defence to an action in trespass where animals stray off the 'home' common.

Quia Emptores	Statute of Edward I 1290.
Quit rents	Dealing with the transfer of interests in land.
Reeves	An official supervising, eg, the management and stocking of a common.
Registered land	Land whose ownership is registered under the Land Registration Acts 1925–2002.
Regulated pasture	Pasture regulated by an inclosure award and owned by the graziers in undivided shares.
Reservation	An area of land or some interest in land kept back out of a conveyance or other deed by the vendor.
Right in gross	Such as a *profits à prendre* where the right is held without being annexed to any land
Right of way	An easement and a legal interest in land entitling the grantee to pass and re-pass over another's land.
Rights of common	Has various definitions under different statutes, but generally rights exercised by commoners in common with the owner of the soil such as rights to graze.
Seigniorial	Associated with a feudal lord.
Servient land	Land over which an easement or a *profit à prendre* is exercised.
Servient tenement	See servient land.
Several vesture	A right to all the products of the soil of another exercisable by several or separate persons.
Several	See Severalty.
Severalty	Where a property or interest in property is held by two or more persons, it is held in severalty where each has a distinct and ascertained share as apposed to joint ownership (or tenancy).
Severance compensation	Compulsory purchase compensation where land is severed.
Shack	See common of shack.
Sheep heaves	An area of land where a hefted flock of sheep graze, hefting means that the sheep have learnt and keep to the boundaries of that land.
Sheepheaf	See Sheep heaves.
Sheepwalk	See Sheep heaves.
Sites of special scientific interest	An area of nature conservation notified under the Wildlife and Countryside Act 1981.

Sole pasture	A right to graze usually held by a single person, or where held by more, each holding a stint of equal size.
Sole profit	A *profit à prendre* where the owner of land has granted to another person or persons the whole and exclusive right such as a right to pasture, and retains no such right himself.
Sole vesture	See a sole profit, a sole vesture is the right to all the produce of the land excluding timber.
Stint	A distinct and equal share in a right such as a right of pasture normally entitling a stint holder to a fixed number of animals.
Stint holders	See Stint.
Stinted pasture	See Stint, there are various other names such as Cattlegate, Beastgate, Cowgrasses, Beastgrasses, Cow-leaze and Pasturegate.
Strays	Animals found on a common not belonging to any of the commoners.
Surcharging	Animals found on a common in excess of the numbers permitted to be present.
Tenancy	See leasehold.
Tenants in common	Form of co-ownership by which the individuals hold distinct shares.
Tenement	Land capable of being owned by a tenure, such as a freehold or leasehold.
Term of years absolute	One of two legal estates in land, see leasehold.
Time immemorial	See Legal memory.
Turbary	Right to take peat or turves for fuel.
Vesture	Right to take all the produce of the land excluding timber.
Vicinage	See *pur cause de vicinage*.
Villeins	The inhabitants of a feudal manor required to work for the lord.
Warrens	A free warren is a right to keep beasts and birds, namely, hare, rabbit, pheasant, partridge and wild duck.
Waste land of the manor	The unenclosed lands of a manor that may or may not be subject to rights of common.
Wayleaves	A statutory right to lay a pipe or cable across private land.

Chapter 1

BACKGROUND

1.1 INTRODUCTION

The registration requirements under the Commons Registration Act 1965 would present any author with a problem as to the arrangement of a book on the law of commons and town and village greens. There are strong arguments in favour of starting with that Act, and treating all subjects and issues thereafter in terms of the definitions of common land and rights of common under that Act. The difficulty with that approach is that the reader may not understand the legal and historical context in which that Act came to apply, or the terms and definitions that were, and to a lesser extent, are now, relevant. We have therefore first dealt with the historical and legal context, and explained a number of legal concepts and principles, before examining in detail the effect of the 1965 Act.

1.2 WHAT IS COMMON LAND?

Aside from any statutory definitions, common land is that land over which commoners are entitled to exercise rights of common, such as grazing their animals. The rights are exercisable together with, or to use the technical expression, *in common* with, others.[1] All or part of the open uninclosed waste area of the unit of land ownership known since the Norman conquest as 'the manor', would have been common land. The owner of the manor and, therefore, of the common land, was the lord of the manor.[2]

However, some lands were known as *commonable lands*. Although their origin and purpose are discussed elsewhere in this book,

---

[1]   The expression 'common land' has particular meanings under different statutes. The definition of 'common land' under the Commons Registration Act 1965 is considered later in this chapter.

[2]   However, the position is not always so clear: see Chapter 5.

commonable lands were generally arable lands that were cropped in strips by individuals but which were, as a whole, subject to rights of common, usually grazing, when the crops had been removed and during the fallow year.[1] Under the Commons Registration Act 1965, commonable lands fall within the definition of *common land* for registration purposes.[2]

It is a popular misconception that common land belongs to everyone and that the public have rights of access over all common land. Rights of access have largely been restricted to metropolitan commons and certain other commons to which s 193 of the Law of Property Act 1925 has been applied. Generally, there has been no public right of access to rural commons, such as those in the upland and hill areas that are still used for grazing purposes. When the Countryside and Rights of Way Act 2000 (CROW Act 2000) fully comes into force, there will then be a general public right of access on foot over all registered common land.[3]

The meaning of 'common land' can actually be much more complicated than the introductory explanation set out above. There has been much legislation concerning common land and the expression may have slightly different meanings under different Acts and for different purposes.

1.3   WHAT ARE RIGHTS OF COMMON?

In the case of the uninclosed land in a manor, rights of common were originally held by the freehold (and copyhold) tenants of the lord of the manor.[4] They were local people who lived and worked within the manor and were often referred to as *commoners*. Rights of common were also held by the owners of commonable lands. As the author of one treatise put it:[5]

---

[1]   See Chapters 2 and 3.

[2]   Section 22(1).

[3]   Registered common land is that registered under Commons Registration Act 1965.

[4]   Prior to 1926 interests in land included freeholds and copyholds. Strictly, only freeholders held *rights* of common, as incidences of their grants; copyhold tenants had *rights* as part of the custom of the appropriate manor.

[5]   Woolrych *A Treatise on the Law of Rights of Common* (1824), at p 13.

'A Right of Common is an incorporeal hereditament, and may be said to exist where two or more, by virtue of a grant, prescription, or custom, take, in common with each other, from the soil of a third person, a part of the natural profits thence produced.'

The more usual rights of common are:

– grazing or pasturage;
– pannage: to put pigs in woodland to graze on acorns and beech mast;
– piscary: to take fish;
– turbary: to take peat turves for fuel;
– estovers: the Saxon word was bote; it consisted of wood and timber and was expressed as house-bote (firewood, and wood for repairing a house), plough or cart-bote (making and repairing agricultural implements) and hay-bote (for repairing fences);
– rights in the soil: right to take sand, gravel, stone, marl and other minerals.

Today, the principal legal interests that can exist in land are the two legal estates (freehold and leasehold) and legal interests such as easements and *profits à prendre*.[1] *Profits à prendre* are rights to take something from another's land and therefore include rights of common. Rights of common are therefore capable of being legal interests in land today.[2]

1.4   WHAT ARE TOWN AND VILLAGE GREENS?

A town or village green is usually that part of the local common that lies within or immediately around the centre of a town (in reality, and in most cases, an expanded village) or village and, accordingly, would have been subject to rights of common. However, town and village greens are often used for a wide range of recreational, leisure and husbandry purposes, and therefore may not necessarily be subject to rights of common.

---

[1]   Law of Property Act 1925, s 1; under Commonhold and Leasehold Reform Act 2000, s 2, an application can be made to register a freehold estate in land as a freehold estate in commonhold land. This is likely to be restricted to blocks of flats.

[2]   Rights of common are more fully explained in Chapters 3 and 4.

Because of their recreational and leisure value, town and village greens have been accorded more and more legislative protection and management control.[1] As such, they are registrable under the Commons Registration Act 1965.[2]

1.5   FACTUAL BACKGROUND

Common land comprises some 550,000 hectares – about 4% of the total land area in England and Wales. There are some 367,000 hectares in England (about 3% of the total land area), of which nearly 50% (180,000 hectares) is either wholly or partially designated as Sites of Special Scientific Interest. In England, over 48% of common land lies mainly within National Parks, and 31% is wholly or partially within Areas of Outstanding Natural Beauty. Surprisingly, just over 51% of all registered commons in England, are less than 1 hectare in area, and only 1.3% are 1,000 hectares or more in area. Just over half of England's common land is in Cumbria and North Yorkshire.[3]

1.6   HISTORICAL BACKGROUND

Common land has had a significant role in the agricultural life of England and Wales. However during the eighteenth and nineteenth centuries substantial areas of common land were inclosed and apportioned out to the larger landowners in the locality. The effect of inclosure was to end the commoners' rights and to divide up the inclosed land among the larger landowners. That was especially true of the more agriculturally fertile land. However, by the mid-nineteenth century there was increasing concern about the role that common land provided or could provide for wider recreational purposes. Thus, legislation in that century made provision for rights of public access for recreational purposes in relation to, for example, commons in metropolitan areas.

---

[1]   See Chapter 9.

[2]   Section 1(1)(a), for example by custom or use as of right for 20 years: *R v Oxfordshire County Council, ex parte Sunningwell Parish Council* [2000] AC 335.

[3]   These facts and figures are taken in part from the website of the Department of Food and Rural Affairs (DEFRA): www.defra.gov.uk.

The role of common land in the agricultural economy of any locality originally operated within a legal context of manorial courts and the freehold and copyhold tenants of the manor. That legal framework was partially dismantled by the reforms of property law in 1922–1925 when copyholds were abolished.[1] After 1925 most of the principal purposes of the manorial courts no longer existed and the management of common land and the regulation of the rights of the commoners through the manorial courts virtually ceased to take place. In any event, the role of common land in agricultural practices became significantly less important in the lowland and more densely populated areas of the country. It was against that background that a Royal Commission produced a report in 1958.[2]

The Commission's principal recommendations were the creation of a statutory register of common land, its ownership and the rights of commoners, the creation of public rights of access over all commons, and provisions for the regulation and management of commons primarily with regard to the changing expectations of the general public that common land had an important role to play in the future. Parliament enacted the Commons Registration Act 1965 to give effect to the first of these recommendations. But it was not until the CROW Act 2000 that Parliament enacted legislation that will give the public a right of access on foot to all registered common land where such a right did not already exist.

1.7   COMMONS REGISTRATION ACT 1965

The Commons Registration Act 1965 required the registration of all common land, town and village greens, the ownerships of common land and of rights of commons.[3] The 1965 Act contained its own, and rather wide, definition of *common land* that was, and remains, relevant for registration purposes:[4]

'In this Act, unless the context otherwise requires, –

"common land" means –

---

[1]   Law of Property Act 1922.

[2]   *Royal Commission Report on Common Land.*

[3]   See Chapter 8.

[4]   Section 22(1).

(a) land subject to rights of common (as defined in this Act) whether those rights are exercisable at all times or only during limited periods;

(b) waste land of a manor not subject to rights of common;

but does not include a town or village green or any land which forms part of a highway. '

'Rights of common' are defined as including:[1]

'... cattlegates or beastgates (by whatever name known) and rights of sole or several vesture or herbage or of sole or several pasture, but does not include rights held for a term of years or from year to year.'

This definition is considered in more detail later in this book, but it is wider than the initial definition of common land adopted at the commencement of this chapter, including both commonable land and waste land of the manor not subject to rights of common.

Of 7,039 common land units in England, only 34.6% had registered rights of common and these commons accounted for nearly 88% of the total area of common land. Of the commons with registered rights, 65% had five registered rights or less and 13.7% had 20 rights or more. Rights to graze cattle were registered on 20% of commons, sheep on 16%, horses and ponies on 13% and estovers (the right to take wood for certain purposes) on 10%. There are approximately 24,157 rights entries on the registers, although this represents a complex situation because of duplication of rights and cross-referencing between adjacent commons. In relation to the ownership of commons, some 1,900 commons had no known owners. At the time of registration, 1,787 commons were in private ownership, 679 had private owners for parts of the land, 1,230 were owned by parish and other councils and 431 were owned by a variety of organisations including charities and trusts.[2]

---

[1] Commons Registration Act 1965, s 22(1).

[2] See the DEFRA website

1.8   FUTURE DEVELOPMENTS

1.8.1   Rights of common

In November 2000, in the *Rural White Paper*,[1] the Government stated that it was committed to legislate on common land as soon as Parliamentary time allowed. Its objective was:

> 'to provide for the protection of all commons for the benefit of future generations; ... we want to increase our ability to tackle over-grazing wherever it occurs and to provide fairer and more effective systems of registration and management. We will also look to improve the arrangements for town and village greens.'

In 2002 the Government published its *Common Land Policy Statement*. The Statement contained proposals for future legislation with a view to securing the future of common land and village greens, and to protect the features and characteristics that make such land so valuable. The Government proposes to restrict the grounds for the de-registration of common land. Its intention is to protect the land from any uses that would reduce its value to the community as a whole. At present, when all rights of common over a particular area of common land have been extinguished, it may be possible to de-register that land provided that it is not waste land of a manor. There are, apparently, approximately 2,500 commons that have no registered owner. These unclaimed commons amount to over 25,000 hectares.[2] The Government proposes that unclaimed common land should be vested in a suitable body which will be empowered to deliver effective management. Further, the vesting of ownership in a local authority or other body should be revocable in the event of an owner subsequently providing evidence of title within a specified period.

1.8.2   Fencing and other works

Section 194 of the Law of Property Act 1925 requires the consent of the Secretary of State or the National Assembly for Wales for fencing or other works that impede access to common land. However, that

---

[1]   *Rural White Paper: Our Countryside: The Future – A Fair Deal for Rural England* (DEFRA, 2000).

[2]   Curiously the number of unclaimed commons is higher in the Statement than the number disclosed on the DEFRA website.

section applies only to land subject to rights of common extant on 1 January 1926. The Government plans to extend the protection of s 194 to all registered common land with the exception of metropolitan commons, which will remain subject to their own legislation. Section 194 contains a number of exceptions; these will be retained save that consent will be required for works connected with the taking or working of minerals. It is proposed that, in future, the following criteria should to be taken into account before deciding whether to allow fencing or works that will prevent or impede access:

– the interests of the public;
– the rights of the owners and commoners;
– the need for effective management of the common;
– the conservation of wildlife and its habitats and of natural and historical features; and
– impacts on rights of public access.

A number of improvements in the operation of s 194, such as its enforcement, are also to be brought forward.

1.8.3   Town and village greens

In relation to town and village greens, the *Common Land Policy Statement 2002* refers to the effect of s 98 of the CROW Act 2000. Where an application is made for registration of land as a town or village green, on the basis of at least 20 years' qualifying use by the public, it is proposed that there should be a prescribed 2-year period from the date on which such public use of the land is challenged in which to lodge a registration application. The Government also proposes to introduce a formal mechanism by which landowners could clearly indicate that, although use of the land may continue for the time being, the nature of the use has ceased to meet the criteria for registration as a town or village green. A number of more detailed proposals to improve the registration arrangements relating to town and village greens have also been put forward.

(a)   Parking

The parking of vehicles on town or village greens and vehicular access ways across such land has always been controversial. Legislation will be sought to provide a power for landowners, leaseholders and any management body that has responsibility for the custody and care of town or village green land to grant consent for temporary parking on the green without contravening the legislative provisions that generally protect greens. The power would be subject to appropriate controls by the Secretary of State or the National Assembly for Wales.

(b) *Private rights of vehicular access*

Section 68 of the CROW Act 2000 contains provisions that enable owners of premises, where the appropriate criteria are met, to obtain a right of vehicular access to their premises across land over which it is otherwise an offence to drive, including a town or village green. However, that provision does not resolve the problem as to whether driving over such land would still be an offence under s 12 of the Inclosure Act 1857 and/or s 29 of the Commons Act 1876. The Government proposes to resolve this problem in future legislation so that s 68 easements are protected. However, it also proposes to reinforce observance of the existing legislation to the effect that no further vehicular access ways across land that remains registered as town or village greens should be created. That will be subject to certain exceptions where the creation of an access way would be in the interests of the local community, for example, to provide access to a public facility such as a village hall.

In respect of access ways that are already in use, but do not qualify for an easement under s 68 of the CROW Act 2000, the Government proposes that no easement granted by the landowner shall be lawful without the consent of the Secretary of State or the National Assembly for Wales. That proposal will include the possibility of the provision of alternative private land as a contribution to the green in compensation for the interruption of its enjoyment. Controls will also be introduced that require the consent of the Secretary of State or the National Assembly for Wales for any improvements to existing access ways.

Finally, the Statement sets out a number of proposals relating to the agricultural use and management of common land. The Government's proposals are concerned here with commons that are actively used for agricultural activities, such as grazing. The principal proposal is to develop statutory provisions to enable commons and management associations to operate more effectively.

The primary purpose of the associations would be to manage grazing practices and the exercise of rights of grazing. The possible measures may include:

- limitations on and monitoring of the exercise of rights in order to achieve sustainable grazing levels to take full account of conservation requirements;
- fixing of periods during which animals may or may not be turned out onto the commons;
- clearance of animals for disease control or other reasons;
- marking of any animals grazing the commons;
- removal and, if necessary, disposal of unmarked animals or those not on the land by virtue of a right of common or other lawful authority;
- regulation of supplementary feeding;
- restrictions on the turning out of entire animals (uncastrated males) (on grounds of public safety and proper animal husbandry);
- maintenance of local registers of active and inactive graziers;
- controls of lending or leasing of rights;
- raising of funds;
- appointment of reeves or shepherds; and
- referring cases of erroneous or over-quantified rights' registrations to the registration authority and/or the Commons Commissioners.

More detailed proposals include legislation to prohibit the severance of rights and the granting of new grazing rights in gross over a common; existing rights in gross will remain unaffected by this. A grazing right in gross is a right granted to a person, as such, and not granted as a right attached to a specific piece of land owned by that person.

Chapter 2

HISTORICAL DEVELOPMENT

2.1   INTRODUCTION

This chapter sets out a brief outline of the historical development of common land and common rights. The following extract from the *Royal Commission Report on Common Land* sets the scene:[1]

> 'The common lands of England and Wales are in general of immemorial antiquity. In certain cases they may be of comparatively recent origin, but in the main they are, in England, as old as English society. In Wales their origin is not less ancient. Just as the Port Meadow at Oxford is the oldest surviving institution in that city, older by centuries than the University, so the common lands of England and Wales are generally the most ancient institution we now possess; older by far than Parliament, older even than the manor within whose organisation and control they subsequently fell.'

2.2   PRE-1066

2.2.1   The importance of agricultural practices

The law of commons has never been an abstract set of rules devised by law-makers of long ago. Rather it was agricultural practices, centuries old, that gave rise to customs and practices that, in due course, came to shape the law of commons. Although many of the terms associated with the law of commons now appear archaic, and some of the legal concepts may seem somewhat opaque, they developed to give structure and form to the prevalent agriculture systems of the day. Accordingly, the law of commons cannot be understood without some knowledge of those agricultural practices that came to shape and influence the form of the law.

---

[1]   WG Hoskins *History of Common Land and Common Rights*, Appendix II, at para 1.

(a)   The rural economy

There are two aspects of the development of the law of commons
that need to be recognised. First, the importance of agriculture in the
economy of England and Wales. It was the largest sector of the
economy and the principal employer until well into the nineteenth
century. Not only was agriculture important for obvious reasons of
human survival, there were periods in English history when the
export of agricultural products was a considerable contributor to the
generation of national wealth, the wool industry during the
Elizabethan period being a prime example. The second feature in the
association of agriculture with the development of the law of
commons was the changing nature of agricultural practices. In the
earliest periods of the agricultural history considered below, the
efficient use of land and the nature of the agriculture practised,
demanded the co-operation of those working the land – the farmers
and smallholders; sharing the use of fallow land for grazing
purposes was in everyone's best interests.[1] Similarly sharing the use
of unploughed or uncultivated land, and the resources it provided,
was both necessary and sensible for the efficient continuation of
rural communities. People needed wood for heating and cooking,
the construction of buildings and tools, and for making fences and
repairing hedges. But uncultivated land provided other resources,
such as grazing for animals, acorns or beech mast for pigs, and
gravel, stone, clay and sand for making roads and, importantly,
constructing buildings.

There is a further important factor that shaped the customs and
practices associated with agriculture. Most of the country consisted
of agricultural communities and the transport infrastructure was,
generally, rudimentary. Accordingly the movement of resources
between one community and another was quite often extremely
difficult, especially during the winter months. High value, low rate,
resources might be moved from one part of the country to another,
but low value, bulky and heavy resources, such as sand, stone, hay,
straw wood or timber, were far less likely to be transported over
large distances between agricultural communities. A high degree of
co-operation was necessary to maintain the self-sufficiency of
agricultural communities in respect of the commonly consumed
resources.

---

[1]   The fallow land was the land put down to grass and resting between crop rotations.

(b)   The open-field systems

An important contribution made to the development of rights of common was the open-field system of agriculture. This was a system of farming that was predominantly arable but required additional tracts of pasture (meadows for hay and other permanent pasture for grazing). Although the open-field system was largely confined to the arable areas of England, it did exist elsewhere. Under this system, individuals would till strips of land within the open field to grow crops. After the crops were harvested, the whole of the open field would be thrown open to all for the grazing of animals. However, the open-field system also required meadow land to grow grass for hay and, although this too was cut on an individual basis, the whole of the common meadow would be thrown open for grazing purposes once the hay crop had been taken. Arable cropping was carried out on a strict rotation basis so that every third or fourth year was a fallow year when only a grass crop, which took few nutrients from the soil, would be grown. During a fallow year animals would graze the fallow land and dung it at the same time.

(c)   Royal Commission Report on Common Land

The *Royal Commission Report on Common Land* assists our understanding in the use of the wilder and uninclosed parts of England and Wales:[1]

'Extensive common lands existed not only in the original woods of pre-Conquest England, or on the open moorlands of northern and western England and Celtic Wales, but also in the widespread marches and fens that border the coasts of this country. Of this type the fens and marshes that surrounded the Wash, in Lincolnshire, Norfolk and Cambridgeshire, furnish perhaps the best documented example, though they may be regarded – like the woods of Kent or the uplands of Devon – as typical of their class in any part of the country.

Here we find, too, inter-commoning over a wide area of country. The great wastes of the fens, much of them drying out in the summer months, were managed by groups of villages adjacent to them. Sometimes the group was determined by geographical proximity, sometimes by ancient administrative arrangements of which only

[1]   WG Hoskins *History of Common Land and Common Rights*, Appendix II.

echoes may now survive; but whichever the arrangement these groups and their rights were sharply defined and clear differentiated. At first these wastes were treated as common fen, and the group of villages was the managing authority. At a later date, when the partition of the common fen among the individual villages and its appropriation by manorial lords took effect, the villages claimed that their right to inter-common in the fen had existed from time out of mind. Once again we see that common rights are older than the manor, and once again the inference is, as in Kent and elsewhere, that they go back to the earliest days of the Old English settlement.'

2.2.2   The Celts

Although this section deals with the position pre-1066, it is difficult to identify any useful or relevant starting date. Crop rotation and the efficient use of fallow and uncultivated land are the features that form the genesis of the development of customs that later became more formalised as the law of commons. It is believed that, in Celtic times, crop rotation was practised. There was probably a 4-year crop rotation so that each year one of four fields would be kept fallow and uncultivated. Continuously cropping land soon exhausts its manurial value, therefore, allowing an area to lie fallow each year enabled the nutrients to be restored. Apart from any natural rebalancing of soil nutrients, in the absence of an intensively grown crop, the fallow land would be grazed by animals. The dung from these animals and that collected from farmsteads would be used to fertilise the soil. Celtic people were tribal and survival of a tribe depended upon co-operation. One can assume that tribal customs and practices dictated the form of crop rotation and regulated the use of the fallow land, and the cropped land during the winter, by animals belonging to the tribe and its members.

The Roman Invasion placed substantial demands upon agriculture, but also brought with it a number of improvements. Although the invaders required greater quantities of grain, farm implements were much improved, as well as storage methods. However, the system of crop rotation, as such, remained. Even the Romans found that you cannot grow a cereal or any other crop in the same field year after year without yields beginning to deteriorate; fallow land was still required, and cropped land was still available for pasturing animals after a crop was harvested.

2.2.3 Anglo-Saxon period

With the withdrawal of the Romans one might assume that no substantial change in the pattern of agricultural activities would have occurred, other than those changes consequential to changes in the nature of the market for produce and the loss of regularisation that the Romans had no doubt imposed. However, the Anglo-Saxon period leading up to the Norman Invasion was probably the most influential in shaping and refining those agricultural practices that influenced the development of what we now call the law of commons. During the Anglo-Saxon period the method of cultivation was that of the common or open-field system. The cultivated land of each community was divided up into two or three open and uninclosed fields. Each field was divided into a number of strips; a strip was about an acre in size. It was usually a furlong (40 rods) in length, and 4 rods in breadth.[1] A member of a community would own strips scattered between the open fields. In accordance with the custom and practice of the community, at least one open field would be required to remain fallow every year. After the crops were harvested each year and during its fallow year, all members of the community were entitled to allow their cattle to pasture this field as it was, during its fallow year, a 'common' field and the members of the community had common rights of grazing over it.

Land within a common field, or other land, on the fringes of a village, which was not suitable for cultivation of crops, was used as common pasture over which, again, the villagers had common rights. Also, stretching out beyond the common fields, and probably to the boundaries with the next community, were the waste lands over which all had rights to graze their animals and take resources, such as timber. In some cases adjoining communities might share common rights over such waste land.

Such farming practices, associated with the open or common field system, with the use of crop rotation and the common use of fallow and waste lands, continued up to the sixteenth and seventeenth centuries in most parts of the country.

---

[1] See Seebohm *Village Community*, at chapter 1 and Holdsworth *A History of English Law* (2nd edn) vol II, at pp 56–78.

Anglo-Saxon land ownership was generally of three kinds: Folkland, Bookland, or Laneland. Those who owned Folkland were free men owning land that was kept within the family and which was subject to the customs of the locality. These individuals were the cultivators, owning land that they cultivated under the open or common field system. Bookland was originally of ecclesiastical origin, and the incidence of such ownership was governed by the book; it was often a superior form of tenure.[1] Accordingly Folkland held by the cultivators might also be Bookland held by some superior chief, or the Church. It is this form of ownership which probably formed the basis of the titles held by the lords of manorships after the Norman Invasion. Laneland was land held by way of a temporary loan or gift for a period of time, usually for a term of three lives. Whilst Bookland was usually land granted by the King, Laneland represented more of a commercial arrangement within lower levels of land ownership.[2]

What is significant about these forms of land ownership is that they illustrate a more communal, co-operative form of ownership at one end, namely Folkland, to more individual notions of private ownership and rights in the form of both Bookland and Laneland.[3] If the origins of the law of commons are to be found anywhere, the open or common field system and the form of that ownership known as Folkland are the most likely candidates.

Again the *Royal Commission Report on Common Land* helps us to understand the refinement and articulation of common rights:[4]

> 'The history of common rights in England ... may be viewed as that of an increasing limitation of rights to more sharply defined classes of user. This limitation arose naturally from the pressure of a growing population upon a fixed supply of land throughout historic times. The degree of pressure, and hence the chronology of the limitation of common rights, varied according to local circumstances. But whatever the local variations, the general picture is clear.

---

[1]   'The book' is the law to which the land was subject: see Holdsworth *A History of English Law* (2nd edn) vol II, at p 68.

[2]   Ibid, at pp 56–78.

[3]   See Holdsworth *A History of English Law* (2nd edn) vol II.

[4]   WG Hoskins *History of Common Land and Common Rights*, Appendix II, at paras 7, 8 and 9.

At first there was abundant land for everyone, and too few people to colonise or farm it. Common rights had no need of definition and therefore could hardly be said to exist. The first limitation we detect is a restriction of these ancient customary practices in a given area to the men of one particular shire. It is at this point that we may speak of the origin of common rights. Where there is no limitation, there can be no rights. Before this date we ought to speak of customary practices rather than of rights; and these might well go back to the earliest generations of pastoral farming in Britain. We next observe a limitation of common rights to a particular *region* in a county. Examples from Kent are the woodland region of the Chart, and the marshes subject to Wye. As late as 1086 Doomsday Book refers to a pasture in Suffolk which is common to all the men of the hundred of Coleness and to no-one else.

The process of limitation of common rights had generally gone much farther than this by the time of the Norman Conquest. In a great number of places common pastures and other common rights were now limited or appropriated to particular manors, or particular vills, or particular boroughs ...

The process of limitation and appropriation continued over several centuries. Common rights often, perhaps generally, became restricted to a particular class of inhabitant within a borough, or a vill, or a manor. The last stage of limitation was reached when even this restriction had to be narrowed by introducing the conception of a *stint* for every right in the common pasture. Instead of each commoner of the borough, manor or vill being free to pasture as many beasts as he liked, the growing shortage of pasture compelled each commoner to agree to a quota according, generally, to the size of his farm.'

2.3 NORMAN CONQUEST

Following the Norman Conquest in 1066 William I divided up the land as he saw fit. He rewarded his followers, and those Anglo-Saxons who came over to him, with grants of land. By such grants, his followers held the lands upon certain conditions of homage and services. William I was the overlord; his followers held land from him as his chief tenants.[1] The structure of the so-called feudal system so imposed was as follows. The chief tenants owed obligations to the King but, in turn, were entitled to rely on the obligations owed to them by their tenants and villains. The principal unit was the manor and the lord of the manor was usually a chief tenant of the King.[2] Within the manor would be one or more villages. One must bear in mind that the imposition of the structure of the manorship upon Anglo-Saxon village communities encountered a number of difficulties. First, there would have been a language difficulty with the lord of the manor generally speaking only Norman-French, and the villains only Anglo-Saxon. Secondly, any significant interference with the system of agricultural practices, described above, would have been likely to bring chaos and even starvation to the communities. Thirdly, many holders of a manorship would frequently have been away on business with the King, or providing military service for him and they would have left in charge their stewards to manage their affairs in their absences.

The profound effect of the imposition of the manorial system on the previous system of villages is explained in the *Royal Commission Report on Common Land*:[3]

'There can be little doubt that originally common land was common property. Outside the valuable arable and meadows of the villages and towns there was for several centuries no need or incentive to appropriate the wild wastes of the moors, heaths, fens, marshes, and woods, into private hands. Customary practices of grazing animals, of taking turf ... and wood for fuel and building ..., of fishing ..., of taking the fruits of Nature, developed unchecked and unchallenged in that large and ample world where there was more than enough for all. The appropriation of these common lands into private ownership is one of the profoundest and at the same time most obscure changes in English history. We see it developing as early as the ninth century; and it was probably the general result of the imposition of manorial system upon an original village communal system. The process of appropriating common land into private ownership was still far from

---

[1]   See Harpum et al, ed, *Megarry & Wade: The Law of Real Property* (6th edn, Sweet & Maxwell), at para 2–002.

[2]   The idea of a manor was not completely new as the seigniorial concept was known to the Anglo-Saxons.

[3]   WG Hoskins *History of Common Land and Common Rights*, Appendix II, at para 14.

complete at the making of Doomsday Book (1086). But in general common lands and wastes … had passed into the private ownership of manorial lords by the early thirteenth century, leaving to the peasantry only their customary rights over the surface. Even these surface rights were not safe from the growing claims of many lords, and the agrarian history of the thirteenth century is full of battles between lords and peasants over questions of common rights. Common rights were the mere shadow (though a valuable shadow) of the substance that had once been; but even the shadow had to be fought for and jealously guarded.'

Against that background the agricultural practices and customs of a village were merely absorbed into the manorial system. The lord would often have to conform to the communal system of agriculture, and conform to the rules that governed the use of the uninclosed or waste lands. These rules were asserted against him by his freehold tenants as well as the whole community.[1] The manor was a source of wealth and services for the lord of the manor. Where agricultural practices could be developed, such as by drainage or the cultivation of waste or uncultivated land, the lord of the manor would have a powerful incentive to advance such matters. He derived additional income from higher rents, but his own freehold and other tenants derived obvious benefits as well.

2.3.1   Manorial courts

With the advent of the manor came courts that regulated various aspects of manorial life. Manorial courts were the institutions through which the lord of the manor was able to regulate and resolve land ownership problems, deal with the obligations to provide services and also deal with issues arising from customs of the agricultural practices. Formerly there were three separate courts: the Court Leet; the Court Baron; and the Customary Court. In the Court Leet local by-laws could be made to control animals grazing on the fallow land in the system of open fields, whereas in the Customary Court, by-laws could be made and enforced to control animals on the manorial waste. These courts were normally presided over by the lord's steward, who acted as judge and kept the records. The customary tenants were required to appear and

---

[1]   See Holdsworth *History of English Law* (2nd edn) vol 7, at p 146.

acted like a jury in deciding whether or not a practice was a custom of the manor.

The Court Baron was concerned with the wider enforcement of law and order within the manor. It also recorded the names of new tenants and their heirs. The steward acted as a clerk and kept the records, and the beadle kept order.[1]

2.3.2   Approvement

One of the common issues between the lord of the manor and his tenants was whether he could approve the common or waste land of the manor without their consent. The word 'approve' meant enclose and bring into cultivation the common land. This would be of commercial advantage to the lord of the manor if he could add it to the land that he held or occupied himself – the lord's demesne. It could also be indirectly to his advantage in that he could let such approved land and derive rents from it. However, it was not necessarily to the advantage of all of the manor's tenants. Because of the uncertainty as to whether the lord of the manor could approve without consent, the Statute of Merton (1235–1236) was enacted to clarify the position and to provide that a lord could approve the common or waste land of the manor without his tenants' consent provided that he left them a sufficiency of common for their purposes. A further Commons Act was passed in 1285 to extend the right of approvement where commoners had rights of common across the commons of two adjoining manors; this Act also prohibited legal actions against a person who had erected a windmill, sheepcote or cowshed, or made necessary enlargements of his curtilage on the common or waste land.

Between 1086 (Doomsday Book) and 1348 (the Black Death) the population of England and Wales trebled.[2] The increase in the population, and the demands it put on agriculture, resulted in the approvement or inclosure of large tracts of the open waste lands which contributed to the disappearance of what had hitherto been common land. The approvement or inclosure of waste lands was in the interests of both the lord of the manor and the more important of

---

[1]   See Jessel *The Law of the Manor* (1998), at chapter 13.

[2]   Royal Commission on Common Land, Appendix II, at para 18.

his tenants who were agriculturally more productive, and many thousands of farms were created during this period.

2.4   INCLOSURE MOVEMENTS

2.4.1   Changes in agricultural practices

Changes in agricultural practices were to alter the significance of the manor and hastened the inclosure of the common lands. The open field system with its strict crop rotation and its regulated grazing of the fallow land, was much shaped by the use of the ox as the principal means of ploughing land. In time the ox was replaced by the horse which meant that land could be ploughed more efficiently. However, the horse was less suited to grazing the fallow lands and required large quantities of hay during the winter.[1] The increased use of the horse, and the decline in the use of oxen, altered the balance in the need for open uninclosed land as against cultivated land, and changed the practice of using the fallow land for communal grazing purposes in favour of the cutting of hay that could only be done on an individual, rather than a communal basis. A further factor was the rise in sheep farming during the fifteenth and sixteenth centuries. The open fields, the strip fields and other areas that had been used for arable crops, and customary grazing of the intervening fallow areas, were much more profitably used by sheep for grazing purposes. Indeed many villages were cleared and destroyed in order to facilitate sheep farming.[2]

By the seventeenth and eighteenth centuries further developments in agricultural machinery enabled the less productive areas of common land to be reclaimed, cultivated and used for arable cropping or higher quality pasturage. Inclosure of common land proceeded at a great pace during this period,[3] however, serious concerns were being expressed about the consequences of inclosing common land. As it was put in the *Royal Commission Report on Common Land*:[4]

---

[1]   See Jessel, *The Law of the Manor* (1998), at chapter 3.

[2]   Ibid.

[3]   The legislation is considered at Chapter 7.

[4]   WG Hoskins *History of Common Land and Common Rights*, Appendix II, at para 50.

'The disappearance of millions of acres of common lands caused great local hardships. It was not only the economic loss to the commoner, fatal though that often was. The disappearance of a familiar and perhaps beautiful part of the ancient peasant world often caused the deeper pain. ...

Much of the inclosed common land was ploughed up for corn, especially in eastern England, and it was generally believed that the total food production of the nation had thereby increased. But many honest observers in their own localities thought quite otherwise, and William Cobbett said so most pungently of all. Horton Heath was a common of 150 acres. Cobbett reckoned that

> "the cottagers produced from their little bits, in food, for themselves, and in things to be sold at market, more than any neighbouring farm of 200 acres ... I learnt to hate a system that could lead English gentlemen to disregard matters like these! That could induce them to tear up 'wastes' and sweep away occupiers like those I have described! Wastes indeed! Give a dog an ill name. Was Horton Heath a waste? Was it a 'waste' when a hundred, perhaps, of healthy boys and girls were playing there on a Sunday, instead of creeping about covered with filth in the alleys of a town?"[1]

Quite aside from the process of approvement and inclosure was the refinement and restriction on the exercise of customary rights or rights of common. In most cases these became necessary because of pressures on the use of land, hence the regulation imposed by the stint, and the restriction on the numbers of animals that could be placed on the common.[2]

2.5   LEISURE AND RECREATION

The development and growth of the towns and cities in England during the nineteenth century brought an increased demand for land for recreational and leisure purposes. Indeed the growth was so rapid that many areas of uninclosed common land and other wastes became surrounded by urban development. The legislation

---

[1]   See William Reitzel (ed) *The Progress of a Plough Boy to a Seat in Parliament*.

[2]   See Chapter 3.

passed in the nineteenth century was therefore primarily directed to restricting the inclosure of common land, and to providing, in certain cases, public rights of access to certain urban commons for recreational purposes.[1] Thus, in the Inclosure Act 1845, common land in the neighbourhood of a town could not be inclosed except by order, and no town or village green could be inclosed under the Act. The Act also made provision for the appropriation of areas for the purposes of exercise and recreation for the inhabitants of a neighbourhood.

By the twentieth century the exercise of commoners' rights had largely died out in many parts of the country. Although grazing rights in the hill and upland areas of England and Wales remain important even today, most of the common land in the lowland areas was rarely used by the commoners in exercise of their rights. The most recent legislation has been concerned with protecting common land by requiring registration[2] and by creating public rights of access on foot over registered commons.[3]

---

[1] This is considered in more detail in Chapter 10.

[2] Commons Registration Act 1965.

[3] CROW Act 2000.

Chapter 3

CLASSIFICATION OF COMMON LANDS

3.1   INTRODUCTION

This chapter describes the different types of land that have been, or can be, subject to rights of common. Not all such land was manorial waste of the manor. Rights of common were exercised over commonable lands at the appropriate times of the year (between reaping and sowing), and in fallow years. Woodlands and forests have been subject to special rights of common. In particular parts of the country, what were originally local customs have resulted in lands being subject to, what was called, common of shack and gated or stinted pastures.

3.2   MANORIAL WASTE

In *Potter v North (Sir Henry)*, in an argument put by the Attorney-General to the Court of King's Bench, it was said that:[1]

> 'Upon the creation of manors, the lords took as much as was for their own use into their demesnes, they distributed as much as was convenient amongst their tenants; what was left was called the lord's waste, which was neglected by the lord because he had before taken into his demesnes what he had need of.'

That needs to be put in context. Within a manor, the lands fell into three broad categories: first the lord's demesne land, namely the land that he occupied and had cultivated for his use and that of his household; secondly, land held by the other freeholders within the manor and the copyhold tenants; thirdly, the waste land of the manor as described above, this land was uninclosed and uncultivated land.

---

[1]   1 Ventr 383 at 395; 86 ER 245, at 252.

Not all the waste lands of a manor were necessarily subject to rights of common. Such rights depended upon any grants (express or implied) of rights of common in relation to the freehold owners, and the custom of the manor in relation to the copyhold tenants. Where such rights did exist, the rights would have been appropriate to the nature of the waste, or the relevant part of the waste. Thus, for example, if the waste consisted entirely of land suitable for grazing purposes, one would expect rights of common of pasture, but not the other rights, such as rights to take estovers. On the other hand, waste that consisted partly or mainly of woodland, might be subject to rights of common of estovers and, possibly, rights of common of pannage but not necessarily rights of common of pasture. In any event, where the woodland part of the waste was subject to rights of common of pannage, such rights or customs were sometimes subject to restrictions.[1]

In the case of waste lands adjoining the sea, the boundary is the mean high water mark. If land is added by accretion, such land acquires the character of the land to which it is added. As Farwell J said in *Mercer v Denne*:[2]

> 'Further, the opinion of text-writers, dealing with the analogous cases of accretion to copyholds and wastes of manors ... Hall on the Sea Shore (2nd ed p 113; p 789 of Mr. Stuart Moore's edition) concludes that the land which has accreted to the lord as freehold must be subject to the copyhold interest of the tenant of the land to which it has been added, or, if waste, to the local customs, common, &c., prescribed for by the tenants in respect of such waste.'

Under the Commons Registration Act 1965, common land is defined as land subject to rights of common and waste land of a manor not subject to rights of common.[3] Accordingly, all waste land was registrable, whether or not it was subject to rights of common. Further, waste land of a manor not subject to rights of common was registrable even where the ownership of the waste land had passed to a person who does not own the manorship.[4]

---

[1]   See Chapter 4.

[2]   [1904] 2 Ch 534, at 560, *affirmed* [1905] 2 Ch 538.

[3]   Section 22(1).

[4]   See *Hampshire County Council v Milburn* [1990] 2 All ER 257.

3.3 COMMONABLE LANDS AND SIMILAR RIGHTS

3.3.1 Commonable lands

The word 'commonable' is used in different contexts and in several statutes to mean different things. It is a word often used in connection with rights of common over waste land. Therefore, it does not follow that wherever that word is found, it necessarily has the meaning now to be ascribed to it.[1] However, in general terms, commonable lands are those lands owned or held in severalty during part of the year, but which are subject to rights in common after the severalty crop has been removed and during fallow years.[2] Severalty means individual ownership of the appropriate share. It is usually associated with the original open field system whereby individuals owned strips of the open field. The strips were cultivated for arable crops. When the crops had been removed, then the whole open field would be open to those who held rights of common to graze their animals. The persons holding such rights would either be the individual owners of the strips, that is the severalty owners, or they and other persons.

3.3.2 Lammas lands or half-year lands

Lammas lands were usually meadows used for the purposes of growing grass for taking a hay crop. These lands were the open arable and meadow lands, strips of which were owned or held in severalty during part of the year, and which were commonable to persons holding the severalty rights and to other classes of commoners when the severalty crop or hay had been removed.[3] On Lammas Day,[4] after the appropriate crops had been removed, the fields were then open to all those entitled to exercise rights in common, usually of pasturage. Jessel MR said in *Baylis v Tyssen-Amhurst*:[5]

---

[1] See Gadsden *The Law of Commons* (1988), at p 18, where the author recognises the inherent problems in attempting a definition.

[2] *Halsbury's Laws of England* (4th edn) vol 6, at para 506.

[3] Ibid, at para 517.

[4] Lammas Day was 1 August (or 12 August under the old calendar).

[5] (1877) 6 ChD 500 at 507.

'... lammas lands, that is, lands which, as I understand the meaning of the term, belong to a person who is absolutely the owner in fee simple, to all intents and purposes, for half the year, and the other half of the year he is still the owner in fee simple, subject to a right of pasturage over the lands by other people. Now what that right of pasturage is, of course must be determined by usage, or, as lawyers call it, prescription, which means an implied grant by a former owner of the lammas lands to other people who have the right of pasturage.

Now, in the first place, this right of pasturage, as far as I can understand it, over lammas lands, is always a right annexed to the ownership of some other lands. I use the term "annexed" advisedly. That right, of course, must be determined on the ordinary principles of law, and those principles, as I understand them, say, that where the right is annexed to other lands, the right must have some connection with those other lands to make it what is called appurtenant; that is, there must be some relation between the enjoyment of the right and the enjoyment of those other lands. You may have various connections. The commonest of all is where the right enjoyed is with respect of the beasts which plough the land. The beasts used for ploughing are fed in winter from the land which they plough, and in the summer, in ordinary commons, they go upon the commons. Or it may be the other way, like these lammas lands, where the lands are cultivated till August, and then the beasts are driven upon them in the winter months. That is one connection. It may be the plough beasts.

There may be various other connections. You might, for instance, have a right to depasture so many beasts as are required to manure the land. You might have various other suggested connections between the beasts used on the land and the number of beasts that might depasture. You might require the beasts for various purposes on the land occupied; and those beasts, not exceeding a certain number, might be depastured on the lammas lands or the common lands, as the case may be. But in all ways there must be some connection between the occupation of the lands in respect of which the right is enjoyed and the right itself, which connection from its nature must be to a certain extent limit the right enjoyed. You might say for every beast used on the land, not exceeding one beast per acre, there might be a right of common. But used in some way on the land, I think the beasts must be, to make the right appurtenant; otherwise I do not see what the meaning of the word "appurtenant" is. It is a right appurtenant to the land.'

3.3.3 Shack

Shack is the grain from the ear of the corn that falls to the ground, usually during the harvesting process. A common of shack is similar to the rights over lammas lands in that the land may be held in severalty for part of the year, but after harvest, those persons having the common of shack may put their beasts upon the shack land so that the grain that has fallen to the ground can be consumed. The origin of the right may have arisen in the nature of *vicinage*; in other words because of the difficulties of inclosures, and for the general convenience of all concerned, it was customary to allow the beasts of all the severalty owners onto the lands of all to clean up the fallen grains.[1] The actual practice will depend upon the custom and usage of the particular locality.[2] As with lammas lands, there must be some quantity or measure of the common of shack in terms of the number of beasts. The rule of *levancy* and *couchancy* will apply in the absence of any other rule.[3] The literal meaning of this rule is that the number of beasts a person may put on the shack land is that number that could be maintained on that person's own land during the winter.[4]

In some localities, custom and usage permitted a severalty owner to enclose his own part of the open field. If he did so, then he not only brought to an end the common of shack over his severalty piece of land, but he also brought to an end his right of common of shack over the remaining uninclosed severalty pieces.[5]

3.3.4 Stinted pastures

Stinted pastures have various names, such as cattlegate, beastgate (Suffolk), cowgrasses, beastgrasses, cow-leaze (Epping Forest), and pasturegate. 'Gated' and 'stinted' mean the same thing, the terms denote the number of animals that the holder of the right is entitled to put on the common. Cattlegate is probably the most common term to describe these various rights; cattlegates are found mainly in the north of England. The lord of the manor may own the soil but

---

[1] See *Corbet's case* (1585) 7 Co Rep 5a, 77 ER 417.

[2] *Cheesman v Hardham* (1818) 1 B & Ald 706 at 711.

[3] Ibid.

[4] As explained in *Robertson v Hartopp* (1889) 43 ChD 484 at 516, a case concerning appendant rights.

[5] See *Corbet's case* (1585) 7 Co Rep 5a, 77 ER 417.

subject to the right of pasture by the cattlegate owners.[1] Alternatively the ownership of the soil may be held by the cattlegate owners themselves as tenants in common.[2]

Similar to cattlegates are the sheep heaves also found in the north of England. These were small plots of pasture, found in the middle of the waste land of the manor, the ownership of which belonged to a person other than the lord of the manor. However, there is doubt as to whether sheep heaves ever existed as such and, in any event, they must now be regarded as obsolete.[3]

3.3.5　Regulated pastures

Where an order of inclosure was made under the Inclosure Act 1845, this could provide for the conversion of land into a regulated pasture; the ownership of the soil would then belong to the owners of the stints as tenants in common. The rights of common were extinguished but the management of the regulated pasture was vested in the stint holders. Strictly, the land ceased to be common land.

3.3.6　Commons Registration Act 1965

The wide definition of common land in this Act includes land subject to rights of common 'whether those rights are exercisable at all times or only during limited periods'.[4] Accordingly, most of the rights described under this heading of commonable lands are such rights and the land over which they are exercisable is therefore common land for the purposes of the 1965 Act, and such land, and the rights of common over it, fell to be registered under the Act. In the case of regulated pastures, it is doubtful whether such rights are capable of registration under the 1965 Act as they would not, following an inclosure award, have any longer been rights of common as such.[5]

---

[1]　*Rigg v Earl of Lonsdale* (1857) 1 H&N 923.

[2]　*R v Whixley Inhabitants* (1786) 1 Term Rep 137.

[3]　See Gadsden *the Law of Commons* (1988), at p 98.

[4]　Section 22(1).

[5]　See Gadsden *the Law of Commons* (1988), at p 38.

3.4   THE OLD ROYAL FORESTS

A 'forest' has a particular meaning. It is not necessarily woodland, but it describes an area of land that was formerly subject to 'forest law'. Forests were large areas of land over which the King had exclusive hunting rights in the exercise of his prerogative. The forest laws protected those rights.[1] The King's hunting rights and the forest laws that protected them, overlay the ownership of land by others within the forest and the rights of commoners over common land. There were special courts to enforce the laws: the Court of Attachment had summary jurisdiction and the Court of Swainmote was concerned with the more serious offences; sentence was pronounced by the Chief Justice in Eyre. The principal officers were the wardens and verderers, and below them the keepers and the reeves. The latter marked and controlled the cattle of the commoners. By the seventeenth century these special courts no longer sat. In 1829 the residual royal powers were vested in the Commissioner of His Majesty's Woods and Forests.[2]

The remnants of the original Royal forests include the New Forest in Hampshire, the Forest of Dean in Gloucestershire, Epping Forest, near London and Ashdown Forest in Sussex. There were originally 68 Royal forests but most were divided up into private ownership and wholly or partially inclosed.

Rights of common over land within a Royal forest could be acquired by prescription, even by a class of persons consisting of the inhabitants of a parish. The foundation for prescription is a grant (even though implied) and it could be assumed that the Crown could make such a grant in derogation of its forestral rights, especially as the same were oppressive upon the inhabitants.[3] Rights of common of pasture in a forest were generally limited to horses and cattle,[4] although the right to pasture sheep has been claimed.[5] In some forests there were prescriptive rights of pasture by sheep but in others the common of pannage existed. However, a common

---

[1]   Forest laws were abolished by Wild Creatures and Forest Laws Act 1971. Forests were protected before the Norman invasion: see *the Laws of Canute*, Winchester 1016.

[2]   See WA Gordon *The Law of Forestry* (1955), at pp 66-68.

[3]   *Willingdale v Maitland* (1866) LR 3 Eq 103.

[4]   See *Leicester Forest Case* (1607) Cro Jac 155.

[5]   See WA Gordon *The Law of Forestry* (1955), at p 70.

feature of all the forests was that any rights were subject to restrictions and controls in the interests of the preservation of the game for the King. For instance in some forests there was a 'fence month' or a winter heyning. These were periods during which the forest was closed for the protection of deer either during fawning or in winter when pasture was reserved only for the deer.[1] In the Forest of Dean, rights of common have never been admitted by the Crown, and animals are only permitted by sufferance.

---

[1] See *Halsbury's Laws of England* (4th edn) vol 6, at para 514. In the New Forest, the *fence month* was 15 days before and after midsummer day.

Chapter 4

CLASSIFICATION OF RIGHTS OF COMMON

4.1 INTRODUCTION

The right of commoners to let their animals graze on common land is the right that most readers understand as amounting to rights of common. Behind this relatively simple concept lie two formative matters. First, the history, origin and nature of agricultural practices as explained in Chapter 2 which has had considerable effect on the legal form of rights of common. Secondly, the development of the law relating to rights of common, both the common law, and the customary law enforced in the manorial courts, has given rights of common, in their various forms, certain legal characteristics.

In this chapter, rights of common are first classified and explained according to their legal form and consequence. Later in the chapter the various kinds of rights of common are described. Although some mention may be made in this chapter of the various statutory provisions that regulate or are concerned with the registration of rights of common, this chapter is primarily concerned with the common law and customary law relating to rights of common and not with any analysis of various statutory definitions which may be relevant for specific purposes.

4.1.1 Effect of the Commons Registration Act 1965

Whilst some explanation of the different types of rights of common, and their origin and legal development, may be interesting, the consequences of the Commons Registration Act 1965 renders such background of little significance today. All rights of common that existed prior to 31 July 1970 were required to be registered.[1] Further, any rights of common that existed prior to that date, but which were

---

[1] Section 1(1).

not then registered under the Act cannot any longer be exercisable.[1] However, provision is made for the registration of new rights of common that may be created since 31 July 1970.[2] The 1965 Act also provides that where a right of common consists of or includes a right to graze animals that is not limited by number, then the right was required to be registered by reference to a stated number of animals. Indeed the right could not, after the registration had become final, be exercised in relation to more than the specified and registered number of animals.[3] The effect of that provision means that many of the interesting and difficult problems related to stinted pastures, where the numbers of animals might have varied according to the conditions from time to time, are now only of interest for historical reasons. The basic rule now is whether a particular right of common is registered and, if it is a right of grazing, what are the specified number of animals that were registered. If the right existed prior to 31 July 1970, but was not registered, it cannot any longer be exercised.

The reader should therefore be careful with the material that follows in this chapter. Much of it would have been relevant to the process of registration under the 1965 Act where applicants were seeking to establish rights of common for the registration process, but today serves only to explain rights of common that have been registered.

4.2   CLASSIFICATION OF RIGHTS OF COMMON

In *Hampshire County Council v Milburn*,[4] Lord Templeman made reference to the manorial system which the Normans partly inherited and partly established, and identified three categories of land that were comprised in a typical manor:[5]

> 'The demesne land belonged to the lord of the manor. The copyhold land was divided between the tenants of the lord of the manor. The remainder of the land consisted of uncultivated land, referred to as the waste of the manor. The waste was the natural source of grazing, fodder and fuel for all the inhabitants of the manor. The waste land

---

[1]   Section 1(2)(b).

[2]   Commons Registration (New Land) Regulations 1969, SI 1969/1843.

[3]   Section 15.

[4]   [1990] 2 All ER 257.

[5]   Ibid, at 258e.

belonged to the lord of the manor subject to the rights of the tenants to enjoy in common the fruits or some of the fruits of the soil in the manner of a "profit à prendre". The rights of the commoners varied from manor to manor. The extent of the right of any particular commoner depended on the origin of the right and might depend on the size and situation of land held by the commoner. A grant of arable land to a freeman prior to 1290 entitled him by common law to the use of the manorial waste for such purposes as were necessary for the maintenance of his husbandry. Common rights could also be acquired by grant, custom or prescription. The right of a commoner was the right "to eat the grass with the mouths of his cattle, or to take such other produce of the soil as he may be entitled to".'

4.2.1 The forms of landownership and rights of common

Lord Templeman's description of the model of the English manor may be a little too simple. Within the manor, there were three types of owners (or tenants as they would originally have been called): freeholders; customary freeholders; and copyholders. The lord of the manor would have been a freeholder, although others might have come to acquire freeholds from the lord. Customary freeholders and copyholders were both tenants of the lord. A customary freehold was a superior type of copyhold, the freeholder holding his interest by the custom of the manor and holding a copy of the manorial court roll, the copyholder holding merely at the will of the lord.

The distinction between these different types of ownership was important in relation to the acquisition of rights of common. Only the true freeholder could acquire a right of common by grant. Customary freeholders and copyholders could only acquire such rights according to the custom of the manor, and not by prescription. Customary freeholds and copyholds were abolished in 1922.¹

4.2.2 Rights of common as legal interests

There are various ways in which rights of common fall to be classified. Under English law of property, rights of common are interests in land, generally referred to as incorporeal hereditaments. Provided certain formalities are satisfied concerning their grant (or

---

¹ Law of Property Act 1922.

presumed grant, if acquired by prescription), they are legal interests in land.[1] Rights of common fall within that category of legal interests in land known as *profits à prendre*. As Lord Lindley in *Duke of Sutherland v Heathcote* said:[2]

> 'A *profit à prendre* is a right to take something off another person's land; such a right does not prevent the owner from taking the same sort of thing from off his own land; the first right may limit, but does not exclude, the second.'

A *profit à prendre* falls within, and shares many of the legal characteristics of, the same broad category of legal interests in land as easements. Easements are concerned with the right to use another person's land such as through the exercise of a right of way, whereas a *profit à prendre* is concerned with the right to take something from another's land. Although rights of common are *profits à prendre*, historically they came first. In *Gale on Easements*[3] the authors state that:

> 'A *profit à prendre* may be enjoyed to the exclusion of all other persons, in which case it is termed a "sole" or "several" profit. On the other hand, a profit may be enjoyed in common with one or more persons, including the owner of the servient land, when it is call a profit "in common" or right of common. Every right of common is, therefore, a *profit à prendre*, but not every *profit à prendre* is a right of common.'

This book is not concerned with those *profits à prendre* that are not rights of common. Thus, for example, the grant to a grantee that he alone to the exclusion of all others may fish a river belonging to the grantor is a *profit à prendre* 'sole' or 'several', but cannot be a right of common.

4.2.3   Rights of common classified by legal form

Turning to the legal form of rights of common, the common law has recognised the following classification:

(1)   rights of common appendant;

---

[1]   Law of Property Act 1925, s 1(2).

[2]   [1892] 1 Ch 475 at 484.

[3]   (17th edn), at para 1–129.

(2)   rights of common appurtenant;

(3)   rights of common in gross; and

(4)   rights of common *pur cause de vicinage* (by reason of vicinage).

The precise origin or classification of any right of common that was registered under the Commons Registration Act 1965 is no longer particularly relevant. Rights of common appendant can no longer be created. As they cannot be created, there is no scope for the registration of any such rights under the 1965 Act as newly created rights. The same is also probably true of rights of common *pur cause de vicinage*; all such rights would have been registered and no such new rights can now be created. The precise characteristics of rights of common appendant, and rights of common *pur cause de vicinage*, therefore, no longer have to be considered in any detail as any such rights that existed prior to 31 July 1970 have either been registered with specific numbers of animals or, if they were not registered, can no longer be exercised.[1]

What follows is, therefore, a brief explanation of the legal characteristics of each of these four categories.

(a)   Rights of common appendant

A right of common appendant is said to be annexed to land by operation of law and it probably only existed as a common of pasture.[2] Prior to the statute Quia Emptors 1290, the lord of a manor could create a new tenure, that is grant a new interest in land, by what was called subinfeudation. Where the lord of the manor granted an interest in arable land to a freeholder by subinfeudation, the freeholder obtained as appendant to the arable land the right to pasture certain animals. These were animals necessary to plough and manure the land granted to him, and no more in number. This was explained by Park B in *Dunraven (Earl) v Llewellyn*,[3] where he first sets out an extract from Lord Coke's Commentaries on the Statute of Merton:[4]

---

[1]   Section 1(2)(b) of the 1965 Act.

[2]   Harpum et al (eds) *Megarry & Wade: The Law of Real Property* (6th edn, Sweet & Maxwell), at para 18–083.

[3]   (1850) 15 QB 791.

[4]   At p 810 referring to the statute 20 H 3, c, 4.

'By this recital [of that statute] a point of the ancient common law appeareth, that when a Lord of a manor (whereon was great waste grounds) did enfeoff others of some parts of arable land, the feoffees ad manutenend servitium socae, should have common in the said wastes of the Lord for two causes. One, as incident to the feoffment, for the feoffee could not plough, and manure his ground without beasts, and they could not be sustained without pasture, and by consequence the tenant should have common in the wastes of the Lord for his beasts, which do plough and manure his tenancy, as appendant to his tenancy, and this was the beginning of common appendant. The second reason was for maintenance and advancement of agriculture, and tillage, which was much favoured in law.'

Park B then said:

'This right, therefore, is not a common right of all tenants, but belongs only to each grantee, before the statute of quia emptores, of arable land, by virtue of his individual grant, and as an incident thereto: and it is as much a peculiar right of the grantee as one derived by express grant, or by prescription, though it differs in its extent, being limited to such cattle as are kept for ploughing and manuring them the arable land granted, and as are of a description fit for that purpose; whereas the right by grant or prescription has no such limits, and depends on the will of the grantor.'

The extent of a right of common appendant in pasture is more fully explained below.

(b)   Rights of common appurtenant

A right of common appurtenant is a right that is attached to a particular piece of land and passes to successors in title on any disposal, such as by way of sale or will. Such a right does not arise automatically by way of operation of law as in the case of a right of common appendant; a right of common appurtenant is created by grant, but if no grant can be shown, may be established by prescription. The basis for prescription is, in effect, an implied grant.

(c)   Right of common in gross

A right of common in gross is a right that lies in either grant or prescription, but the right is not attached to the ownership of any particular piece of land. Accordingly the owner of a right of common in gross may own any particular piece of land or no land at all, and is entitled to dispose of that right independently from the disposal of any land.[1] The origin of the right of common in gross is probably to be found in those situations where the lord of the manor had more than sufficient waste to meet the needs of those commoners with rights of common appendant and or appurtenant, and therefore granted rights of common in gross to others who may or may not have held any land. The right may be acquired by grant or prescription.[2] Where a right of common of pasture appurtenant is held, this right can be severed from the dominant land to which it was originally attached; the right of common then becomes a right in gross.[3] On Dartmoor severance of a common of pasture appurtenant is forbidden.[4]

(d)   Rights of common by reason of vicinage

There is a very simple idea behind the nature of this right of common. Where the waste lands of two separate manors adjoin, it may be difficult in practice to restrain the grazing animals of the commoners of one manor from going into the waste of the adjoining manor. The background is explained in Blackstone's *Commentaries*:[5]

> 'Common *because of vicinage*, or neighbourhood, is where the inhabitants of two townships which lie contiguous to each other, have usually intercommoned with one another; the beasts of the one straying mutually into the other's fields, without any molestation from either. This is indeed only a permissive right, intended to excuse what in strictness is a trespass in both, and to prevent a multiplicity of suits ...'

Further, in *Jones v Robin* Parke B said:[6]

> 'It must be considered to be established that a common, or as it is sometimes called feeding, ... pur cause de vicinage, is not properly a right of common or profit à prendre but rather an excuse for a trespass

---

[1] 2 BL Com 34.

[2] *Tyrringham's Case* (1584) 4 Co Rep 36b.

[3] *Bettison v Langton* [2002] 1 AC 27, [2001] 3 All ER 417; *Bunn v Channen* (1813) 5 Taunt 244.

[4] Dartmoor Commons Act 1985, s 8.

[5] (23rd edn, 1854), Book 2, chapter 3, at pp 34–35.

[6] (1847) 10 QB 620 at 632, 116 ER 235 at 240.

.... Lord Coke says that the person entitled cannot put in his cattle into the adjoining waste, but they must escape into it ...'

In *Newman v Bennet* Waller LJ said:[1]

'While [a right of common by reason of vicinage] ... may be useful as a shield against trespass (and ... distress ...), it is still a right of common, though limited in character because it is determinable. It can be determined by fencing off, and however impracticable that might be ... it is a theoretical possibility.'

The limitation on the number of animals that are entitled to the benefit of a right of common by reason of vicinage was explained in *Commissioners of Sewers v Glasse* when Jessel MR said:[2]

'In common of vicinage there is a limitation of the right of this sort. Neither party can put on the commons more beasts than his own common will maintain ...'

Rights of common by reason of *vicinage* will therefore be restricted to grazing. The extent of these rights and the conditions for their existence, are considered further below.

The subject matter of rights of common, of whatever legal form, is now explained.

4.3   RIGHTS OF COMMON OF PASTURE

The right of common of pasture is the right that is, and was, most frequently encountered. In essence, it is the right of an owner of land within the manor to graze animals on the waste lands of the manor or, in the case of the open field system, of the owner of a strip in the open field to graze animals after crops have been taken or in the fallow year. As explained above, the right of common of pasture existed in any of the four legal forms of rights of common known to the common law. However, it is probably correct that rights of common appendant and rights by reason of *vicinage* will only involve rights of common to pasture animals. In respect of each of

---

[1]   [1980] 3 All ER 449 at 454c.

[2]   (1874) LR 19 Eq 134, at 161.

the rights to pasture animals, described below, it is not an incident of the right to be able to bring extra feed on to the common land, although shepherding by a vehicle over a large area would be a reasonable use if exercised with minimum interference with the landowner's rights.[1]

4.3.1 Rights of common of pasture appendant

(a) Registration

The effect of the Commons Registration Act 1965 was to render the legal characteristics of rights of common of pasture appendant obsolete. If such rights existed prior to 31 July 1970, they were required to be registered.[2] If they were registered, and the rights were not in respect of a definite number of animals, registration required a specified number of animals to be entered.[3] If the right of common existed prior to 31 July 1970, and was not registered, the right can no longer be exercised.[4] What follows is therefore a description of the origin and legal characteristics of rights of common of pasture appendant, but there is little practical significance in the characteristics of this particular right today.

(b) Origin and creation

It was explained above that this was a right that arose by operation of law where there was a grant of land by a lord of the manor before the statute of Quia Emptores.[5] The right only arose in respect of what was described as *anciently* arable land. Provided the land was originally arable land at the time of the grant (before 1290), the fact that later it came to be used for pasture land, or that a house was built on part of it, will not change the status of *anciently* arable land for the purposes of a claim to retain the right of common of pasture appendant.[6]

---

[1] *Besley v John* [2003] All ER D 481 (Oct), CA.

[2] Section 1.

[3] Section 15.

[4] Section 1(2)(b).

[5] 1290.

[6] *Tyrringham's Case* (1584) 4 Co Rep 36b, where it was considered that an appendant right could not have been created after 1189.

Because a right of common of pasture appendant does not depend upon actual grant or prescription, it is not necessary to prove actual user of the right in order to establish a claim. Proof only that the land of the claimant was *anciently* arable land is sufficient to give rise to the existence of the right by operation of law. Accordingly, there are only two grounds for defeating a claim: first, that it can be shown that the alleged *anciently* arable lands were never granted by the lord of the manor prior to 1290; and, secondly, where the character of the land in respect of which the claim is made has so altered, by change of use or development, that no right could any longer be exercised.[1]

(c) Limitation on numbers of animals

There is a limit on the number and type of animals in respect of which a common of pasture appendant can be exercised. Although the number of animals that might originally have been turned out upon the common may have been limited to the number required, from time to time, for the proper farming of the land of the commoner, the common law came to apply the rule of *levancy* and *couchancy* which meant the number of animals that would be lying within the buildings and could be kept there throughout the winter.[2] However, in *Robertson v Hartopp* Fry LJ said that he thought the principle of *levancy* and *couchancy* was more the measure of capacity of the land than a condition to be actually and literally complied with by the cattle lying down and getting up, or by their being fed off the land.[3]

(d) Type of animals

The type of animals in respect of which the right may be exercised is also limited. Farm animals were normally referred to by the generic word 'cattle'. The right was confined to animals needed for the purposes of ploughing (horses and oxen) and animals needed to manure the arable land, such as cattle proper and sheep. Other animals, such as pigs and goats, could not have been used in the exercise of a right of common appendant. It was also important that the animals turned onto the common in the exercise of a right of

---

[1]   *Carr v Lambert* (1866) LR 1 Exch 168 and *Scrutton v Stone* (1893) 9 TLR 478, affirmed (1893) 10 TLR 157.

[2]   *Scholes v Hargreaves* (1792) 5 Term Rep 46.

[3]   (1889) 43 ChD 484.

common appendant were those animals belonging to the commoner for the purpose of ploughing or manuring his arable land, or borrowed for that special purpose.[1]

(e) Miscellaneous characteristics

Because a right of common of pasture appendant arises by operation of law, the normal rules of prescription do not apply. However, the right implies prescription, in the sense that the commoner is using land belonging to another (the lord of the manor) for grazing his animals. It is partly for that reason that only a freeholder within the manor acquired an appendant right. Further, the lord of the manor himself did not have *rights* of common of pasture over his own waste lands. The extent to which the lord of the manor put animals on the waste lands of the manor that were otherwise necessary for ploughing and manuring the arable land within his own demesne lands, was really an incident of his own rights as lord of the manor and owner of the soil.[2]

The right of common of pasture appendant could not arise in respect of the use of the open field system.

4.3.2 Rights of common of pasture appurtenant

In *Bettison v Langton* Lord Nichols explained the background to rights of common of pasture appurtenant:[3]

'For centuries many farmers whose lands adjoin the local common have enjoyed the right to put out their sheep and cattle to graze on the common. The animals wintered on the farms, but in the summer months they were let out to graze on the open common. ... These rights have feudal origins ... Traditionally grazing rights are an adjunct of the lands of the farmers who own the rights. The rights had their origin in actual or presumed grant, usually the latter. The law assumes that long continued use must have had a lawful origin. The number of animals that a farmer was entitled to depasture on the common was limited to the animals his land could support through the winter. The language was picturesque: the right was limited to the

---

[1]   *Rumsey v Rawson* (1669) 1 Vent 18.

[2]   *Musgrave v Inclosure Commissioners* (1874) LR 9 QB 162; *Baring v Abbingdon* (1892) 2 Ch 374.

[3]   [2001] 3 All ER 417 at 419.

number of beasts "levant and couchant" ("getting up and lying down") on the farmer's holding in the winter months. These rights could be passed on or sold, but only with the farm to which they were appurtenant. They were to be enjoyed by the occupier for the time being. They could not be sold separately, or "severed", from the farm.'

(a) Customary freeholds and copyholds

Unlike a right of common of pasture appendant, which was restricted to grants of freehold land prior to 1290, rights of common of pasture appurtenant may be exercisable by freeholders whose estates were, prior to 1922, copyholds and customary freeholds.[1] Indeed, a right of common of pasture appurtenant could be claimed by a person who did not own land within the manor but came to use the waste land of the manor for grazing his animals, and who acquired a right by prescription.[2]

(b) Registration

Any right of common of pasture appurtenant that existed prior to 31 July 1970 was required to be registered, and if the right was not in respect of a definite number of animals, a definite number of animals had to be specified for registration purposes.[3] If such rights were not registered, they can no longer be exercised.[4] Rights of common of pasture appurtenant can still be created by express grant (and probably by prescription over land that is not registered common land).[5] Any such new rights are therefore capable of registration.[6]

4.3.3 Right of common *pur cause de vicinage*

This is a right that cannot exist alone save as an addition to some other right of common, such as a right of common appendant, appurtenant, or in gross. The primary right is exercisable by the commoner over a particular common and the additional right of *vicinage* is exercisable over an adjoining common that is contiguous

---

[1] *Robertson v Hartopp* (1889) 43 Ch D 484; *Hall v Byron* (1877) 4 Ch D 667.

[2] *Sacheverell v Porter* (1637) W Jo 396; *Clarkson v Woodhouse* (1782) 5 Term Rep 412n.

[3] Commons Registration Act 1965, ss 1 and 15.

[4] Ibid, s 1(2)(b).

[5] This is more fully considered in Chapters 6 and 8.

[6] Commons Registration (New Land) Regulations 1969.

with the first one. The commoner has no primary right over the neighbouring common but he does have the subsidiary and additional right of *vicinage*. The right can be terminated by the erection of a fence between the two adjoining commons.[1]

The requirement to register rights of common under the Commons Registration Act 1965 gave rise to difficulties in the case of rights of *vicinage*. Apparently some rights of this nature were registered, and others were not. The preliminary question is whether they should have been registered. That seems doubtful because a right of *vicinage* is not a substantive right of common, it is more a customary recognition that animals on adjoining commons will stray and, in effect, provide no more than a defence to trespass proceedings.[2]

4.3.4 Common of pasture in gross

This right may be without limit as to the number of animals that can be put on the common, or may be specified as to a number certain. In practice such a right is more likely to be for a number certain, especially where the right arose by prescription. That is because the prescription would have been in respect of a number certain, such as by reference to the principle of *levancy* and *couchancy*.[3]

4.3.5 Right of foldcourse

This right is sometimes referred to as sheepwalk or foldage, or sometimes free fold. This began as a right of the lord of the manor to have the sheep of his tenants on his land so that they would manure it. Although not originally a right of common, where it remains, it has acquired the characteristics of a right of common.[4]

4.4 COMMON OF TURBARY

This is the right to take turf or peat for heating purposes. It is a right that has to be appurtenant to a house or building. Turfs or peat cut

---

[1] *Gullett v Lopes* (1811) 13 East 348, 104 ER 404.

[2] *Newman v Bennett* [1980] 3 All ER 449, a right of common limited in character.

[3] *Mellor v Spateman* (1669) 1 Saund 339.

[4] *Robinson v Duleep Singh* (1878) 11 ChD 798.

can only be consumed within the house, and cannot be sold.[1] Where in the common or waste the right may be exercised depends on the custom of the particular manor.[2]

4.5   COMMON OF ESTOVERS

This is the right to take the products of the soil in the form of wood or timber. The Saxon word for estovers was bote; it consisted of wood and timber and was expressed as house-bote (firewood, and wood for repairing a house), plough or cart-bote (for making and repairing agricultural implements) and hay-bote (for repairing fences). If the right is in the form of house-bote, the right is in respect of the house or building as it existed at the date of the grant or period of prescription. Although the right is not lost if the building is rebuilt, it will not extend to enable wood or timber to be taken for the purposes of building or repairing any enlargement to the original building.[3]

Generally the right is to take underwood and trees of little value, such as birch, willow, alder or hazel.[4] Accordingly, the more valuable trees, such as oaks, are less likely objects of estovers. The right of estovers is not necessarily limited to wood or timber and may include heather or bracken as fodder or litter for cattle.[5] A right to estovers is never without limitation. It may be limited by reference to cartloads or by reference to the needs of the holding to which the right is attached.[6]

4.6   COMMON OF PISCARY

A right of common of piscary is a right to fish with others in a river or water belonging to a further person. The right can either be appurtenant or in gross. It may exist in a non-navigable river but it

---

[1]   *Valentine v Penny* (1605) Noy 145, 74 ER 1107.

[2]   *Maxwell v Martin* (1830) 6 Bing 522, 130 ER 1382 and *Clarkson v Woodhouse* (1782) 5 Term Rep 412, 101 ER 231.

[3]   *A-G v Reynolds* [1911] 2 KB 888 and *Luttrel's Case* (1601) 4 Co Rep 84b.

[4]   *Earl de la Warr v Miles* (1881) 17 ChD 535.

[5]   *Smith v Earl Brownlow* (1870) LR 9 Eq 241; *Earl de la Warr v Miles* (1881) 17 ChD 535.

[6]   *Earl de la Warr v Miles* (1881) 17 ChD 535; *Earl Pembroke's Case* (1636) Clay 47.

cannot exist in a tidal navigable river as the soil of such a river is presumed to be owned by the Crown.[1] A common of piscary may be created by grant, in which case the extent of the rights granted are a matter of agreement between the parties. However, if a common of piscary is claimed by prescription, it can only be appurtenant to a house, and the fish taken are those for use in the house.[2]

4.7   COMMON IN THE SOIL

There are a wide variety of rights of common to take parts of the soil such as marl (for manuring), sand, stone or other minerals. The right may be appurtenant or held in gross and can be acquired by grant or by prescription.[3] In the case of land that was originally held as a copyhold tenement, the right can be claimed by custom, but not by prescription.[4] The characteristics of both the rights of estovers and of turbary apply, namely that the products must be used in connection with the land or building to which the right attaches. Although where the right exists in gross, it will usually be limited in some form of quantity.

4.8   COMMON IN PANNAGE

The right of common of pannage (or mast) is similar to the right of pasturage. Pannage is to put pigs into woodlands to enable them to feed on such things as acorns and beech mast. The right will usually have been limited to the appropriate times of the year when the acorns and beech mast will be on the ground.[5] In the case of Royal forests, the time of pannage began on Holy-rood Day, 15 days before Michaelmas and ended 40 days after Michaelmas.[6]

---

[1]   *Ward v Cresswell* (1741) Willes 265; *A-G for British Colombia v A-G for Canada* [1914] AC 153.

[2]   *Clayton v Corby* (1843) 5 QB 415; *Lord Chesterfield v Harris* [1908] 2 Ch 397.

[3]   *Gateward's Case* (1607) 6 Co Rep 59b.

[4]   *Rogers v Brenton* (1847) 10 QB 26; *Heath v Deane* [1905] 2 Ch 86.

[5]   *Chilton v Corporation of London* (1878) 7 ChD 562.

[6]   *Manwood's Forest Laws* (4th ed, 1717), at p 230, quoted in Gordon, *Law of Forestry* (1955), at p 70.

4.9   RIGHTS OF SOLE

4.9.1   General meaning

Where the owner of the soil retains the right to use his own land for, say, the grazing of pasture, and grants rights of pasture to others, those rights of pasture are rights of common; they may be exercised in common with the owner of the soil. However, where the owner grants to another person or persons the whole and exclusive right to pasture, and retains no such right himself, he has granted a sole profit. The distinction between rights of common and a sole right depends entirely on whether the owner of the soil has retained any right of the same nature or product that he has granted.

The words 'sole' and 'several' probably mean the same thing and are interchangeable in use in this context.[1]

A sole right (or profit) can be granted to one person. Having granted that right the owner cannot grant any more rights of the same nature in the same land. A sole right may be granted by the same grant to several persons, such as to all the tenants of a particular manor.[2] In the usual case of a grant of rights of sole in pasture, each share would be known as a stint, or beastgate or cattlegate. The shares or stints can be acquired by others – even by the owner of the soil.[3]

The owner or owners of rights of sole, say of pasture, may be able to exclude the owner of the soil from putting his own cattle on the land to take any of the pasture, but the owner of the soil may exercise any other rights of ownership, such as the taking of game.[4]

4.9.2   Vesture

Vesture includes all the produce of the land excluding timber. It includes corn, grass, underwood and all that can be cut by the scythe.[5] A right of vesture does not include any right to the non-agricultural products that can be dug out of the soil.[6] A right of sole

---

[1]   Gadsden *Law of Commons*, at chapter 3.

[2]   *Hoskins v Robins* (1671) 2 Wms Saund 324, 85 ER 1123.

[3]   *Lonsdale (Earl) v Rigg* (1856) 11 Ex 654, 156 ER 992.

[4]   Ibid.

[5]   Co Litt 4b.

[6]   *Re Tenants of Owning* (1587) 4 Leon 43, 74 ER 718.

vesture might be exercisable by the owner (or owners) of the sole at limited periods of the year leaving the owner of the soil to take agricultural produce, such as a hay crop outside those periods.

4.9.3 Herbage

This is a sole right to take grass by cutting or grazing.[1] The right is less than vesture but more than a right of pasture, which does not include the cutting of grass.

4.9.4 Pasture

The sole right in pasture, whether held by a single person (a single stint), or more usually by a number of persons (each holding a stint), permits such persons to take the grass only through the mouths of their cattle.[2] Where there is more than one stint in a sole pasture, each stint is of equal size. Stints may have specified numbers of animals attached to them. This right is common in the north of England and is frequently owned in gross. That means that the right is not attached to the land, if any, belonging to the owner of the right. Sole rights of pasture are assignable.[3]

4.9.5 Other sole rights

A *profit à prendre* is a right and a legal interest to take a specified product from land belonging to the owner of the soil. Such a right is not confined to vesture, herbage or pasture, but can include the right to take or dig some specified product out of the soil, such as marl or sand. However, sole *profits à prendre* that are not sole rights to vesture, herbage or pasture are not registrable under the Commons Registration Act 1965; they are not further considered in this book.

4.9.6 Commons Registration Act 1965

Chapter 8 explains the registration requirements of this Act. The registrable rights include 'cattlegates or beastgates (by whatever name known) and rights of sole or several vesture or herbage or of

---

[1]   *Earl de la Warr v Miles* (1881) 17 ChD 535.

[2]   *Cox v Glue* (1848) 5 CB 533, at 548, 136 ER 987, at 993.

[3]   *Welcome v Upton* (1840) 6 M&W 536, 151 ER 524.

sole or several pasture'.[1] Sole rights of vesture, herbage and pasture were therefore registrable, and the land over which such rights are exercisable is common land under the 1965 Act.[2]

---

[1]   Sections 1(1)(b) and 22(1).

[2]   Section 22(1).

Chapter 5

OWNERSHIP OF COMMON LAND

5.1 INTRODUCTION

As discussed in Chapters 1 and 2, common land was that part of the manor that was not occupied by the copyhold tenants, nor was it part of the lord's demesne lands. It was that part of uninclosed land which was available and used by the copyhold tenants, the customary freeholders and the other freeholders in common with the lord of the manor for, principally, the grazing of animals and the taking of estovers. Therefore, originally, the owner of the common lands was the lord of the manor. The lord of the manor would have held the common lands of the manor under one of the freehold titles.

In the case of commonable lands, that is those lands subject to the open-field system or similar, such open fields were owned in strips of approximately 1 acre each by the various several owners.

This chapter addresses the nature, incidents and liabilities of the ownership of the common lands.

5.2 LORD OF THE MANOR

It is necessary to explain the ownership of common lands in the wider context of the ownership of a manor in its lord. The lord of the manor normally held the manorship directly from the Crown. Under the original feudal arrangements, the manor was held upon terms by which the lord of the manor owed certain duties to the King such as of homage (or loyalty) and the provision of services (such as military). The lord of the manor was, in effect, in control of the whole of the geographical area of the manor and all who lived within it. Save for the free men within the manor, all others would originally have been serfs required to work for and provide services to the lord of the manor. Because of his legal and actual control over all that was within the boundaries of the manor, and of its inhabitants, the lord of the manor enjoyed many rights and incidents of his ownership. The extent of these rights is well illustrated by the deemed effect of a conveyance of a manor set out in s 62(3) of the Law of Property Act 1925:

> 'A conveyance of a manor shall be deemed to include and shall by virtue of this Act operate to convey, with the manor, all pastures, feedings, wastes, warrens, commons, mines, minerals, quarries, furzes, trees, woods, underwoods, coppices, and the ground and soil thereof, fishings, fisheries, fowlings, courts leet, courts baron, and other courts, view of frank pledge and all that to view of frank pledge doth belong, mills, mulctures, customs, tolls, duties, reliefs, heriots, fines, sums of money, amerciaments, waifs, estrays, chief-rents, quitrents, rents charge, rents seck, rents of assize, fee farm rents, services, royalties jurisdictions, franchises, liberties, privileges, easements, profits, advantages, rights, emoluments, and hereditaments whatsoever, to the manor appertaining or reputed to appertain, or, at the time of conveyance, demised, occupied, or enjoyed with the same, or reputed or known as part, parcel, or member thereof.'[1]

These fall into two broad groups: corporeal hereditaments (those matters that physically exist, such as wastes, warrens, etc); and incorporeal hereditaments (those matters that cannot be physically touched, but are in the nature of rights or benefits, such as fisheries, the holding of courts and the entitlement to rents, etc). A full explanation of the nature of all the incidents of the ownership of the lord of the manor is beyond the scope of this book. What is clear is that the ownership of the wastes and commons is but one of the incidents of that ownership.

Increasingly the ownership of a common has become severed from the ownership of the lord of the manor. Where that has taken place, the person owning the common lands, which were originally part of the manor, will generally enjoy the same characteristics of ownership of that soil, as the lord of the manor would have done so had he retained its ownership. However, such an owner would not enjoy all the other and usual incidents of the ownership of a manor.

---

[1]   Many of the expressions set out above are explained in the glossary to this book.

5.3   OWNERSHIP OF THE SOIL OF COMMON LAND

The ownership of the soil of the common is capable of being held under the two legal estates in land, namely the fee simple absolute in possession (freehold) or term of years absolute (lease).[1] The normal presumption is that the owner of the soil owns everything upwards to the heavens and downwards to the centre of the earth subject only to the rights of the commoners. Subject to any statutory restrictions, the owner may use the common lands for any purposes he chooses provided he does not interfere with the commoners' rights. Thus, for example, if the common land is extensive, and the number of persons owning rights of common is limited, the common land may have spare capacity for the grazing of animals. In such circumstances the owner of the soil is entitled to grant licences to strangers to pasture animals.[2] Subject, again, to not interfering with the rights of the commoners, the owner of the soil is entitled to shoot over and take game on the common. He is therefore entitled to grant shooting rights to a third party.[3]

One of the principal characteristics of the ownership of the soil of the common is the right of the lord or owner of the soil to pasture his own animals on the common. This right was not dependent upon there being a sufficiency of common land, or pasture on it, for the commoners.[4] Indeed, in those limited cases in which a right to exclude the lord from the common arises, such a right is a sole or several pasture or herbage and is not a right of common at all. Somewhat confusingly, such rights in sole or several pasture or herbage, are included in the definition of rights of common in the Commons Registration Act 1965.[5]

The expression 'the lord of the manor' may therefore be synonymous with the expression 'owner of the soil of the common'. However, care must be taken in understanding some of the earlier decided authorities as to whether the expression 'lord of the manor'

---

[1]   Law of Property Act 1925, s 1(1). The new legal estate of commonhold is not relevant to the ownership of common land.

[2]   See *Mellor v Spateman* (1669) 1 Saund 339 at 345; *Atkinson v Teesdale* (1772) 2 Wm BL 817.

[3]   *Ewart v Graham* (1859) 7 HL Cas 331.

[4]   Co Litt 122a.

[5]   Co Litt 122a and Commons Registration Act 1965, s 22(1).

means, strictly that, or is simply being used to indicate the owner of the soil.

5.3.1   Powers of leasing

A distinction must be made between the power of the lord of the manor to grant leases of common land and his power to grant leases of the waste land of the manor. The lord of the manor has power to grant leases of common land, although any leases so granted will be subject to the rights of the commoners. However, there is a limited power in the Inclosure Act 1773, s 15 by which the lord of the manor may, with the consent of three-quarters of persons having rights of common on the wastes and commons, grant a lease for a term not exceeding 4 years of any part not exceeding one-twelfth in area of such wastes and commons. The lease must be granted for the best and most improved yearly rent that can, by public auction, be obtained and the net rents shall then be applied in the draining, fencing or otherwise improving the residue of those wastes and commons.

In the case of the waste land of a manor that is not subject to rights of common, such land only retains that particular status for so long as it has the physical characteristics of being 'open, uncultivated and unoccupied'.[1] The effect of the lord of the manor granting any lease of any waste lands of the manor not subject to rights of common must surely mean that the land is no longer unoccupied, thus causing such land to cease to be waste land.

5.3.2   Right to grant grazing rights

Consistent with the proposition that the owner of a common may grant leases of it, the owner may grant grazing rights provided there is sufficient pasture left for the commoners.[2]

5.3.3   Grazing for the owner's animals

The essential characteristic of land subject to rights of common is that those rights are rights in common with the owner of the soil. Accordingly, the lord or owner of the soil has a right to pasture his

---

[1]   See *Attorney-General v Hanmer* (1858) 27 LJ Ch 837.

[2]   *Smith v Feverell* (1675) 2 Mod Rep 6, 86 ER 909; *Arlett v Ellis* (1827) 7 B&C 346.

own animals on the common. It is irrelevant that there may not be enough grazing for the commoners' animals.[1]

5.3.4   Trees, timber and woodland

The owner may plant trees on common land provided such planting does not interfere with the sufficiency of pasturage. The owner is also entitled to those trees that grow naturally on common land. Where the trees completely exclude the ability of the commoners to exercise their rights of common, the commoners may then abate the nuisance by felling the trees.[2] But if the effect of the trees is merely to prevent the commoners from enjoying their rights of common as beneficially as they are entitled to, the commoners cannot then fell the trees by way of self-abatement, and must bring legal proceedings for nuisance.[3]

5.3.5   Rights to game

The owner of the soil has a right to take game from the common land and the waste land of the manor, and may grant shooting rights to third parties.[4] The grant of such a right is a *profit à prendre*.

5.3.6   Warrens

The beasts and birds of a warren are hare, rabbit, pheasant, partridge and wild duck.[5] What is known as a 'free warren' is a right to keep beasts and birds of a warren. It is not a characteristic of the ownership of the manor, or of the soil of a common. It could have been acquired by direct grant of franchise from the Crown or by prescription (which assumes such a grant).[6] One particular type of warren was known as the cone-burrow (or coney-burrow). This was a warren used for the keeping of rabbits. Where the owner of the soil was entitled to exercise free warren, he could make or enlarge cone-

---

1   Co Litt 122a; *Arlett v Ellis* (1827) 7 B&C 346.

2   *Sandgrove v Kirby* (1797) 1 Bos & P 13.

3   *Hope v Osborne* [1913] 2 Ch 349.

4   *Ewart v Graham* (1859) 7 HL Cas 331; *Wickham v Hawker* (1840) 7 M&W 63.

5   *Fitzhardinge (Lord) v Percell* [1908] 2 Ch 139.

6   2 Bl Com 38.

burrows provided such works did not interfere with the sufficiency of grazing or other rights to which the commoners were entitled.[1]

5.3.7 Rights to minerals

In principle the lord or owner of the soil was always entitled to take minerals or other materials from the soil of the common. However, the exercise of such rights must not interfere with the sufficiency of the grazing or other rights to which the commoners are entitled.[2] In practice, the biggest constraint on the extraction of minerals from common land will be the need to obtain the necessary planning permission.

5.3.8 Right to drive

The lord of the manor had the right to drive the common. This meant an entitlement to round up and collect all the animals with a view to establishing whether any animals were present that did not belong to commoners or whether any of the commoners had more than their entitlement by way of numbers of animals on the common.[3]

5.3.9 Prescription or custom

All the various rights set out above might be limited by prescription or the custom of the manor.[4]

5.3.10 Right of approvement

The Commons Acts 1236 and 1285, which are still in force, authorised the approvement of common land. Approvement was the right of inclosing lands subject to rights of common, provided there was no interference with the sufficiency of those rights.[5] In practice, the right of approvement is now virtually obsolete because

---

1 *Gresill v Hoddesden* (1608) Yelv 143, 80 ER 96.

2 *Robinson v Duleep Singh* (1876) 11 Ch D 798.

3 *Thomas v Nicholls* (1681) 3 Lev 40.

4 *Wolstanton Ltd v Newcastle-under-Lyme Borough Council* [1940] AC 860, [1940] 3 All ER 101.

5 *Arlett v Ellis* (1827) 7 B&C 346; *Betts v Thompson* (1871) 6 Ch App 732.

of later legislation imposing restrictions on the inclosure of commons.[1]

5.3.11 Wayleaves and easements

Because the lord of the manor is the owner of the soil, subject only to the rights of common, he is free to grant wayleaves. Any grant must not interfere with the rights of common. Such grants may include rights to the utility services to lay pipes and cables over or under the common. Special problems have arisen in the case of easements over common land; these are considered below.

5.4   COMMONABLE LANDS

Commonable lands include lands subject to the open field system and also lammas lands and shack lands.[2] These lands will not necessarily have been owned by the lord of the manor. Their origin lay in the open-field system of agriculture by which individuals owned strips of the open field, of about 1 acre. They were known as several owners, because they individually owned those strips – distinct shares of the open field. After harvest, that is between reaping and sowing, the whole open field would then be thrown open to all owners (and occasionally others) to pasture their animals and manure the land. That would also have occurred during the fallow year. Accordingly, such land was subject to rights of common between reaping and sowing and, according to the custom, in the fallow years. During the time of the year when a crop was being grown, the individual owners were owners as such, and had all the rights and incidents of such ownership. In rural areas, the open field may well have been held in freehold by the lord of the manor, and the individual strips of land held by the lord's tenants under either customary freehold or copyhold. In some urban areas, the town or borough would have owned the common field for the benefit of all, and granted leases of strips to farmers. There are very few examples today of working open field systems.[3]

---

[1]   See Chapter 7.

[2]   Chapter 3.

[3]   Laxton, in Nottinghamshire, and Laugharne in Wales, are two examples.

5.5   EASEMENTS OVER COMMON LAND

As explained above, the owner of the soil of common land is entitled, as a matter of land law, to do as he wishes with the common provided he does not interfere with the rights of the commoners. He can therefore grant rights to shoot, or additional rights of common such as of pasture where there is an excess of sufficiency of pasture for the existing commoners.[1] Both of these types of grant are grants capable of being *profits à prendre*, which, together with easements, are legal interests in land sharing certain similar legal characteristics.

However, the grant of an easement over common land, such as an easement (or right) of way, can give rise to certain problems. In the case of an *express* grant of a right of way, the grantee cannot carry out works, such as the creation of a road surface that will either interfere with the rights of the commoners or will breach a number of statutory provisions that prohibit works on commons.[2] Such works may amount to an inclosure, or may otherwise require the consent of the Secretary of State.[3] Where a common is owned by a parish or other council, such as under the Open Spaces Act 1906, it may well be a breach of the duties of such an owner, as a trustee for the benefit of the enjoyment of the public to grant such rights.[4]

The position of the implied grant of an easement, such as a right of way over common land, is even more fraught. In *Hanning v Top Deck Travel Group Ltd*, the Court of Appeal decided a right of way could not be acquired by prescription where the user relied on was in breach of law.[5] The user relied on was use by vehicles, and such use was a breach of the Law of Property Act 1925, s 193(4), a section which had application to the common in question. That decision was said to be wrong by the defendants in *Bakewell Managements Ltd v Brandwood* on the ground that prescription assumes an implied grant, and a grant by the owner would negate what would otherwise be any unlawful user contrary to the Law of Property Act

---

[1]   *Ewart v Graham* (1859) 7 HL Cas 331 (shooting rights); *Wickham v Hawker* (1840) 7 M&W 63 (rights to hawk, hunt, fish and fowl); *Smith v Feverall* (1675) 2 Mod 6, 86 ER 909.

[2]   These are fully discussed in Chapter 11.

[3]   Such as under Law of Property Act 1925, s 194.

[4]   Open Spaces Act 1906, s 10.

[5]   (1993) 68 P&CR 14.

1925, s 193(4). The Court of Appeal disagreed and followed *Hanning* deciding that it was correctly decided.[1]

The effect of *Hanning* was to cause great difficulties to the many owners of properties with a sole means of access over adjoining common land. Even where the Law of Property Act 1925, s 193(4) did not apply, the similar provisions in the Road Traffic Acts, which prohibited driving vehicles over land that was not a road, would have application.

Section 68 of the CROW Act 2000 was enacted to address these difficulties where a right of way could have been acquired by prescription, but for the fact that the necessary user would have been an offence. Under s 68, the Vehicular Access across Common and Other Land (England) Regulations 2002[2] were made. The regulations apply to any land crossed by a way used as a means of access for vehicles to particular premises. The owner of the premises may apply to the owner of the common land for the creation of an easement. In the case of any dispute, the matter is referred to the Lands Tribunal. Compensation is payable: 0.25% of the value of the claimant's premises where the premises existed on 31 November 1905, or 0.5% where they existed on 30 November 1930.

The time-limits for making claims are far from clear. By reg 6(2), an application for an easement had to be made before 3 July 2003 in respect of a way that was then still being used and in respect of which a prescriptive right could have been acquired but for the unlawful user (generally, 20-year user). Many owners of premises with access over common land will have been unaware of this time-limit. Where the use of the relevant way ceases at a date after 3 July 2003, the application must be made within 12 months of such cessation.

The right to apply for an easement only arises where the user 'would otherwise have been sufficient to create on or after the prescribed date, and to keep in existence, an easement giving a right of way for vehicles'.[3] The prescribed date was 5 May 1993. The literal meaning of this limitation is that if the 20-year prescriptive

---

period expired prior to this prescribed date, no claim can be made. The possible answer to this conundrum is to contend for a 20-year prescription period under the Prescription Act 1832; the prescriptive period is that immediately before the action or suit.[1] An alternative claim based on the doctrine of a lost modern grant does assume a grant on the date when user of the way first commenced and, if s 68(1) has the effect its literal interpretation suggests, would fall foul of the prescribed date bar if the 20-years' user expired before that date.

There is a strict timetable for the service by the landowner of notices under regs 7 and 8 of the 2002 Regulations. Where no notices are served, the claimant becomes entitled to an easement as of right upon payment into court of the compensation sum.[2]

---

[1]   Prescription Act 1832, s 4.

[2]   Regulations 14 and 15.

Chapter 6

CREATION AND TRANSFER OF RIGHTS OF COMMON

6.1   INTRODUCTION

There are a number of ways in which rights of common were created in the past. In the case of rights enjoyed by copyholders (including customary freeholds – a type of copyhold), until the abolition of copyhold in 1922, rights akin to rights of common were acquired by copyholders by custom. Otherwise, rights of common were attached to freehold interests. These rights were of four kinds: rights appendant; rights appurtenant; rights in gross; or rights *pur cause de vicinage*.[1] Rights of common appendant must have existed prior to 1290,[2] and cannot therefore any longer be created. The other rights were capable of being created by grant or reservation, prescription or statute. These are the only methods by which rights of common can still be created today.

Save for the case of rights of common in gross, rights of common pass on the transfer of the land to which they are attached (the dominant land). Rights of common in gross are not attached to any land, and can therefore be transferred as such. Certain formalities are necessary for the transfer of any rights of common.

All rights of common subsisting at the time of the Commons Registration Act 1965 were required to be registered under that Act.[3] At the end of the registration period (31 July 1970) 'no rights of common shall be exercisable over any such land unless they are

---

[1]   See Chapter 4.

[2]   Possibly prior to 1189, see *Tyrringham's Case* (1584) 4 Co Rep 36b.

[3]   Section 1.

registered either under this Act or under the Land Registration Acts 1925 and 1936'.[1]

The 1965 Act defines common land as including land subject to rights of common.[2] Provision is made for the registration of new commons.[3] New rights of common can still be created over land that is not registered common land by grant (or reservation), by prescription and by statute. It is much more questionable whether new rights can be created, at least by prescription, over registered commons. In very limited circumstances rights of common can be created by statute.

This chapter also deals with the protection of rights of common, together with the legal and extra-legal remedies available to commoners where rights are being interfered with.

6.2   CREATION

6.2.1   Custom

Custom arises in two separate circumstances: custom in connection with the rights of the copyholders of a manor and originally enforceable in the manorial courts, although ultimately by the common law courts; and custom enforceable at common law.

(a)   Custom and copyholders

The copyholders in a manor did not own freehold legal estates. As rights of common proper were part of freehold interests, the rights of the copyholders to exercise similar rights on the uninclosed lands within the manor arose and were protected by the customs of the manor. Although copyholds started as grants of tenancies at the will of the lord of the manor, over time the copyhold interest acquired recognition as an estate of its own and was at the will of the lord only in name. Customs determined the characteristics of these estates, how long they lasted, how they could be inherited, and what additional rights ran with them. Customs varied from manor to manor, although manors in a particular locality or area of the

---

[1]   Section 1(2)(b).

[2]   Section 22(1).

[3]   Section 13 and Commons Registration (New Land) Regulations 1969, SI 1969/1843.

country may have shared common customs. Customs were enforceable against the lord of the manor and others, eventually, in the common law courts.[1]

Customs concerned a number of matters within the manor, such as inheritance, services, as well as the use of the uninclosed lands. Customs were enforceable in and regulated by the customary court of the manor. This court would have regulated the use of the waste land of the manor by controlling the number of animals, and the times of the year when they could be let out.[2] The manorial courts were held until the abolition of copyhold in 1922.[3] Their use and effectiveness in relation to the control of customary rights exercisable over the uninclosed waste lands of the manor began to peter out following the alterations in agricultural practices and the inclosure of the commons. However, it seemed unlikely that the precise rights to use the waste land of the manor by the copyholders remained unchanged throughout the history of the manor. Accordingly, although these rights lay in custom, and would normally be of long usage, it seems possible that alterations in the local custom would have arisen from time to time and, accordingly, new rights created notwithstanding the strict rule in the common law courts that a custom must have existed prior to 1189.

Customary rights of common can therefore no longer be created. Where the common law rule that a customary right cannot exist if it can be shown not to have existed prior to 1189 applies, it may be possible to show by reference to decisions of the respective manorial courts that a particular customary right to use waste land of the manor was confirmed by a manorial court, and then became converted, with the conversion of the copyhold title, to a freehold interest. In practice this is no longer relevant in respect of registered commons because any unregistered rights of common that existed when the Commons Registration Act 1965 came into force can no longer be exercised.[4]

---

[1]　In the sixteenth century the action of ejectment in the common law courts was extended to protect the interests of copyholders: see Simpson, *An Introduction to the History of Land Law* (1961), at p 145.

[2]　See Jessel, *The Law of the Manor*, at chapter 13.

[3]　Law of Property Act 1922.

[4]　Section 1(2)(b).

(b)   Custom and the common law

Outside the manorial courts, custom was enforceable at common law. However, a custom was only enforceable if local, ancient, reasonable and certain. Of these requirements, ancient meant that the custom had come into existence before 1189.[1] The effect of the abolition of copyhold was to convert the copyhold into a freehold, and the customary rights of the copyholders to use the waste lands of the manor into rights of common.[2]

Custom is important in relation to town and village greens. The use of the green for the recreational purposes of the local inhabitants may be a custom that the common law will enforce.[3]

6.2.2   Express grant

(a)   Formal requirements

By 'grant' is meant a grant by deed of a legal interest. A right of common is a *profit à prendre* and capable of being a legal interest in land.[4] A *profit à prendre* can only exist as a legal interest if it is granted by deed.[5] To create a legal interest, the grant must be for an interest equivalent to an estate in fee simple absolute in possession or a term of years absolute.[6] A profit granted for any other term, such as for a life, will only be an equitable interest notwithstanding that the grant lies in a deed.[7] Further, an enforceable contract to grant a profit will only give the grantee an equitable right.[8] In the case of any contract or agreement made on or after 27 September 1989, the contract or agreement must comply with the Law of Property (Miscellaneous Provisions) Act 1989, s 2. In the case of an agreement to grant a *profit à prendre* made before 27 September 1989, there must either be a sufficient memorandum in writing that

---

[1]   The commencement of legal memory; the accession of Richard I; see *Hammerton v Honey* (1876) 24 WR 603.

[2]   Law of Property Act 1922, Sch 12.

[3]   See Chapter 9.

[4]   Law of Property Act 1925, s 1(2)(a).

[5]   Ibid, s 52(1).

[6]   Ibid, s 1(2)(a).

[7]   Ibid, s 1(3).

[8]   *White v Taylor (No 2)* [1969] 1 Ch 160.

satisfies the Law of Property Act 1925, s 40 or the agreement must be supported by part performance.[1]

If the owner of land grants a *profit à prendre* to be enjoyed by one party to the exclusion of all other persons, the profit is a 'sole' or 'several' profit. Whereas if the profit is granted to a person to be enjoyed with a number of other persons, including the owner of the land, it is called a profit 'in common'. It follows that every right of common is a *profit à prendre*, but not every *profit à prendre* is a right of common.[2]

(b)   Competence of the grantor

The grantor of a *profit à prendre* must have the necessary competence to grant the intended interest or interests. Thus persons entitled only to rights of common over common land would have no power to grant an easement of way over the common.[3] A person who owns a lease of land could grant a *profit à prendre* out of that lease for a term that was less than the term of the lease, but that person could not grant a *profit à prendre* in perpetuity.

(c)   Exclusive right of grazing

In *Anderson v Bostock*[4] it was held that the grant of an exclusive right of grazing over a moor could not exist as an appurtenant right to land. Grazing rights have to be related to the needs or use of the dominant tenement and could not be of an exclusive and unlimited nature for such appurtenant rights are unknown to the law. An exclusive right to grazing without limit did not therefore pass to successors in title as an appurtenant right.

6.2.3   Reservation

A *profit à prendre* may be created by the express reservation of such a right in a deed of conveyance of the affected land. The purchaser acquires the land subject to the reserved rights. A reservation operates without a re-grant.[5] However, any ambiguity will be

---

[1]   *Mason v Clarke* [1955] AC 778.

[2]   See *Gale on Easements* (17th edn), at paras 1–S129.

[3]   *Paine & Co v St Neots Gas & Coke Co* [1939] 3 All ER 812.

[4]   [1976] Ch 312.

[5]   Law of Property Act 1925, s 65.

construed against the purchaser of the land as if there had been a re-grant by that person.[1] In practice the circumstance where rights of common might be created by reservation is probably limited to that where existing common land is sold and the owner reserves for himself rights of common.

6.2.4 Prescription

Any *profit à prendre* that lies in grant is capable of being acquired by prescription. Prescription is the legal idea by which the law concludes that there has been a grant of a *profit à prendre* by implication: an implied grant.

There are three methods of claiming a *profit à prendre* by prescription:

- at common law;
- under the doctrine of a lost modern grant; or
- under the Prescription Act 1832.

Each method is based on the idea that there has been a grant by deed. Rights of common appendant arise by operation of law and do not lie in grant. Accordingly, such rights cannot be acquired by prescription. An acquisition of a *profit à prendre* by way of prescription is not the same as the acquisition of customary rights.[2]

Under any of the three methods of prescription, there must be user of the claimed right, as of right, without permission, without secrecy, and without force. There is a further general requirement that the right claimed must be continuously used during the prescriptive period. However, continuity has regard to the nature of the right. Thus a claim to a right of pasturage during certain times of the year does not require user outside those periods.[3]

---

[1]   *St Edmundsbury & Ipswich Diocesan Board of Finance v Clark (No 2)* [1975] 1 WLR 468.

[2]   See *Halsbury's Laws of England* (4th edn) vol 6, at para 555 and *Hammerton v Honey* (1876) 24 WR 603; *Tyson v Smith* (1838) 9 Ad & El 406; *Mercer v Denne* [1905] 2 Ch 538; see also Chapter 3.

[3]   *White v Taylor (No 2)* [1969] 1 Ch 160 at 192, [1969] 1 All ER 1015.

(a) Prescription at common law

Prescription at common law requires user since time immemorial (1189). In practice, proof of user for a sufficiently long period of time, exceeding 20 years, will normally suffice.[1] A claim based on prescription at common law can be defeated by showing that there could not have been such user so far back as 1189. Unity of ownership of the land over which the right is asserted and the land in respect of which the right is exercised will defeat a claim under this method of prescription because a person cannot have a profit over his own land. Further, such a claim will be defeated if there is evidence that the claimed right was not, as a matter of fact, exercised at some point since 1189.[2]

(b) Lost modern grant

The doctrine of lost modern grant evolved to address some of the problems that arose in relation to proving user back to 1189 in the case of prescription at common law. Under this doctrine, there is a presumption that a grant was made of the right, but the grant has been lost.[3] The normal prescriptive period is a minimum of 20 years.[4] The claim can only be defeated by showing that there could not have been a capable grantor or grantee at the time of the supposed 'lost' grant. The fact that the person asserting the right believed, when so doing, that he had and was entitled to, a right, does not negate a claim to a right of common under the doctrine of lost modern grant.[5]

Where a person, purportedly entitled to rights of common that existed when the Commons Registration Act 1965 came into force, failed to appeal a decision of the Commons Commissioner not to confirm an application for the registration of those rights, those rights would cease to be exercisable under s 1(2)(b) when the Commissioner decided the application was void and not at the

---

[1] *R v Joliff* (1823) 2 B&C 54.

[2] *Addington v Clode* (1775) 2 WmBl 989; *R v Ashby Folville Inhabitants* (1866) LR 1 QB 213; *Bryant v Foot* (1868) LR 3 QB 497.

[3] *Cowlam v Slack* (1812) 15 East 108; *Tehidy Minerals Ltd v Norman* [1971] 2 QB 528, [1971] 2 All ER 475.

[4] *Tehidy Minerals Ltd v Norman* [1971] 2 QB 528, [1971] 2 All ER 475.

[5] *Earl de la Warr v Miles* (1881) 17 ChD 535.

earlier date of 31 July 1970. Lost modern grant cannot operate until the date of the Commissioner's decision.[1]

A right cannot be acquired by prescription where the acts justifying the right, for example grazing or the taking of estovers, would themselves be unlawful,[2] or there could never have been any lawful grant.[3]

(c)   The Prescription Act 1832

This Act provides for a minimum prescriptive period of 30 years without interruption. The right becomes absolute and indefeasible where a full period of 60 years is established unless the right was enjoyed by consent or agreement made by deed in writing.[4] The two periods of 30 years and 60 years are those immediately before any legal proceedings in which the issue is brought into question.[5] However, no act amounts to an interruption of user unless it has been submitted to or acquiesced in for one year. Consequently, a period of 29 years and one day, or 59 years and one day, is sufficient to found a right provided legal proceedings are commenced immediately on the expiration of the relevant 30- or 60-year period, so that a full year's interruption is not achieved. All the other requirements for the establishment of the profit by prescription apply under this Act. However, an oral consent given at the commencement of the 60-year period will not defeat a claim.[6]

6. 3   THE COMMONS REGISTRATION ACT 1965

The creation of rights of common (as distinct from a *profit à prendre* that does not amount to a right of common, such as a 'sole' or

---

[1] *Dynevor (Lord) v Richardson* [1995] Ch 173. As the registration of the land as common land was earlier deemed void, this case is no authority for the proposition that a right of common can be acquired by prescription over registered common land; it leaves the question open.

[2] *Hanning v Top Deck Travel Group Ltd* (1993) 68 P&CR 14; *Bakewell Management Ltd v Brandwood* [2003] 1 WLR 1429; see also Chapter 5.

[3] *Neaverson v Peterborough RDC* [1902] 1 Ch 557; *Mill v New Forest Commissioners* (1856) 18 CB 60.

[4] Section 1.

[5] Section 4.

[6] *Tickle v Brown* (1836) 4 Ad & El 369; *Earl de la Warr v Miles* (1881) 17 ChD 535.

'several' profit), has been profoundly affected by the Commons Registration Act 1965. In order to understand the consequences for the creation of rights of common by prescription, one needs first to understand the position in relation to the creation of rights by *express* grant.

6.3.1 Express grant of rights of common over registered commons

By s 1(2) of the 1965 Act, no rights of common shall be exercisable over any common land that has been registered under the Act unless those rights are registered under the 1965 Act or under the Land Registration Acts 1925 and 1936. All rights of common that existed at the commencement of the 1965 Act therefore had to be registered, or could not after the end of the registration period thereafter be exercised.

However, s 1(2) appears to allow for the registration of new rights of common coming into existence after the end of the registration period of 31 July 1970. In theory the owner of the soil to a registered common could create new or additional rights of common by express grant. Such expressly granted rights of common would not be exercisable over any registered common land until those rights were, themselves, registered under the Act. However, there seems to be no provision for the amendment of existing registers of rights of common to allow for such new rights of common to be entered on existing registers.

Section 13 makes provision for regulations to provide for the amendment where:

> 'any rights registered under this Act are apportioned, extinguished or released, or are varied or transferred in such circumstances as may be prescribed.'

But there is no reference to rights that are created over registered commons, although it might be possible to contend that upon the creation of new rights existing registered rights are varied. Further, the consequential Commons Registration (New Land) Regulations 1969 specifically provide that no application can be entertained for the registration of rights of common over existing registered common land.[1]

6.3.2   Grant of new rights over land not registered as common land

The position is different in relation to the creation by express grant of rights of common over any land that is not, at the time, registered common land. Such land will, upon the express grant of rights of common over it, become common land in respect of which a new registration can be effected under the 1965 Act, together with the newly created rights of common.[2]

6.3.3   Acquisition of rights by prescription and the Commons Registration Act 1965

(a)   *Registered commons*

The acquisition of rights of common by prescription is founded upon the assumption of a grant (an implied grant). Accordingly, there is no reason why the observations in relation to express grants above should not also apply in principle to prescription. During the prescriptive period, the person without any common rights but who is asserting a right of common by user as of right over an existing registered common, is arguably not exercising *rights of common* within the meaning of s 1(2)(b). That subsection must be referring to rights that ought to have been registered prior to 31 July 1970, and were not, in other words, rights that were legal interests and capable of registration.

Section 1(2)(b) does not make it unlawful to use a common for a purpose that, upon the completion of a prescriptive period would, in the absence of the Act, then be a right of common acquired by prescription. There is therefore no reason why rights of common cannot be purportedly prescribed against a registered common. But on completion of the 20-year (or under the Prescription Act 1832, 30-year) prescriptive period, the law assumes an implied grant at the commencement of the prescriptive period. However, it is arguable

---

[1]   Regulation 3(2).

[2]   Commons Registration Act 1965, s 1 and Commons Registration (New Land) Regulations 1969, SI 1969/1843, reg 3.

that s 1(2)(b) might then have effect. The easement acquired by prescription cannot be exercised. The contrary argument is that if the right did not exist when the Act came into force, the right did not require registration. The real difficulty, which is common to the creation of new express grants of rights of common, and to the acquisition of rights by prescription, is that the Act contains no clear provisions to add newly acquired rights over existing registered commons. One is left with the possible argument that the registered rights of common have been varied.[1]

(b) Rights acquired by prescription over land not registered as common land

The position is quite different where rights have been acquired by prescription over land that is not registered as common land. Such land becomes new common land in respect of which a new registration can be effected under the 1965 Act, together with the newly created rights of common.[2]

6.4 TRANSFER

Rights of common appendant or appurtenant will pass with the conveyance of the land to which they are attached.[3] However, a right of common appendant passes with the land and can never be severed from it; it was acquired by operation of law, and not by grant.[4] Rights of common appurtenant can be severed from the land to which they are attached and then become rights of common in gross.[5]

Rights of common are interests in land, they are incorporeal hereditaments, and can only be conveyed or transferred by deed.[6] In the absence of express mention, in any deed or transfer of the

---

[1]   Section 13. But Knox J in *Dynevor v Richardson* [1995] 1 All ER 109 would not seem to have precluded the acquisition of prescriptive rights in all cases.

[2]   Commons Registration Act 1965, s 1 and Commons Registration (New Land) Regulations 1969, SI 1969/1843, reg 3.

[3]   Law of Property Act 1925, s 62.

[4]   *Bennett v Reeve* (1740) Willes 227.

[5]   *Bunn v Channen* (1813) 5 Taunt 244. Under Dartmoor Commons Act 1985, s 8 there is a prohibition against severance.

[6]   Law of Property Act 1925, s 51.

dominant land to which rights of common are attached, such rights will pass pursuant to the word-saving provision in s 62(1) of the Law of Property Act 1925.[1]

The Commons Registration Act 1965 required rights of common to be registered. These rights were widely defined and included cattlegates or beastgates, rights of sole or several vesture or herbage or of sole or several pasture.[2] All such rights existing prior to 31 July 1970 were required to be registered.[3] Upon the transfer of any registered rights, application should be made to register the transfer and the new owner as owner on the register of rights of common.[4]

6.5   STATUTE

Rights of common may be created by statute. The effect of many inclosure awards made under private, and later, the public inclosure Acts of the nineteenth century, was the creation or variation of rights of common.

However, today, the most common circumstance for the creation of rights of common over land not subject to the same is in connection with compulsory acquisition of common land. The compulsory purchase order may include suitable 'exchange' land to replace common land that is proposed to be acquired. The order may provide for the vesting of the exchange land in persons, and subject to the same rights, as the land being compulsorily acquired. The confirming Secretary of State must certify his satisfaction.[5]

6.6   PROTECTION OF RIGHTS OF COMMON

Rights of common are legal interests in land. Commoners are entitled to exercise their rights without interference or obstruction.

---

[1]   *White v Williams* [1922] 1 KB 727; *White v Taylor (No 2)* [1969] 1 Ch 160, [1968] 1 All ER 1015.

[2]   Section 22(1).

[3]   Section 4.

[4]   Section 13 and Commons Registration (General) Regulations 1966, SI 1966/1471, reg 29(1), as amended by Commons Registration (General) (Amendment) Regulations 1968, SI 1968/658.

[5]   Acquisition of Land Act 1981, s 19(1); see also Chapter 12.

6.6.1   Extent of rights of common

The rights of the commoners are limited:[1]

> 'The interest which a commoner has in the common is, in the legal phrase, to eat the grass with the mouths of his cattle, or to take such other produce of the soil as he may be entitled to. Apart from this, he must not meddle at all with the soil, nor with the fruits or produce, even though by doing so he may eventually improve and meliorate the common.'

In the case of rights of pasturage, the rights were quantified and registered under the Commons Registration Act 1965.[2] In respect of other rights, such as of estovers or of turbary, the extent of the rights must be determined in accordance with the principles considered in Chapter 4.

6.6.2   Liability for damage to the soil

Where the commoner is properly exercising his rights of common, he is not liable to the owner of the soil of the common for any damage that is directly and unavoidably caused by that exercise, for example by his cattle eating a stack put on the common by the owner.[3]

6.6.3   Legal remedies for interference with rights of common

(a)   *The scope of likely interference*

The commoner might suffer damage in a number of different ways. One or more of his fellow commoners might put more animals upon the common than they are entitled to which could diminish the available grazing. The commoner's animals might be physically prevented from grazing on the whole, or more likely part, of the common by the actions of either the owner of the soil or some third party. Each case needs to be separately considered.

---

[1]   *Halsbury's Laws of England* (4th edn) vol 6, at para 652 adapted from 1 Roll Abr 406, quoted in 1 Saund 353a.

[2]   Section 15.

[3]   *Farmor v Hunt* (1611) Yelv 201; Cro Jac 271; *sub nom Farmer v Hunt* 80 ER 132.

(b)   Overstocking by other commoners

Where there is unlawful overstocking by another commoner, there is a right of *surcharging* to recover damages for the wrong.[1] Where there are two adjoining commons, the commoners of each common may enjoy rights *pur cause de vicinage* over the common that adjoins the one over which they have substantive rights. Whilst that gives a commoner a defence if his animals are found on the common adjoining his home common, it would not do so if he is over-stocking by reference to the rights he has on his own home common.

One solution to overstocking is for the commoners to persuade the owner of the soil to exercise his right to drive the common and remove the animals that are not entitled to be present.[2]

(c)   Physical obstruction

Physical obstruction might occur by a person erecting a building or other works on the common, such as fences, or otherwise destroying or unlawfully removing the subject matter of the right of common. Where a person interferes with, or obstructs, the lawful exercise of a right of common, the appropriate remedy is nuisance for what is called *disturbance* to the right. Rights of common fall within that category of legal interests in land known as *profits à prendre*. Such rights, together with easements, are protected by, primarily, the law of nuisance. Damages and/or an injunction are the appropriate remedies.[3]

A commoner may bring legal proceedings for the wrongful taking of the subject-matter of his rights of common, such as the consumption of the pasture, and also for any wrong that, if not stopped, could grow into a legal right such as an easement.[4]

6.6.4   Self-help abatement

Abatement is the removal of the cause of the interference by the injured commoner without any recourse to the courts. A person

---

[1]   See precedent in *Atkin's Court Forms*, vol 8(2).

[2]   See Chapter 5.

[3]   *King v Brown, Durant & Co* [1913] 2 Ch 416; *Fitzgerald v Firbank* [1897] 2 Ch 96.

[4]   *King v Brown, Durant & Co* [1913] 2 Ch 416.

suffering a nuisance is, in principle, entitled to abate it.[1] The law does not favour abatement and it should be restricted to simple cases that would not justify the expense of legal proceedings and urgent cases that required an immediate remedy.[2] A prior request is required, especially where the person liable in law did not actually cause the injury or entry is required on the wrong-doer's property,[3] and abatement must be exercised without delay.[4]

The scope of abatement is probably quite limited. In *Hope v Osborne* it was held that a commoner cannot abate a nuisance caused by another party that merely interferes with his rights of common. His right of abatement is limited to a nuisance that wholly prevents him from exercising his rights.[5] Further, no more must be done than is strictly necessary to abate the nuisance.[6] For example, a commoner would be entitled to remove a fence that had been wrongly erected on the common preventing access by his animals.[7] However, the decision of the Court of Appeal in *Burton v Winters*[8] shows that there are limitations on the right to use the self-help remedy of abatement. It is a summary remedy justified only in clear and simple cases or in an emergency. The right ceases on the refusal of a court to grant an injunction.

6.6.5 Statutory remedies

A number of statutory provisions create statutory offences for interferences with commons.[9] In appropriate cases, such as unlawful fencing, commoners might find a more effective remedy by having recourse to these provisions by making a complaint and request for action to the body responsible for enforcement.

---

[1]   *Baten's Case* (1610) 9 Co Rep 54b; *Perry v Fitzhowe* (1845) 8 QB 775.

[2]   *Gale on Easements* (17th edn), at para 14–06, relying on *Burton v Winters* [1993] 1 WLR 1077.

[3]   *Lemmon v Webb* [1894] 3 Ch 1.

[4]   *Moffett v Brewer* (1848) Iowa 1 Greene 348; see also *Burton v Winter* [1993] 1 WLR 1077 and *Co-operative Wholesale Society v British Railway Board* [1995] NPC 200.

[5]   [1913] 2 Ch 349.

[6]   *Roberts v Rose* (1865) LR 1 Exch 82.

[7]   *Cooper v Marshall* (1757) 1 Burr 259 and *Kirby v Sadgrove* (1797) 1 Bos & P 13 (fence erected by lord of the manor inconsistent with the grant of rights of common); see also *Arlett v Ellis* (1827) 7 B&C 346.

[8]   [1993] 1 WLR 1077.

[9]   See Chapter 11.

Chapter 7

INCLOSURE AND EXTINGUISHMENT OF RIGHTS OF COMMON

7.1   INTRODUCTION

There are various ways in which rights of common can be brought to an end. Some of these depend upon the actions of parties or the characteristics of the subject matter of the right of common. The inclosure of commons – once an important cause of the extinguishment of rights of common – is now virtually obsolete. Compulsory purchase has now become much more important in this context and this is considered separately at Chapter 12.

Where any rights of common have been terminated or extinguished, or any land ceased to be common land, then appropriate amendments and deletions can be made to the registers of common land and rights.[1]

7.2   EXTINGUISHMENT WITHIN THE CONTROL OF THE PARTIES

7.2.1   Unity of ownership

The essential characteristic of a right of common is that it is a *profit à prendre* exercisable for the benefit of one parcel of land (the benefited land) over another parcel of land (the common land). If both the benefited land and the common land come to be within the ownership of the same person, the rights of common are extinguished. As Coke said:[2]

---

[1]   Commons Registration Act 1965, s 13.

[2]   Co Litt 313a, quoted in *Gale on Easements* (17th edn), at para 12–02.

'[Profits à prendre] are said to be extinguished when they are gone forever, et tunc moriuntur, and can never be revived; that is, when one man hath as high and perdurable an estate in the one as in the other.'

There will not be extinguishment where, say, the freehold owner of the common acquires a lease of the dominant or benefited land to which rights of common are attached. Although the rights of common may be suspended for the duration of his ownership of the lease of the benefited land, once the lease has terminated, the rights are revived.[1]

7.2.2   Abandonment and non-use

Mere non-use of rights of common will generally be insufficient to establish an intention to abandon. As Alderson B said in *Ward v Ward*:[2]

'The presumption of abandonment cannot be made from the mere fact of non-user. There must be other circumstances in the case to raise that presumption. The right is acquired by adverse enjoyment. The non-user, therefore, must be the consequence of something which is adverse to the user.'

The period of non-user is therefore not particularly relevant. Non-use of a right of way for 175 years did not raise any presumption of abandonment in one case.[3] Much more relevant is whether the owner of the rights of common has made changes to the benefited land such as to show that he no longer has use for or intends to assert his rights of common. Demolishing a house with a right of common or turbary, with no intention of erecting a replacement, shows intentional abandonment.[4] In the case of rights of common of pasture, whether appendant or appurtenant, altering the character and use of the benefited land such that it could no longer be used for

---

[1]   Co Litt 313a.

[2]   (1852) 7 Ex Ch 838 at 839 quoted in *Gale on Easements* (17th edn), at para 12–56.

[3]   *Benn v Hardinge* (1992) 66 P&CR 246

[4]   *Moore v Rawson* (1824) 3 B&C 332.

supporting the animals entitled to the pasturage, such as by building houses, does raise the presumption of abandonment.[1]

7.2.3 Express release

Rights of common will be extinguished if the owner of the rights enters into an express deed of release. There has been doubt as to whether releasing rights of common over part of the affected land releases the whole of the right.[2]

7.3 BY STATUTE

7.3.1 Generally

Rights of common may be extinguished by statute in a number of ways. The most obvious today arises upon the exercise of powers of compulsory acquisition. Schedule 4 to the Compulsory Purchase Act 1965 contains a procedure for the determination of compensation to commoners and the extinction of their rights.[3] There are powers under the Town and Country Planning Act 1990 under which easements and other rights can be overridden.[4] Local planning authorities have wide powers to acquire land, compulsorily or by agreement, for planning purposes.[5] They may also appropriate land from one purpose to another.[6] Where any land has been acquired or appropriated by a local planning authority for planning purposes, the authority may appropriate the land for any other purpose for which they are authorised to acquire land.[7] However, the right to appropriate land which is common land is subject to ministerial consent.[8] But where land has been acquired or appropriated for planning purposes, any building or other works carried out in

---

[1]   *Carr v Lambert* (1866) LR 1 Ex Ch 168; *Re Yateley Common, Hampshire* [1977] 1 All ER 505, [1977] 1 WLR 840.

[2]   *Rotherham v Green* (1597) Cro Eliz 593; *Miles v Etteridge* (1692) 1 Show 349. But compare with *Benson v Chester* (1799) 8 Term Rep 396.

[3]   *Lewis v Mid Glamorgan County Council* [1995] 1 All ER 760; see also Chapter 12.

[4]   See s 237.

[5]   See ss 226–227.

[6]   Local Government Act 1972, s 122.

[7]   See s 232(1) of the 1990 Act.

[8]   Section 232(2) of the 1990 Act and s 122 of the 1972 Act.

accordance with planning permission authorises the interference with any easement or rights affecting that land. Two comments are called for here. First, the mere grant of planning permission will not, of itself, authorise works or building on common land; the additional controls considered in Chapter 11 have to be complied with. Secondly, a change of use is not authorised.[1]

Inclosure is now only possible under the authority of a statute. This is considered further below.

7.3.2   Commons Registration Act 1965

Rights of common existing prior to the expiration of the registration period on 31 July 1970, but not registered by that date, are not thereafter exercisable.[2] That status of non-exercisability amounts to a type of statutory extinguishment of the rights. However, non-exercisability, as a concept, appears to leave the possibility of the rights becoming exercisable at some point. It is possible that the legislature decided to leave the issue of what should happen to unregistered but registrable rights to a future piece of legislation.

7.4   INCLOSURE

7.4.1   Inclosure before 1845

The right of approvement was the first process by which surplus waste came to be inclosed. The right to do so was confirmed by the Commons Act 1236, as extended by the Commons Act 1285. Generally the lord of the manor was required to leave sufficient pasture on the uninclosed waste or common for the commoners.[3] Today any approvement under the Commons Acts 1236–1285 requires the consent of the Secretary of State.[4]

---

1   *Thames Water Utilities Ltd v Oxford City Council* [1999] 1 EGLR 167.

2   Section 1(2)(b).

3   *Arlett v Ellis* (1827) 7 B&C 346; *Robertson v Hartopp* (1889) 43 ChD 484.

4   Law of Commons Amendment Act 1893.

Prior to 1845 a number of private Acts were passed authorising inclosure on a local basis.[1]

7.4.2   Inclosure post-1845

The Inclosure Act 1845 provided a comprehensive procedure for the inclosure of commons. A number of subsequent Acts made amendments to that Act. However, the Commons Act 1876 introduced a requirement that inclosure should not proceed without the approval of the Inclosure Commissioners and of Parliament. Such approval to be given only where the inclosure would be of benefit to the neighbourhood.

(a)   *Inclosure Act 1845*

By s 11 of the 1845 Act, the following descriptions of land could be inclosed:

–   all land subject to any rights of common whatsoever, and whether such rights may be exercised or enjoyed at all times, or may be exercised or enjoyed only during limited times, seasons or periods, or be subject to any suspension or restriction whatsoever in respect of the time of the enjoyment thereof;

–   all gated and stinted pastures in which the property of the soil or of some part thereof is in the owners of the cattlegates or other gates or stints, or any of them;

–   all gated and stinted pastures in which no part of the property of the soil is in the owners of the cattlegates or other gates or stints, or any of them;

–   all land held, occupied, or used in common, either at all times or during any time or season, or periodically, and either for all purposes or for any limited purpose, and whether the separate parcels of the several owners of the soil shall or shall not be known by metes or bounds or otherwise distinguishable;

–   all land in which the property or right of or to the vesture or herbage, or any part thereof, during the whole or any part of the year, or the property or right of or to the wood or under-wood growing and to grow thereon, is separated from the property of the soil;

---

[1]   Apparently 4,000 such Acts were passed between 1745 and 1845: see *Halsbury's Laws of England* (4th edn) vol 6, at para 704.

–   and all lot meadows and other lands the occupation or enjoyment of the separate lots or parcels of which is subject to interchange among the respective owners in any known course of rotation or otherwise.

The New Forest and the Forest of Dean were excluded.[1]

Land within 15 miles of London or within certain distances of large towns was not to be inclosed without the previous direction of Parliament in each case.[2] In fact there is further legislation considered below in relation to the protection of metropolitan commons. Town and village greens were not to be inclosed, although there was provision for directing that greens should be allotted to the church wardens and overseers of the poor.[3]

The Act made provision for the making of applications for inclosure or regulation of a common by persons representing at least one-third in value of the interests in the affected land. An assistant Commissioner of the Inclosure Commissioners would hold a local inquiry, and would then report to the Inclosure Commissioners. If the Inclosure Commissioners were satisfied that inclosure or regulation should proceed, they would prepare a draft provisional order. Following further deposit of the draft provisional order, it would then be reported to Parliament and Parliament would confirm the order as a confirmatory Act. Following confirmation by Act of Parliament, a valuer was appointed to put the details of the Act into effect. One important matter was to deal with claims for compensation by commoners whose rights were affected or terminated. The valuer would also direct the allotment of the inclosed common between the persons entitled. This appeared in an award. A number of details such as ownership of roads and ways, fencing, and straightening out boundaries, were also done in the award. Some land was allotted for public purposes, such as setting out new roads, and the residue was then divided and allotted between the various persons interested, including the lord of the manor and the other persons who had rights of common.

---

[1]   Section 13.

[2]   Section 14.

[3]   Section 15 and see Chapter 9.

(b) Commons Act 1876

This Act considerably restricted inclosure under the 1845 Act. The Inclosure Commissioners had to be persuaded that the application for inclosure would be for the benefit of the neighbourhood, and with a view to that benefit they were required to consider inserting the following provisions:[1]

- free access to be secured to any particular points of view;
- particular trees or objects of historical interest were to be preserved;
- there was to be reserved, where a recreation ground was not set out, a privilege of playing games or of enjoying other species of recreation at such times and in such manner and on such parts of the common as might have been thought suitable;
- carriage roads, bridle paths, and footpaths over the common were to be set out as appeared most commodious;
- any other specified thing was to be done which it might be thought equitable and expedient, regard being had to the benefit of the neighbourhood.

That Act considerably altered the policy direction behind the inclosure and reflected a growing concern about the loss of common land in terms of its recreational and wider public benefit value.

(c) Inclosure today

These Acts, and others, made provision for the regulation of commons, including metropolitan commons.[2] Although the provisions relating to inclosure in the Inclosure Act 1845 and the Commons Act 1876 are still on the statute book, these powers have not been used for some considerable time, and must be regarded in the present political climate as being virtually obsolete.

---

[1] Section 7
[2] See Chapter 11.

Chapter 8

REGISTRATION OF COMMON LAND AND RIGHTS OF COMMON

8.1   INTRODUCTION

The Commons Registration Act 1965 gave effect to one of the recommendations of the *Royal Commission Report on Common Land*.[1] The 1965 Act made provision for the registration of commons, the ownership of common land and of rights of common. It also made provision for the registration of town and village greens.

In some respects the law of commons became frozen by the 1965 Act. Thereafter, the status of common land, and whether any rights of common could be exercised, depended entirely upon the entries in the registers. Further, rights of common of pasture, that had previously been held without stint, or limitation of numbers, but which depended on the carrying capacity of the land to which the rights were attached (*levancy* and *couchancy*), had to be registered with specified animal numbers. It is likely that excessive numbers were registered in many cases, but in any event the register determined the extent of the right.

The Act, however, has thrown up certain questions such as: can new rights of common be granted over an existing common and, if so, should these be registered? Can rights of common be acquired by prescription? Does the registered entry of rights of common determine for ever the extent of those rights?

---

[1]   Cmnd 462 1958.

8.2   REGISTRATION: COMMONS

8.2.1   Registration

Section 1 of the Commons Registration Act 1965 required the registration of:

(a)   land in England or Wales which is common land or a town or village green;

(b)   rights of common over such land; and

(c)   persons claiming to be or found to be owners of such land or becoming the owners thereof by virtue of the 1965 Act.

It also directed that no rights of common over land which was capable of being registered under the 1965 Act could be registered under the Land Registration Acts of 1925 and 1936 (and their statutory successor, the Land Registration Act 2002).

The registration requirement was a continuing obligation. Although the initial registration period expired on 31 July 1970, and any rights of common not registered could not thereafter be exercised,[1] provision was made for registration of new commons coming into existence after that period.[2]

8.2.2   Meaning of common land and rights of common

(a)   Common land

'Common land' was defined as meaning:[3]

'(a)   land subject to rights of common (as defined in this Act) whether those rights are exercisable at all times or only during limited periods;

(b)   waste land of a manor not subject to rights of common; but does not include a town or village green or any land which forms part of a highway.'

---

[1]   Commons Registration Act 1965, s 1(2)(b). This would probably include rights acquired by prescription where the prescriptive period had already been satisfied.

[2]   Ibid, s 13.

[3]   Ibid, s 22(1).

Common land therefore has a specific meaning for the purposes of the 1965 Act. It is either land subject to rights of common, or it is waste land of a manor, not subject to rights of common. Although each needs to be considered in turn, the meaning of rights of common is crucial to both. As both expressions – common land and rights of common – are more widely defined under the Act than such expressions would have been understood prior to the Act, certain land and rights that would not have been understood as either common land or rights in common became registrable.

(b)   Rights of common

The Act defines 'rights of common' as including:

> 'Cattlegates or beastgates (by whatever name known) and rights of sole or several vesture or herbage or of sole or several pasture, but does not include rights held for a term of years or from year to year.'

The first thing to note is that this is not an exclusive definition. Accordingly, rights of common, exercised by the commoners together with the owner of the relevant land, fall within this definition.[1]

Cattlegates and beastgates are stints or rights to pasture a specified number of beasts on land. Rights of sole or several vesture, herbage or pasture were rights exercisable by the sole owners to the exclusion of the owner of the land, and were not, strictly, rights of common because the owner was excluded.[2] It follows that land, which was not regarded as common land prior to the 1965 Act, is treated as common land for the purposes of this Act.

Rights attached to leases and tenancies or held for periods of time equivalent to leases or tenancies were excluded. Thus, the freehold owner of land with attached rights of common was required to register his rights but, if the land is let to a farming tenant, together with the rights, the tenant's interest in the rights are not registered. Rights of sole of pasture are frequently let for defined or periodic terms less than a fee simple, either together with a tenancy of land or quite separate from any tenancy; such rights are not registrable.

---

[1]   See Chapter 4.

[2]   Ibid.

8.2.3   Land subject to rights of common

Returning to the definition of common land, if land is subject to rights of common, defined as widely as they are under the Act, then the common should have been registered, and its ownership and the rights of common over it.

Such land specifically includes land where the rights of common are exercisable at all times or only during limited periods. Rights exercisable at all times cause no problems. However, rights exercisable only during limited periods could be more problematical. In Chapter 3, reference was made to commonable lands, such as Lammas lands, or other lands that were derived from the open-field system of agriculture. Individuals owned strips of the open fields but the land was subject to rights of pasture in favour of all the owners during specified periods of the year (usually between reaping and sowing). The land would not normally have been regarded as the open 'common or waste' of a manor as commonly understood, but regarded by its owners as 'their' land subject only to the mutual rights at certain times of the year. Whilst the registration requirements alone may not be of much consequence to the owners, such owners might now be startled to discover that, as such commons are registered commons, there are now to be public rights of access on foot over all such commons.[1]

8.2.4   Waste land of the manor not subject to rights of common

Waste land of the manor not subject to rights of common would have been owned by the lord of the manor. It would have been his land which, because it was not subject to rights of common, he could have inclosed. Most of it would have been roadside waste, and few would have regarded it as common land as generally understood. However, it was registrable under the 1965 Act, and its meaning was important.

In *A-G v Hanmer*[2] Watson B said:

> 'The true meaning of "wastes", or "waste lands", or "waste grounds of the manor", is the open, uncultivated and unoccupied lands parcel of

---

[1]   CROW Act 2000.

[2]   (1858) 27 LJ Ch 837 at 840.

the manor, or open lands parcel of the manor other than the demesne lands of the manor.'

As Lord Templeman said in *Hampshire County Council v Milburn*:[1]

'The manorial system which the Normans partly inherited and partly established displayed a variety of local laws and customs but in general there were three categories of land comprised in a manor. The demesne land belonged to the lord of the manor. Copyhold land was divided between the tenants of the lord of the manor. The remainder of the land consisted of uncultivated land, referred to as the waste of the manor. The waste land was the natural source of grazing, fodder and fuel for all the inhabitants of the manner. The waste land belonged to the lord of the manor subject to the rights of the tenants to enjoy in common the fruits or some of the fruits of the soil.'

The only difficulty with that description of the lands within the manor is that Lord Templeman did not add as a fourth category 'waste land not subject to any rights of common'.

Under the 1965 Act, any waste land that was subject to rights of common fell within the definition of 'common land', and was as such registrable. However, there was a separate requirement to ensure that waste land of the manor not subject to rights of common should also be registered. What if such waste land became separated, or severed from the ownership of the manor as such? Did such land cease to be waste land *of* the manor if it was no longer held *with* the manor? In *Re Chewton Common, Christchurch, Borough of Christchurch v Milligan*[2] Slade J said:

'The phrase "waste land of a manor" [in the 1965 Act], used in relation to a particular piece of land in the context of a statute passed some forty years after copyhold tenure had been abolished [in 1925], does not as a matter of legal language by any means necessarily import that the ownership of the land still rests with the Lord of the relevant manor. ... It is permissible to construe the phrase in this particular context of a post-1925 statute as meaning waste land which was once waste land of a manor in the days when copyhold tenure still existed.'

---

[1]   [1990] 2 All ER 257 at 258.

[2]   [1977] 3 All ER 509 at 514–515, [1977] 1 WLR 1242 at 1249–1250.

That approach was approved by the House of Lords in *Hampshire County Council v Milburn*.[1] Lord Templeman said:[2]

> '... but the [1965] Act provided that waste land "not subject to rights of common" should be registered, whether there was an identifiable owner of that land or not and the Act did not provide for registration of such land to be vacated once the owner had been identified. The Royal Commission [on common land] clearly thought that common land should be preserved for the benefit of the public and registration was the first step to that end. Parliament cannot have intended that every identifiable piece of waste land which was required to be registered under the Act should cease to be affected by the Act by the voluntary act of the owner for the time being. ... "Waste land of a manor" means "waste land now or formerly of a manor" or "waste land of manorial origin".'

The House of Lords disapproved of the decision of the Court of Appeal in *Box Parish Council v Lacey*[3] where it had refused the registration of Box Hill Common, formerly waste land of the manor of Box, because it had become severed from the lordship of the manor in 1878.

The meaning of 'waste land of the manor' was also considered in *Re: Britford Common*[4] where Slade J said that:[5]

> 'It is implicit in [the definition in section 22 of the 1965 Act] that waste land of the manor must be (a) parcel of a manor; (b) open and uncultivated; (c) unoccupied; and (d) not comprised in the demesne lands of the manor. If it complies with all these four conditions, it constitutes "waste land of a manor".'

In the light of his later decision in *Re Chewton Common*, Slade J would probably have qualified condition (a) to read 'is or was parcel of a manor'.

---

[1]   [1990] 2 All ER 257.

[2]   Ibid, at 262.

[3]   [1980] Ch 109, [1979] 1 All ER 113.

[4]   [1977] 1 All ER 532.

[5]   Ibid, at 539.

The status of land as 'waste land of the manor' is not necessarily altered if such land should be the subject of compulsory acquisition. In *Lewis v Mid Glamorgan County Council*[1] the House of Lords was concerned with the compulsory acquisition of common land for the purposes of constructing a reservoir pursuant to the powers granted by a local Act. Although no notice to treat was served on the commoners as required by s 5 of the Compulsory Purchase Act 1965, the compensation procedure in Sch 4 to that Act was invoked and compensation was agreed and paid to the commoners' committee. The Water Authority later abandoned the reservoir project and sold the land to the local authority for use as a golf course. The House of Lords decided that although the local Act sanctioned the construction of the reservoir on the common, there was no Parliamentary sanction for the golf course development. Neither the local Act nor the Compulsory Purchase Act 1965, although providing for the compulsory acquisition of rights vested in the lords of the manor and the commoners, altered the classification of land as waste land of the manor. The land therefore remained part of the common. Although the rights of common may have been extinguished, the land was still waste land of the manor, not subject to rights of common, and was common land within the meaning of s 22(1)(b) of the 1965 Act.

8.3   REGISTRATION: TOWN OR VILLAGE GREENS

The definition of 'common land' excludes a town or village green or any land which forms part of a highway.[2] However, a town or village green is capable of being registered as such.[3] Accordingly, common land and greens are mutually exclusive. However, a green falling within the definition of a town or village green could be subject to rights of common. The Act appears to allow the registration of rights of common over a green even though the green is not common land.[4]

Section 22(1) of the 1965 Act defines a town or village green as meaning:

---

[1]   [1995] 1 All ER 760.

[2]   Commons Registration Act 1965, s 22(1).

[3]   Ibid, s 1(1)(a).

[4]   Ibid, ss 1(1) and 4(1).

'(1) ... land which has been allotted by or under any Act for the exercise or recreation of the inhabitants of any locality or on which the inhabitants of any locality have a customary right to indulge in lawful sports and pastimes or which falls within subsection (1A) of this section.

(1A) Land falls within this subsection if it is land on which for not less than twenty years a significant number of the habitants of any locality, or of any neighbourhood within a locality, have indulged in lawful sports and pastimes as of right, and either

(a)   continue to do so, or

(b)   have ceased to do so for not more than such period as may be prescribed, or determined in accordance with prescribed provisions.'[1]

The three classes of green within this definition are discussed in Chapter 9. Class A is allotted land; Class B is land where the inhabitants have customary rights; and Class C, as originally enacted, is land where the inhabitants of any locality indulged in sports and pastimes as of right for not less than 20 years. With effect from 30 January 2001, the amended definition of a Class C green requires that the user must be by a *significant* number of inhabitants of a locality or neighbourhood within a locality, and (in the absence of any regulations under s 22(1A)(b)) that user must *continue* to the date of any application for registration.[2]

Although a highway cannot be registered as part of a common, there is no similar prohibition in the case of the registration of a green.[3]

8.4   REGISTRATION PROCESS

8.4.1   The registration authorities

The registration authorities for the purposes of the Act are:

–   where land is situated in a county or unitary authority, the county council or the unitary authority, respectively; and

---

[1]   Commons Registration Act 1965, ss 22(1) and (1A).

[2]   *Oxfordshire County Council v Oxford City Council* [2004] EWHC 12, [2004] PLSCS 16.

[3]   Commons Registration Act 1965, s 22(1).

– where land is situated in Greater London, a London borough council in which the land is situated.[1]

Where part of any land is in the area of one registration authority and part in that of another, the authorities may, by agreement, provide for one of them to be the registration authority in relation to the whole of the land.[2]

8.4.2 The Registers

For the purposes of registering common land, town and village greens, rights of common and the ownership of such land, the registration authorities are required to maintain:

– a register of common land; and
– a register of town or village greens.[3]

In the case of East Sussex County Council, many of its records, including registers required to be maintained under s 3, were destroyed by fire. Accordingly, the Commons Registration (East Sussex) Act 1994 was enacted to enable the county council to reconstitute its registers.

Any register maintained under the Act is required to be open to inspection by the public at all reasonable times.[4]

8.4.3 Original application and provisional registration

In respect of any application made before 31 July 1970, this was required to be entered by the registration authority on the registers as a provisional registration, and so described.[5] In the case of an application for the registration of any land as common land or as a town or village green, such an application could have been made by any person. In any event, a registration authority was entitled to register any land as common land or a town or village green notwithstanding that no application had been made for that

---

[1] Commons Registration Act 1965, s 2.

[2] Ibid, s 2(2).

[3] Ibid, s 3.

[4] Ibid, s 3(2).

[5] Ibid, s 4(1).

registration by any other person.[1] The registration authority was required, in any event, to register any land in any case where it registered any rights over it.[2]

A registration remained provisional until it became final in accordance with the provisions of the 1965 Act. An application would become final following the expiration of the various procedures for the making and hearing of objections. In the case of an undisputed application, that is where either no objection was made to the registration under s 4 or if objections were made and all of them were withdrawn, the registration became final at the end of the period during which such objections could have been made, or at the date of the withdrawal.[3]

8.4.4   Notification and objections to registration

Section 5 of the 1965 Act made provision for the giving of notices by the registration authority of applications for registration, and for the making of objections. The time-limits for the making of an application for registration under s 4, and for advancing objections under s 5, have now long expired.

8.4.5   Exemptions

Certain land is exempted from registration.[4] The registration requirements of the 1965 Act did not apply to the New Forest, Epping Forest or the Forest of Dean. Also, the requirements did not apply to any land exempted under an order made by the Minister. The Commons Registration (Exempted Land) Regulations 1965[5] made provision for such exemption, although the criteria for the selection or commons exempted from registration are not entirely clear. The exempted commons are distributed throughout England, although there are a number located in the South East, including Mitcham Common and Kenley Commons in London, and Oxshott Heath, Esher in Surrey.

---

[1]   Commons Registration Act 1965, s 4(2)(a).

[2]   Ibid, s 4(2)(b).

[3]   Ibid, s 7.

[4]   Ibid, s 11.

[5]   SI 1965/2001.

8.4.6 Quantification of grazing rights

Where a right of common consisted of or included a right, not limited by number, to graze animals or animals of any class, such a right was treated, for the purposes of registration, as exercisable in relation to no more animals, or animals of that class, than a definite number.[1] Any application for the registration of such a right was required to state the numbers of animals to be entered on the registers, or as the case may be, the numbers of animals of different classes to be so entered.[2] When any such registration became final, the right was accordingly exercisable in relation to animals not exceeding the number of animals registered or such other number as Parliament might later determine.[3]

8.4.7 Subsequent registration under the Land Registration Acts

If the ownership of any land has been registered under the Commons Registration Act 1965 and, subsequently, that ownership is registered under the Land Registration Acts,[4] then when the Land Registry inform the registration authority of that subsequent registration, the authority must delete the entry in the ownership register under the 1965 Act.[5]

8.5 EFFECT OF REGISTRATION

8.5.1 Effect of provisional registration

Until a registration became final under the Act, a provisional registration was not conclusive as to the matters registered. Accordingly, any rights of common that had provisional registration depended upon proof of title, through express grant or evidence supporting prescription, for their validity. A provisional registration remained subject to objection and the determination of any objections by a Commons Commissioner.[6]

---

[1] Commons Registration Act 1965, s 15(1).

[2] Ibid, s 15(2).

[3] Ibid, s 15(3).

[4] Land Registration Acts 1925 and 1936, now the Land Registration Act 2002.

[5] Commons Registration Act 1965, s 12.

[6] Ibid, ss 5 and 6.

8.5.2   Effect of final registration

If no objection was made to a provisional registration, or if all objections were withdrawn, the registration became final at the end of the objection period or the withdrawal of the objection.[1] If an objection was made to the provisional registration of land as common land, or as a green, or to the provisional registration of any ownership or rights of common over such land, the registration became final upon the decision of the Commons Commissioner dismissing all such objections.[2]

The effect of registration of any land as common land or as a town or village green, or of any rights of common over any such land, is conclusive evidence of the matters registered.[3] This can mean that land achieving final registration under the 1965 Act as common land retains that legal status even where the land never fell within the definition of common land under the Act. In *Corpus Christi College, Oxford v Gloucestershire County Council*,[4] land that had never been waste land of the manor was provisionally registered as common land, and rights of common over it were also provisionally registered. The owners successfully objected to the provisional registration of the rights of common, and these were deleted from the register. There was no objection to the provisional registration of the land as common land. The Court of Appeal held that even though the land was not subject to rights of common, and had never been waste land of the manor, s 10 of the Act deemed the land common land: the final registration of the land as common land was conclusive as to that status.

A court will not normally go behind a registration that has become final by virtue of s 10. Thus *R v Norfolk County Council, ex parte Perry*,[5] where a bungalow had been built on land in the ownership of the applicant, the land had acquired final registration status following a provisional registration to which no objections were made. It was held that the registration was conclusive.

---

1   Commons Registration Act 1965, s 7(1).

2   Ibid, s 6.

3   Ibid, s 10.

4   [1982] 3 WLR 849, [1982] 3 All ER 995.

5   (1996) 74 P&CR 1.

One effect of the conclusive nature of a final registration of land as common land is that such land is regarded as registered common for the purpose of the public rights of access under the CROW Act 2000.[1]

Another effect of the conclusive registration of land as a town or village green may depend on the basis of the rights over the land claimed by the applicants. If the green was registered on the basis of the proof of customary rights, those rights may be exercised. However, if the green was registered on the basis of 20 years' use by inhabitants indulging in sports and pastimes,[2] it has been doubted whether the Act confers rights on the public.[3] However, in *Oxfordshire County Council v Oxford City Council*[4] Lightman J decided that the act of registration does not confer on land the status of a green; the status is acquired independently of the registration process. He stated that the existence of a green of whichever class, whether established with or without the benefit of the presumption arising by reason of registration, gives rise to the rights of the local inhabitants ordinarily incident to the status of such a green. In the case of a Class C green (20 years of sports and pastimes), registration merely records and confirms its prior existence.

8.6   EFFECT OF FAILURE TO REGISTER

8.6.1   Unregistered rights no longer exercisable

(a)   *Rights of common*

The registration period ceased on 31 July 1970. After the end of that period, no land capable of being registered under the 1965 Act shall be deemed to be common land or a town or village green unless it was so registered, and no rights of common shall be exercisable over any such land unless they were registered under either the 1965 Act or under the Land Registration Acts 1925 to 2002: see s 1(2) of the 1965 Act.

---

[1]   See Chapter 10.

[2]   Under s 22(1A) of the 1965 Act.

[3]   *New Windsor Corporation v Mellor* [1975] Ch 380 per Lord Denning MR at pp 391H–392G; and *R (Laing Homes Ltd) v Buckinghamshire County Council* [2003] EWHC 1578 (Admin); [2003] 3 PLR 60.

[4]   [2004] EWHC 12, [2004] PLSCS 16.

The words in s 1(2) that 'no rights of common shall be exercisable over any such land unless they are registered ... .,' mean that where rights of common existed prior to the expiration of the registration period, and were therefore lawfully exercisable, the effect of non-registration meant that such rights were lost completely. It also meant that if no rights of common were registered in respect of land that had been common land, such land ceased to be common land. Thus in *Central Electricity Generating Board v Clwyd County Council*[1] the County Council provisionally registered an area of land as common land notwithstanding that an application to register the rights of common had not been made within the prescribed period of time. It was held that since 'common land' means land subject to rights of common, and no rights of common were registered within the prescribed period, any rights which might have existed were no longer exercisable by virtue of s 1(2) of the 1965 Act. Further, the fact that such rights of common were no longer exercisable meant that they had been extinguished and the area was no longer common land. However, the decision in that case was brought into question in *Corpus Christi College, Oxford v Gloucestershire County Council*.[2]

The same point arose in *Re Turnworth Down*[3] where, again, rights of common had not been registered within the prescribed period. However, the complication in this case was that the relevant rights – rights to cut furze – had been awarded under an inclosure award made pursuant to a private Act of Parliament of 1801. In relation to an application to register the land as common land, it was argued on behalf of the applicant that, as the right to cut furze had been created by statute, they could only be extinguished if that statute was repealed by a subsequent statute, and s 1(2)(b) of the 1965 Act did not have that effect. That argument was rejected. It was held that all rights of common including those created by an earlier Act were subject to the provisions of the 1965 Act and that, therefore, the failure to register the rights to cut furze within the prescribed period meant that such rights had been extinguished. It followed that the land was not subject to rights of common and could not be registered as common land.

---

[1]   [1976] 1 WLR 151.

[2]   [1982] 3 WLR 849, [1982] 3 All ER 995.

[3]   [1977] 2 All ER 105.

Where an application was made to register rights of common, and the Commons Commissioner upholds an objection, there was a period by which an appeal could be brought. If such an appeal was not brought, s 1(2)(b) operates to extinguish a provisional registration of rights when that provisional registration becomes void as a result of the Commons Commissioner's determination.[1]

(b)   Town and village greens

In respect of town or village greens, in *Oxfordshire County Council v Oxford City Council*,[2] Lightman J decided that the provision in s 1(2) of the 1965 Act that non-registration had the effect that the land shall not be deemed to be a green, means that the rights of local inhabitants in respect of greens registrable but unregistered by 31 July 1970 were extinguished, and a fresh period of qualifying user is required to revive the green. That period would be 20 years in respect of a Class C green.

8.6.2   Unclaimed land: town or village green

Section 8 makes provision for the vesting of unclaimed land. Where the registration of any land as common land or as a town or village green became final, then unless the land was registered under the Land Registration Acts,[3] the registration authority was required to refer the question of ownership to a Commons Commissioner.[4]

After the giving of notices by the registration authority, the Commons Commissioner was required to inquire into the matter and, if satisfied that any person was the owner, direct the registration authority to register that person as owner.[5] If the Commons Commissioner was not so satisfied, and the land was a town or village green, he was required to direct that the registration authority register as owner a specified local authority.[6] The local authorities were, in the case of land where there was a parish or

---

[1]   *Lord Dynevor v Richardson* [1995] 1 All ER 109.

[2]   [2004] EWHC 12, [2004] PLSCS 16.

[3]   Land Registration Acts 1925 and 1936, now Land Registration Act 2002.

[4]   Commons Registration Act 1965, s 8(1).

[5]   Ibid, s 8(2).

[6]   Ibid, s 8(3).

community council, such a council, ie in London, the London borough council, elsewhere, the district council.[1]

On registration of the ownership of a town or village green in the name of the appropriate local authority, then, unless the land was regulated under the Commons Act 1899, ss 10 and 15 of the Open Spaces Act 1906 (power to manage and make byelaws) would apply as if the authority had acquired ownership under the 1906 Act.[2]

8.6.3   Unclaimed land: common land

Where the registration of any land as common land became final, but no person was registered under the Land Registration Acts as the owner of the land,[3] then, until the land is vested under any provisions that Parliament might later make, any local authority for the area became entitled to take such steps for the protection of the land against unlawful interference as could be taken by an owner in possession of the land, and the authority may institute proceedings for any offence committed in respect of the land.[4]

8.7   AMENDMENTS, RECTIFICATIONS AND NEW COMMONS

8.7.1   The amendment of registers

Regulations under s 13 of the 1965 Act provide for the amendment of the registers where:

– any land registered under the Act ceases to be common land or a town or village green; or
– any land becomes common land or a town or village green; or
– any rights registered under the Act are apportioned, extinguished or released, or are varied or transferred in such circumstances as may be prescribed.

---

[1]   Commons Registration Act 1965, s 8(5).

[2]   Ibid, s 8(4); see also Chapters 9 and 11 for powers of management.

[3]   Land Registration Acts 1925 and 1936, now Land Registration Act 2002.

[4]   Commons Registration Act 1965, s 9.

8.7.2 Creation of rights of common after 31 July 1970

There are two principal ways in which rights of common can be created:

– by express grant or reservation;
– by prescription, namely actual use as of right for the minimum 20-year prescriptive period.

The way in which rights of common can be created or acquired is explained in more detail in Chapter 6. The Commons Registration (New Land) Regulations 1969 make provision for the registration of land becoming common land for the first time after 2 January 1970 and of rights in respect of such land. However, neither the 1965 Act, nor the 1969 Regulations permit registration of rights of common created after 2 January 1970 over land that was registered under s 4 of the 1965 Act.[1]

The Commons Registration (New Land) Regulations 1969 provide for those cases where, after 2 January 1970:

– any land becomes common land;
– any land becomes a town or village green.

Such land may be included in the appropriate register and that there can be registration of the rights of common over such land.[2] Where rights of common are created by express grant by deed after 2 January 1970, and they are created over land that is not at the time of creation registered common land, then such land would have become common land at the date of such creation. Accordingly, both the new common land and the new rights of common are capable of being registered under reg 3 of the 1969 Regulations.

The position concerning the acquisition of rights of common over land that is not common land by prescription is less clear. Prescription depends upon establishing user as of right for the minimum 20-year prescription period. Whilst the right might have been exercisable as of right during the 20-year period, the right does not become a *profit à prendre* and a legal interest in land until the first day after the expiration of the 20-year period. That is the day upon

---

[1] Commons Registration (New Land) Regulations 1969, SI 1969/1843, reg 3(2). See further Chapter 6.

[2] Ibid, reg 3(1).

which rights of common acquired by prescription can be said to have been 'created'. For the purposes of reg 3 of the 1969 Regulations, that would be the date when the land over which such rights have been acquired, where it is not already registered common land, 'becomes common land'. Such rights thereafter become registrable. Accordingly, it would not seem to matter that some part of the 20-year prescriptive period preceded 3 January 1970. Until the expiration of the 20-year period, it cannot be said that rights of common were exercisable, within the meaning of s 1(2)(b) of the 1965 Act, because although the person exercising those rights may have thought he was entitled to do so and was exercising them 'as of right' he was not actually exercising rights of common as such. Accordingly, the purported exercise of rights prior to 3 January 1970 was not at that time capable of registration and therefore are not rights that cease to be exercisable by virtue of s 1(2)(b). Accordingly, provided the prescriptive period had not expired prior to 31 July 1970, it is arguable that such rights can still be registered over land that is not common land.

It would seem that the same argument could be applied to the acquisition of rights of common by prescription where the whole of the prescriptive 20-year period falls after 2 January 1970. Indeed, this approach appears to be confirmed by the notes to the forms prescribed by the 1969 Regulations. Note 5 to form 31, which is concerned with the registration of rights of common over new common land after 2 January 1970, sets out how land can become subject to rights of common:

– by or under an Act of Parliament;
– by a grant by the owner of land of rights of common over it;
– by rights of common being acquired over it by prescription;
– by substitution or exchange for other land which has ceased to be common land under:
  (a) ss 147 and 148 of the Inclosure Act 1845; or
  (b) para 11 of Sch 1 to the Acquisition of Land (Authorisation Procedure) Act 1946;[1] or
  (c) any other enactment providing, on the exchange of land, for the transfer of rights trusts or incidents attaching to the land given in exchange from that land to the land taken in exchange and vice versa.

---

[1]   See now Acquisition of Land Act 1981.

8.7.3 Town or village greens

The position of new town or village greens is slightly different. In *Oxfordshire County Council v Oxford City Council*,[1] Lightman J decided that although non-registration of a green that existed prior to 31 July 1970 meant that the rights of the inhabitants over the green were extinguished,[2] rights over a green were not dependent on registration and a fresh period of user by the local inhabitants could give rise to the creation of a green (Class C) as registration does not confer rights.[3] Where an application is made to register a Class C green after the date when the amended definition came into force (30 January 2001), that amended definition does not apply where any 20-year period of unamended Class C user is satisfied before that date; continuity of user to the date of the application for registration is not required. However, where the 20-year period ends after 29 January 2001, the amended definition of a Class C green applies so that the inhabitants must be a *significant number* and the user must *continue* to the date of the application for registration.[4]

8.7.4 New common land and land registration

Regulation 3(3) of the Commons Registration (New Land) Regulations 1969 provides that no person may be registered under the 1969 Regulations as the owner of any land which is already registered under the Land Registration Acts 1925 to 1966. However, the position concerning rights of common has become more complicated following the commencement of the Land Registration Act 2002. Prior to the coming into force of that Act, the general principle under the Land Registration Act 1925, and the Land Registration Rules 1925,[5] was that rights of common were neither required nor capable of substantive registration, although were capable of being entered as appurtenant rights to a substantively registered interest. In other words, on the registration of the transfer of land having the benefit of rights of common, such benefit might be described in the Property Register of the registered title. It

---

[1] [2004] EWHC 12, [2004] PLSCS 16.

[2] By virtue of s 1(2) of the 1965 Act.

[3] Not applying *New Windsor Corporation v Mellor* [1975] Ch 380 per Lord Denning MR at pp 391H–392G; *R (Laing Homes Ltd) v Buckinghamshire County Council* [2003] EWHC 1578 (Admin), [2003] 3 PLR 60.

[4] *Oxfordshire County Council v Oxfordshire City Council* [2004] EWHC 12, [2004] PLSCS 16.

[5] SR&O 1925/1093.

followed that rights of common that were not registered in any way under the Land Registration Act 1925 were binding on purchasers of a registered title.[1]

The Land Registration Act 2002 provides that where easements or profits (and the latter include rights of common) are granted or reserved after the Act comes into force, they will not override a subsequent registrable disposition unless they are first registered.[2] However, the grant of a right of common that is registrable under the Commons Registration Act 1965 is not registrable under the 2002 Act.

8.7.5   Applications to register new commons and greens

Where an application is made under the Commons Registration (New Land) Regulations 1969, the registration authority must send notice to every person believed to be an owner, lessee, tenant or occupier of any part of the land affected by the application, or to be likely to wish to object to the application. It must also publish a notice and affix a notice on any part of the land where possible. The notices must give not less than six weeks within which objections can be made.[3] The registration authority must then consider any objections that are in writing and shall send the applicant a copy of every statement in objection. It shall not reject the application without giving the applicant a reasonable opportunity of dealing with the matters contained in the statements of objection and with any other matter in relation to the application which appears to the authority to afford prima facie grounds for rejecting the application.[4] If the registration authority accepts an application, it makes the necessary registration as a registration under s 13 of the 1965 Act.[5] However, it should not normally make a decision without first holding a non-statutory inquiry or hearing.[6] If the registration

---

[1]   They were overriding interests within the meaning of Land Registration Act 1925, s 70(1).

[2]   See s 27(2)(d).

[3]   Commons Registration (New Land) Regulations 1969, SI 1969/1843, reg 5.

[4]   Ibid, reg 6.

[5]   Ibid, reg 7.

[6]   *R (Cheltenham Builders Ltd) v South Gloucestershire District Council* [2003] EWHC 2803 (Admin).

authority rejects the application, it must give to the applicant the reasons for the rejection.

In the case of an application to register a green that has come into existence after 31 July 1970, the application cannot be amended but the registration authority is not required to accept each and every of the grounds or dates used in an application for registration of land as a green. Thus the statement of the date on which the land became a green is a guide to the case intended to be made by the applicant, but it is not and cannot be taken to be writ in stone. A registration authority may register as a green a lesser area than that advanced in an application provided it is not substantially different and where it considers that the part omitted does not have the status of a green.[1] Guidance is also given in *Oxfordshire County Council v Oxford City Council* as to how an application for registration of a green should be considered where either some of the land is inaccessible or is crossed with tracks that are, or may become, public rights of way.[2]

The 1969 Regulations do not contain any further rights of appeal, whether by way of a public local enquiry or a hearing before the Commons Commissioners. If an application for registration of new common land or of a new town or village green or of rights of common over new common land is rejected, the only remedy available to the disappointed applicant is to make an application for judicial review into the High Court. On the other hand, if an application succeeds or partly succeeds, and the registration authority then effects an amendment or addition to the registers pursuant to s 13 of the 1965 Act, s 14 of the 1965 Act empowers the High Court to order that a register be amended if it appears to the court that no amendment or a different amendment ought to have been made and that the error cannot be corrected in pursuance of regulations made under the Act, and that the court deems it just to rectify the register.[3] Alternatively, an application can be made for judicial review.[4]

---

[1]　*Oxfordshire County Council v Oxford City Council* [2004] EWHC 12, [2004] PLSCS 16.

[2]　Ibid

[3]　Section 14(b); the public have an interest: see also *Re Anstey Common* [1985] 1 Ch 329, 341A

[4]　*R (Cheltenham Builders Ltd) v South Gloucestershire District Council* [2003] EWHC 2803 (Admin).

8.7.6 Land ceasing to be common land and alterations to rights of common

Provision is made by the Commons Registration (General) Regulations 1966[1] for the amendment of the registers where land has ceased to be common land, or rights of common have been altered or varied in some way.[2]

Land would cease to be common land within the meaning of s 22(1) of the 1965 Act where it was no longer subject to rights of common.[3] That might happen where, for example, there has been a release of the rights of common to the owner of the soil, or where the ownership of the soil and of the lands to which rights of common are attached are merged together in a single owner. Regulation 27 of the 1966 Regulations permit the owner of the soil to apply for the removal of the land from the registers.

Following the compulsory purchase of common land, land may be provided by way of exchange and as substituted land.[4] There are also provisions for exchange of land in ss 147 and 148 of the Inclosure Act 1845. Regulation 28 of the 1966 Regulations provides for the amendment of the registers to accommodate such substituted land.

Where any right of common has been apportioned, varied, extinguished or released, or, having become a right in gross, has been transferred, application can be made under reg 29 of the 1966 Regulations for the amendment of the register.[5]

---

[1]   SI 1966/1471.

[2]   Section 13 of the 1965 Act.

[3]   In *Corpus Christi College, Oxford v Gloucestershire County Council* [1982] 3 All ER 995, the Court of Appeal decided that land had not ceased to be common land, within the meaning of s 13 of the 1965 Act, where the provisional registration of rights of common had not been confirmed, and no objection had been made against the registration of the land as common land.

[4]   See Chapter 12 and Acquisitions of Land Act 1981, s 19(2).

[5]   See also Chapter 6.

8.7.7　Rectification

The High Court has power to order the amendment of a register under the 1965 Act, where it deems it just, in the following circumstances:[1]

- if the registration of any land or rights of common has become final and the court is satisfied that any person was induced by fraud to withdraw an objection to the registration or to refrain from making an objection; or
- the register has been amended in pursuance of s 13 and it appears to the court that no amendment or a different amendment ought to have been made and that the error cannot be corrected in pursuance of regulations under the Act. The court is not restricted to errors of law and can consider the overall merits of the amendment.[2] The court has a wide discretion.[3]

8.7.8　Dwelling-houses and rectification

The Commons Registration Act 1965 contained a defect. No adequate requirement was made so that when land was provisionally registered, the owner should be notified of that provisional registration. Accordingly, there were occasions when land consisting of a dwelling-house, or ancillary to a dwelling-house, was given final registration without the relevant owners making an objection.

That defect was addressed by the Common Land (Rectification of Registers) Act 1989. This provided that where land consisting of a dwelling-house or land ancillary to a dwelling-house has had that characteristic since 5 August 1945, a notice could be given by any person within 3 years of the Act objecting to the inclusion of such land on either the register of common land or of town or village greens.[4] On receipt of such a notice, the registration authority was

---

[1]　Section 14.

[2]　*R v Suffolk County Council, ex parte Steed* (1995) 70 P&CR 487. Alternatively, a registration can be quashed by judicial review: see *R (Cheltenham Builders Ltd) v South Gloucestershire District Council* [2003] EWHC 2803 (Admin).

[3]　*Secretary of State for Health v Birmingham City Council* (per Vinelott J) (unreported) 20 July 1995; see also *Oxfordshire County Council v Oxford City Council* [2004] EWHC 12, [2004] PLSCS 16.

[4]　Section 1(1)–(2).

required to refer the matter to a Commons Commissioner to inquire into it and make a decision as to whether the register required modification.[1]

In *Re Land at Freshfields*[2] the applicant owned an area of land, adjoining his house and garden, that had been used as pasture for grazing cattle and growing hay. This area had been registered as common land under the 1965 Act. The Commons Commissioner had been entitled to dismiss the applicant's application under the 1989 Act to have the land removed from the register; the land could not be described as 'garden' within the meaning of the 1989 Act. However, in *Storey v Commons Commissioner*[3] the Commissioner was wrong to conclude that an orchard some distance from a dwelling-house could not be part of the 'garden'; it was a question of fact whether land was 'garden'. Land did not have to be used and enjoyed as ancillary to a single dwelling-house for the whole period after 5 August 1945.

8.8   COMMONS COMMISSIONERS AND APPEALS

As explained above, in relation to the hearing of objections to provisional registrations, Commons Commissioners dealt with these and made decisions binding on the registration authorities. The Lord Chancellor appointed Commons Commissioners from lawyers and a panel of assessors with special knowledge to assist the Commissioners.[4] Provision was made for the award of costs.[5]

Any person aggrieved by the decision of a Commons Commissioner as being erroneous in law is entitled to require a case to be stated for the decision of the High Court.[6]

Where a registration authority is required to make a decision about altering or adding an entry to the registers under s 13, it should

---

[1]   Section 1(4).

[2]   (1993) 66 P&CR 9.

[3]   (1993) 66 P&CR 206, applying *Cresstock Investments Ltd v Commons Commissioner* [1992] 1 WLR 1088.

[4]   Commons Registration Act 1965, s 17(1).

[5]   Ibid, s 17(4).

[6]   Ibid, s 18(1).

normally consider holding a non-statutory inquiry or hearing.[1] The person holding the inquiry would be appointed by the authority and would not hold the position of a Commons Commissioner.

However, the issue as to whether a Commons Commissioner has jurisdiction to determine whether land has become a town or village green is to be considered by the Court of Appeal.[2]

---

[1] *R (Cheltenham Builders Ltd) v South Gloucestershire District Council* [2003] EWHC 2803 (Admin), following *R v Suffolk County Council, ex parte Steed* (1995) 70 P&CR 487 at 500.

[2] *R (Witney) v Commons Commissioners* (unreported) 29 November 2003.

Chapter 9

TOWN AND VILLAGE GREENS

9.1   INTRODUCTION

What is a town or village green? In *New Windsor Corporation v Mellor*,[1] Lord Denning MR explained the background to customary rights to a village green:[2]

> 'Today we look back far in time. To a town or village green. The turf is old. Animals have grazed there for hundreds of years. Nowadays they are pleasant stretches of grass where people sit and talk. Sometimes they play cricket or kick a ball about. But in mediaeval times it was the place where young men mustered with their bows and arrows. They shot at the butts. There might be stocks there where offenders were put for their petty misdemeanours. In the month of May they set up a maypole and danced around it. We have no record of when it all began.'

He then introduced an excerpt from the poem 'Forefathers' by Edmund Blunden:

> 'On the green they watched their sons
>
> Playing til too dark to see,
>
> As their fathers watched them once,
>
> As my father once watched me.'

Town and village greens are the quintessential features of the village in England and Wales and, to a lesser extent, the smaller county towns. Although today associated with leisure activities, their pre-1066 origins no doubt lay in the obvious need for some form of open

---

[1]   [1975] 1 Ch 380.

[2]   Ibid, at 386c

space in any village where communal activities of one sort or another, whether for leisure or non-leisure purposes, could be carried out. By the Norman period the following description would have been true of many village greens:[1]

> 'Through the village ran the highway. This was not a metalled road as we know it but a broad area, muddy in winter and dusty in summer, along which travellers made their way as best they could, detouring round potholes and rough patches over the adjoining land. Wandering pedlars sold their goods on the green and visiting showmen set up their booths there. The young folk met and the older ones gossiped in good weather and cottagers put out their geese to graze.'

Many town or village greens would have been, and may remain, subject to rights of common, particularly rights of pasture. But the town or village greens that have never been subject to rights of common were almost certainly always part of the waste lands of the manor.[2] In the nineteenth century, it was the practice for Inclosure Commissioners to allot areas in a town or village for recreational purposes, in connection with the inclosing of commons. Town or village greens are also frequently subject to customary rights for leisure and other purposes, whether or not they are either part of the waste lands of the manor or subject to rights of common.

An area may look like a town or village green, because it is an open, probably green, space within or near the centre of a town or a village. However, town or village greens do not all have the same origins, and the public will not necessarily enjoy public rights of access for the same purposes over each of them.

This chapter considers the legal basis of town and village greens, and their regulation and protection. Although the registration process of town or village greens under the Commons Registration Act 1965 was considered more fully in Chapter 8, the Act is briefly considered here because its registration requirements have considerably enhanced the significance of town and village greens. One important consequence of the Act has been the uncertainty of

---

[1]   See Jessel *The Law of the Manor* (1998), at p 8.

[2]   See Chapter 2.

the rights that registration might confer on the local inhabitants[1] in respect of what are called Class C greens, as explained below.

9.2 REGISTRATION OF GREENS UNDER THE COMMONS REGISTRATION ACT 1965

9.2.1 Registration

Section 1(1) of the 1965 Act provides that:

'There shall be registered, in accordance with the provisions of this Act and subject to the exceptions mentioned thereon –

(a) land in England or Wales which is common land or a town or village green;

(b) rights of common over such land; and

(c) persons claiming to be or found to be owners of such land or becoming the owners thereof by virtue of this Act.'

Section 3 of the 1965 Act requires the registration authorities to maintain a separate register of town or village greens. As originally enacted, the 1965 Act defined a town or village green as meaning:[2]

'... land which has been allotted by or under any Act for the exercise or recreation of the inhabitants of any locality or on which the inhabitants of any locality have a customary right to indulge in lawful sports and pastimes *or on which the inhabitants of any locality have indulged in such sports and pastimes as of right for not less than 20 years.'*

The definition of a Class C green was amended with effect from 30 January 2001; the italicised words set out above were deleted and replaced with 'or which falls within subsection (1A) of this section', together with the following:[3]

---

[1] *R v Oxfordshire County Council, ex parte Sunningwell Parish Council* [2000] 1 AC 335, *per* Lord Hoffmann at 347c, and *R (Laing Homes Ltd) v Buckinghamshire County Council* [2003] EWHC 1578, at [47], [2003] 3 PLR 60. But see now *Oxfordshire County Council v Oxford City Council* [2004] EWHC 12, [2004] PLSCS 16.

[2] Section 22(1).

[3] Subsections 22(1A) and (1B) were introduced by CROW Act 2000, s 98 with effect from 30 January 2001.

'(1A) Land falls within this subsection if it is land on which for not less than twenty years a significant number of the inhabitants of any locality, or of any neighbourhood within a locality, have indulged in lawful sports and pastimes as of right, and either –

   (a)   continue to do so, or

   (b)   have ceased to do so for not more than such period as may be prescribed, or determined in accordance with prescribed provisions.

(1B) If regulations made for the purposes of paragraph (b) of subsection (1A) of this section provide for the period mentioned in that paragraph to come to an end unless prescribed steps are taken, the regulations may also require registration authorities to make available in accordance with the regulations, on payment of any prescribed fee, information relating to the taking of any such steps.'

The Act provides for three classes of greens, a classification referred to by Carnwath J in *R v Suffolk County Council, ex parte Steed*:[1] Class A, allotted land; Class B, land subject to customary right to indulge in lawful sports and pastimes; and Class C, land on which for more than 20 years a significant number of inhabitants indulged in lawful sports and pastimes (as amended). The unamended definition of a Class C green applies whenever the 20-year qualifying period of user (which can be any period of 20 years) expired prior to 30 January 2001; that user does not have to continue up to the date of any application to register the green. The amended definition of a Class C green, which requires the additional requirement of a significant number of local inhabitants, although they can be of any locality within a neighbourhood, and that the user continues to the date of any application to register the green, applies where the 20-year qualifying period had not expired by 30 January 2001. In other words, the amended definition is not engaged by every application after that date.[2]

---

[1]   [1995] QB 487 at 491; also by Lord Hoffmann in *R v Oxfordshire County Council, ex parte Sunningwell Parish Council* [1999] 2 EGLR 94 at 95E and by Sullivan J in *R (Cheltenham Builders Ltd) v South Gloucestershire District Council* [2003] EWHC 2803.

[2]   *Oxfordshire County Council v Oxford City Council* [2004] EWHC 12, [2004] PLSCS 16.

9.2.2 Effect of non-registration

In respect of town or village greens existing at the date when the 1965 Act came into force, the period of registration expired on 31 July 1970. The 1965 Act then provides that at the end of that period 'no land capable of being registered under the Act shall be deemed to be ... a town or village green unless it is so registered'.[1] It has been said that whilst land subject to a customary right to indulge in lawful sports and pastimes (Class B) might cease to have that status by reason of non-registration, land falling within the other two classes of town or village greens would probably retain their status.[2] However, in *Oxfordshire County Council v Oxford City Council*[3] Lightman J decided that the act of registration does not confer on land the status of a green; the status is acquired independently of the registration process. He stated that the existence of a green of whichever class, whether established with or without the benefit of the presumption arising by reason of registration, gives rise to the rights of the local inhabitants ordinarily incident to the status of such a green. In the case of a Class C green, registration merely records and confirms its prior existence. Accordingly, he decided that the provision in s 1(2) of the 1965 Act that non-registration had the effect that the land shall not be deemed to be a green meant that the rights of local inhabitants in respect of greens registrable but unregistered by 31 July 1970 were extinguished, and a fresh period of qualifying user is required to revive that green. That period would be 20 years in respect of a Class C green

9.2.3 New greens

Where any land becomes a town or village green after 31 July 1970, the 1965 Act makes provision for the amendment of the registers so that a new town or village green can be included.[4] The procedure usually requires the registration authority to hold a non-statutory inquiry or hearing; a decision to register may be challenged by judicial review or by an application under s 14 of the 1965 Act.[5] Only

---

[1]   Section 1(2)(a).

[2]   See Gadsden *The Law of Commons*, at p 385.

[3]   [2004] EWHC 12, [2004] PLSCS 16.

[4]   Section 13 and Commons Registration (General) Regulations 1966, SI 1966/1471 as amended by Commons Registration (New Land) Regulations 1969, SI 1969/1843.

[5]   *R (Cheltenham Builders Ltd) v South Gloucestershire District Council* [2003] EWHC 2803.

Class C greens can now come into existence. Class C greens within the meaning of the unamended definition may be registered where the 20-year qualifying period was satisfied prior to 30 January 2001 (any period of 20 years will suffice). Where the 20-year qualifying period expires after that date, the amended definition of a Class C green applies, and the user must be by a significant number of inhabitants, and continue until the date of the application for registration.[1] Guidance on the form and treatment of applications was considered in Chapter 8.

The appropriate classes of green that may be registered as town or village greens are now considered.

9.3   CLASS A: ALLOTTED LAND

This category of land is described as 'land which has been allotted by or under any Act for the exercise or recreation of the inhabitants of any locality'.[2] Prior to the enactment of the Inclosure Act 1845, inclosure awards frequently allotted areas of land, particularly town and village greens, for the purposes of exercise and of recreation. The Inclosure Act 1845 contained several provisions for the allotment of land for exercise and recreation in the award of the Inclosure Commissioners.

Under the 1845 Act any existing town or village green could not be subject to inclosure.[3] Further, it was lawful for the Commissioners to allot any existing green to the church wardens and overseers of the poor of the parish to hold that land in trust to allow the same to be used for the purposes of exercise and recreation, provided that such allotted green should be of equal or greater extent to any previously existing. The boundary of such an allotted green was to be marked where it adjoined inclosed land.[4]

When first enacted, the 1845 Act required the Inclosure Commissioners to consider allotting part of the waste lands of the manor for the purposes of exercise and recreation. An allotment of

---

[1]   *Oxfordshire County Council v Oxford City Council* [2004] EWHC 12, [2004] PLSCS 16.

[2]   Commons Registration Act 1965, s 22(1).

[3]   Section 15. See also Chapter 7 for an explanation of this Act.

[4]   Section 15.

between 4 and 10 acres was to be provided according to the size of the population of the parish.[1] Allotments for exercise and recreation would normally be made to the church wardens and overseers of the relevant parishes.[2] It has been said that the effect of allotments for exercise and recreation was to extinguish any rights of common over the affected land.[3] This seems doubtful as the provision dealing with the extinguishment of rights of common appears to be directed to the allotments that were made for the purposes of inclosure. The management obligations in relation to allotted greens or areas for exercise and recreation are considered below. It became the invariable practice of the Inclosure Commissioners after 1845 to allot land for the purposes of exercise and recreation.

Although the nature and origin of customary rights is considered below, it was quite usual for greens allotted under s 15 of the 1845 Act to have been subject to customary rights.

9.4 CLASS B: CUSTOMARY RIGHTS TO INDULGE IN LAWFUL SPORTS AND PASTIMES

Customary rights are recognised by the common law where certain requirements are satisfied. Such rights must have been exercisable only by members of some identifiable local community, in relation to a particular locality.[4] They must be certain, reasonable and continuous, and have existed from time immemorial (1189). In *Mercer v Denne* it was said that:[5]

> 'Most cases with regard to validity of custom are difficult of decision. The fact is that reason recoils from the proposition that legal memory goes back to an arbitrary date at the beginning of the reign of Richard I., A.D. 1189, and, if one finds proof of uninterrupted modern usage, there is a natural inclination to presume the previous existence of the custom right back to 1189, even though the facts may be such as to

---

[1] Section 31.

[2] Section 73.

[3] See Gadsden *The Law of Commons*, at p 380 relying on s 106 of the 1845 Act.

[4] *R v Oxfordshire County Council, ex parte Sunningwell Parish Council* [2000] AC 335 and *R v Suffolk County Council, ex parte Steed* (1995) 70 P&CR 487.

[5] *Mercer v Denne* [1905] 2 Ch 538, *per* Vaughan Williams LJ at 577.

force upon reason the conclusion that the modern usage could not in fact have been adopted for more than a few generations.'

It seems certain that, apart from allotted greens (considered above), town or village greens had their origins as either waste lands of the manor or as land subject to rights of common. Either way the owner of the soil would have been the owner of the manor. Customary rights can therefore be acquired over both waste lands of the manor and land subject to rights of common. It is also clear that the customary rights can be acquired over land that would not ordinarily be described as a town or village green, they might be acquired over an area of private land, if the necessary requirements are satisfied.[1]

The requirements for establishing a customary right are as follows.

9.4.1   Local inhabitants

A customary right may only be exercised by the members of some identifiable local community. The definition of 'any locality', in s 22(1) of the 1965 Act, therefore probably means '*the* locality'. As Sir George Jessel MR said in *Hammerton v Honey:*[2]

> 'What must be the usage proved? It must not only be consistent with the custom alleged, but, if I may use the expression, not too wide. For instance, if you allege a custom for certain persons to dance on a green, and you prove in support of that allegation, not only that some people danced, but that everybody else in the world who chose danced and played cricket, you have got beyond your custom.'

In *Bourke v Davis*[3] it was said that a custom is good if confined to inhabitants of a particular district. In *Edward v Jenkins*, Kekewich J, after considering the decision in *Fitch v Rawling*[4] said:[5]

---

[1]   *Hall v Nottingham* (1875) 1 Ex D 1.

[2]   (1876) 24 WR 603.

[3]   (1889) 44 ChD 110.

[4]   (1795) 2 H Bl 393.

[5]   [1896] 1 Ch 308, at 313.

'I do not, therefore, find in any of the cases anything that would justify me in saying that the use of the word "district" means more than the particular division known to the law in which the particular property is situate. It may be situate in a parish, or in a manor, or there might be some other division. But I cannot see how a number of parishes can, without specific evidence, be said to be situated in a particular district so that land in one of the parishes is land in a particular district.'

Although *Fitch v Rawling* was not referred to in *Ministry of Defence v Wiltshire County Council*,[1] Harman J decided that the residents of three streets in the vicinity of the open land in question did not constitute a defined body of persons recognised in law as an entity, such as a parish or manor, and were therefore not capable of exercising a customary right.

In *Edwards v Jenkins*,[2] Kekewich J decided that a custom could not be claimed on behalf of the inhabitants of three parishes, because three parishes did not constitute a district, such as a parish or a manor. In *New Windsor Corporation v Mellor*[3] Lord Denning MR said that he did not think that that was correct. He added:

'So long as the locality is certain, that is enough.'

Gadsden suggests this observation is highly persuasive and that it ought to be a question of fact in each case as to the extent of the locality which is relevant for establishing a customary right, and that there is no reason why a housing estate, whatever its extent, should not be regarded as a locality.[4] There must, however, be some doubt about that approach. Customary rights must be ancient, certain, reasonable and continuous. They are 'ancient' if they are shown to have commenced prior to 1189, the beginning of legal memory. Apart from the fact that a housing estate today can probably be shown not to have existed in 1189, this approach, and Lord Denning's disapproval, fails to take into account that a customary

---

[1]   [1995] 4 All ER 931.

[2]   [1896] 1 Ch 308.

[3]   [1975] 1 Ch 380.

[4]   See Gadsden *The Law of Commons*, at p 379.

right must, at least in theory, lie in grant. As Heath J said in *Fitch v Rawling:*[1]

> 'The lord might have granted such a privilege, as is claimed by the …
> custom, before the time of memory.'

That recognises the unlikelihood of any grant being made by the lord of the manor in favour of inhabitants outside the manor, or possibly the parish. In *R (Cheltenham Builders Ltd) v South Gloucestershire District Council*, Sullivan J concluded that 'locality' was an administrative unit.[2]

9.4.2   Ancient, certain, reasonable and continuous

The other essential characteristics of a custom are: immemorial existence, reasonableness, certainty, and continuity.[3] Although every custom must have been in existence since 1189, there is a presumption of such immemorial existence if proof of user in living memory is shown. However, that presumption is rebuttable by proof that the user could not have taken place since 1189.[4]

Reasonableness has no single test, but embraces notions of reasonableness considered in relation to all the circumstances, the nature of the custom, the land over which it is claimed and consistency with other rights and laws.[5] Certainty requires definite limits to the rights claimed, the locality it is claimed over and the persons claiming it.[6] Continuity requires the absence of interruption since 1189. That does not mean use everyday, or even every year, but no interruption to the exercise of the right as a right. It certainly does not mean that the right must be capable of being exercised

---

[1]   (1795) 2 H. Bl. 393 at 399.

[2]   [2003] EWHC 2803 (Admin).

[3]   *Halsbury's Laws of England* (4th edn) vol 21(1), at para 606.

[4]   *Hammerton v Honey* (1876) 24 WR 603.

[5]   *Wolstanton Ltd v Newcastle-under-Lyme Borough Council* [1940] AC 860, [1940] 3 All ER 101, HL.

[6]   *Hammerton v Honey* (1876) 24 WR 603.

every day as many rights are only claimed in respect of defined periods each year.[1]

9.4.3   Nature of the activities

Both non-leisure and leisure activities have been recognised as customary rights. Thus in *Mercer v Denne*[2] a custom was established for fishermen drying nets on land. The relevance of the nature of the activity that founds a customary right arises because of the registration requirements of the Commons Registration Act 1965 and the various provisions that protect and regulate town and village greens. For the purposes of the 1965 Act, where a customary right is claimed, this is limited to where the inhabitants of any locality have a customary right to indulge in lawful sports and pastimes. As we shall see below, in relation to the regulation and management of town and village greens, the various provisions are restricted to town and village greens used for recreational purposes. Accordingly, the only customary rights that are generally relevant to town and village greens are those involving recreational pastimes.

Customary rights which have been upheld include archery,[3] dancing,[4] and playing cricket.[5]

9.4.4   Conclusions

The requirements set out above will prevent the establishment of a customary right at common law in many circumstances. The additional category of greens, based on 20 years' use for lawful sports and pastimes addressed some of the defects in establishing such user as a customary right.

---

[1]   *New Windsor Corporationn v Mellor* [1974] 2 All ER 510.

[2]   [1905] 2 Ch 538.

[3]   *New Windsor Corporation v Mellor* [1975] 1 Ch 380.

[4]   *Hall v Nottingham* (1875) 1 Ex D 1.

[5]   *Fitch v Rawling* (1795) 2 H Bl 393.

9.5   CLASS C: USE OF LAND FOR LAWFUL SPORTS AND PASTIMES AS OF RIGHT FOR 20 YEARS

9.5.1   Deficiencies in requirements for customary rights

This category was amended by the Countryside and Rights of Way Act 2000, with effect from 30 January 2001. The amendment introduced the need for a *significant* number of inhabitants to have indulged in lawful sports and pastimes, and that such inhabitants could be the inhabitants not merely of a locality, but also of any neighbourhood within a locality – this latter change addressing the difficulty in *Ministry of Defence v Wiltshire County Council*.[1] The purpose of this category is clear. Under the common law an easement or a profit may be acquired by implication which arises where a minimum of 20 years' use without permission, without secrecy, and without force, can be established (30 years for profits under the Prescription Act 1832). A claim to customary rights can be defeated by showing that the rights could not have been exercised before 1189. Accordingly, a claim to public rights of exercise and recreation would fail at common law.[2] The identification of the locality has also caused problems. The requirements of this third category are as follows.

9.5.2   Significant number of inhabitants

A significant number of inhabitants must have indulged in lawful sports and pastimes. There is little guidance on the meaning of a 'significant number of the inhabitants' of either any locality or of a neighbourhood within a locality in the Act. This should be given its ordinary meaning such that a claim by only a few inhabitants could constitute a 'significant number' in appropriate cases. In *R (Alfred McAlpine Homes Ltd) v Staffordshire County Council*, it was held that a 'significant number' need not be considerable or substantial; it was a matter of impression for the decision-maker on the evidence put before him and what mattered was that the number of people using the land in question had to be sufficient to indicate that their use of the land signifies that it is a general use by the local community for informal recreation, rather than occasional use by individuals as

---

[1]   [1995] 4 All ER 931.

[2]   *New Windsor Corporation v Mellor* [1975] 1 Ch 380 at 391.

trespassers.[1] It is not necessary that a significant number of inhabitants must be the applicants for registration as a town or village green. In one case only four local residents made the application.[2]

9.5.3　Any locality or neighbourhood within a locality

A claim can be made by the inhabitants of any locality, or of any neighbourhood within a locality. The meaning of 'the inhabitants of any locality' was considered above in relation to customary rights. A 'locality' suggested a manor or a parish or some other recognised unit. It is insufficient if the land is used predominantly by inhabitants of the village.[3] What is now clear is that an area less than a locality is sufficient to support a claim. This circumvents the problem that the applicants faced in *Ministry of Defence v Wiltshire County Council* where the residents of three streets were held not to constitute a locality.[4] But a 'locality' is not an arbitrary line on a map; it means an administrative unit and a 'neighbourhood' within a locality means an area with a sufficient degree of cohesiveness.[5]

9.5.4　As of right

The applicants must show that the inhabitants have indulged in lawful sports and pastimes *as of right*. The meaning of *as of right* was considered in *R v Oxfordshire County Council, ex parte Sunningwell Parish Council*.[6] In this case the church authorities were the owners of 10 acres of glebe land on which they had obtained planning permission to build some houses. The parish council contended that the glebe was land on which the inhabitants of the locality had indulged in sports and pastimes as of right for not less than 20 years. The House of Lords decided that where a use had to be established

---

[1]　[2002] 2 PLR 1, at para 71.

[2]　*R (Beresford) v Sunderland City Council* [2002] QB 874.

[3]　*R v Oxfordshire County Council, ex parte Sunningwell Parish Council* [1999] 2 EGLR 94, at 99D.

[4]　[1995] 4 All ER 931.

[5]　*R (Cheltenham Builders Ltd v South Gloucestershire District Council* [2003] EWHC 2803 (Admin).

[6]　[1999] 2 EGLR 94 in which *R v Suffolk County Council, ex parte Steed* [1997] 1 EGLR 131 was said to be wrongly decided.

as of right, user that was apparently *as of right* could not be discounted merely because many of the users over a long period were subjectively indifferent as to whether a right existed, or even had private knowledge that it did not. It was sufficient that the glebe was used predominantly by inhabitants even if there was occasional use by non-inhabitants. A balance had to be struck between neighbourly tolerance of trespass and the acquisition of rights by user; there had been sufficient quality of user as of right. Toleration was not inconsistent with user as of right.[1]

In *R (Beresford) v Sunderland City Council,* the commons registration authority had refused an application for an area to be registered as a town green, pursuant to s 13 of the 1965 Act, on the ground that the inhabitants had indulged in sports and pastimes with the permission or implied licence of the landowner; the inhabitants had not indulged in sports or pastimes *as of right.*[2] The House of Lords held that the claim to a use of the land *as of right* was not defeated by implied permission. The land had been owned by public or local authorities and their provision of the land was not, on the evidence, indicative of a precatory permission; the application for registration of the area as a town green could proceed.

In *R (Laing Homes Ltd) v Buckinghamshire County Council,* Sullivan J had to consider whether rights could be exercisable, *as of right,* over some fields used for taking an annual hay crop. In concluding that the matter had to be remitted to the registration authority for reconsideration, he said that the proper approach was to consider how the exercise of the activities appeared to the owner of the land:[3]

> 'Thus, the proper approach is not to examine the extent to which those using the land for recreational purposes were interrupted by the landowner's agricultural activities, but to ask whether those using the fields for recreational purposes were interrupting [the landowners' licensee's] agricultural use of the land in such a manner, or to such an extent, that [the landowners] should have been aware that the recreational users believed that they were exercising a public right. If the starting point is, "how would the matter have appeared to [the

---

[1]   [1999] 2 EGLR 94, at 99F.

[2]   [2004] 1 All ER 160, [2003] 3 WLR 1306, on appeal from [2001] 3 PLR 120.

[3]   *R (Laing Homes Ltd) v Buckinghamshire County Council* [2003] EWHC 1578 (Admin) at para 82, [2003] 3 PLR 60.

landowners]?" it would not be reasonable to expect [the landowners] to resist the recreational use of their field so long as such use did not interfere with their licensee's ... use of them, for taking an annual hay crop.'

Sullivan J also considered that public statements made by members of the public against the development of the fields, in relation to planning applications, were inconsistent with a claim *as of right*.[1] The problem with showing 'user as of right' was considered in *R (Cheltenham Builders Ltd) v South Gloucestershire District Council*.[2]

9.5.5   20-year period and lack of continuity

The amendments made by the Countryside and Rights of Way Act 2000 (s 22(1A)(a)) require either that the use is continuing or has ceased to do so for no more than a prescribed period of time. One of the difficulties faced by the claimants in *Ministry of Defence v Wiltshire County Council* was that they had to show a 20-year use up to the date of the application for registration of an area as a town or village green.[3] The prescribed period allows for the possibility that the landowner may have prevented use for a period of time sufficient to negate 20-years' user continuing up to the date of application. The prescribed period is likely to be about 2 years. Where an application was withdrawn after the landowner objected, there had not been continuity of user as of right thereafter.[4]

However, until there is a prescribed period, the provision in s 22(1A)(a) which relates to a green that is used by a significant number of the inhabitants of any neighbourhood within a locality who indulge in lawful sports and pastimes as of right and who continue to do so, means that the use must continue until the time of an application for registration or of the commencement of proceedings vindicating the existence of the green.[5] In relation to the required 20-year period of user to establish a Class C green, any

---

[1]   *R (Laing Homes Ltd) v Buckinghamshire County Council* [2003] EWHC 1578 (Admin) at para 82, [2003] 3 PLR 60.

[2]   [2003] EWHC 2803 (Admin).

[3]   [1995] 4 All ER 931.

[4]   *R (Cheltenham Builders Ltd) v South Gloucestershire District Council* [2003] EWHC 2803 (Admin).

[5]   In *Oxfordshire County Council v Oxford City Council* [2004] EWHC 12, [2004] PLSCS 16.

period of 20 years is sufficient and it need not be the 20-year period immediately before the application for registration. The applicant can select any 20 years prior to the application.[1] In the case of greens falling within the amended definition of a Class C green that came into force on 29 January 2001, an application may be made at any time thereafter so long as user is continuing.[2]

9.5.6   Lawful sports and pastimes

Finally, the expression 'lawful sports and pastimes' was considered in *R v Oxfordshire County Council, ex parte Sunningwell Parish Council*.[3] The rights claimed were for:[4]

> '... such outdoor pursuits as walking their dogs, playing family and children's games, flying kites, picking blackberries, fishing in the stream and tobogganing down the slope when snow falls.'

Lord Hoffmann said that 'sports and pastimes' was a composite class, so that an activity that was a sport or a pastime would be within it.[5] In *R (Laing Homes Ltd) v Buckinghamshire County Council* Sullivan J considered that the use of footpaths for walking dogs through fields might not constitute the necessary sports or pastimes.[6] The situation where the public use defined tracks over land can cause difficulties as to whether the use of those tracks will give rise to public rights of way only, or rights of user as a Class C green. Also, where tracks across land are already public rights of way can a Class C green user be established? In *Oxfordshire County Council v Oxford City Council*,[7] Lightman J stated that in the first situation the user of the tracks will generally only establish public rights of way unless the user is wider in scope or the tracks are of such character that user of them cannot give rise to a presumption of

---

[1]   *Oxfordshire County Council v Oxford City Council* [2004] EWHC 12, [2004] PLSCS 16.

[2]   Ibid.

[3]   [1999] 2 EGLR 94.

[4]   Ibid, at 95C.

[5]   [1999] 2 EGLR 94, at 98L.

[6]   *R (Laing Homes Ltd) v Buckinghamshire County Council* [2003] EWHC 1578 (Admin), [2003] 3 PLR 60. Dog-walking and playing with children was accepted by Carnwath J in *R v Suffolk County Council, ex parte Steed* (1995) 70 P&CR 487 at 503.

[7]   [2004] EWHC 12, [2004] PLSCS 16.

dedication at common law as a public highway, but user of such tracks for pedestrian recreational purposes may readily qualify as user as a Class C green. The answer must depend how the matter would have appeared to the owner of the land.[1] In the second situation the user will generally be referable to the public rights of way unless the user is only explicable to a Class C green; the matter being viewed from the position of the landowner.

9.5.7 Effect of registration of green based on 20 years of public use

Curiously, if the green is registered on the basis, not of a custom, but of use by the public for 20 years for sports or pastimes, the 1965 Act gives the public no rights to carry out those activities. The activities are not, of course, exercisable, as of right, as a custom.[2]

9.6 REGULATION AND PROTECTION

9.6.1 Ownership

Town or village greens that were allotted for exercise or recreation for the inhabitants of any locality, under the Inclosure Act 1845, or earlier Inclosure Acts, will usually now be owned by the parish or town council, or, in urban areas, the district or borough council. In the case of town or village greens subject to customary rights, or which have been registered as such under the Commons Registration Act 1965, on the ground that they have been used for sports and pastimes for at least 20 years, their ownership is far less certain. The land may be privately owned and may never have been a green properly so described. A town or village green is more usually part of the uninclosed land in what was, or remains, a village. That land would originally have been owned by the lord of the manor.

Under s 1(1)(a) of the Commons Registration Act 1965, land in England or Wales which is a town or village green was required to

---

[1] [2004] EWHC 12, [2004] PLSCS 16 and *R v Oxfordshire County Council, ex parte Sunningwell Parish Council* [2001] 1 AC 335, pp 352H–353A.

[2] *New Windsor Corporation v Mellor* [1975] Ch 380 per Lord Denning MR at 391H–392G; and *R (Laing Homes Ltd) v Buckinghamshire County Council* [2003] EWHC 1578 (Admin), [2003] 3 PLR 60.

have been registered. There should also have been registered persons claiming to be or found to be owners of such land.[1] Where any land was registered as a town or village green, but no person was registered as its owner, either under the Commons Registration Act 1965 or the Land Registration Acts 1925 and 1936, there is provision under the 1965 Act for the ownership of a town or village green to be vested in a local authority.[2] In the case of land in a parish or community where there is a parish or community council, that council is the appropriate local authority. If the land is regulated by a scheme under the Commons Act 1899, the appropriate local authority is the parish or community council only if the powers of management under Part I of the 1899 Act are being exercised by that council.[3] In the case of land in a London borough, the local authority is the borough council.[4] In all other cases, the appropriate local authority is the council or the district in which the land is situated.[5]

9.6.2   Effect of rights of common

No doubt many town or village greens were subject to rights of common[6] and such land would have been subject to the rights of the commoners. Whether the rights of recreation prevail over, or are subject to, the rights of the commoners or the rights of the owner to any produce, probably depends upon the manner by which the recreational rights were acquired. In *Fitch v Fitch*[7] it was held that the rights of an owner to cut hay prevailed over the recreational rights of the local inhabitants. However, one can see that there may be circumstances where the recreational rights were acquired by such use as did prevail over the rights of the commoners or the owner. The possible conflict between the recreational rights of the local inhabitants and the rights of commoners remains because rights of common were registrable under the Commons Registration Act 1965 in respect of a town or village green.[8] Although the

---

[1]   Section 1(1)(c).

[2]   Commons Registration Act 1965, s 8(3).

[3]   Ibid, s 8(5)(a).

[4]   Ibid, s 8(5)(b).

[5]   Ibid, s 8(5)(c).

[6]   *Ratcliffe v Jowers* (1891) 8 TLR 6 (Barnes Green, London).

[7]   (1797) 2 Esp 543.

[8]   Section 4(1).

definition of *common* land under the Commons Registration Act 1965 excludes a town or village green,[1] rights of common may nonetheless be registered and exercised over a town or village green.[2]

9.6.3 Management powers and duties

There are several statutory provisions that contain management powers and duties. These statutory provisions are not restricted to town or village greens.

(a) *Metropolitan Commons Acts 1866 – 1878*

These Acts applied to land which was subject to rights of common in 1866, the whole or any part of which was situated within the Metropolitan Police District as defined at the date of the passing of the Act.[3] Under the 1866 Act, schemes of regulation were made for many metropolitan commons, including bylaws and regulations for the prevention of nuisances and the preservation of order.[4] It would appear that the purpose of a scheme under the 1866 Act is:

> 'for the establishment of local management with a view to the expenditure of money on the drainage, levelling, and improvement of a metropolitan common, and to the making of bylaws and regulations for the prevention of nuisances and the preservation of order thereon.'

(b) *Commons Act 1899*

Under this Act the council of an urban district may make a scheme for the regulation and management of any common within their district with a view to the expenditure of money on the drainage, levelling and improvement of the common, and to the making of bylaws and regulations for the prevention of nuisances and the preservation of order on the commons.[5] Although this Act was principally concerned with the making of schemes of regulation

---

[1] Section 22(1).

[2] Section 4(1).

[3] Sections 3 and 4.

[4] Section 6.

[5] Section 1. See further at Chapter 11.

affecting commons, the expression 'common' was deemed to include any town or village green.[1]

(c)   Open Spaces Act 1906

This Act contains a number of powers for trustees and local authorities in relation to the management of open spaces. An 'open space' is defined as meaning any land, whether inclosed or not, on which there are no buildings or of which not more than one-twentieth part is covered with buildings, and the whole or the remainder of which is laid out as a garden or is used for purposes of recreation, or lies waste and unoccupied.[2] That definition would plainly include a town or village green. Under the Act, a local authority includes a parish council.[3] Land may be acquired by, or transferred to, a local authority pursuant to powers under the Act.[4] Where an open space has been acquired by a local authority under the Act, that authority is required to hold and administer the open space in trust for the public and may carry out works of improvement.[5] There is a power to make bylaws.[6]

(d)   Criminal offences: nuisance and inclosure

Section 12 of the Inclosure Act 1857 makes it an offence to create nuisances of various forms on an allotted town or village green without lawful authority.[7] Section 29 of the Commons Act 1876 deems encroachment, enclosure or any erection on a green a public nuisance. These two provisions apply to greens, however, and whenever created and whether registered under the 1965 Act or not, including Class C greens.[8] If land has the status of a green prior to its registration, the owner might fear prosecution for acts contrary to these two provisions. These offences require *mens rea* and cannot give rise to any exposure to prosecution where the existence of the green is not established and known. The language of the legislation

---

[1]   Section 15.

[2]   Section 20.

[3]   Section 1.

[4]   See ss 2–7 and 9.

[5]   Section 10.

[6]   Section 15.

[7]   Such as the erection of an electric fence: *Rabett v Poole* (unreported county court decision).

[8]   *Oxfordshire County Council v Oxford City Council* [2004] EWHC 12, [2004] PLSCS 16.

makes plain that the prohibited acts continue 'once and for all' and not 'continuing' offences. Accordingly, putting up a building in ignorance of the fact that the land is a green is no offence, and it is not a criminal offence to refrain from removing it when the true facts are known.[1]

9.6.4 Buildings and other works on town or village greens

Parish councils and others owning town or village greens may wish to carry out works, such as the provision of car parks and the erection of buildings, such as sports pavilions or public lavatories. A number of provisions prevent the erection of works, or make it a criminal offence to carry out certain activities on town or village greens, although much may depend on the precise legal status of the green in issue.[2] Where the green is subject to customary rights of sports and pastimes, and such activities have been acquired by 20 years' use, no works can be carried out that would interfere or obstruct the lawful exercise of those rights. The test is probably whether the rights can be exercised as conveniently as before.[3] The erection of a cricket pavilion on a small part of a very large village green is hardly likely to give rise to an actionable interference with the lawful rights of the inhabitants. Indeed, the very same inhabitants may have been pressing for just such a facility. But the construction of a car park on a relatively small green might well constitute an actionable interference.

In the case of greens that have been allotted under an inclosure award, a number of provisions make the carrying out of works on those greens a criminal offence.[4] The Commons Act 1876 prohibits any encroachment or inclosure on a green, although it does allow works carried out with a view to its better enjoyment.[5] This would include the erection of a cricket pavilion.

---

[1]   *Oxfordshire County Council v Oxford City Council* [2004] EWHC 12, [2004] PLSCS 16.

[2]   Section 94 of Law of Property Act 1925 requires ministerial consent to any fence or inclosure on a green that is common land.

[3]   See *Gale on Easements* (17th edn), at chapter 13.

[4]   Inclosure Act 1848, s 10, Inclosure Act 1857, s 12, and Commons Act 1876, s 29.

[5]   Section 29. See *Rabett v Poole* (unreported county court decision).

9.6.5   Driving on greens

Driving vehicles over town and village greens can be a criminal offence. Under the Road Traffic Act 1972, s 36 it is an offence to drive a motor vehicle without lawful authority onto any common land or any other land of whatever description not being land forming part of a road. There is an exception where a person drives no more than 15 yards for the purposes of parking.

Some town or village greens may be subject to dedication for the purposes of the Law of Property Act 1925, s 193. Under that provision any person who, without lawful authority, drives on such land commits a criminal offence.[1]

Because it is unlawful to drive on a village green, a right of way cannot be acquired by prescription, as the user would have been in breach of the law.[2]

---

[1]   Section 193(4).

[2]   See Chapter 6.

Chapter 10

PUBLIC ACCESS TO COMMONS

10.1 INTRODUCTION

Prior to the widespread inclosure of common land, up to the nineteenth century, the common land to a village was proportionately larger in extent than today (if indeed any remains) and socially and economically more important. For the reasons explained in Chapter 2, common land played an important role in the rural economy. To local people, almost entirely employed in agriculture, or activities related to agriculture, there simply was no notion of public rights of access onto the common separate from the rights and incidents of rights of common. With the massive urbanisation of the nineteenth century, and the disengagement of many people from agricultural activities, many commons came to be seen to have separate or additional recreational purposes. Separate from the exercise of rights of common, the use of common land for general recreational purposes must be authorised by the law in some manner. Common land is, after all, land owned by the owner of the soil and, so far as that person is concerned, is subject only to the rights of common.

Outside the exercise of rights of common, the law authorises recreational use, which would otherwise be a trespass on common land, by the recognition of customary or other common law rights or by statute. The most significant statutory rights of access are now found in the CROW Act 2000.

In practice, the public may have rights of access over common land (or, for that matter, town and village greens) along public highways. Public highways include public footpaths and bridleways.

10.2   COMMON LAW RIGHTS OF ACCESS TO COMMONS

The common law has come to recognise two principal recreational rights over land. Neither category is unique to common land. Common law rights of access for recreational use may arise over private land that is not common land, and customary rights are frequently found in relation to town and village greens, which may not necessarily have been subject to rights of common.

10.2.1 Easement of recreation

In *Re Ellenborough Park*,[1] it was held that the owner of land could have, for the benefit of that land, an easement over land adjoining or nearby that permitted the owner full enjoyment of a pleasure ground. A similar right was held to be an easement in the earlier case of *Duncan v Louch*,[2] and a right of common use of a garden was an easement in *Mulvaney v Gough*.[3]

The rights in *Re Ellenborough Park* were expressly granted in conveyances of a number of properties surrounding the pleasure ground in question. However, any right that lies in grant is also capable of being acquired by implied grant, such as where there has been a use of land, without force, without secrecy, and without permission.[4] Whilst it may be theoretically possible for an individual landowner to seek to claim an implied easement in this way, it is far more likely that where common land has been used for recreational purposes by one person in the locality, it will have been enjoyed by many others. In such circumstances the particular owner may not necessarily be asserting an implied easement for the direct benefit of his property, but he may be asserting as a member of a class, the public, rights of a customary nature, considered below.

---

[1]   [1956] 1 Ch 131.

[2]   (1845) 6 QB 904.

[3]   [2002] 3 EGLR 72.

[4]   *Gale on Easements* (17th edn, 2002), at paras 4–73 to 4–86.

10.2.2 Customary rights

From time to time the courts have upheld customary rights. In *New Windsor Corporation v Mellor*[1] Lord Denning MR explained the background to customary rights:

'Today we look back far in time. To a town or village green. The turf is old. Animals have grazed there for hundreds of years. Nowadays they are pleasant stretches of grass where people sit and talk. Sometimes they play cricket or kick a ball about. But in mediaeval times it was a place where young men mustered with their bows and arrows. They shot at the butts. There might be stocks there where offenders were put for their petty misdemeanours. In the month of May they set up a maypole and danced around it. We have no record of when it all began.'

He then continued:[2]

'The villagers have an undoubted right to play games on their green. But whence comes their right? Not in deeds or in statutes. Only in custom from time immemorial. Rarely has it ever been challenged, ... To be good, of course, a custom must be reasonable. ... The result is that, in many village greens, no one knows who is the owner of the land. But everyone knows that the villagers have a right to play games on it. If anyone should disturb or hinder the exercise of that right, any one of the inhabitants can sue to enforce the right of all, stating that he does so on behalf of himself and all others. ... He can stop any fences being erected, or any holes being dug, or pipes laid, if they would interfere unreasonably with the exercise by the villagers of their right. And such a right, once acquired by custom, cannot be lost by disuse or abandonment. It can only be abolished or extinguished by Act of Parliament. ... in my opinion, [the land in question] is subject to a customary right in the inhabitants to indulge in lawful sports and pastimes on that land.'

---

[1]   [1975] 1 Ch 380.

[2]   Ibid, at p 386F.

Customary rights must be exercisable only by members of some identifiable local community.[1] The rights must be exercisable as of right in relation to a particular locality.[2]

Customary rights must be ancient, certain, reasonable and continuous.[3] A custom is said to be 'ancient' if it commenced prior to 1189 – the beginning of legal memory. However, in practice proof of long user will be sufficient, unless there is evidence that the custom commenced after 1189.[4] A customary right can still be established even where the nature of the custom changes. The playing of cricket, for example, may replace the playing of some earlier types of games.

Although customary rights may well arise in relation to a common properly so called, they are more likely to be found in respect of town and village greens, where this topic is more fully explored.[5]

10.3   COUNTRYSIDE AND RIGHTS OF WAY ACT 2000 (CROW ACT 2000)

When the CROW Act 2000 is fully in force, it will provide the public with a new right of access on foot only to registered common land, as well as other open uncultivated land such as mountain, moor, heath and down. All such land will be known as 'Access Land'.[6] Save in the case of registered common land, other areas of Access Land have first to be identified by a mapping exercise that is being carried out by the Countryside Agency. The CROW Act 2000 contains provisions for the exclusion or restriction of public access onto Access Land.

---

[1]   *R v Oxfordshire County Council, ex parte Sunningwell Parish Council* [2000] AC 335.

[2]   *R v Suffolk County Council, ex parte Steed* (1995) 70 P&CR 487. However, in *Ministry of Defence v Wiltshire County Council* [1995] 4 All ER 931, the residents of three streets were held not to constitute a locality. See also *R (Laing Homes Ltd) v Buckinghamshire County Council* [2003] EWHC 1978 (Admin), [2003] 3 PLR 60.

[3]   *Lockwood v Wood* (1844) 6 QB 64.

[4]   *Simpson v Wells* (1872) LR 7 QB 214.

[5]   See Chapter 9.

[6]   Occupiers Liability Act 1957 will not apply to persons exercising a right of access. In any event, any duty of care excludes certain risks: see s 13(1)–(2).

10.3.1 Rights of access

Section 2(1) of the CROW Act 2000 contains the general right of the public to enter and remain on any 'Access Land' for the purposes of open air recreation on foot only. Such rights of access may only be exercised where 'Access Land' has been included on a conclusive map prepared by the Countryside Agency (or the Countryside Council for Wales). Section 1 of the Act defines Access Land as meaning any land which:

(a) is shown as open country on a map in conclusive form issued by the appropriate countryside body;

(b) is shown on such a map as registered common land;

(c) is registered common land in any area outside Inner London for which no such map relating to registered common land has been issued;

(d) is situated more than 600 metres above sea level in any area for which no such map relating to open country has been issued; or

(e) is dedicated to the purposes of access under s 16 of the Act.

However, Access Land does not include 'excepted land' or land which is treated by s 15(1) of the Act as being accessible to the public apart from the CROW Act 2000.[1]

'The appropriate countryside body' means, in relation to England, the Countryside Agency, and, in relation to Wales, the Countryside Council for Wales.

The following definitions are important. 'Open country' is land which appears to the appropriate countryside body as consisting wholly or predominantly of mountain, moor, heath or down, and is not registered common land.[2] 'Registered common land' means:

(a) land which is registered as common land under the Commons Registration Act 1965, and whose registration under that Act has become final; or

(b) subject to an exception considered below, land which was registered as common land under the 1965 Act on 30 November 2000 – the date when the CROW Act 2000 was enacted – or on

---

[1]   Section 1(1).

[2]   Section 1(2).

any date after that day but has subsequently ceased to be registered as common land under the 1965 Act on the register of common land in which it was included, by reason of having ceased to be common land within the meaning of the 1965 Act. Accordingly, the general rule is that where common land was on 30 November 2000, or some subsequent date, registered under the 1965 Act, but is then removed, it remains 'registered common land' for the purposes of the public rights of access under the CROW Act 2000. The exceptions to the general rule are as follows. Land that is omitted from the register of common land under the 1965 Act following an application to amend the register of common land made before 30 November 2000, and land that ceases to be common land by reason of powers of compulsory purchase or the provision of substitute common land under the 1965 Act.[1]

10.3.2 Exceptions

Schedule 1 to the CROW Act 2000 sets out a list of 'excepted land'; such land cannot be Access Land to which the public will have rights of access. The excepted land includes the following:

(1) land on which the soil is being, or has at any time within the previous 12 months been, disturbed by any ploughing or drilling undertaken for the purposes of planting or sowing crops or trees;

(2) land covered by buildings or the curtilage of such land;

(3) land within 20 metres of a dwelling;

(4) land used as a park or garden;

(5) land used for the getting of minerals by surface working (including quarrying);

(6) land used for the purposes of a railway or tramway;

(7) land used for the purposes of a golf course, racecourse or aerodrome;

(8) land which does not fall within any of the categories above, but which is covered by works used for the purposes of a statutory undertaking or for telecommunications apparatus, or the curtilage of any such land;

(9) land where development is being carried out such that it will fall within any of the categories set out above;

---

[1] Section 1(3) and (4).

(10) land within 20 metres of a building which is used for housing livestock, not being a temporary or moveable structure;

(11) land covered by pens in use for the temporary reception or detention of livestock;

(12) land habitually used for the training of racehorses; and

(13) land the use of which is regulated under the Military Lands Acts. Whilst the exceptions set out above may make some sense in relation to Access Land other than registered common land, it is not easy to see how the exceptions will work in practice in relation to registered common land itself. There must be many cases of dwellings or buildings used for housing livestock that are located within 20 metres of the boundaries of existing common land. As explained above, Access Land is required to be mapped[1] and, strictly, any area of registered common land to which one or more of the exceptions set out above apply, must not be excluded from the draft, provisional and conclusive maps. Although no marked or physical boundary will appear on the ground, the public will be trespassing if they pass into the 20-metre boundary around dwellings and livestock buildings and it is unclear how that could ever be adequately 'policed'.[2]

10.3.3 Restrictions

The Act contains certain provisions for the exclusion or restriction of the public right of access.[3] The owner (or any tenant) of Access Land may give notice to the appropriate countryside body in accordance with regulations excluding or restricting access to any land on one or more days specified in the notice.[4] The number of days on which access is excluded or restricted is limited to 28 in each calendar year.[5] Access may not be excluded or restricted on Christmas Day, Good Friday or any Bank Holiday or on more than 4 days in any

---

[1] Strictly, it is all registered common land and all open country that must be mapped. The maps may therefore include areas that will not be Access Land because one or more of the exceptions will apply.

[2] But see s 20 for duty of Countryside Agency to inform the public of the extent of Access Land.

[3] See Chapter 11.

[4] Access to the Countryside (Exclusions and Restrictions) (England) Regulations 2003, SI 2003/2713 and Access to the Countryside (Exclusions and Restrictions) (Wales) Regulations 2003, SI 2003/142.

[5] Ibid. For the manner and form of notice, see reg 4.

calendar year which are either Saturday or Sunday, on any Saturday between 1 June and 11 August, in any year, or on any Sunday between 1 June and 30 September in any year.[1]

It is likely that the purpose of this provision allowing exclusion or restriction of access on a certain number of days in each calendar year is to enable shooting to take place. As that is unlikely over registered common land, this particular exclusion may have little importance in relation to such land.

Section 23 contains provisions allowing the restriction on dogs onto Access Land.[2] During specified periods, the right of access onto land consisting of moor managed for the breeding and shooting of grouse may not be exercised with dogs. Similarly, the owner of land used in connection with lambing may take steps such that the right of access may only be exercised by persons who do not take dogs into any field or inclosure on land in which there are sheep. As any field or inclosure is unlikely to include registered common land, this exclusion will not be relevant where common land is used for the pasturing of sheep.

Public rights of access may also be excluded or restricted where the appropriate countryside body allows an application by the owner for the purposes of land management.[3] The public rights of access may also be excluded or restricted for the purpose of avoiding risk of fire or danger to the public.[4] Public rights of access may also be excluded or restricted on certain grounds of nature conservation and heritage preservation.[5] Regulations provide for the giving of notices, the making of directions and for appeals.[6]

---

[1]   Section 22.

[2]   Access to the Countryside (Exclusions and Restrictions) (England) Regulations 2003, SI 2003/2713, reg 5 and Access to the Countryside (Exclusions and Restrictions) (Wales) Regulations 2003, SI 2003/142.

[3]   Section 24.

[4]   Section 25.

[5]   Section 26.

[6]   See note 2 above.

10.3.4 Additional land open to access

Certain other land, which cannot be Access Land, is treated as being accessible to the public apart from the CROW Act 2000. Such land includes:

(a) common land to which the Law of Property Act 1925, s 193 applies (see below);
(b) public rights of access to land within the meaning of Part I of the Commons Act 1899;
(c) an access agreement or access order under Part V of the National Parks and Access to the Countryside Act 1949; or
(d) public rights of access under the Ancient Monuments and Archaeological Areas Act 1979, s 19.

10.3.5 By-laws

The CROW Act 2000 contains provisions for the making of by-laws regulating public rights of access,[1] for the appointment of wardens,[2] and for the erection and maintenance of notices indicating boundaries of Access Land and any exclusions or restrictions.[3]

10.3.6 Mapping of open country

By s 4 of the Act, it is the duty of the Countryside Agency to prepare maps showing all open country, and all registered common land. In respect of Wales, the same duty falls on the Countryside Council for Wales. A map prepared under this section must distinguish between open country and registered common land, but need not distinguish between different categories of open country.[4] The Countryside Agency (or the Countryside Council for Wales) may decide not to show areas of open country which are so small that their inclusion would serve no useful purpose and may determine that any boundary of an area of open country is to be treated as coinciding with a particular physical feature. In other words, where

---

[1] Section 17.
[2] Section 18.
[3] Section 19.
[4] Section 4(4).

commonsense suggests that natural features would provide a natural boundary, that decision can be made.[1]

By s 5 of the Act, the Countryside Agency (or Countryside Council for Wales) is required to:

(a) issue in draft form any map prepared by them under s 4;
(b) consider representations received by them within a prescribed period with respect to the showing of, or the failure to show, any area of land on the map as registered common land or as open country;
(c) confirm the map with or without modifications;
(d) if the map has been confirmed without modifications, issue it in provisional form; and
(e) if the map has been confirmed with modifications, prepare a map incorporating the modifications, and issue that map in provisional form.[2]

10.3.7 Representations against maps

Regulation 5 of the Access to the Countryside (Maps in Draft Form) (England) Regulations 2001[3] provides that where the Countryside Agency has issued a map in draft form, it shall, as soon as reasonably practicable on or after the date of issue, publish a notice that (amongst other things):

(a) invites representations with respect of the showing of, or the failure to show, any area of land on the map in draft form as registered common land or open country;
(b) states that representations on the map in draft form must be made so as to be received by the Agency within a period of 3 months beginning with the date of issue;
(c) states the manner in which representations must be made to the Countryside Agency including the effect of reg 12(2) and (3); and
(d) states the general effect of the right conferred on the public by s 2(1).

---

[1]   Section 4(5).

[2]   Access to the Countryside (Correction of Provisional and Conclusive Maps) (England) Regulations 2003, SI 2003/1591 provide for the correction of provisional and conclusive maps.

[3]   SI 2001/3301.

Regulation 12(1) provides that where the Countryside Agency has issued a map in draft form, it shall consider:

'... any representations, with respect to the showing of, or the failure to show, any area of land on the map as registered common land or as open country, received by them within a period of three months beginning with the date of issue.'

That duty is limited to, in effect, a consideration of discrepancies between the map of registered common land under the Commons Registration Act 1965, and the draft map prepared by the Countryside Act under the CROW Act 2000. Regulation 12(2) makes provision for the information that must be contained in any representation, so as to identify the representator, the location and extent of the land to which the representation relates, and the interest in the land that the representator has.

The scope of the representations that can be made by or on behalf of, for example, landowners, in relation to the maps in draft form, is extremely limited. In the case of common land, the representation right is limited to making representations that the Countryside Agency map in draft form includes land that is *not* registered common land. That will require a very careful comparison of the relevant maps. If there is a discrepancy, then a landowner may wish to consider making a representation. There is no general right to object to the inclusion of registered common land on the maps that are being prepared by the Countryside Agency.

10.3.8 Consultations

Regulation 4 of the Regulations makes provision for consultation of the maps in draft form. The persons who are to be consulted include only those listed in the Schedule to the Regulations. These include the Countryside Council for Wales and the Historic Buildings and Monuments Commission for England. In any event, the consultation requirement is limited to an invitation to make representations in respect to the showing of, or the failure to show, any area of land on the map in draft form as registered common land (or as open country).

10.3.9 Confirmation of maps

When the Countryside Agency has considered any representations received by it with respect of the showing of, or the failure to show, any area of land on the map as registered common land, its duty under s 5 of the CROW Act 2000 is to confirm the map with or without modifications. If the map is confirmed without modifications, the Countryside Agency must issue it in provisional form, and if the map has been confirmed with modifications, it must prepare a map incorporating the modifications, and issue that map in provisional form.[1]

10.3.10 Appeals

By s 6 of the Act, any person having an interest in any land may appeal against the showing of that land on a map in provisional form as registered common land or as open country. In the case of land in England, the appeal is to the Secretary of State and in Wales, it is to the National Assembly for Wales.[2] An appeal relating to the showing of any land as registered common land may be brought only on the ground that the land is not registered common land.[3] Accordingly, the right of appeal in relation to common land is limited to the case where land is shown on a map in provisional form as registered common land, where it should not be so included, as it is not common land registered under the Commons Registration Act 1965. In relation to any land that is shown as open country, an appeal may only be brought on the ground that the land does not consist wholly or predominantly of mountain, moor, heath or down, or the discretion to use as the boundary of the area of open country some particular physical feature has not been exercised properly.[4]

Under s 7 of the Act, the Secretary of State (or the National Assembly for Wales) may hold either a hearing or a public local inquiry.[5] The Secretary of State will appoint an inspector to hold the

---

[1]   Section 5. There are powers of correction in Access to the Countryside (Correction of Provisional and Conclusive Maps) (England) Regulations 2003, SI 2003/1591.

[2]   Section 6(1).

[3]   Section 6(2).

[4]   Section 6(3).

[5]   Section 7.

hearing or public local inquiry and to prepare a report containing conclusions and recommendations. Following the hearing of the appeal, and the consideration of the inspector's report, the Secretary of State (or the National Assembly for Wales) may approve the whole or part of the map which is the subject of the appeal, with or without modifications, or require the Countryside Agency (or the Countryside Council for Wales) to prepare a new map relating to all or part of the area covered by the map which is the subject of the appeal.[1] Under s 8 of the CROW Act 2000, the Secretary of State (or the National Assembly for Wales) may appoint any person to exercise on his or its behalf the function of determining any appeals or any matters involved in such appeals.

10.3.11   Maps in conclusive form

The Countryside Agency (or the Countryside Council for Wales) is required to issue a map in conclusive form where no appeal has been brought under s 6 within the time-limit or, where an appeal has been brought, the appeal has been determined by the map or part of it being approved without modifications, or the appeal has been withdrawn. Where an appeal has been determined by the map or part of it being approved with modifications, the appropriate countryside body must then prepare a map in conclusive form incorporating the modifications.[2]

Under s 10, maps in conclusive form must be reviewed from time to time. The first review should be undertaken not more than 10 years after the issue of the map in conclusive form, and subsequent reviews at not more than 10-year intervals.

10.4   SECTION 193 OF LAW OF PROPERTY ACT 1925

Section 193 of the Law of Property Act 1925 provides for public access over common lands in the following circumstances:

> 'Members of the public shall, subject as hereinafter provided, have rights of access for air and exercise to any land which is a metropolitan common within the meaning of the Metropolitan Commons Acts 1866

---

[1]   Section 6(4).

[2]   Section 9.

to 1898, or manorial waste, or a common, which is wholly or partly situated within an area which immediately before 1 April 1974 was a borough or urban district, and to any land which at the commencement of this Act is subject to rights of common and to which this section may from time to time be applied in manner hereinafter provided.'

That subsection makes provision for access to specified categories of commons and other land in the circumstances explained below. However, when the CROW Act 2000 comes fully into force, s 193 will be repealed and public rights of access will come under the CROW Act 2000.

10.4.1 Definition of a common under s 193

The terms 'manorial waste, or a common' are not expressly defined for the purposes of s 193. 'Manorial waste' probably has the same meaning as the waste land of a manor. In *Attorney-General v Hanmer*[1] it was said that:

> 'The true meaning of "wastes", or "waste lands", or "waste grounds of the manor", is the open, uncultivated and unoccupied lands parcel of the manor, or open lands parcel of the manor other than the demesne lands of the manor.'

In *Hampshire County Council v Millburn*[2] Lord Templeman accepted that, for the purposes of the Commons Registration Act 1965, s 22(1) meant:

> '..."waste land of a manor" means "waste land now or formerly of a manor" or "waste land of manorial origin".'

It therefore may not matter that a particular area of manorial waste is no longer actually held with, and is part of, a manor.

The word 'common' was probably meant to have a wide general meaning. Section 193(1) itself separately distinguishes land 'subject to rights of common' in connection with the dedication of rural commons. That supposes that land might be a common without

---

[1]   (1858) 27 LJ Ch 837 at 840.

[2]   [1990] 2 All ER 257 at 262j.

necessarily being land subject to rights of common. Somewhat confusingly, s 193(1)(d) provides that rights of access under the section shall cease to apply to any land over which the commonable rights are extinguished under any statutory provision. That poses the question as to whether the two expressions, within the same subsection, of 'rights of common' and 'commonable rights' were intended to have the same or different meanings. It is unlikely that those expressions were intended to have different meanings. The expression 'commonable rights' was probably used merely as a more convenient linguistic description of the land to which rights of access would cease where commonable rights were extinguished.

10.4.2 Metropolitan commons

The Metropolitan Commons Act 1866 defined the term 'common' as meaning land subject at the time of the passing of the Act to any right of common, and any land subject to be included under the provisions of the Inclosure Act 1845.[1] Land subject to be included under the provisions of the Inclosure Act 1845 is widely defined as all lands subject to any rights of common whatsoever, and whether such rights may be exercised or enjoyed at all times, or may be exercised or enjoyed only during times, seasons or periods.[2] The 1866 Act applies to any commons, as so defined, the whole or any part of which is situated within the Metropolitan Police District as defined at the date of the passing of the Act.[3]

10.4.3 Borough or urban commons

Prior to 1 April 1974, local government in England and Wales consisted of the first tier county councils and the second tier of urban and rural district councils. Additionally, there were separate unitary authorities known as county borough councils. Accordingly, the public have had rights of access for air and exercise since 1 January 1926 over any common or manorial waste that fell within the boundaries of a pre-April 1974 borough or urban district council. This was never very logical as some commons in rural areas actually fell within urban district council boundaries, and conversely some

---

[1]   Section 3 as amended by Metropolitan Commons Act 1869, s 2.

[2]   Section 11 continues with a very full description of such lands.

[3]   Section 4. The extent of the Metropolitan Police District was defined by Metropolitan Police Act 1829, ss 4 and 34 and Metropolitan Police Act 1839, s 2.

commons or manorial wastes in urban and built up areas fell outside those boundaries and were within the areas of rural district councils.

10.4.4 Rural common subject to dedication

Section 193 of the Law of Property Act 1925 did not automatically create rights of air and exercise in favour of the public over rural commons, that is those commons lying outside the boundaries of pre-April 1974 borough and urban district council areas. By s 193(2):

> 'The lord of the manor or other person entitled to the soil of any land subject to rights of common may by deed, revocable or irrevocable, declare that this section shall apply to the land, and upon such deed being deposited with the Minister the land shall, so long as the deed remains operative, be land to which this section applies.'

Since 1926, the owners of a large number of commons have executed deeds of dedication under s 193. However, a large number of commons remain without the benefit of such dedication and, accordingly, in the absence of any other statutory provisions, are not subject to general public rights of access. The impact of the CROW Act 2000 was considered above.

The provision for the dedication applies only to land 'subject to rights of common'. Accordingly, even if land can fall within the definition of a 'common', if it is not subject to rights of common, s 193 cannot be applied to it by dedication.

10.4.5 Extent of rights of public access

Where s 193 applies to a manorial waste or a common, the public has access for 'air and exercise'. The right does include the right to ride horses over such common land, as riding would have been a normal way of taking air and exercise in 1925.[1]

Section 193(4) contains limitations on what may be done on a common to which the section applies:

---

[1] *R v Secretary of State for the Environment, Transport and the Regions, ex parte Billson* [1998] 2 All ER 587, contrary to Gadsden *The Law of Commons* (1988), at chapter 11.

'Any person who, without lawful authority, draws or drives upon any land to which this section applies any carriage, cart, caravan, truck, or other vehicle, or camps or lights any fire thereon, or who fails to observe any limitation or condition imposed by the Minister under this section in respect of any such land, shall be liable [of a criminal offence].'

The Minister can make an order, known as an order of limitation, on the application of any person entitled to the soil of the land, or entitled to any commonable rights affecting the land. An order of limitation may impose such limitations and conditions as to the exercise of the rights of access or as to the extent of the land to be affected as, in the opinion of the Minister, are necessary or desirable for preventing injury to the land or any interest in the land, or for protecting objects of historical interest.[1] An order of limitation will be published in the form of permanent notices on or near the affected land.

10.4.6 Effect of subsequent legislation

Two statutes, subsequent to s 193, need to be considered. Under the Commons Registration Act 1965,[2] land over which rights of common were exercised was required to be registered. The 1965 Act also provides that s 1(2) shall not affect the application to any land registered under the Act of the Law of Property Act 1925, s 193.[3] Section 1(2) provides that where there was a failure to register rights of common, they shall cease to be exercisable. The purpose of that saving provision was probably included to ensure that if rights of common were not exercised, and that non-exercisability was deemed to be equivalent to extinguishment, the rights of access under s 193 would continue.[4]

---

[1] Section 193(1)(b).

[2] Section 1(2)(b).

[3] Section 21(1).

[4] See *Central Electricity Generating Board v Clwyd County Council* [1976] 1 WLR 151.

10.5   ADDITIONAL STATUTORY RIGHTS OF ACCESS

10.5.1   Commons Act 1876

This Act contains provisions for the regulation and inclosure of commons other than metropolitan commons within the meaning of the Metropolitan Commons Acts 1866 and 1869.[1] A provisional order, which requires confirmation as an Act of Parliament, may make provision for the benefit of the neighbourhood and, in particular, may provide for free access to be secured to any particular points of view, and that there be reserved, where a recreation ground is not set out, a privilege of playing games or of enjoying other forms of recreation at such times and in such manner and on such parts of the common as may be thought suitable.[2] Bylaws may be made for regulating public access.

10.5.2   Commons Act 1899

This Act contains provisions for the regulation of any common within the area of a district council. The scheme of regulation may contain any of the provisions for the benefit of the neighbourhood which are mentioned in the Commons Act 1876, s 7.[3] The Commons (Schemes) Regulations 1982[4] and the Commons (Schemes) (Welsh Forms) Regulations 1982[5] make provision for a model form of scheme. Paragraph 4 of the model scheme provides that:

> 'The inhabitants of the neighbourhood shall have a right of free access to every part of the common and a privilege of playing games and of enjoying other kinds of recreation thereon, subject to any bylaws made by the Council under this Scheme.'

The scheme also includes provisions for the making of bylaws regulating the use of, and activities on, a regulated common.

---

[1]   A 'metropolitan common' is defined by Metropolitan Commons Act 1866, s 4 as any common the whole or any part of which is situated within the Metropolitan Police District as defined at the passing of that Act.

[2]   Section 7.

[3]   Section 1.

[4]   SI 1982/209.

[5]   SI 1982/667.

10.5.3 National Parks and Access to the Countryside Act 1949

This Act makes provision for the making of access orders or access agreements under which the public has access for open air recreation to 'open country', being any area that consists wholly or predominantly of mountain, moor, heath, down, cliff or foreshore.[1] Schedule 2 to the Act sets out a number of general restrictions that must be observed by persons exercising the right of access. The effect of the interrelationship between the statutory right of access and the general restrictions is that any person who fails to comply with the restrictions when on land the subject of an access order or agreement is treated as a trespasser. Unlike a deed of dedication under the Law of Property Act 1925, s 193, where criminal sanctions are imposed on those breaching the prohibited acts, there are no criminal sanctions affecting visitors to land within access orders or access areas. In the past, the attraction to a landowner in entering into an access agreement, rather than a deed of dedication, is that compensation and/or grants have been available.

10.6 LOCAL ACTS

Many commons are regulated by individual local Acts of Parliament. Although each Act must be carefully considered as to its terms, many make provision for public rights of access. Such Acts include the Epping Forest Act 1878, the Wimbledon and Putney Common Act 1871, the Dartmoor Commons Act 1985 and the Ashdown Forest Act 1974.

---

[1] Sections 59–65.

Chapter 11

REGULATION AND MANAGEMENT OF COMMON LANDS

11.1 INTRODUCTION

Common land was largely regulated and managed according to the customs of the manor. This took place through the manorial courts acting through the steward to the lord of the manor. However, the nineteenth century legislation on commons introduced powers of regulation and management concerning the exercise of rights of common and of public recreation and access where so provided. During the twentieth century legislation was concerned with the protection of the scientific and ecological aspects of common land.

11.2 MANAGEMENT BY THE OWNER OF THE SOIL

All common land is owned by someone. Where commons are owned by local authorities, these authorities may have active management policies. These are usually directed to the management of the common for public recreation in respect of those commons to which the public have rights of access. Local authorities will generally be able to use most of the powers referred to below.

In the case of commons owned by non-local authorities, where the owner also possesses the manorship, such persons will have all the powers of management incidental to the ownership of any legal estate in land, subject only to the rights of the commoners and the various statutory prohibitions against inclosure, fencing or the making of erections.

In the case of commons in the upland areas where the use is primarily for grazing purposes by those holding rights of common, the owner of the common may himself utilise his own right to pasture his animals. He may, therefore, take a fairly active interest in the careful management of the common in the wider general interests of the commoners.[1]

In those cases where commons are owned by non-local authority owners and where commoners' rights are no longer actively exercised, the principal value of the common may lie in public access and recreation where that is authorised. Such owners may have little incentive in most cases to pursue active management policies for public recreation and access purposes. However, access agreements have been made under s 64 of the National Parks and Access to the Countryside Act 1949. The effect of such agreements is to permit access to the public to open land. The access agreement may make provision for payments by the local planning authority to the owner in consideration of the making of the agreement and by way of contributions towards expenditure.

11.3   REGULATION OF NON-METROPOLITAN COMMONS

A series of Acts between the Inclosure Act 1845 and the Commons Act 1899 make provision for the regulation of commons.[2] Although now repealed, the Inclosure Act 1845, s 113 made provision for a regulated pasture. The procedure, and the powers of the Inclosure Commissioners, the Assistance Commissioner, and the valuer were the same in relation to the making of a provisional order, and an award in the case of inclosure.[3] The basic steps – the making of a draft provisional order, its advertisement and submission to the Secretary of State for approval, and subsequent confirmation of the provisional order by Parliament – are the same as in the case of inclosure orders.[4] Where an order provided for the regulation of a common, the order could include provision for the adjustment of rights. This included the determination of the persons entitled to rights of common, what those rights should be, and the rights and liabilities of the owner.[5] However, the order could make provision for the improvement of the common. This might include the

---

[1]   See Chapter 5 on the incidence of the ownership of common land.

[2]   Inclosure Act 1845, Commons Act 1876, Commons (Expenses) Act 1878, Commons Act 1879, Communable Rights Compensation Act 1882, and Commons Act 1899.

[3]   See Chapter 7.

[4]   Ibid.

[5]   Commons Act 1876, s 4.

draining, manuring or levelling of the common, the planting of trees, the making of by-laws and regulations, the general management of the common, and the appointment from time to time of conservators.[1] Following the confirmation of the Act, an award would then be made of a regulated pasture. The effect of this was that:[2]

'All rights of common, and all rights whatever by the [regulation] intended to be extinguished, belonging to or claimed by any person whomsoever, in or upon such lands, shall cease, determine, and be forever extinguished.'

The ownership of a regulated pasture would be with the stint holders in proportion to the value of their respective stints.[3] The award normally gave powers of management and control to the stint holders.

The provisions related to regulated pastures are no longer in force. Strictly, a regulated pasture is not land subject to rights of common.[4] However, under the Commons Registration Act 1965, s 11 and the Commons Registration (Exempted Land) Regulations 1965, there was exempted from registration regulated pasture where no rights of common had been exercised over the land for at least 30 years. Nevertheless, some regulated pastures have been registered.

11.4   REGULATION OF METROPOLITAN COMMONS

Provision was made for the regulation of metropolitan commons under a number of Acts.[5] Under the Metropolitan Commons Acts, a 'common' was defined as meaning land that was on 10 August 1866 subject to any rights of common and land that could be the subject of inclosure under the Inclosure Act 1845.[6] A metropolitan common was any common, the whole or any part of which was situated

---

[1]   Commons Act 1876, s 5.

[2]   Inclosure Act 1845, ss 106 and 114.

[3]   Ibid, s 116.

[4]   Ibid.

[5]   Metropolitan Commons Act 1866, Metropolitan Commons Amendment Act 1869, Metropolitan Commons Act 1887, and Metropolitan Commons Act 1898.

[6]   Metropolitan Commons Act 1866, s 3.

within the Metropolitan Police District on 10 August 1866. Section 5 of the Metropolitan Commons Act 1866 prohibited inclosure of metropolitan commons, except for the purposes of widening a highway. The purposes of the Metropolitan Commons Acts were to create schemes for the establishment of local management, the carrying out of improvements, and the making of by-laws.[1]

11.5   REGULATION OF COMMONS UNDER THE COMMONS ACT 1899

The Commons Act 1899 contained powers for urban district councils to make schemes for the regulation and management of any common within their district with a view to the expenditure of money on the drainage, levelling, and improvement of the common, and to the making of by-laws and regulations for the prevention of nuisances and the preservation of order on the common.[2] When a scheme is made, it must be advertised, and objections can then be made to it.[3] The council can approve the scheme unless objections of dissent are received from the owner or persons representing at least one-third in value of the ownership in the common.[4] A draft scheme is prescribed by regulations.[5] The scheme provides for the works that may be carried out to improve and manage the common, and also the rights of free access. Compensation is payable to any person with an interest in a common made the subject of a scheme.[6] There are powers to make by-laws.[7]

11.5.1   Commons Act 1908

This Act regulates the turning out onto commons of entire animals (uncastrated males). The Act contains powers by which the persons entitled to turn animals onto a common may resolve at a meeting by a majority in value of their interest to make regulations. These may

---

[1]   Metropolitan Commons Act 1866, s 6. None of the provisions of Commons Act 1876 were applicable to any metropolitan common: s 35.

[2]   Section 1.

[3]   Section 2.

[4]   Ibid.

[5]   Commons (Schemes) Regulations 1982, SI 1982/209.

[6]   Section 6.

[7]   Section 10.

determine the times and the conditions under which entire animals of any class or description or age specified in the regulation may be put on the common.[1] The Act provides that regulations require the confirmation of the Secretary of State.[2]

11.6   LOCAL REGULATION OF COMMONS

A number of commons are subject to specific Acts for their regulation. These include the New Forest,[3] Epping Forest,[4] Ashdown Forest[5] and Dartmoor[6]. The local Acts generally provide for the regulation and management of the respective commons, and for public access subject to by-laws.

11.7   NATURE RESERVES AND SITES OF SPECIAL SCIENTIFIC INTEREST

Nearly 50% of the common land in England is wholly or partially designated as a site of special scientific interest. The Wildlife and Countryside Act 1981 makes provision for sites of special scientific interest.[7] The notification of such a site specifies the flora, fauna, or geological or physiographical features by reason of which the land is of special interest, and any operations likely to damage that flora or fauna or those features.[8]

11.7.1 Notification

Where a site has been notified, the owner or occupier of any such land shall not carry out any of the operations specified in the notification unless:

---

[1]   Section 1.

[2]   Ibid.

[3]   New Forest Acts 1877 to 1970.

[4]   Epping Forest Acts 1878 and 1880.

[5]   Ashdown Forest Act 1974.

[6]   Dartmoor Commons Act 1985.

[7]   Section 28.

[8]   Section 28(4).

- written notice has been given to English Nature (or the Countryside Council for Wales); and
- one of the specific conditions is fulfilled.[1]

The conditions, one only of which need be satisfied, are as follows:

- the operation is carried out with the written consent of English Nature (or the Countryside Council for Wales);
- the operation is carried out in accordance with the terms of an agreement;[2] or
- that 4 months have expired from the giving of the notice.[3]

The purpose of the procedure requiring an owner or occupier of land to notify an intention to carry out a notifiable operation is to enable the English Nature (or the Countryside Council for Wales) to give consent or to offer to enter into an agreement. The purpose of an agreement is to achieve the protection of the site through the use of acceptable activities and operations.

11.7.2 Special orders

In certain cases, special protection for certain areas of special scientific interest can be achieved by the making of an order.[4] Such a site will be one where there is a need to secure the survival of any kind of animal or plant or to comply with some international obligation. The additional protection under a site protected by an order is that the 4-month period of protection is extended to 12 months.[5]

11.7.3 Effect of sites of special scientific interest

The possible consequences to commoners of the designation of a common as a site of special scientific interest are illustrated by the decision in *Owen v Blathwayt*.[6] In that case, a number of tenanted farms enjoyed sheep-grazing rights over land that had once been a

---

1   Section 28(5)(a).

2   Under National Parks and Access to the Countryside Act 1949, s 60 or Countryside Act 1968, s 15.

3   Section 28(6).

4   Section 29.

5   Section 29(6).

6   [2002] EWHC 2231, [2003] P&CR 28.

common. The land was designated as a site of special scientific interest but English Nature consented to one of the tenants grazing animals on the land, provided there was no more than a specified number during winter months and a higher specified number during the rest of the year. As these numbers were substantially lower than the number of animals that could be maintained on the tenant's holding, this led to a dispute with the other tenants with similar sheep-grazing rights as to whether a rule of priority applied so that the first grantee of rights could displace the others on the land. The court held that all tenants claiming grazing rights had to regard themselves as having equal status. The same principles would probably apply to common land.

The House of Lords in *Bettison v Langton* confirmed that where rights of common of pasture are appurtenant to land, they may be severed from the land and be held by a purchaser (and his successors) in gross.[1] The requirement under the Commons Registration Act 1965 to register specific numbers of animals resulted in excessive numbers being entered, which is now giving rise to severe overgrazing and conservation management problems. Where rights of common of grazing are severed from land, this will produce enormous problems in enforcing conservation policies under, for example, the Wildlife and Countryside Act 1981.[2]

In *Southern Water Authority v The Nature Conservancy Council*, the term 'occupier' was given a wide interpretation as including anyone with a stable relationship with the land and which was not transient. Accordingly, the persons holding common rights would fall within that status and be entitled to notification, and subject to the obligations in relation to sites of special scientific interest.[3]

11.7.4 Future developments

The difficulties of reconciling conservation regulation under the Wildlife and Countryside Act 1981 and the rights of commoners, with registered rights under the Commons Registration Act 1965 has

---

[1] [2001] 3 All ER 417.

[2] Sydenham, 'Managing Common Land for Environmental Benefit: The Difficulties After Bettison v Langton', *Environmental Law Review*, 4.1(1), March 2002.

[3] [1992] 3 All ER 481.

long been a subject for discussion.[1] Although the Commons Registration Act 1965, s 13 permits the amendment of the registers following the transfer of common rights, there is no duty to notify changes in ownership. The commons registers are often out of date, inaccurate, and unrepresentative of the current land use on the common. This makes for difficulties in identifying all commoners with registered rights, especially having regard to the powers and duties of English Nature under the Wildlife and Countryside Act 1968, s 28.[2] Proposals have been advanced for the introduction of legislative regulation of the numbers of stock that can be grazed on commons in order to address the acute problems in some areas of overgrazing, often arising out of inflated numbers of animals registered under the Commons Registration Act 1965.[3] The Department of the Environment Transport and the Regions, has produced guidance on the management of commons, together with a model constitution for a commons association.[4]

11.8   THE COUNTRYSIDE AND RIGHTS OF WAY ACT 2000 (CROW ACT 2000)

The rights of public access that will in due course be available under this Act are explained in Chapter 10. 'Access Land', under the CROW Act 2000, includes all registered common land. There are limited rights for owners of Access Land to exclude or restrict public access, for example:

–   along specified routes or ways;
–   by entering the land only at a specified place or places;
–   by persons who do not take dogs on the land; or
–   by persons who satisfy any other specified conditions.[5]

The Act also makes provision for the exclusion or restriction of access where the appropriate authority makes a direction for the

---

[1]   Rodgers, 'Environmental Management of Common Land: Towards a Legal Framework?', *Environmental Law Review*, March 2002.

[2]   Ibid.

[3]   Ibid.

[4]   *The Good Practice Guide on Managing the Use of Common Land* (DETR, 1998); and *MAFF Guidelines for Joint ESA Agreements with Commoners*.

[5]   Sections 2(1) and 21(3).

purposes of the management of the land by its owner.[1] There is also a right to seek the exclusion or restriction of access for no more than 28 days each calendar year.[2] It will be some time before it is clear how these management arrangements will operate under this Act, especially in relation to common land. But one can see the likelihood of restrictions on access during, for example, the lambing season.[3]

11.9 FENCES ON COMMONS

There are two matters here, namely whether there are any obligations to fence or provide some other form of stockproof inclosure around the boundary of a common, to prevent the escape of animals, and whether, and in what circumstances, fencing can be erected on a common.

11.9.1 Duty to fence

A duty on owners of properties adjoining a common may arise as a matter of custom to fence to prevent the animals on the common straying out.[4] In an earlier case the same result was achieved by the implication of an easement to fence; the obligation falling on the owners of properties adjoining the common.[5] The standard of fencing must be suited to the animals likely to be upon the common.[6]

11.9.2 Right to erect fences

In the case of commonable lands, stinted and regulated pastures, that have been the subject of allotment or regulation schemes, the terms of the award will determine liability as to fencing.

---

[1]   Section 24(1).

[2]   Section 22.

[3]   See now Access to the Countryside (Exclusions and Restrictions) (England) Regulations 2003, SI 2003/2713 and Access to the Countryside (Exclusions and Restrictions) (Wales) Regulations 2003, SI 2003/142.

[4]   *Egerton v Harding* [1975] QB 62.

[5]   *Crow v Wood* [1971] 1 QB 77.

[6]   *Coaker v Willcocks* [1911] 1 KB 649, *affirmed* [1911] 2 KB 124.

With regard to fencing on common land, the Law of Property Act 1925, s 194(1) provides that:

'The erection of any building or fence, or the construction of any other work, whereby access to land to which this section applies is prevented or impeded, shall not be lawful unless the consent of the [Secretary of State] thereto is obtained, ...'

Section 194 applies to any land which at the commencement of the 1925 Act was then subject to rights of common (1 January 1926).[1] The restrictions on buildings or fences cease to apply to any land over which the rights of common are extinguished under any statutory provision, or to any land over which the rights of common are otherwise extinguished if the county council in which the land is situated passes a resolution and that is approved by the Secretary of State.[2]

The Secretary of State gave consent to the erection of fences on Ashdown Forest; the purpose of the fences was to manage sheep with a view to maintain the 'openness' of parts of the forest.

11.10   DRIVING VEHICLES OVER COMMON LAND

It is an offence under the Road Traffic Act 1988 to drive a motor vehicle without lawful authority upon any common land not forming part of a road. The Law of Property Act 1925, s 193 applies to urban commons and commons to which the section was specifically applied to by declaration from time to time.[3] In respect of common land to which s 193 applies:

'Any person who, without lawful authority, draws or drives upon any land to which this section applies any carriage, cart, caravan, truck, or other vehicle, or camps or lights any fire thereon, or who fails to observe any limitation or condition imposed by the Minister under this section in respect of any such land, shall be liable on summary conviction to a fine ...'

---

[1]   Section 194(4). A temporary electric fence is unauthorised: see *Rabett v Poole* (unreported county court decision).

[2]   Section 194(3).

[3]   See Chapter 10.

11.11   NATIONAL TRUST COMMON LAND

Under s 29 of the National Trust Act 1971, the Trust is required to keep all commons open and unbuilt on as open spaces for recreation and the enjoyment of the public. Under s 23 of the National Trust Act 1971, ministerial consent is required for any buildings or other works on Trust-owned commons if public access would be affected.

CHAPTER 12

COMPULSORY ACQUISITION AND COMMON LANDS

12.1 INTRODUCTION

Many public authorities and other bodies have powers of compulsory purchase. These powers may authorise the compulsory acquisition of land or of rights over land. Common land is not immune from compulsory acquisition, although there are a number of procedural safeguards. There are special provisions for the assessment of compensation payable to the owners of common land, and to the commoners.

A full explanation of the legislation and powers of compulsory acquisition is beyond the scope of this book. However, the basic principles are as follows. The power to acquire land or rights in land is found in an Act of Parliament. Powers in public Acts of Parliament are available to central government and local authorities for such purposes as the acquisition of land and rights for the purposes of creating and improving public highways (see the Highways Act 1980). Other legislation contains powers to acquire land for specific projects, such as the Channel Tunnel Railway (see the Channel Tunnel Railway Act 1996). Increasing use is made of the powers in the Transport and Works Act 1992 to make works orders for such projects as railways and light tramways. A power to acquire land or rights compulsorily is exercisable only after the making and confirmation of a compulsory purchase order or, in the case of the Transport and Works Act 1992, a works order. Such orders are made by the authority possessing powers of compulsory acquisition and then confirmed by the relevant Secretary of State. It is in relation to the procedures for the making and confirmation of compulsory purchase orders that the legislation contains special provisions concerning common land.

12.2   COMPULSORY ACQUISITION OF LAND

Where a compulsory purchase order authorises the purchase of any land forming part of a common, open space or fuel or field garden allotment, the order is subject to what is called special Parliamentary procedure unless excluded by a certificate issued by the Secretary of State (see the Acquisition of Land Act 1981, s 19(1)).

12.2.1   Certificate excluding special Parliamentary procedure

The Secretary of State may only issue a certificate where he is satisfied:

'(a) that there has been or will be given in exchange for land as described above, other land, not being less in area and being equally advantageous to the persons, if any, entitled to rights of common or other rights, and to the public, and that the land given in exchange has been or will be vested in the persons in whom the land purchased was vested and subject to the like rights, trusts and incidents as attached to the land purchased, or[1]

(b) that the land is being purchased in order to secure its preservation or improve its management,[2] or

(c) that the land does not exceed 250 square yards in extent or is required for the widening or drainage of an existing highway or partly for the widening and partly for the drainage of such a highway and that the giving in exchange of other land is unnecessary, whether in the interests of the persons, if any, entitled to rights of common or other rights or in the interests of the public.'[3]

In relation to the above exclusions, the word 'common' is defined as including any land subject to be inclosed under the Inclosure Acts 1845 to 1882, and any town or village green.[4] The word 'open space' is defined as meaning any land laid out as a public garden, or used

---

[1]   Section 19(1)(a).

[2]   Section 19(1)(aa).

[3]   Section 19(1)(b).

[4]   Section 19(4).

for the purposes of public recreation, or land being a disused burial ground.[1]

In *Greenwich London Borough Council v the Secretary of State for the Environment*,[2] the court had to consider the meaning of the words 'equally advantageous' in paragraph (a) above. In connection with a compulsory purchase order that included some ancient woodland, a certificate had been issued in respect of exchange land that was to be planted with trees. However, during a period of about 15 years, to enable the trees to become established, the public would only have restricted access. Hutchison J said:

> 'It seemed likely that Parliament would have intended to permit a degree of flexibility, leaving it to the Secretary of State to judge whether advantages of one sort could be off set against advantages of a different sort.'

He added that the Secretary of State acted lawfully if he was:

> 'satisfied of equal advantage at the date of exchange on the basis that advantages that the exchange land would have in the future meant that it was equally advantageous to users of the order land and the public at large at the date of exchange.'

Where the Secretary of State is proposing to give a certificate, he must direct the acquiring authority to give public notice of his intention so to do.[3] The Secretary of State then affords an opportunity to all persons interested to make representations and objections in relation to his proposal to give a certificate. After causing a public local inquiry to be held in any case where it appears to him to be expedient so to do, and having regard to any representations or objections made, the Secretary of State may give his certificate. Before doing so he is required to consider any representations and objections made and, if an inquiry has been held, the report of the person who held the inquiry.[4]

---

[1]   Section 19(4).

[2]   [1993] Env LR 344.

[3]   Section 19(2).

[4]   Section 19(2).

12.2.2 Exchange land

A compulsory purchase order may provide for the vesting of exchange land in the persons and is subject to the same rights as the land being compulsorily acquired. It may also provide for the discharging of the land being compulsorily acquired of all rights to which it was previously subject.[1] There is one exception to this; that arises where the Secretary of State gives a certificate where land is already common or open space land and is being purchased in order to secure its preservation or improve its management.

Although the Secretary of State is not bound to hold a public local inquiry, he should only decline to do so where the issues relating to the provision of, for example, exchange land are relatively straightforward and can be fully covered in written submissions, and where it would be difficult to see how the Secretary of State could obtain further assistance. Exchange land does not have to replicate the land being compulsorily acquired.[2]

12.2.3 Special Parliamentary procedure

Where a certificate is not issued, as described above, a compulsory purchase order is of no effect until it has been laid before Parliament by the Secretary of State and comes into force in accordance with the provisions of the Statutory Orders (Special Procedure) Act 1945. A notice of an intention to lay an order before Parliament must be published in the *London Gazette*.[3] A period of time is allowed for the presentation of petitions by way of general objection or for the amendment to the order. A petition may be presented by any person in accordance with the standing orders of Parliament. Petitions may be of general objection, or for some amendment. An order may be annulled by resolution of either House of Parliament, or referred to a joint committee of both Houses for consideration of any petition.[4] If the joint committee report that the order should not be approved, or if amendments are made which are unacceptable to the Secretary of State, the order can only be authorised by the introduction of a

---

[1] Section 19(2A).

[2] *Waltham Forest District Council v Secretary of State for the Environment* [1993] EGCS 34.

[3] Statutory Orders (Special Procedures) Act 1945, s 2(1).

[4] Sections 3–5.

Bill and its confirmation by Acts of Parliament.[1] In those cases where the committee report the order without amendment, it will come into operation without further formal confirmation procedures.[2]

Special Parliamentary procedure provides Parliament with a measure of control over controversial proposals for the compulsory acquisition of common land. The procedure also allows the making of petitions for consideration by an appropriate committee.

12.3   ACQUISITION OF RIGHTS OVER COMMONS

Where a compulsory purchase order authorises the acquisition of a right over land forming part of a common, open space or fuel or field garden allotment, it shall be subject to special Parliamentary procedure except where excluded by a certificate of the Secretary of State.[3] The Secretary of State may only issue a certificate excluding special Parliamentary procedure where he is satisfied that:

(a) the land, when burdened with the right sought to be compulsorily acquired, will be no less advantageous to those persons in whom it is vested and other persons, if any, entitled to rights of common or other rights, and to the public, than it was before;[4] or

(b) the right, which is being acquired compulsorily, is being acquired in order to secure the preservation or improvement of the management of the land;[5] or

(c) there has been or will be given in exchange for the right being compulsorily acquired additional land that will be adequate to compensate the owner of the common and those entitled to rights of common or other rights over it for the disadvantages which will result from the acquisition of the right. The additional land must either have been, or will be vested in the owner of the land over which the right is to be acquired, and be

---

[1]   Section 6(2).

[2]   Section 6(1).

[3]   Acquisition of Land Act 1981, Sch 3, para 6(1).

[4]   Ibid, para 6(1)(a).

[5]   Ibid, para 6(1)(aa).

made subject to the like rights as attached to that land apart from the compulsory purchase order;[1] or

(d) the land affected by the right to be acquired does not exceed 250 square yards in extent, and the giving of other land in exchange for the right is unnecessary, whether in the interests of the persons, if any, entitled to rights of common of other rights or in the interests of the public.[2]

Where land is being acquired by a compulsory purchase order under the Highways Act 1980, a certificate can be issued under paragraph (d) above where, in the alternative to the land being acquired not exceeding 250 square yards, only rights are required in connection with the widening or drainage of an existing highway or in connection partly with the widening and partly with the drainage of such a highway.[3]

Where the Secretary of State is proposing to issue a certificate under any of the grounds set out above, the procedures for publicity, the making of objections and representations and the holding of a local public inquiry or otherwise, more fully explained at para **12.2.1** above, will apply.

Where a compulsory purchase order is concerned with the acquisition of rights, and no certificate can be issued excluding special Parliamentary procedure, or the Secretary of State decides not to do so, the special Parliamentary procedure described at para **12.2.3** above will apply.

12.4   COMPENSATION FOR THE FREEHOLD

12.4.1 Value of land taken

In the case of the acquisition of common land, the freehold will have to be compulsorily acquired. There are no special rules for the assessment of compensation for the acquisition of such a freehold. The owner of the freehold will be entitled to the value of his interest assessed in accordance with the compensation rules. These rules are

---

[1]   Acquisition of Land Act 1981, Sch 3, para 6(1)(b).

[2]   Ibid, para 6(1)(c).

[3]   Ibid, para 6(2).

set out in the Land Compensation Act 1961. Certain rules concern the basis of finding the open market value of the freehold interest; in broad terms, one assumes a sale by a willing seller in the open market.[1] Further rules deal with any planning assumptions that can be made; these may be relevant to the determination of the open market value.[2]

Where a piece of common land is being compulsorily acquired, the freehold is unlikely to have a very high value. However, the following factors should be considered:

(a) The value of the residue of rights left to the owner of the soil, such as his entitlement to timber, minerals or any rights he has in common with the commoners, such as rights of grazing.

(b) Whether the rights of the commoners might be extinguished, such as by merger. This is believed to have occurred in respect of Copthorne Common where the owner of the soil was able to acquire the property of the only remaining commoner with registered common rights. By combining in one ownership the land to which common rights were attached with the ownership of the soil of the common land itself, the rights of common were released by the merger of the two interests; the land was no longer subject to common rights.

(c) All commons within the Metropolitan Police District, or within the areas once boroughs or urban districts (as they existed before local government reorganisation in 1974), are subject to a public right of access for air and exercise. A similar right applies to commons outside those areas if the owner of the soil has made a declaration allowing for this under s 193 of the Law of Property Act 1925. Most common land is registered common land under the Commons Registration Act 1965. All registered common land is land over which the public will have rights of access under the CROW Act 2000.

(d) Where the soil of a common carries with it ownership of the lord of the manor, a manorship may have considerable value. Whether this adds to the value of the land taken, or goes to any claim for injurious affection or severance, will depend on the circumstances.

---

[1]   Land Compensation Act 1961, s 5(2).

[2]   Ibid, ss 14–18.

12.4.2 Injurious affection and severance compensation

In addition to the value of any land taken, compensation is also payable for the effect of severance or injurious affection on any retained land of a claimant owner.[1] It follows that the owner of the soil may have a claim for compensation for the diminution in value of the retained part of the common. There may be a similar claim where the ownership of the soil is with the lord of the manor, and the retained interest in the manorship is similarly diminished in value.

12.4.3 Payment of compensation and conveyance

The compensation in respect of the right in the soil of any of the land subject to compulsory purchase and subject to any rights of common must be paid to the lord of the manor, if he is so entitled, or to any other such party who owns the soil, other than the commoners.[2] On payment or tender to the lord of the manor, or such other party as is entitled to the ownership of the soil, of the compensation agreed or awarded in respect of the right in the soil of any common land, the lord of the manor or such other party shall convey the land to the acquiring authority. The conveyance has the effect of vesting the land in the acquiring authority as if the lord of the manor or other party had owned the freehold at the time of executing the conveyance.[3] In default of such a conveyance, it shall be lawful for the acquiring authority, if it thinks fit, to execute a deed poll and, after paying the compensation monies into court, the land shall vest absolutely in the acquiring authority.[4]

The provisions discussed in this section apply only where the commoners are not also entitled to ownership of the soil. In the case of a common where the soil is owned by the commoners, not infrequent in Wales, the compensation provisions discussed under the next heading are appropriate.

---

[1] Compulsory Purchase Act 1965, s 7.

[2] Ibid, Sch 4, para 1(1).

[3] Ibid, para 2(1)–(2).

[4] Ibid, para 2(3).

12.5 COMPENSATION FOR THE COMMONERS

Schedule 4 to the Compulsory Purchase Act 1965 sets out the procedure for the assessment of compensation payable to the commoners on the compulsory acquisition of common land.

Two situations are covered by these provisions: the assessment of compensation where the commoners are also the owners of the soil, and the assessment of compensation payable to the commoners where the right in the soil does not belong to the commoners. In either situation, compensation must be determined by agreement between the acquiring authority and a committee of the persons entitled to commonable or other rights in the land appointed under the provisions of Sch 4.[1]

12.5.1 Meeting of commoners

The acquiring authority may convene a meeting of the commoners having rights over the land subject to compulsory purchase after giving notice in a local newspaper and fixing a notice on the door of the parish church in the locality.[2] The meeting may appoint a committee consisting of not more than five commoners, and the decision of the majority of persons present at the meeting shall bind the minority and all absent parties.[3]

The acquiring authority may negotiate with the committee. If a sum of compensation is agreed, that agreement is binding on all persons interested in the commonable rights. Compensation may be paid to the committee or any three of them. The compensation may be apportioned by the committee among the commoners, according to their respective interests, and the acquiring authority is not bound to see to the apportionment or to the application of the compensation, nor are they liable for any misapplication or non-application of the compensation.[4] If the committee fails to agree with the acquiring

---

[1] Compulsory Purchase Act 1965, Sch 4, para 3.

[2] Ibid, para 4.

[3] Ibid, para 4(5).

[4] Ibid, para 5(1)–(3).

authority as to the amount of compensation, the dispute is referred to and determined by the Lands Tribunal.[1]

Where there has been a failure to hold an effective meeting, or the meeting fails to appoint a committee, the amount of the compensation is determined by a surveyor selected from the members of the Lands Tribunal.[2] On the payment of compensation to the committee, or any three of them or, where appropriate, into court, the acquiring authority may execute a deed poll; this will vest in the authority the common land freed and discharged from all the commonable rights.

Where the committee has difficulties in apportioning compensation, or there are difficulties about its investment, there are a number of powers that deal with this particular problem.[3]

12.5.2 Exchange land

Where the acquiring authority has provided exchange land to replace the common land being acquired, the granting of an exchange land certificate does not, by itself, preclude the payment of compensation to the commoners.[4] In one case the Lands Tribunal considered that the value of commoners' rights transferred to the exchange land represented in whole, or in part, the compensation which was payable for the acquisition of the rights in common which subsisted in the land acquired.[5]

12.5.3 Valuation of rights of common

Most common rights, such as grazing rights, are attached to land. In certain areas the existence of such rights is a significant factor in the value of farmland. If the land to which common rights are annexed is valued, first with those rights and, second, after those rights have been acquired as a result of the taking of the common, the difference can be said to be attributable to the value of the common rights. As

---

[1]   Compulsory Purchase Act 1965, Sch 4, para 5(4).

[2]   Ibid, para 6.

[3]   See Inclosure Act 1852, s 22, and Commonable Compensation Rights Act 1882, s 2.

[4]   *McKay v The City of London Corporation* (1966) 17 P&CR 264.

[5]   *Lay v Norfolk County Council* [1997] RVR 9 and *Freeman v Middlesex County Council* (1965) 16 P&CR 253.

the value of common rights over the same common may differ from holding to holding, the procedure of treating for compensation through a committee rather than directly is not always satisfactory.

12.5.4 Disputes

If there is disagreement among the commoners as to how the compensation should be apportioned or invested, the committee may make application in writing to the Secretary of State at the Department of the Environment, Food and Rural Affairs, who has powers to make an award binding on the parties.[1]

12.5.5 Effect of payment of compensation

The payment of compensation does not alter the status of the land as common land, as such. Therefore, unless inclosure is authorised, the land remains common land and cannot be inclosed. Further, the procedure under Sch 4 does not extinguish any public rights of access, only the commoners' rights.[2]

---

[1]   Inclosure Acts 1852–54 and Commonable Compensation Rights Act 1882.

[2]   *Lewis v Mid-Glamorgan County Council* [1995] 1 All ER 760.

APPENDIX

LEGISLATION

Commons Registration Act 1965   179
Law of Property Act 1925, ss 193–194   192
Inclosure Act 1857, s 12   195
Commons Act 1876, s 29   196
Countryside and Rights of Way Act 2000, ss 1–46, 68 and
   Schs 1–4   197

Commons Registration (General) Regulations 1966,
   SI 1966/1471   241
Commons Registration (New Land) Regulations 1969,
   SI 1969/1843   260
Vehicular Access across Common and other Land (England)
   Regulations 2002, SI 2002/1711   293

COMMONS REGISTRATION ACT 1965

(1965 c 64)

An Act to provide for the registration of common land and of town or village greens; to amend the law as to prescriptive claims to rights of common; and for purposes connected therewith

[5 August 1965]

1 Registration of commons and towns or village greens and ownership of and rights over them

(1) There shall be registered, in accordance with the provisions of this Act and subject to the exceptions mentioned therein –

   (a) land in England or Wales which is common land or a town or village green;
   (b) rights of common over such land; and
   (c) persons claiming to be or found to be owners of such land or becoming the owners thereof by virtue of this Act;

   and no rights of common over land which is capable of being registered under this Act shall be registered [in the register of title].

(2) After the end of such period, not being less than three years from the commencement of this Act, as the Minister may by order determine –

   (a) no land capable of being registered under this Act shall be deemed to be common land or a town or village green unless it is so registered; and
   (b) no rights of common shall be exercisable over any such land unless they are registered either under this Act or [in the register of title].

(3) Where any land is registered under this Act but no person is registered as the owner thereof under this Act or [in the register of title], it shall –

   (a) if it is a town or village green, be vested in accordance with the following provisions of this Act; and
   (b) if it is common land, be vested as Parliament may hereafter determine.

Amendment – Land Registration Act 2002, s 133, Sch 11.

2 Registration authorities

(1) The registration authority for the purposes of this Act shall be –

   (a) in relation to any land situated in any county . . . , the council of that county [or, if the county is a metropolitan county, the council of the metropolitan district in which the land is situated] . . . ; and

(b)   in relation to any land situated in Greater London, the [council of the London borough in which the land is situated];

except where an agreement under this section otherwise provides.

(2)   Where part of any land is in the area of one registration authority and part in that of another the authorities may by agreement provide for one of them to be the registration authority in relation to the whole of the land.

Amendment – Local Government Act 1972, s 272(1), Sch 30; Local Government Act 1985, s 16, Sch 8.

3   The registers

(1)   For the purposes of registering such land as is mentioned in section 1(1) of this Act and rights of common over and ownership of such land every registration authority shall maintain –

(a)   a register of common land; and
(b)   a register of town or village greens;

and regulations under this Act may require or authorise a registration authority to note on those registers such other information as may be prescribed.

(2)   Any register maintained under this Act shall be open to inspection by the public at all reasonable times.

4   Provisional registration

(1)   Subject to the provisions of this section, a registration authority shall register any land as common land or a town or village green or, as the case may be, any rights of common over or ownership of such land, on application duly made to it and accompanied by such declaration and such other documents (if any) as may be prescribed for the purpose of verification or of proving compliance with any prescribed conditions.

(2)   An application for the registration of any land as common land or as a town or village green may be made by any person, and a registration authority –

(a)   may so register any land notwithstanding that no application for that registration has been made, and
(b)   shall so register any land in any case where it registers any rights over it under this section.

(3)   No person shall be registered under this section as the owner of any land which is registered [in the register of title] and no person shall be registered under this section as the owner of any other land unless the land itself is registered under this section.

(4)   Where, in pursuance of an application under this section, any land would fall to be registered as common land or as a town or village green, but the land is already so registered, the registration authority shall not register it again but shall note the application in the register.

(5) A registration under this section shall be provisional only until it has become final under the following provisions of this Act.

(6) An application for registration under this section shall not be entertained if made after such date, not less than three years from the commencement of this Act, as the Minister may by order specify; and different dates may be so specified for different classes of applications.

(7) Every local authority shall take such steps as may be prescribed for informing the public of the period within which and the manner in which applications for registration under this section may be made.

Amendment – Land Registration Act 2002, s 133, Sch 11.

5   Notification of, and objections to, registration

(1) A registration authority shall give such notices and take such other steps as may be prescribed for informing the public of any registration made by it under section 4 of this Act, of the times and places where copies of the relevant entries in the register may be inspected and of the period during which and the manner in which objections to the registration may be made to the authority.

(2) The period during which objections to any registration under section 4 of this Act may be made shall be such period, ending not less than two years after the date of the registration, as may be prescribed.

(3) Where any land or rights over land are registered under section 4 of this Act but no person is so registered as the owner of the land the registration authority may, if it thinks fit, make an objection to the registration notwithstanding that it has no interest in the land.

(4) Where an objection to a registration under section 4 of this Act is made, the registration authority shall note the objection on the register and shall give such notice as may be prescribed to the person (if any) on whose application the registration was made and to any person whose application is noted under section 4(4) of this Act.

(5) Where a person to whom notice has been given under subsection (4) of this section so requests or where the registration was made otherwise than on the application of any person, the registration authority may, if it thinks fit, cancel or modify a registration to which objection is made under this section.

(6) Where such an objection is made, then, unless the objection is withdrawn or the registration cancelled before the end of such period as may be prescribed, the registration authority shall refer the matter to a Commons Commissioner.

(7) An objection to the registration of any land as common land or as a town or village green shall be treated for the purposes of this Act as being also an objection to any registration (whenever made) under section 4 of this Act of any rights over the land.

(8)   A registration authority shall take such steps as may be prescribed for informing the public of any objection which they have noted on the register under this section and of the times and places where copies of the relevant entries in the register may be inspected.

(9)   Where regulations under this Act require copies of any entries in a register to be sent by the registration authority to another local authority they may require that other authority to make the copies available for inspection in such manner as may be prescribed.

6   Disposal of disputed claims

(1)   The Commons Commissioner to whom any matter has been referred under section 5 of this Act shall inquire into it and shall either confirm the registration, with or without modifications, or refuse to confirm it; and the registration shall, if it is confirmed, become final, and, if the confirmation is refused, become void –

> (a)   if no appeal is brought against the confirmation or refusal, at the end of the period during which such an appeal could have been brought;
> (b)   if such an appeal is brought, when it is finally disposed of.

(2)   On being informed in the prescribed manner that a registration has become final (with or without modifications) or has become void a registration authority shall indicate that fact in the prescribed manner in the register and, if it has become void, cancel the registration.

(3)   Where the registration of any land as common land or as a town or village green is cancelled (whether under this section or under section 5(5) of this Act) the registration authority shall also cancel the registration of any person as the owner thereof.

7   Finality of undisputed registrations

(1)   If no objection is made to a registration under section 4 of this Act or if all objections made to such a registration are withdrawn the registration shall become final at the end of the period during which such objections could have been made under section 5 of this Act or, if an objection made during that period is withdrawn after the end thereof, at the date of the withdrawal.

(2)   Where by virtue of this section a registration has become final the registration authority shall indicate that fact in the prescribed manner in the register.

8   Vesting of unclaimed land

(1)   Where the registration under section 4 of this Act of any land as common land or as a town or village green has become final but no person is registered under that section as the owner of the land, then unless the land is registered [in the register of title], the registration authority shall refer the question of the ownership of the land to a Commons Commissioner.

(2) After the registration authority has given such notices as may be prescribed, the Commons Commissioner shall inquire into the matter and shall, if satisfied that any person is the owner of the land, direct the registration authority to register that person accordingly; and the registration authority shall comply with the direction.

(3) If the Commons Commissioner is not so satisfied and the land is a town or village green he shall direct the registration authority to register as the owner of the land the local authority specified in subsection (5) of this section; and the registration authority shall comply with the direction.

(4) On the registration under this section of a local authority as the owner of any land the land shall vest in that local authority and, if the land is not regulated by a scheme under the Commons Act 1899, sections 10 and 15 of the Open Spaces Act 1906 (power to manage and make byelaws) shall apply in relation to it as if that local authority had acquired the ownership under the said Act of 1906.

[(5) Subject to subsection (6) of this section, the local authority in which any land is to be vested under this section is –

(a) if the land is in a parish or community where there is a parish or community council, that council, but, if the land is regulated by a scheme under the Commons Act 1899, only if the powers of management under Part I of that Act are, in accordance with arrangements under Part VI of the Local Government Act 1972, being exercised by the parish or community council;

(b) if the land is in a London borough, the council of that borough; and

(c) in any other case, the council of the district in which the land is situated.

(6) Where –

(a) any land has been vested in a district council in accordance with subsection (5)(c) of this section, and

(b) after the land has been so vested a parish or community council comes into being for the parish or community in which the land is situated (whether by the establishment of a new council or by adding that parish or community to a group of parishes or communities for which a council has already been established),

then, if the circumstances are such that, had the direction under subsection (3) of this section been given at a time after the parish or community council had come into being, the land would in accordance with subsection (5)(a) of this section have been vested in the parish or community council, the district council shall, if requested to do so by the parish or community council, direct the registration authority to register the parish or community council, in place of the district council, as the owner of the land; and the registration authority shall comply with any such direction.

(7) The council of any district, parish or community affected by any registration made in pursuance of subsection (6) above shall pay to the other of those councils so affected such sum, if any, as may be agreed between them to be appropriate to take account of any sums received or to be received, or any

expenditure incurred or to be incurred, in respect of the land concerned, and, in default of agreement, the question of what sum, if any, is appropriate for that purpose shall be determined by arbitration.]

Amendment – Land Registration Act 2002, s 133, Sch 11, para 7(1), (2); Local Government Act 1972, s 189(2).

9   Protection of unclaimed common land

Where the registration under section 4 of this Act of any land as common land has become final but no person is registered under this Act or [in the register of title] as the owner of the land, then, until the land is vested under any provision hereafter made by Parliament, any local authority in whose area the land or part of the land is situated may take such steps for the protection of the land against unlawful interference as could be taken by an owner in possession of the land, and may (without prejudice to any power exercisable apart from this section) institute proceedings for any offence committed in respect of that land.

Amendment – Land Registration Act 2002, s 133, Sch 11

Modification – in relation to any registered common which is within any National Park for which a National Park authority is the local planning authority and is not owned by or vested in any other body which is a local authority – Environment Act 1995, s 70, Sch 9.

10   Effect of registration

The registration under this Act of any land as common land or as a town or village green, or of any rights of common over any such land, shall be conclusive evidence of the matters registered, as at the date of registration, except where the registration is provisional only.

11   Exemption from registration

(1)   The foregoing provisions of this Act shall not apply to the New Forest or Epping Forest nor to any land exempted from those provisions by an order of the Minister, and shall not be taken to apply to the Forest of Dean.

(2)   The Minister shall not make an order under this section except on an application made to him before such date as may be prescribed.

(3)   The Minister shall not make an order under this section with respect to any land unless it appears to him –

  (a)   that the land is regulated by a scheme under the Commons Act 1899 or the Metropolitan Commons Acts 1866 to 1898 or is regulated under a local Act or under an Act confirming a provisional order made under the Commons Act 1876; and

  (b)   that no rights of common have been exercised over the land for at least thirty years and that the owner of the land is known.

(4)   The Minister shall, before dealing with any application under this section, send copies thereof to the registration authority and to such other local authorities as may be prescribed, and shall inform those authorities whether he has granted or refused the application; and those authorities shall take such

steps as may be prescribed for informing the public of the application and its grant or refusal.

(5) If any question arises under this Act whether any land is part of the forests mentioned in subsection (1) of this section it shall be referred to and decided by the Minister.

12 Subsequent registration under Land Registration Acts 1925 and 1936

The following provisions shall have effect with respect to the registration [in the register of title] of any land after the ownership of the land has been registered under this Act, that is to say –

(a) . . .

(b) if the registration authority is notified by the Chief Land Registrar that the land has been registered [in the register of title] the authority shall delete the registration of the ownership under this Act and indicate in the register in the prescribed manner that it has been registered under those Acts.

Amendment – Land Registration Act 2002, s 133, Sch 11, (4); Land Registration Act 1997, s 4(2), Sch 2, Pt I.

13 Amendment of registers

Regulations under this Act shall provide for the amendment of the registers maintained under this Act where –

(a) any land registered under this Act ceases to be common land or a town or village green; or

(b) any land becomes common land or a town or village green; or

(c) any rights registered under this Act are apportioned, extinguished or released, or are varied or transferred in such circumstances as may be prescribed;

. . .

Amendment – Law of Property Act 1969, s 16(2), Sch 2, Part I.

14 Rectification of registers

The High Court may order a register maintained under this Act to be amended if –

(a) the registration under this Act of any land or rights of common has become final and the court is satisfied that any person was induced by fraud to withdraw an objection to the registration or to refrain from making such an objection; or

(b) the register has been amended in pursuance of section 13 of this Act and it appears to the court that no amendment or a different amendment ought to have been made and that the error cannot be corrected in pursuance of regulations made under this Act;

and, in either case, the court deems it just to rectify the register.

15   Quantification of certain grazing rights

(1)   Where a right of common consists of or includes a right, not limited by number, to graze animals or animals of any class, it shall for the purposes of registration under this Act be treated as exercisable in relation to no more animals, or animals of that class, than a definite number.

(2)   Any application for the registration of such a right shall state the number of animals to be entered in the register or, as the case may be, the numbers of animals of different classes to be so entered.

(3)   When the registration of such a right has become final the right shall accordingly be exercisable in relation to animals not exceeding the number or numbers registered or such other number or numbers as Parliament may hereafter determine.

16   Disregard of certain interruptions in prescriptive claims to rights of common

(1)   Where during any period a right of common claimed over any land was not exercised, but during the whole or part of that period either –

   (a)   the land was requisitioned; or
   (b)   where the right claimed is a right to graze animals, the right could not be or was not exercised for reasons of animal health;

   that period or part shall be left out of account, both –

   (i)   in determining for the purposes of the Prescription Act 1832 whether there was an interruption within the meaning of that Act of the actual enjoyment of the right; and
   (ii)   in computing the period of thirty or sixty years mentioned in section 1 of that Act.

(2)   For the purposes of the said Act any objection under this Act to the registration of a right of common shall be deemed to be such a suit or action as is referred to in section 4 of that Act.

(3)   In this section 'requisitioned' means in the possession of a Government department in the exercise or purported exercise of powers conferred by regulations made under the Emergency Powers (Defence) Act 1939 or by Part VI of the Requisitioned Land and War Works Act 1945; and in determining in any proceedings any question arising under this section whether any land was requisitioned during any period a document purporting to be a certificate to that effect issued by a Government department shall be admissible in evidence.

(4)   Where it is necessary for the purposes of this section to establish that a right to graze animals on any land could not be or was not exercised for reasons of animal health it shall be sufficient to prove either –

   (a)   that the movement of the animals to that land was prohibited or restricted by or under the Diseases of Animals Act 1950 or any enactment repealed by that Act; or

(b)   that the land was not, but some other land was, approved for grazing under any scheme in force under that Act or any such enactment and the animals were registered, or were undergoing tests with a view to registration, under the scheme.

17   Commons Commissioners and assessors

(1)   The Lord Chancellor shall –

(a)   appoint to be Commons Commissioners such number of [persons who have a 7 year general qualification, within the meaning of section 71 of the Courts and Legal Services Act 1990,] as he may determine; and

(b)   draw up and from time to time revise a panel of assessors to assist the Commons Commissioners in dealing with cases calling for special knowledge;

and shall appoint one of the Commons Commissioners to be Chief Commons Commissioner.

[(1A) A Commons Commissioner shall vacate his office on the day on which he attains the age of seventy years; but this subsection is subject to section 26(4) to (6) of the Judicial Pensions and Retirement Act 1993 (power of Lord Chancellor to authorise continuance in office up to the age of seventy-five years).]

(2)   Any matter referred under this Act to a Commons Commissioner shall be dealt with by such one of the Commissioners as the Chief Commons Commissioner may determine, and that Commissioner may sit with an assessor selected by the Chief Commons Commissioner from the panel appointed under this section.

(3)   If at any time the Chief Commons Commissioner is for any reason unable to act, the Lord Chancellor may appoint another Commons Commissioner to act in his stead.

(4)   A Commons Commissioner may order any party to any proceedings before him to pay to any other party to the proceedings any costs incurred by that party in respect of the proceedings; and any costs so awarded shall be taxed in the county court according to such of the scales prescribed by county court rules for proceedings in the county court as may be directed by the order, but subject to any modifications specified in the direction, or, if the order gives no direction, by the county court, and shall be recoverable in like manner as costs awarded in the county court.

(5)   The Minister shall pay to the Commons Commissioners and assessors appointed under this section such fees and such travelling and other allowances as the Minister may, with the approval of the Treasury, determine, and shall provide the Commons Commissioners with such services and facilities as appear to him required for the discharge of their functions.

Amendment – Courts and Legal Services Act 1990, s 71(2), Sch 10; Judicial Pensions and Retirement Act 1993, s 26, Sch 6 (for savings see s 27, Sch 7 thereof).

18   Appeals from Commons Commissioners

(1)   Any person aggrieved by the decision of a Commons Commissioner as being erroneous in point of law may, within such time as may be limited by rules of court, require the Commissioner to state a case for the decision of the High Court.

(2)   So much of section 63(1) of the Supreme Court of Judicature (Consolidation) Act 1925 as requires appeals to the High Court to be heard and determined by a Divisional Court shall not apply to an appeal by way of case stated under this section, but no appeal to the Court of Appeal shall be brought against the decision of the High Court in such a case except with the leave of that Court or the Court of Appeal.

19   Regulations

(1)   The Minister may make regulations –

(a)   for prescribing the form of the registers to be maintained under this Act and of any applications and objections to be made and notices and certificates to be given thereunder;

(b)   for regulating the procedure of registration authorities in dealing with applications for registration and with objections;

(c)   for prescribing the steps to be taken by registration authorities for the information of other local authorities and of the public in cases where registrations are cancelled or modified;

(d)   for requiring registration authorities to supply by post, on payment of such fee as may be prescribed, such information relating to the entries in the registers kept by them as may be prescribed;

(e)   for regulating the procedure of the Commons Commissioners and, in particular, for providing for the summoning of persons to attend and give evidence and produce documents and for authorising the administration of oaths, and for enabling any inquiry or proceedings begun by or before one Commons Commissioner to be continued by or before another;

(f)   for enabling an application for the registration of rights of common attached to any land to be made either by the landlord or by the tenant and for regulating the procedure where such an application is made by both;

(g)   for enabling the Church Commissioners to act with respect to any land or rights belonging to an ecclesiastical benefice of the Church of England which is vacant;

(h)   for treating any registration conflicting with another registration as an objection to the other registration;

(i)   for requiring, before applications for registration are entertained, the taking of such steps as may be specified in the regulations for the information of persons having interests in any land affected by the registration;

(j)   for the correction of errors and omissions in the registers;

(k)   for prescribing anything required or authorised to be prescribed by this Act.

(2) The regulations may make provision for the preparation of maps to accompany applications for registration and the preparation, as part of the registers, of maps showing any land registered therein and any land to which rights of common registered therein are attached, and for requiring registration authorities to deposit copies of such maps with such Government departments and other authorities as may be prescribed.

(3) The regulations may prescribe the payment of a fee not exceeding five pounds on an application made after the end of such period as may be specified in the regulations.

(4) The regulations may make different provision with respect to different circumstances.

(5) Regulations under this Act shall be made by statutory instrument which shall be subject to annulment in pursuance of a resolution of either House of Parliament.

20 Orders

(1) Any order made by the Minister under any provision of this Act may be varied or revoked by subsequent order made thereunder.

(2) Any such order, other than an order made under section 11 of this Act, shall be made by statutory instrument.

(3) Any statutory instrument made under this section shall be subject to annulment in pursuance of a resolution of either House of Parliament.

21 Savings

(1) Section 1(2) of this Act shall not affect the application to any land registered under this Act of section 193 or section 194 of the Law of Property Act 1925 (rights of access to, and restriction on inclosure of, land over which rights of common are exercisable).

(2) Section 10 of this Act shall not apply for the purpose of deciding whether any land forms part of a highway.

22 Interpretation

(1) In this Act, unless the context otherwise requires –

'common land' means –

(a) land subject to rights of common (as defined in this Act) whether those rights are exercisable at all times or only during limited periods;

(b) waste land of a manor not subject to rights of common;

but does not include a town or village green or any land which forms part of a highway;

'land' includes land covered with water;

'local authority' means ... the council of a county, ... London borough or county district, the council of a parish ... ;

'the Minister' means the Minister of Land and Natural Resources;

'prescribed' means prescribed by regulations under this Act;

['register of title' means the register kept under section 1 of the Land Registration Act 2002;]

'registration' includes an entry in the register made in pursuance of section 13 of this Act;

'rights of common' includes cattlegates or beastgates (by whatever name known) and rights of sole or several vesture or herbage or of sole or several pasture, but does not include rights held for a term of years or from year to year;

'town or village green' means land which has been allotted by or under any Act for the exercise or recreation of the inhabitants of any locality or on which the inhabitants of any locality have a customary right to indulge in lawful sports and pastimes [or which falls within subsection (1A) of this section].

[(1A) Land falls within this subsection if it is land on which for not less than twenty years a significant number of the inhabitants of any locality, or of any neighbourhood within a locality, have indulged in lawful sports and pastimes as of right, and either –

(a)   continue to do so, or
(b)   have ceased to do so for not more than such period as may be prescribed, or determined in accordance with prescribed provisions.

(1B) If regulations made for the purposes of paragraph (b) of subsection (1A) of this section provide for the period mentioned in that paragraph to come to an end unless prescribed steps are taken, the regulations may also require registration authorities to make available in accordance with the regulations, on payment of any prescribed fee, information relating to the taking of any such steps.]

(2)   References in this Act to the ownership and the owner of any land are references to the ownership of a legal estate in fee simple in any land and to the person holding that estate, and references to land registered [in the register of title] are references to land the fee simple of which is so registered.

Amendment – Local Government Act 1985, s 102(2), Sch 17; Local Government Act 1972, s 272(1), Sch 30; Land Registration Act 2002, s 133, Sch 11; Countryside and Rights of Way Act 2000, s 98(1), (2); Countryside and Rights of Way Act 2000, s 98(1), (3); Land Registration Act 2002, s 133, Sch 11, para 7(1), (6).

23   Application to Crown

(1)   This Act shall apply in relation to land in which there is a Crown or Duchy interest as it applies in relation to land in which there is no such interest.

(2)   In this section 'Crown or Duchy interest' means an interest belonging to Her Majesty in right of the Crown or of the Duchy of Lancaster, or belonging to the Duchy of Cornwall, or belonging to a Government department, or held in trust for Her Majesty for the purposes of a Government department.

24   Expenses

There shall be defrayed out of moneys provided by Parliament any expenses of the Minister under this Act and any increase attributable to this Act in the sums payable under any other Act out of moneys so provided.

25   Short title, commencement and extent

(1)   This Act may be cited as the Commons Registration Act 1965.

(2)   This Act shall come into force on such day as the Minister may by order appoint, and different days may be so appointed for different purposes; and any reference in any provision to the commencement of this Act is a reference to the date on which that provision comes into force.

(3)   This Act does not extend to Scotland or to Northern Ireland.

LAW OF PROPERTY ACT 1925

(1925 c 20)

PART XI

MISCELLANEOUS

Commons and Waste Lands

193   Rights of the public over commons and waste lands

(1)   Members of the public shall, subject as hereinafter provided, have rights of access for air and exercise to any land which is a metropolitan common within the meaning of the Metropolitan Commons Acts, 1866 to 1898, or manorial waste, or a common, which is wholly or partly situated within [an area which immediately before 1st April 1974 was] a borough or urban district, and to any land which at the commencement of this Act is subject to rights of common and to which this section may from time to time be applied in manner hereinafter provided:

Provided that –

     (a)   such rights of access shall be subject to any Act, scheme, or provisional order for the regulation of the land, and to any byelaw, regulation or order made thereunder or under any other statutory authority; and

     (b)   the Minister shall, on the application of any person entitled as lord of the manor or otherwise to the soil of the land, or entitled to any commonable rights affecting the land, impose such limitations on and conditions as to the exercise of the rights of access or as to the extent of the land to be affected as, in the opinion of the Minister, are necessary or desirable for preventing any estate, right or interest of a profitable or beneficial nature in, over, or affecting the land from being injuriously affected, [for conserving flora, fauna or geological or physiographical features of the land,] or for protecting any object of historical interest and, where any such limitations or conditions are so imposed, the rights of access shall be subject thereto; and

     (c)   such rights of access shall not include any right to draw or drive upon the land a carriage, cart, caravan, truck, or other vehicle, or to camp or light any fire thereon; and

     (d)   the rights of access shall cease to apply –

         (i)   to any land over which the commonable rights are extinguished under any statutory provision;

         (ii)   to any land over which the commonable rights are otherwise extinguished if the council of the county[, county borough] [or metropolitan district] . . . in which the land is situated by resolution assent to its exclusion from the operation of this section, and the resolution is approved by the Minister.

(2) The lord of the manor or other person entitled to the soil of any land subject to rights of common may by deed, revocable or irrevocable, declare that this section shall apply to the land, and upon such deed being deposited with the Minister the land shall, so long as the deed remains operative, be land to which this section applies.

(3) Where limitations or conditions are imposed by the Minister under this section, they shall be published by such person and in such manner as the Minister may direct.

(4) Any person who, without lawful authority, draws or drives upon any land to which this section applies any carriage, cart, caravan, truck, or other vehicle, or camps or lights any fire thereon, or who fails to observe any limitation or condition imposed by the Minister under this section in respect of any such land, shall be liable on summary conviction to a fine not exceeding [level 1 on the standard scale] for each offence.

(5) Nothing in this section shall prejudice or affect the right of any person to get and remove mines or minerals or to let down the surface of the manorial waste or common.

(6) This section does not apply to any common or manorial waste which is for the time being held for Naval, Military or Air Force purposes and in respect of which rights of common have been extinguished or cannot be exercised.

Amendment – Local Government Act 1972, s 189(4); Countryside and Rights of Way Act 2000, s 46(3), Sch 4; Local Government (Wales) Act 1994, s 66(6), Sch 16; Local Government Act 1985, s 16, Sch 8; Local Government Act 1972, s 272(1), Sch 30; Countryside and Rights of Way Act 2000, ss 46(1)(a), 102, Sch 16, Pt I; maximum fine increased and converted to a level on the standard scale by the Criminal Justice Act 1982, ss 37, 38, 46.

194 Restrictions on inclosure of commons

(1) The erection of any building or fence, or the construction of any other work, whereby access to land to which this section applies is prevented or impeded, shall not be lawful unless the consent of the Minister thereto is obtained, and in giving or withholding his consent the Minister shall have regard to the same considerations and shall, if necessary, hold the same inquiries as are directed by the Commons Act 1876 to be taken into consideration and held by the Minister before forming an opinion whether an application under the Inclosure Acts 1845 to 1882 shall be acceded to or not.

(2) Where any building or fence is erected, or any other work constructed without such consent as is required by this section, the county court within whose jurisdiction the land is situated, shall, on an application being made by the council of any county [or county borough] ... or district concerned, or by the lord of the manor or any other person interested in the common, have power to make an order for the removal of the work, and the restoration of the land to the condition in which it was before the work was erected or constructed, but any such order shall be subject to the like appeal as an order made under section thirty of the Commons Act 1876.

(3)   This section applies to any land which at the commencement of this Act is subject to rights of common:

Provided that this section shall cease to apply –

(a)   to any land over which the rights of common are extinguished under any statutory provision;

(b)   to any land over which the rights of common are otherwise extinguished, if the council of the county[, county borough] [or metropolitan district] . . . in which the land is situated by resolution assent to its exclusion from the operation of this section and the resolution is approved by the Minister.

(4)   This section does not apply to any building or fence erected or work constructed if specially authorised by Act of Parliament, or in pursuance of an Act of Parliament or Order having the force of an Act, or if lawfully erected or constructed in connexion with the taking or working of minerals in or under any land to which the section is otherwise applicable, or to any [telecommunication apparatus installed for the purposes of a telecommunications code system] [electronic communications apparatus installed for the purposes of an electronic communications code network].

Amendment – Local Government (Wales) Act 1994, s 66(6), Sch 16; Local Government Act 1972, s 272(1); Sch 30; Local Government Act 1985, s 16, Sch 8; Telecommunications Act 1984, s 109, Sch 4; Communications Act 2003, s 406(1), Sch 17.

Modification –Environment Act 1995, s 70, Sch 9.

INCLOSURE ACT 1857

(1857 c 31)

12 Proceedings for prevention of nuisances in town and village greens and allotments for exercise and recreation

And whereas it is expedient to provide summary means of preventing nuisances in town greens and village greens, and on land allotted and awarded upon any inclosure under the said Acts as a place for exercise and recreation: If any person wilfully cause any injury or damage to any fence of any such town or village green or land, or wilfully and without lawful authority lead or drive any cattle or animal thereon, or wilfully lay any manure, soil, ashes, or rubbish, or other matter or thing thereon, or do any other act whatsoever to the injury of such town or village green or land, or to the interruption of the use or enjoyment thereof as a place for exercise and recreation, such person shall for every such offence, upon a summary conviction thereof before two justices, upon the information of any churchwarden or overseer of the parish in which such town or village green or land is situate, or of the person in whom the soil of such town or village green or land may be vested, forfeit and pay, in any of the cases aforesaid, and for each and every such offence, over and above the damages occasioned thereby, any sum not exceeding [level 1 on the standard scale] and it shall be lawful for any such churchwarden or overseer or other person as aforesaid to sell and dispose of any such manure, soil, ashes, and rubbish, or other matter or thing as aforesaid; and the proceeds arising from the sale thereof, and every such penalty as aforesaid, shall, as regards any such town, or village green not awarded under the said Acts or any of them to be used as a place for exercise and recreation, be applied in aid of the rates for the repair of the public highways in the parish, and shall, as regards the land so awarded, be applied by the persons or person in whom the soil thereof may be vested in the due maintenance of such land as a place for exercise and recreation; and if any manure, soil, ashes, or rubbish be not of sufficient value to defray the expense of removing the same, the person who laid or deposited such manure, soil, ashes, or rubbish shall repay to such churchwarden or overseer or other person as aforesaid the money necessarily expended in the removal thereof; and every such penalty as aforesaid shall be recovered in manner provided by the Summary Jurisdiction Act 1848; and the amount of damage occasioned by any such offence as aforesaid shall, in case of dispute, be determined by the justices by whom the offender is convicted; and the payment of the amount of such damage, and the repayments of the money necessarily expended in the removal of any manure, soil, ashes, or rubbish, shall be enforced in like manner as any such penalty.

Amendment – Maximum fine increased and converted to a level on the standard scale by the Criminal Justice Act 1982, ss 37, 38, 46.

COMMONS ACT 1876

(1876 c 56)

PART II

AMENDMENT OF THE INCLOSURE ACTS

Field Gardens and Recreation Grounds

29   Town and village greens

An encroachment on or inclosure of a town or village green, also any erection thereon or disturbance or interference with or occupation of the soil thereof which is made otherwise than with a view to the better enjoyment of such town or village green or recreation ground, shall be deemed to be a public nuisance, and if any person does any act in respect of which he is liable to pay damages or a penalty under section twelve of the Inclosure Act 1857, he may be summarily convicted thereof upon the information of any inhabitant of the parish in which such town or village green or recreation ground is situate, as well as upon the information of such persons as in the said section mentioned.

This section shall apply only in cases where a town or village green or recreation ground has a known and defined boundary.

Amendment – Statute Law Revision Act 1894.

COUNTRYSIDE AND RIGHTS OF WAY ACT 2000

(2000 c 37)

Part I, Part II, s 68 and Schedules 1–4

ARRANGEMENT OF SECTIONS

PART I

ACCESS TO THE COUNTRYSIDE

CHAPTER I

RIGHT OF ACCESS

General

Section
1   Principal definitions for Part 1
2   Rights of public in relation to access land
3   Power to extend to coastal land

Maps

4   Duty to prepare maps
5   Publication of draft maps
6   Appeal against map after confirmation
7   Appeal procedure
8   Power of Secretary of State or Assembly to delegate functions relating to appeals
9   Maps in conclusive form
10 Review of maps
11 Regulations relating to maps

Rights and liabilities of owners and occupiers

12 Effect of right of access on rights and liabilities of owners
13 Occupiers' liability
14 Offence of displaying on access land notices deterring public use

Access under other enactments or by dedication

15 Rights of access under other enactments
16 Dedication of land as access land

Miscellaneous provisions relating to right of access

17   Byelaws
18   Wardens
19   Notices indicating boundaries, etc
20   Codes of conduct and other information

CHAPTER II
EXCLUSION OR RESTRICTION OF ACCESS

21   Interpretation of Chapter II
22   Exclusion or restriction at discretion of owner and others
23   Restrictions on dogs at discretion of owner
24   Land management
25   Avoidance of risk of fire or of danger to the public
26   Nature conservation and heritage preservation
27   Directions by relevant authority: general
28   Defence or national security
29   Reference by relevant advisory body
30   Appeal by person interested in land
31   Exclusion or restriction of access in case of emergency
32   Regulations relating to exclusion or restriction of access
33   Guidance by countryside bodies to National Park authorities

CHAPTER III
MEANS OF ACCESS

34   Interpretation of Chapter III
35   Agreements with respect to means of access
36   Failure to comply with agreement
37   Provision of access by access authority in absence of agreement
38   Appeals relating to notices
39   Order to remove obstruction

CHAPTER IV
GENERAL

40   Powers of entry for purposes of Part I
41   Compensation relating to powers under s 40
42   References to public places in existing enactments
43   Crown application of Part I
44   Orders and regulations under Part I
45   Interpretation of Part I
46   Repeal of previous legislation, and amendments relating to Part 1

PART II

PUBLIC RIGHTS OF WAY AND ROAD TRAFFIC

. . .

68   Vehicular access across common land etc

. . .

Schedules:

Schedule 1—Excepted land for the purposes of Part I

Schedule 2—Restrictions to be observed by persons exercising rights of access

Schedule 3—Delegation of appellate functions

Schedule 4—Minor and consequential amendments relating to Part I

An Act to make new provision for public access to the countryside; to amend the law relating to public rights of way; to enable traffic regulation orders to be made for the purpose of conserving an area's natural beauty; to make provision with respect to the driving of mechanically propelled vehicles elsewhere than on roads; to amend the law relating to nature conservation and the protection of wildlife; to make further provision with respect to areas of outstanding natural beauty; and for connected purposes.

[30 November 2000]

PART I
ACCESS TO THE COUNTRYSIDE

CHAPTER I
RIGHT OF ACCESS

General

1   Principal definitions for Part I

(1)   In this Part 'access land' means any land which –

(a)   is shown as open country on a map in conclusive form issued by the appropriate countryside body for the purposes of this Part,

(b)   is shown on such a map as registered common land,

(c)   is registered common land in any area outside Inner London for which no such map relating to registered common land has been issued,

(d)   is situated more than 600 metres above sea level in any area for which no such map relating to open country has been issued, or

(e)   is dedicated for the purposes of this Part under section 16,

but does not (in any of those cases) include excepted land or land which is treated by section 15(1) as being accessible to the public apart from this Act.

(2)   In this Part –

'access authority' –

(a)   in relation to land in a National Park, means the National Park authority, and

(b)   in relation to any other land, means the local highway authority in whose area the land is situated;

'the appropriate countryside body' means –

(a)   in relation to England, the Countryside Agency, and

(b)   in relation to Wales, the Countryside Council for Wales;

'excepted land' means land which is for the time being of any of the descriptions specified in Part I of Schedule 1, those descriptions having effect subject to Part II of that Schedule;

'mountain' includes, subject to the following definition, any land situated more than 600 metres above sea level;

'mountain, moor, heath or down' does not include land which appears to the appropriate countryside body to consist of improved or semi-improved grassland;

'open country' means land which –

(a)   appears to the appropriate countryside body to consist wholly or predominantly of mountain, moor, heath or down, and

(b)   is not registered common land.

(3)   In this Part 'registered common land' means –

(a)   land which is registered as common land under the Commons Registration Act 1965 (in this section referred to as 'the 1965 Act') and whose registration under that Act has become final, or

(b)   subject to subsection (4), land which fell within paragraph (a) on the day on which this Act is passed or at any time after that day but has subsequently ceased to be registered as common land under the 1965 Act on the register of common land in which it was included being amended by reason of the land having ceased to be common land within the meaning of that Act.

(4)   Subsection (3)(b) does not apply where –

(a)   the amendment of the register of common land was made in pursuance of an application made before the day on which this Act is passed, or

(b)   the land ceased to be common land by reason of the exercise of –

(i)   any power of compulsory purchase, of appropriation or of sale which is conferred by an enactment,

(ii)   any power so conferred under which land may be made common land within the meaning of the 1965 Act in substitution for other land.

2   Rights of public in relation to access land

(1)   Any person is entitled by virtue of this subsection to enter and remain on any access land for the purposes of open-air recreation, if and so long as –

   (a)   he does so without breaking or damaging any wall, fence, hedge, stile or gate, and

   (b)   he observes the general restrictions in Schedule 2 and any other restrictions imposed in relation to the land under Chapter II.

(2)   Subsection (1) has effect subject to subsections (3) and (4) and to the provisions of Chapter II.

(3)   Subsection (1) does not entitle a person to enter or be on any land, or do anything on any land, in contravention of any prohibition contained in or having effect under any enactment, other than an enactment contained in a local or private Act.

(4)   If a person becomes a trespasser on any access land by failing to comply with –

   (a)   subsection (1)(a),

   (b)   the general restrictions in Schedule 2, or

   (c)   any other restrictions imposed in relation to the land under Chapter II,

   he may not, within 72 hours after leaving that land, exercise his right under subsection (1) to enter that land again or to enter other land in the same ownership.

(5)   In this section 'owner', in relation to any land which is subject to a farm business tenancy within the meaning of the Agricultural Tenancies Act 1995 or a tenancy to which the Agricultural Holdings Act 1986 applies, means the tenant under that tenancy, and 'ownership' shall be construed accordingly.

3   Power to extend to coastal land

(1)   The Secretary of State (as respects England) or the National Assembly for Wales (as respects Wales) may by order amend the definition of 'open country' in section 1(2) so as to include a reference to coastal land or to coastal land of any description.

(2)   An order under this section may –

   (a)   make consequential amendments of other provisions of this Part, and

   (b)   modify the provisions of this Part in their application to land which is open country merely because it is coastal land.

(3)   In this section 'coastal land' means –

   (a)   the foreshore, and

   (b)   land adjacent to the foreshore (including in particular any cliff, bank, barrier, dune, beach or flat which is adjacent to the foreshore).

Maps

4   Duty to prepare maps

(1)   It shall be the duty of the Countryside Agency to prepare, in respect of England outside Inner London, maps which together show –

   (a)   all registered common land, and
   (b)   all open country.

(2)   It shall be the duty of the Countryside Council for Wales to prepare, in respect of Wales, maps which together show –

   (a)   all registered common land, and
   (b)   all open country.

(3)   Subsections (1) and (2) have effect subject to the following provisions of this section and to the provisions of sections 5 to 9.

(4)   A map prepared under this section must distinguish between open country and registered common land, but need not distinguish between different categories of open country.

(5)   In preparing a map under this section, the appropriate countryside body –

   (a)   may determine not to show as open country areas of open country which are so small that the body consider that their inclusion would serve no useful purpose, and
   (b)   may determine that any boundary of an area of open country is to be treated as coinciding with a particular physical feature (whether the effect is to include other land as open country or to exclude part of an area of open country).

5   Publication of draft maps

The appropriate countryside body shall –

   (a)   issue in draft form any map prepared by them under section 4,
   (b)   consider any representations received by them within the prescribed period with respect to the showing of, or the failure to show, any area of land on the map as registered common land or as open country,
   (c)   confirm the map with or without modifications,
   (d)   if the map has been confirmed without modifications, issue it in provisional form, and
   (e)   if the map has been confirmed with modifications, prepare a map incorporating the modifications, and issue that map in provisional form.

6   Appeal against map after confirmation

(1)   Any person having an interest in any land may appeal –

   (a)   in the case of land in England, to the Secretary of State, or
   (b)   in the case of land in Wales, to the National Assembly for Wales,

against the showing of that land on a map in provisional form as registered common land or as open country.

(2) An appeal relating to the showing of any land as registered common land may be brought only on the ground that the land is not registered common land.

(3) An appeal relating to the showing of any land as open country may be brought only on the ground that –

(a) the land does not consist wholly or predominantly of mountain, moor, heath or down, and

(b) to the extent that the appropriate countryside body have exercised their discretion under section 4(5)(b) to treat land which is not open country as forming part of an area of open country, the body ought not to have done so.

(4) On an appeal under this section, the Secretary of State or the National Assembly for Wales may –

(a) approve the whole or part of the map which is the subject of the appeal, with or without modifications, or

(b) require the appropriate countryside body to prepare under section 4 a new map relating to all or part of the area covered by the map which is the subject of the appeal.

7 Appeal procedure

(1) Before determining an appeal under section 6, the Secretary of State or the National Assembly for Wales may, if he or it thinks fit –

(a) cause the appeal to take, or continue in, the form of a hearing, or

(b) cause a local inquiry to be held;

and the appeal authority shall act as mentioned in paragraph (a) or (b) if a request is made by either party to the appeal to be heard with respect to the appeal.

(2) Subsections (2) to (5) of section 250 of the Local Government Act 1972 (local inquiries: evidence and costs) apply to a hearing or local inquiry held under this section as they apply to a local inquiry held under that section, but as if –

(a) references in that section to the person appointed to hold the inquiry were references to the Secretary of State or the National Assembly for Wales, and

(b) references in that section to the Minister causing an inquiry to be held were references to the Secretary of State or the Assembly.

(3) Where –

(a) for the purposes of an appeal under section 6, the Secretary of State or the National Assembly for Wales is required by subsection (1) –

(i) to cause the appeal to take, or continue in, the form of a hearing, or

(ii) to cause a local inquiry to be held, and

(b)   the inquiry or hearing does not take place, and

(c)   if it had taken place, the Secretary of State or the Assembly or a person appointed by the Secretary of State or the Assembly would have had power to make an order under section 250(5) of the Local Government Act 1972 requiring any party to pay the costs of the other party,

the power to make such an order may be exercised, in relation to costs incurred for the purposes of the inquiry or hearing, as if it had taken place.

(4)   This section has effect subject to section 8.

8   Power of Secretary of State or Assembly to delegate functions relating to appeals

(1)   The Secretary of State or the National Assembly for Wales may –

(a)   appoint any person to exercise on his or its behalf, with or without payment, the function of determining –

(i)   an appeal under section 6, or

(ii)   any matter involved in such an appeal, or

(b)   refer any matter involved in such an appeal to such person as the Secretary of State or the Assembly may appoint for the purpose, with or without payment.

(2)   Schedule 3 has effect with respect to appointments under subsection (1)(a).

9   Maps in conclusive form

(1)   Where –

(a)   the time within which any appeal under section 6 may be brought in relation to a map in provisional form has expired and no appeal has been brought, or

(b)   every appeal brought under that section in relation to a map has –

(i)   been determined by the map or part of it being approved without modifications, or

(ii)   been withdrawn,

the appropriate countryside body shall issue the map (or the part or parts of it that have been approved without modifications) as a map in conclusive form.

(2)   Where –

(a)   every appeal brought under section 6 in relation to a map in provisional form has been determined or withdrawn, and

(b)   on one or more appeals, the map or any part of it has been approved with modifications,

the appropriate countryside body shall prepare a map which covers the area covered by the map in provisional form (or the part or parts of the map in provisional form that have been approved with or without modifications) and incorporates the modifications, and shall issue it as a map in conclusive form.

(3)   Where either of the conditions in subsection (1)(a) and (b) is satisfied in relation to any part of a map in provisional form, the Secretary of State (as respects England) or the National Assembly for Wales (as respects Wales) may direct the relevant countryside body to issue that part of the map as a map in conclusive form.

(4)   Where on an appeal under section 6 part of a map in provisional form has been approved with modifications but the condition in subsection (2)(a) is not yet satisfied, the Secretary of State (as respects England) or the National Assembly for Wales (as respects Wales) may direct the relevant countryside body to issue a map which covers the area covered by that part of the map in provisional form and incorporates the modifications, and to issue it as a map in conclusive form.

(5)   Where a map in conclusive form has been issued in compliance with a direction under subsection (3) or (4), subsections(1) and (2) shall have effect as if any reference to the map in provisional form were a reference to the part not affected by the direction.

(6)   A document purporting to be certified on behalf of the appropriate countryside body to be a copy of or of any part of a map in conclusive form issued by that body for the purposes of this Part shall be receivable in evidence and shall be deemed, unless the contrary is shown, to be such a copy.

10   Review of maps

(1)   Where the appropriate countryside body have issued a map in conclusive form in respect of any area, it shall be the duty of the body from time to time, on a review under this section, to consider –

   (a)   whether any land shown on that map as open country or registered common land is open country or registered common land at the time of the review, and
   (b)   whether any land in that area which is not so shown ought to be so shown.

(2)   A review under this section must be undertaken –

   (a)   in the case of the first review, not more than ten years after the issue of the map in conclusive form, and
   (b)   in the case of subsequent reviews, not more than ten years after the previous review.

(3)   Regulations may amend paragraphs (a) and (b) of subsection (2) by substituting for the period for the time being specified in either of those paragraphs such other period as may be specified in the regulations.

11   Regulations relating to maps

(1)   Regulations may make provision supplementing the provisions of sections 4 to 10.

(2) Regulations under this section may in particular make provision with respect to –

   (a) the scale on which maps are to be prepared,

   (b) the manner and form in which they are to be prepared and issued,

   (c) consultation with access authorities, local access forums and other persons on maps in draft form,

   (d) the steps to be taken for informing the public of the issue of maps in draft form, provisional form or conclusive form,

   (e) the manner in which maps in draft form, provisional form or conclusive form are to be published or to be made available for inspection,

   (f) the period within which and the manner in which representations on a map in draft form may be made to the appropriate countryside body,

   (g) the confirmation of a map under section 5(c),

   (h) the period within which and manner in which appeals under section 6 are to be brought,

   (i) the advertising of such an appeal,

   (j) the manner in which such appeals are to be considered,

   (k) the procedure to be followed on a review under section 10, including the issue of maps in draft form, provisional form and conclusive form on a review, and

   (l) the correction by the appropriate countryside body of minor errors or omissions in maps.

(3) Regulations made by virtue of subsection (2)(b) or (e) may authorise or require a map to be prepared, issued, published or made available for inspection in electronic form, but must require any map in electronic form to be capable of being reproduced in printed form.

(4) Regulations made by virtue of subsection (2)(k) may provide for any of the provisions of this Chapter relating to appeals to apply (with or without modifications) in relation to an appeal against a map issued in provisional form on a review.

Rights and liabilities of owners and occupiers

12   Effect of right of access on rights and liabilities of owners

(1) The operation of section 2(1) in relation to any access land does not increase the liability, under any enactment not contained in this Act or under any rule of law, of a person interested in the access land or any adjoining land in respect of the state of the land or of things done or omitted to be done on the land.

(2) Any restriction arising under a covenant or otherwise as to the use of any access land shall have effect subject to the provisions of this Part, and any liability of a person interested in any access land in respect of such a restriction is limited accordingly.

(3) For the purposes of any enactment or rule of law as to the circumstances in which the dedication of a highway or the grant of an easement may be presumed, or may be established by prescription, the use by the public or by any person of a way across land in the exercise of the right conferred by section 2(1) is to be disregarded.

(4) The use of any land by the inhabitants of any locality for the purposes of open-air recreation in the exercise of the right conferred by section 2(1) is to be disregarded in determining whether the land has become a town or village green.

13 Occupiers' liability

(1) In section 1 of the Occupiers' Liability Act 1957 (liability in tort: preliminary), for subsection (4) there is substituted –

'(4) A person entering any premises in exercise of rights conferred by virtue of –

(a) section 2(1) of the Countryside and Rights of Way Act 2000, or
(b) an access agreement or order under the National Parks and Access to the Countryside Act 1949,

is not, for the purposes of this Act, a visitor of the occupier of the premises.'

(2) In section 1 of the Occupiers' Liability Act 1984 (duty of occupier to persons other than his visitors), after subsection (6) there is inserted –

'(6A) At any time when the right conferred by section 2(1) of the Countryside and Rights of Way Act 2000 is exercisable in relation to land which is access land for the purposes of Part I of that Act, an occupier of the land owes (subject to subsection (6C) below) no duty by virtue of this section to any person in respect of –

(a) a risk resulting from the existence of any natural feature of the landscape, or any river, stream, ditch or pond whether or not a natural feature, or
(b) a risk of that person suffering injury when passing over, under or through any wall, fence or gate, except by proper use of the gate or of a stile.

(6B) For the purposes of subsection (6A) above, any plant, shrub or tree, of whatever origin, is to be regarded as a natural feature of the landscape.

(6C) Subsection (6A) does not prevent an occupier from owing a duty by virtue of this section in respect of any risk where the danger concerned is due to anything done by the occupier –

(a) with the intention of creating that risk, or
(b) being reckless as to whether that risk is created.'

(3)   After section 1 of that Act there is inserted –

'1A Special considerations relating to access land

In determining whether any, and if so what, duty is owed by virtue of
section 1 by an occupier of land at any time when the right conferred by
section 2(1) of the Countryside and Rights of Way Act 2000 is exercisable in
relation to the land, regard is to be had, in particular, to –

  (a)   the fact that the existence of that right ought not to place an undue
         burden (whether financial or otherwise) on the occupier,
  (b)   the importance of maintaining the character of the countryside, including
         features of historic, traditional or archaeological interest, and
  (c)   any relevant guidance given under section 20 of that Act.'

14   Offence of displaying on access land notices deterring public use

(1)   If any person places or maintains –

  (a)   on or near any access land, or
  (b)   on or near a way leading to any access land,

a notice containing any false or misleading information likely to deter the
public from exercising the right conferred by section 2(1), he is liable on
summary conviction to a fine not exceeding level 1 on the standard scale.

(2)   The court before whom a person is convicted of an offence under
subsection (1) may, in addition to or in substitution for the imposition of a
fine, order him to remove the notice in respect of which he is convicted within
such period, not being less than four days, as may be specified in the order.

(3)   A person who fails to comply with an order under subsection (2) is guilty of a
further offence and liable on summary conviction to a fine not exceeding
level 3 on the standard scale.

Access under other enactments or by dedication

15   Rights of access under other enactments

(1)   For the purposes of section 1(1), land is to be treated as being accessible to the
public apart from this Act at any time if, but only if, at that time –

  (a)   section 193 of the Law of Property Act 1925 (rights of the public over
         commons and waste lands) applies to it,
  (b)   by virtue of a local or private Act or a scheme made under Part I of the
         Commons Act 1899 (as read with subsection (2)), members of the public
         have a right of access to it at all times for the purposes of open-air
         recreation (however described),
  (c)   an access agreement or access order under Part V of the National Parks
         and Access to the Countryside Act 1949 is in force with respect to it, or

(d) the public have access to it under subsection (1) of section 19 of the Ancient Monuments and Archaeological Areas Act 1979 (public access to monuments under public control) or would have access to it under that subsection but for any provision of subsections (2) to (9) of that section.

(2) Where a local or private Act or a scheme made under Part I of the Commons Act 1899 confers on the inhabitants of a particular district or neighbourhood (however described) a right of access to any land for the purposes of open-air recreation (however described), the right of access exercisable by those inhabitants in relation to that land is by virtue of this subsection exercisable by members of the public generally.

16   Dedication of land as access land

(1) Subject to the provisions of this section, a person who, in respect of any land, holds –

(a) the fee simple absolute in possession, or
(b) a legal term of years absolute of which not less than 90 years remain unexpired,

may, by taking such steps as may be prescribed, dedicate the land for the purposes of this Part, whether or not it would be access land apart from this section.

(2) Where any person other than the person making the dedication holds –

(a) any leasehold interest in any of the land to be dedicated, or
(b) such other interest in any of that land as may be prescribed,

the dedication must be made jointly with that other person, in such manner as may be prescribed, or with his consent, given in such manner as may be prescribed.

(3) In relation to a dedication under this section by virtue of subsection (1)(b), the reference in subsection (2)(a) to a leasehold interest does not include a reference to a leasehold interest superior to that of the person making the dedication.

(4) A dedication made under this section by virtue of subsection (1)(b) shall have effect only for the remainder of the term held by the person making the dedication.

(5) Schedule 2 to the Forestry Act 1967 (power for tenant for life and others to enter into forestry dedication covenants) applies to dedications under this section as it applies to forestry dedication covenants.

(6) Regulations may –

(a) prescribe the form of any instrument to be used for the purposes of this section,
(b) enable a dedication under this section to include provision removing or relaxing any of the general restrictions in Schedule 2 in relation to any of the land to which the dedication relates,

    (c)   enable a dedication previously made under this section to be amended by the persons by whom a dedication could be made, so as to remove or relax any of those restrictions in relation to any of the land to which the dedication relates, and

    (d)   require any dedication under this section, or any amendment of such a dedication by virtue of paragraph (c), to be notified to the appropriate countryside body and to the access authority.

(7)   A dedication under this section is irrevocable and, subject to subsection (4), binds successive owners and occupiers of, and other persons interested in, the land to which it relates, but nothing in this section prevents any land from becoming excepted land.

(8)   A dedication under this section is a local land charge.

Miscellaneous provisions relating to right of access

17   Byelaws

(1)   An access authority may, as respects access land in their area, make byelaws –

    (a)   for the preservation of order,

    (b)   for the prevention of damage to the land or anything on or in it, and

    (c)   for securing that persons exercising the right conferred by section 2(1) so behave themselves as to avoid undue interference with the enjoyment of the land by other persons.

(2)   Byelaws under this section may relate to all the access land in the area of the access authority or only to particular land.

(3)   Before making byelaws under this section, the access authority shall consult –

    (a)   the appropriate countryside body, and

    (b)   any local access forum established for an area to which the byelaws relate.

(4)   Byelaws under this section shall not interfere –

    (a)   with the exercise of any public right of way,

    (b)   with any authority having under any enactment functions relating to the land to which the byelaws apply, or(c) with the running of a telecommunications code system or the exercise of any right conferred by or in accordance with the telecommunications code on the running of any such system

    [(c)   with the provision of an electronic communications code network or the exercise of any right conferred by or in accordance with the electronic communications code on the operator of any such network].

(5)   Sections 236 to 238 of the Local Government Act 1972 (which relate to the procedure for making byelaws, authorise byelaws to impose fines not exceeding level 2 on the standard scale, and provide for the proof of byelaws in legal proceedings) apply to all byelaws under this section whether or not the authority making them is a local authority within the meaning of that Act.

(6) The confirming authority in relation to byelaws made under this section is –

    (a) as respects England, the Secretary of State, and

    (b) as respects Wales, the National Assembly for Wales.

(7) Byelaws under this section relating to any land –

    (a) may not be made unless the land is access land or the access authority are satisfied that it is likely to become access land, and

    (b) may not be confirmed unless the land is access land.

(8) Any access authority having power under this section to make byelaws also have power to enforce byelaws made by them; and any county council or district or parish council may enforce byelaws made under this section by another authority as respects land in the area of the council.

18 Wardens

(1) An access authority or a district council may appoint such number of persons as may appear to the authority making the appointment to be necessary or expedient, to act as wardens as respects access land in their area.

(2) As respects access land in an area for which there is a local access forum, an access authority shall, before they first exercise the power under subsection (1) and thereafter from time to time, consult the local access forum about the exercise of that power.

(3) Wardens may be appointed under subsection (1) for the following purposes –

    (a) to secure compliance with byelaws under section 17 and with the general restrictions in Schedule 2 and any other restrictions imposed under Chapter II,

    (b) to enforce any exclusion imposed under Chapter II,

    (c) in relation to the right conferred by section 2(1), to advise and assist the public and persons interested in access land,

    (d) to perform such other duties (if any) in relation to access land as the authority appointing them may determine.

(4) For the purpose of exercising any function conferred on him by or under this section, a warden appointed under subsection (1) may enter upon any access land.

(5) A warden appointed under subsection (1) shall, if so required, produce evidence of his authority before entering any access land in the exercise of the power conferred by subsection (4), and shall also produce evidence of his authority while he remains on the access land, if so required by any person.

(6) Except as provided by subsection (4), this section does not authorise a warden appointed under subsection (1), on land in which any person other than the authority who appointed him has an interest, to do anything which apart from this section would be actionable at that person's suit by virtue of that interest.

19 Notices indicating boundaries, etc

(1) An access authority may erect and maintain –

(a) notices indicating the boundaries of access land and excepted land, and

(b) notices informing the public of –

(i) the effect of the general restrictions in Schedule 2,

(ii) the exclusion or restriction under Chapter II of access by virtue of section 2(1) to any land, and

(iii) any other matters relating to access land or to access by virtue of section 2(1) which the access authority consider appropriate.

(2) In subsection (1)(b)(ii), the reference to the exclusion or restriction of access by virtue of section 2(1) is to be interpreted in accordance with section 21(2) and (3).

(3) Before erecting a notice on any land under subsection (1) the access authority shall, if reasonably practicable, consult the owner or occupier of the land.

(4) An access authority may also, as respects any access land in their area, defray or contribute towards, or undertake to defray or contribute towards, expenditure incurred or to be incurred in relation to the land by any person in displaying such notices as are mentioned in subsection (1)(a) and (b).

20 Codes of conduct and other information

(1) In relation to England, it shall be the duty of the Countryside Agency to issue, and from time to time revise, a code of conduct for the guidance of persons exercising the right conferred by section 2(1) and of persons interested in access land, and to take such other steps as appear to them expedient for securing –

(a) that the public are informed of the situation and extent of, and means of access to, access land, and

(b) that the public and persons interested in access land are informed of their respective rights and obligations –

(i) under this Part, and

(ii) with regard to public rights of way on, and nature conservation in relation to, access land.

(2) In relation to Wales, it shall be the duty of the Countryside Council for Wales to issue, and from time to time revise, a code of conduct for the guidance of persons exercising the right conferred by section 2(1) and of persons interested in access land, and to take such other steps as appear to them expedient for securing the results mentioned in paragraphs (a) and (b) of subsection (1).

(3) A code of conduct issued by the Countryside Agency or the Countryside Council for Wales may include provisions in pursuance of subsection (1) or (2) and in pursuance of section 86(1) of the National Parks and Access to the Countryside Act 1949.

(4) The powers conferred by subsections (1) and (2) include power to contribute towards expenses incurred by other persons.

CHAPTER II

EXCLUSION OR RESTRICTION OF ACCESS

21 Interpretation of Chapter II

(1) References in this Chapter to the exclusion or restriction of access to any land by virtue of section 2(1) are to be interpreted in accordance with subsections (2) and (3).

(2) A person excludes access by virtue of subsection (1) of section 2 to any land where he excludes the application of that subsection in relation to that land.

(3) A person restricts access by virtue of subsection (1) of section 2 to any land where he provides that the right conferred by that subsection –

(a) is exercisable only along specified routes or ways,
(b) is exercisable only after entering the land at a specified place or places,
(c) is exercisable only by persons who do not take dogs on the land, or
(d) is exercisable only by persons who satisfy any other specified conditions.

(4) In this Chapter, except section 23(1), 'owner', in relation to land which is subject to a farm business tenancy within the meaning of the Agricultural Tenancies Act 1995 or a tenancy to which the Agricultural Holdings Act 1986 applies, means the tenant under that tenancy.

(5) Subject to subsection (6), in this Chapter 'the relevant authority' –

(a) in relation to any land in a National Park, means the National Park authority, and
(b) in relation to any other land, means the appropriate countryside body.

(6) Where –

(a) it appears to the Forestry Commissioners that any land which is dedicated for the purposes of this Part under section 16 consists wholly or predominantly of woodland, and
(b) the Forestry Commissioners give to the body who are apart from this subsection the relevant authority for the purposes of this Chapter in relation to the land a notice stating that the Forestry Commissioners are to be the relevant authority for those purposes as from a date specified in the notice,

the Forestry Commissioners shall as from that date become the relevant authority in relation to that land for those purposes, but subject to subsection (7).

(7) Where it appears to the Forestry Commissioners that any land in relation to which they are by virtue of subsection (6) the relevant authority for the purposes of this Chapter has ceased to consist wholly or predominantly of

woodland, the Forestry Commissioners may, by giving notice to the body who would apart from subsection (6) be the relevant authority, revoke the notice under subsection (6) as from a date specified in the notice under this subsection.

22 Exclusion or restriction at discretion of owner and others

(1) Subject to subsections (2) and (6), an entitled person may, by giving notice to the relevant authority in accordance with regulations under section 32(1)(a), exclude or restrict access by virtue of section 2(1) to any land on one or more days specified in the notice.

(2) The number of days on which any entitled person excludes or restricts under this section access by virtue of section 2(1) to any land must not in any calendar year exceed the relevant maximum.

(3) In this section 'entitled person', in relation to any land, means –

    (a) the owner of the land, and

    (b) any other person having an interest in the land and falling within a prescribed description.

(4) Subject to subsection (5), in this section 'the relevant maximum' means twenty-eight.

(5) If regulations are made under subsection (3)(b), the regulations must provide that, in cases where there are two or more entitled persons having different interests in the land, the relevant maximum in relation to each of them is to be determined in accordance with the regulations, but so that the number of days on which access by virtue of section 2(1) to any land may be excluded or restricted under this section in any calendar year does not exceed twenty-eight.

(6) An entitled person may not under this section exclude or restrict access by virtue of section 2(1) to any land on –

    (a) Christmas Day or Good Friday, or

    (b) any day which is a bank holiday under the Banking and Financial Dealings Act 1971 in England and Wales.

(7) An entitled person may not under this section exclude or restrict access by virtue of section 2(1) to any land –

    (a) on more than four days in any calendar year which are either Saturday or Sunday,

    (b) on any Saturday in the period beginning with 1st June and ending with 11th August in any year,

    (c) on any Sunday in the period beginning with 1st June and ending with 30th September in any year.

(8) Regulations may provide that any exclusion or restriction under subsection (1) of access by virtue of section 2(1) to any land must relate to an area of land the boundaries of which are determined in accordance with the regulations.

23   Restrictions on dogs at discretion of owner

(1)   The owner of any land consisting of moor managed for the breeding and shooting of grouse may, so far as appears to him to be necessary in connection with the management of the land for that purpose, by taking such steps as may be prescribed, provide that, during a specified period, the right conferred by section 2(1) is exercisable only by persons who do not take dogs on the land.

(2)   The owner of any land may, so far as appears to him to be necessary in connection with lambing, by taking such steps as may be prescribed, provide that during a specified period the right conferred by section 2(1) is exercisable only by persons who do not take dogs into any field or enclosure on the land in which there are sheep.

(3)   In subsection (2) 'field or enclosure' means a field or enclosure of not more than 15 hectares.

(4)   As respects any land –

(a)   any period specified under subsection (1) may not be more than five years,

(b)   not more than one period may be specified under subsection (2) in any calendar year, and that period may not be more than six weeks.

(5)   A restriction imposed under subsection (1) or (2) does not prevent a blind person from taking with him a trained guide dog, or a deaf person from taking with him a trained hearing dog.

24   Land management

(1)   The relevant authority may by direction, on an application made by a person interested in any land, exclude or restrict access to that land by virtue of section 2(1) during a specified period, if the authority are satisfied that the exclusion or restriction under this section of access by virtue of section 2(1) to the extent provided by the direction is necessary for the purposes of the management of the land by the applicant.

(2)   The reference in subsection (1) to a specified period includes a reference to –

(a)   a specified period in every calendar year, or

(b)   a period which is to be –

(i)   determined by the applicant in accordance with the direction, and

(ii)   notified by him to the relevant authority in accordance with regulations under section 32(1)(d).

(3)   In determining whether to any extent the exclusion or restriction under this section of access by virtue of section 2(1) during any period is necessary for the purposes of land management, the relevant authority shall have regard to –

(a)   the existence of the right conferred by section 22,

    (b)   the extent to which the applicant has exercised or proposes to exercise that right, and

    (c)   the purposes for which he has exercised or proposes to exercise it.

(4)   Where an application under this section relates to land which is not access land at the time when the application is made, the relevant authority shall not give a direction under this section unless they are satisfied that it is likely that the land will be access land during all or part of the period to which the application relates.

25   Avoidance of risk of fire or of danger to the public

(1)   The relevant authority may by direction exclude or restrict access by virtue of section 2(1) in relation to any land during a specified period if the authority are satisfied –

    (a)   that, by reason of any exceptional conditions of weather or any exceptional change in the condition of the land, the exclusion or restriction under this section of access to the land by virtue of section 2(1) to the extent provided by the direction is necessary for the purpose of fire prevention, or

    (b)   that, by reason of anything done, or proposed to be done, on the land or on adjacent land, the exclusion or restriction under this section of access to the land by virtue of section 2(1) to the extent provided by the direction is necessary for the purpose of avoiding danger to the public.

(2)   The reference in subsection (1) to a specified period includes a reference to –

    (a)   a specified period in every calendar year, and

    (b)   a period which is to be –

        (i)   determined by a specified person in accordance with the direction, and

        (ii)   notified by him to the relevant authority in accordance with regulations under section 32(1)(d).

(3)   The relevant authority may exercise their powers under subsection (1) on the application of any person interested in the land, or without any such application having been made.

(4)   In determining on an application made by a person interested in the land whether the condition in subsection (1)(a) or (b) is satisfied, the relevant authority shall have regard to –

    (a)   the existence of the right conferred by section 22,

    (b)   the extent to which the applicant has exercised or proposes to exercise that right, and

    (c)   the purposes for which he has exercised or proposes to exercise it.

(5) Where an application under this section relates to land which is not access land at the time when the application is made, the relevant authority shall not give a direction under this section unless they are satisfied that it is likely that the land will be access land during all or part of the period to which the application relates.

26 Nature conservation and heritage preservation

(1) The relevant authority may by direction exclude or restrict access by virtue of section 2(1) to any land during any period if they are satisfied that the exclusion or restriction of access by virtue of section 2(1) to the extent provided by the direction is necessary for either of the purposes specified in subsection (3).

(2) A direction under subsection (1) may be expressed to have effect –

   (a) during a period specified in the direction,
   (b) during a specified period in every calendar year, or
   (c) during a period which is to be –

      (i) determined by a specified person in accordance with the direction, and
      (ii) notified by him to the relevant authority in accordance with regulations under section 32(1)(d), or

   (d) indefinitely.

(3) The purposes referred to in subsection (1) are –

   (a) the purpose of conserving flora, fauna or geological or physiographical features of the land in question;
   (b) the purpose of preserving –

      (i) any scheduled monument as defined by section 1(11) of the Ancient Monuments and Archaeological Areas Act 1979, or
      (ii) any other structure, work, site, garden or area which is of historic, architectural, traditional, artistic or archaeological interest.

(4) In considering whether to give a direction under this section, the relevant authority shall have regard to any advice given to them by the relevant advisory body.

(5) Subsection (4) does not apply where the direction is given by the Countryside Council for Wales for the purpose specified in subsection (3)(a) or revokes a direction given by them for that purpose.

(6) In this section 'the relevant advisory body' –

   (a) in relation to a direction which is to be given for the purpose specified in subsection (3)(a) or which revokes a direction given for that purpose, means –

      (i) in the case of land in England, English Nature, and

(ii) in the case of land in Wales in respect of which the Countryside Council for Wales are not the relevant authority, the Countryside Council for Wales, and

(b) in relation to a direction which is to be given for the purpose specified in subsection (3)(b) or which revokes a direction given for that purpose, means –

(i) in the case of land in England, the Historic Buildings and Monuments Commission for England, and
(ii) in the case of land in Wales, the National Assembly for Wales.

27 Directions by relevant authority: general

(1) Before giving a direction under section 24, 25 or 26 in relation to land in an area for which there is a local access forum so as to exclude or restrict access to the land –

(a) indefinitely, or
(b) during a period which exceeds, or may exceed, six months,

the relevant authority shall consult the local access forum.

(2) Any direction under section 24, 25 or 26 may be revoked or varied by a subsequent direction under that provision.

(3) Where a direction given under section 24, 25 or 26 in relation to any land by the relevant authority excludes or restricts access to the land –

(a) indefinitely,
(b) for part of every year or of each of six or more consecutive calendar years, or
(c) for a specified period of more than five years,

the authority shall review the direction not later than the fifth anniversary of the relevant date.

(4) In subsection (3) 'the relevant date', in relation to a direction, means –

(a) the day on which the direction was given, or
(b) where it has already been reviewed, the day on which it was last reviewed.

(5) Before revoking or varying a direction under section 24 or 25 which was given on the application of a person interested in the land to which the direction relates ('the original applicant'), the relevant authority shall –

(a) where the original applicant still holds the interest in the land which he held when he applied for the direction and it is reasonably practicable to consult him, consult the original applicant, and
(b) where the original applicant does not hold that interest, consult any person who holds that interest and with whom consultation is reasonably practicable.

(6)   Before revoking or varying a direction under section 26, the relevant authority shall consult the relevant advisory body as defined by section 26(6), unless the direction falls within section 26(5).

28   Defence or national security

(1)   The Secretary of State may by direction exclude or restrict access by virtue of section 2(1)to any land during any period if he is satisfied that the exclusion or restriction of such access to the extent provided by the direction is necessary for the purposes of defence or national security.

(2)   A direction under subsection (1) may be expressed to have effect –

(a)   during a period specified in the direction,
(b)   during a specified period in every calendar year,
(c)   during a period which is to be –

   (i)   determined in accordance with the direction by a person authorised by the Secretary of State, and
   (ii)   notified by that person to the relevant authority in accordance with regulations under section 32(1)(c), or

(d)   indefinitely.

(3)   Any direction given by the Secretary of State under this section may be revoked or varied by a subsequent direction.

(4)   Where a direction given under this section in relation to any land excludes or restricts access to the land –

(a)   indefinitely,
(b)   for part of every year or of each of six or more consecutive calendar years, or
(c)   for a specified period of more than five years,

the Secretary of State shall review the direction not later than the fifth anniversary of the relevant date.

(5)   In subsection (4) 'the relevant date', in relation to a direction, means –

(a)   the day on which the direction was given, or
(b)   where it has previously been reviewed, the day on which it was last reviewed.

(6)   If in any calendar year the Secretary of State reviews a defence direction, he shall –

(a)   prepare a report on all reviews of defence directions which he has undertaken during that year, and
(b)   lay a copy of the report before each House of Parliament.

(7)   In subsection (6) 'defence direction' means a direction given under this section for the purposes of defence.

29   Reference by relevant advisory body

(1)   Subsections (2) and (3) apply where –

(a)   the relevant advisory body has given advice under section 26(4) or on being consulted under section 27(6), but

(b)   in any respect, the relevant authority decide not to act in accordance with that advice.

(2)   The relevant advisory body may refer the decision –

(a)   in the case of land in England, to the [Secretary of State], or

(b)   in the case of land in Wales, to the National Assembly for Wales.

(3)   On a reference under this section the [Secretary of State] or the National Assembly for Wales may, if he or it thinks fit –

(a)   cancel any direction given by the relevant authority, or

(b)   require the relevant authority to give such direction under section 26 as the [Secretary of State] or, as the case may be, the Assembly, think fit.

(4)   Sections 7 and 8 (and Schedule 3) have effect in relation to a reference under this section as they have effect in relation to an appeal under section 6 . . ..

(5)   In this section –

. . .

'the relevant advisory body' has the same meaning as in section 26, except that it does not include the National Assembly for Wales.

Amendment – SI 2002/794, art 5(1), Schs 1 and 2.

30   Appeal by person interested in land

(1)   Subsections (2) and (3) apply where –

(a)   a person interested in any land (in this section referred to as 'the applicant') –

(i)   has applied for a direction under section 24 or 25, or

(ii)   has made representations on being consulted under section 27(5), but

(b)   in any respect, the relevant authority decide not to act in accordance with the application or the representations.

(2)   The relevant authority shall inform the applicant of their reasons for not acting in accordance with the application or representations.

(3)   The applicant may appeal against the decision –

(a)   in the case of land in England, to the [Secretary of State], or

(b)   in the case of land in Wales, to the National Assembly for Wales.

(4)   On appeal under this section the [Secretary of State] or the National Assembly for Wales may, if he or it thinks fit –

(a)   cancel any direction given by the relevant authority, or

(b) require the relevant authority to give such direction under section 24 or 25 as the [Secretary of State] or, as the case may be, the Assembly, think fit.

(5) Sections 7 and 8 (and Schedule 3) have effect in relation to an appeal under this section as they have effect in relation to an appeal under section 6 . . ..

(6) . . .

Amendment – SI 2002/794, art 5(1), Schs 1 and 2.

31 Exclusion or restriction of access in case of emergency

(1) Regulations may make provision enabling the relevant authority, where the authority are satisfied that an emergency has arisen which makes the exclusion or restriction of access by virtue of section 2(1) necessary for any of the purposes specified in section 24(1), 25(1) or 26(3), by direction to exclude or restrict such access in respect of any land for a period not exceeding three months.

(2) Regulations under this section may provide for any of the preceding provisions of this Chapter to apply in relation to a direction given under the regulations with such modifications as may be prescribed.

32 Regulations relating to exclusion or restriction of access

(1) Regulations may make provision –

(a) as to the giving of notice under section 22(1),
(b) as to the steps to be taken under section 23(1) and (2),
(c) as to the procedure on any application to the relevant authority under section 24 or 25, including the period within which any such application must be made,
(d) as to the giving of notice for the purposes of section 24(2)(b)(ii), 25(2)(b)(ii), 26(2)(c)(ii) or 28(2)(c)(ii),
(e) prescribing the form of any notice or application referred to in paragraphs (a) to (d),
(f) restricting the cases in which a person who is interested in any land only as the holder of rights of common may make an application under section 24 or 25 in respect of the land,
(g) as to requirements to be met by relevant authorities or the Secretary of State in relation to consultation (whether or not required by the preceding provisions of this Chapter),
(h) as to the giving of directions by relevant authorities or the Secretary of State,
(i) as to notification by relevant authorities or the Secretary of State of decisions under this Chapter,
(j) as to steps to be taken by persons interested in land, by relevant authorities, by the bodies specified in section 26(6) or by the Secretary of State for informing the public about the exclusion or restriction under this Chapter of access by virtue of section 2(1), including the display of notices on or near the land to which the exclusion or restriction relates,

(k)   as to the carrying out of reviews by relevant authorities under section 27(3) or by the Secretary of State under section 28(4),

(l)   as to the period within which and manner in which appeals under section 30 are to be brought,

(m)   as to the advertising of such an appeal, and

(n)   as to the manner in which such appeals are to be considered.

(2)   Regulations made under subsection (1)(k) may provide for any of the provisions of this Chapter relating to appeals to apply (with or without modifications) on a review under section 27.

33   Guidance by countryside bodies to National Park authorities

(1)   Subject to subsection (3), the Countryside Agency may issue guidance –

(a)   to National Park authorities in England with respect to the discharge by National Park authorities of their functions under this Chapter, and

(b)   to the Forestry Commissioners with respect to the discharge by the Forestry Commissioners of any functions conferred on them by virtue of section 21(6) in relation to land in England.

(2)   Subject to subsection (3), the Countryside Council for Wales may issue guidance –

(a)   to National Park authorities in Wales with respect to the discharge by National Park authorities of their functions under this Chapter, and

(b)   to the Forestry Commissioners with respect to the discharge by the Forestry Commissioners of any functions conferred on them by virtue of section 21(6) in relation to land in Wales.

(3)   The Countryside Agency or the Countryside Council for Wales may not issue any guidance under this section unless the guidance has been approved –

(a)   in the case of the Countryside Agency, by the Secretary of State, and

(b)   in the case of the Countryside Council for Wales, by the National Assembly for Wales.

(4)   Where the Countryside Agency or the Countryside Council for Wales issue any guidance under this section, they shall arrange for the guidance to be published in such manner as they consider appropriate.

(5)   A National Park authority or the Forestry Commissioners shall have regard to any guidance issued to them under this section.

CHAPTER III

MEANS OF ACCESS

34   Interpretation of Chapter III

In this Chapter –

'access land' does not include any land in relation to which the application of section 2(1) has been excluded under any provision of Chapter II either indefinitely or for a specified period of which at least six months remain unexpired;

'means of access', in relation to land, means –

(a)   any opening in a wall, fence or hedge bounding the land (or part of the land), with or without a gate, stile or other works for regulating passage through the opening,

(b)   any stairs or steps for enabling persons to enter on the land (or part of the land), or

(c)   any bridge, stepping stone or other works for crossing a watercourse, ditch or bog on the land or adjoining the boundary of the land.

35   Agreements with respect to means of access

(1)   Where, in respect of any access land, it appears to the access authority that –

    (a)   the opening-up, improvement or repair of any means of access to the land,

    (b)   the construction of any new means of access to the land,

    (c)   the maintenance of any means of access to the land, or

    (d)   the imposition of restrictions –

        (i)   on the destruction, removal, alteration or stopping-up of any means of access to the land, or

        (ii)   on the doing of any thing whereby the use of any such means of access to the land by the public would be impeded,

is necessary for giving the public reasonable access to that land in exercise of the right conferred by section 2(1), the access authority may enter into an agreement with the owner or occupier of the land as to the carrying out of the works or the imposition of the restrictions.

(2)   An agreement under this section may provide –

    (a)   for the carrying out of works by the owner or occupier or by the access authority, and

    (b)   for the making of payments by the access authority –

        (i)   as a contribution towards, or for the purpose of defraying, costs incurred by the owner or occupier in carrying out any works for which the agreement provides, or

        (ii)   in consideration of the imposition of any restriction.

36 Failure to comply with agreement

(1) If the owner or occupier of any access land fails to carry out within the required time any works which he is required by an agreement under section 35 to carry out, the access authority, after giving not less than twenty-one days' notice of their intention to do so, may take all necessary steps for carrying out those works.

(2) In subsection (1) 'the required time' means the time specified in, or determined in accordance with, the agreement as that within which the works must be carried out or, if there is no such time, means a reasonable time.

(3) If the owner or occupier of any access land fails to observe any restriction which he is required by an agreement under section 35 to observe, the access authority may give him a notice requiring him within a specified period of not less than twenty-one days to carry out such works as may be specified in the notice, for the purpose of remedying the failure to observe the restriction.

(4) A notice under subsection (3) must contain particulars of the right of appeal conferred by section 38.

(5) If the person to whom a notice under subsection (3) is given fails to comply with the notice, the access authority may take all necessary steps for carrying out any works specified in the notice.

(6) Where the access authority carry out any works by virtue of subsection (1), the authority may recover the amount of any expenses reasonably incurred by them in carrying out the works, reduced by their contribution under the agreement, from the person by whom under the agreement the cost (apart from the authority's contribution) of carrying out the works would fall to be borne.

(7) Where the access authority carry out any works by virtue of subsection (5), the authority may recover the amount of any expenses reasonably incurred by them in carrying out the works from the person to whom the notice under subsection (3) was given.

37 Provision of access by access authority in absence of agreement

(1) Where, in respect of any access land –

    (a) it appears to the access authority that –

        (i) the opening-up, improvement or repair of any means of access to the land,

        (ii) the construction of any new means of access to the land, or

        (iii) the maintenance of any means of access to the land,

    is necessary for giving the public reasonable access to that land, or to other access land, in pursuance of the right conferred by section 2(1), and

    (b) the access authority are satisfied that they are unable to conclude on reasonable terms an agreement under section 35with the owner or occupier of the land for the carrying out of the works, the access authority may, subject to subsection (3), give the owner or occupier a notice stating that, after the end of a specified period of not less than twenty-one days, the authority intend to take all necessary steps for carrying out the works specified in the notice for the opening-up, improvement, repair, construction or maintenance of the means of access.

(2) A notice under subsection (1) must contain particulars of the right of appeal conferred by section 38.

(3) Where a notice under subsection (1) is given to any person as the owner or occupier of any land, the access authority shall give a copy of the notice to every other owner or occupier of the land.

(4) An access authority exercising the power conferred by subsection (1) in relation to the provision of a means of access shall have regard to the requirements of efficient management of the land in deciding where the means of access is to be provided.

(5) If, at the end of the period specified in a notice under subsection (1), any of the works specified in the notice have not been carried out, the access authority may take all necessary steps for carrying out those works.

38 Appeals relating to notices

(1) Where a notice under section 36(3) or 37(1) has been given to a person in respect of any land, he or any other owner or occupier of the land may appeal against the notice –

(a) in the case of land in England, to the Secretary of State, and
(b) in the case of land in Wales, to the National Assembly for Wales.

(2) An appeal against a notice under section 36(3) may be brought on any of the following grounds –

(a) that the notice requires the carrying out of any works which are not necessary for remedying a breach of the agreement,
(b) that any of the works have already been carried out, and
(c) that the period specified in the notice as that before the end of which the works must be carried out is too short.

(3) An appeal against a notice under section 37(1) may be brought on any of the following grounds –

(a) that the notice requires the carrying out of any works which are not necessary for giving the public reasonable access to the access land in question,
(b) in the case of works to provide a means of access, that the means of access should be provided elsewhere, or that a different means of access should be provided, and
(c) that any of the works have already been carried out.

(4)   On an appeal under this section, the Secretary of State or the National Assembly for Wales may –

    (a)   confirm the notice with or without modifications, or

    (b)   cancel the notice.

(5)   Sections 7 and 8 (and Schedule 3) have effect in relation to an appeal under this section as they have effect in relation to an appeal under section 6.

(6)   Regulations may make provision as to –

    (a)   the period within which and manner in which appeals under this section are to be brought,

    (b)   the advertising of such an appeal, and

    (c)   the manner in which such appeals are to be considered.

(7)   Where an appeal has been brought under this section against a notice under section 36(3) or 37(1), the access authority may not exercise their powers under section 36(5) or section 37(5) (as the case may be) pending the determination or withdrawal of the appeal.

39   Order to remove obstruction

(1)   Where at any time two or more access notices relating to a means of access have been given to any person within the preceding thirty-six months, a magistrates' court may, on the application of the access authority, order that person –

    (a)   within such time as may be specified in the order, to take such steps as may be so specified to remove any obstruction of that means of access, and

    (b)   not to obstruct that means of access at any time when the right conferred by section 2(1) is exercisable.

(2)   If a person ('the person in default') fails to comply with an order under this section –

    (a)   he is liable on summary conviction to a fine not exceeding level 3 on the standard scale, and

    (b)   the access authority may remove any obstruction of the means of access and recover from the person in default the costs reasonably incurred by them in doing so.

(3)   In this section 'access notice' means a notice under section 36(3) or 37(1) in respect of which the period specified in the notice has expired, other than a notice in respect of which an appeal is pending or which has been cancelled on appeal.

CHAPTER IV

GENERAL

40   Powers of entry for purposes of Part I

(1)   A person who is authorised by the appropriate countryside body to do so may enter any land –

   (a)   for the purpose of surveying it in connection with the preparation of any map under this Part or the review of any map issued under this Part,

   (b)   for the purpose of determining whether any power conferred on the appropriate countryside body by Chapter II should be exercised in relation to the land,

   (c)   for the purpose of ascertaining whether members of the public are being permitted to exercise the right conferred by section 2(1),

   (d)   in connection with an appeal under any provision of this Part, or

   (e)   for the purpose of determining whether to apply to the Secretary of State or the National Assembly for Wales under section 58.

(2)   A person who is authorised by a local highway authority to do so may enter any land –

   (a)   for the purpose of determining whether the local highway authority should enter into an agreement under section 35, give a notice under section 36(1) or (3) or section 37(1) or carry out works under section 36(1) or (5), section 37(5) or section 39(2)(b),

   (b)   for the purpose of ascertaining whether an offence under section 14 or 39 has been or is being committed, or

   (c)   for the purposes of erecting or maintaining notices under section 19(1).

(3)   A person who is authorised by a National Park authority to do so may enter any land –

   (a)   for the purpose of enabling the authority to determine whether to exercise any power under Chapter II of this Act in relation to the land,

   (b)   for the purpose of determining whether members of the public are being permitted to exercise the right conferred by section 2(1),

   (c)   in connection with an appeal under any provision of this Part,

   (d)   for the purpose of determining whether the authority should enter into an agreement under section 35, give a notice under section 36(1) or (3) or section 37(1) or carry out works under section 36(1) or (5), section 37(5) or section 39(2)(b),

   (e)   for the purpose of ascertaining whether an offence under section 14 or 39 has been or is being committed, or

   (f)   for the purposes of erecting or maintaining notices under section 19(1).

(4)   A person who is authorised by the Forestry Commissioners to do so may enter any land –

    (a)   for the purpose of determining whether any power conferred on the Forestry Commissioners by Chapter II should be exercised in relation to the land, or

    (b)   in connection with an appeal under any provision of this Part.

(5)   A person acting in the exercise of a power conferred by this section may –

    (a)   use a vehicle to enter the land;

    (b)   take a constable with him if he reasonably believes he is likely to be obstructed;

    (c)   take with him equipment and materials needed for the purpose for which he is exercising the power of entry;

    (d)   take samples of the land and of anything on it.

(6)   If in the exercise of a power conferred by this section a person enters land which is unoccupied or from which the occupier is temporarily absent, he must on his departure leave it as effectively secured against unauthorised entry as he found it.

(7)   A person authorised under this section to enter upon any land –

    (a)   shall, if so required, produce evidence of his authority before entering, and

    (b)   shall produce such evidence if required to do so at any time while he remains on the land.

(8)   A person shall not under this section demand admission as of right to any occupied land, other than access land, unless –

    (a)   at least twenty-four hours' notice of the intended entry has been given to the occupier, or

    (b)   it is not reasonably practicable to give such notice, or

    (c)   the entry is for the purpose specified in subsection (2)(b) and (3)(e).

(9)   The rights conferred by this section are not exercisable in relation to a dwelling.

(10) A person who intentionally obstructs a person acting in the exercise of his powers under this section is guilty of an offence and liable on summary conviction to a fine not exceeding level 2 on the standard scale.

41   Compensation relating to powers under s 40

(1)   It is the duty of a body by which an authorisation may be given under section 40 to compensate any person who has sustained damage as a result of –

    (a)   the exercise of a power conferred by that section by a person authorised by that body to do so, or

    (b)   the failure of a person so authorised to perform the duty imposed on him by subsection (6) of that section,

except where the damage is attributable to the fault of the person who sustained it.

(2) Any dispute as to a person's entitlement to compensation under this section or as to its amount shall be referred to an arbitrator to be appointed, in default of agreement –

   (a) as respects entry on land in England, by the Secretary of State, and

   (b) as respects entry on land in Wales, by the National Assembly for Wales.

42 References to public places in existing enactments

(1) This section applies to any enactment which –

   (a) is contained in an Act passed before or in the same Session as this Act, and

   (b) relates to things done, or omitted to be done, in public places or places to which the public have access.

(2) Regulations may provide that, in determining for the purposes of any specified enactment to which this section applies whether a place is a public place or a place to which the public have access, the right conferred by section 2(1), or access by virtue of that right, is to be disregarded, either generally or in prescribed cases.

43 Crown application of Part I

(1) This Part binds the Crown.

(2) No contravention by the Crown of any provision of this Part shall make the Crown criminally liable; but the High Court may declare unlawful any act or omission of the Crown which constitutes such a contravention.

(3) The provisions of this Part apply to persons in the public service of the Crown as they apply to other persons.

44 Orders and regulations under Part I

(1) Any power to make an order or regulations which is conferred by this Part on the Secretary of State or the National Assembly for Wales is exercisable by statutory instrument.

(2) Any power to make an order or regulations which is conferred by this Part on the Secretary of State or the National Assembly for Wales includes power –

   (a) to make different provision for different cases, and

   (b) to make such incidental, supplementary, consequential or transitional provision as the person making the order or regulations considers necessary or expedient.

(3) No order under section 3 or regulations under paragraph 3 of Schedule 2 shall be made by the Secretary of State unless a draft has been laid before, and approved by a resolution of, each House of Parliament.

(4) Any statutory instrument containing regulations made by the Secretary of State under any other provision of this Part shall be subject to annulment in pursuance of a resolution of either House of Parliament.

45   Interpretation of Part I

(1)   In this Part, unless a contrary intention appears –

'access authority' has the meaning given by section 1(2);

'access land' has the meaning given by section 1(1);

'the appropriate countryside body' has the meaning given by section 1(2);

'excepted land' has the meaning given by section 1(2);

'Inner London' means the area comprising the inner London boroughs, the City of London, the Inner Temple and the Middle Temple;

'interest', in relation to land, includes any estate in land and any right over land, whether the right is exercisable by virtue of the ownership of an estate or interest in land or by virtue of a licence or agreement, and in particular includes rights of common and sporting rights, and references to a person interested in land shall be construed accordingly;

'livestock' means cattle, sheep, goats, swine, horses or poultry, and for the purposes of this definition 'cattle' means bulls, cows, oxen, heifers or calves, 'horses' include asses and mules, and 'poultry' means domestic fowls, turkeys, geese or ducks;

'local highway authority' has the same meaning as in the Highways Act 1980;

'local or private Act' includes an Act confirming a provisional order;

'mountain' has the meaning given by section 1(2);

'open country' has the meaning given by section 1(2);

'owner', in relation to any land, means, subject to subsection (2), any person, other than a mortgagee not in possession, who, whether in his own right or as trustee for another person, is entitled to receive the rack rent of the land, or, where the land is not let at a rack rent, would be so entitled if it were so let;

'prescribed' means prescribed by regulations;

'registered common land' has the meaning given by section 1(3);

'regulations' means regulations made by the Secretary of State (as respects England) or by the National Assembly for Wales (as respects Wales);

'rights of common' has the same meaning as in the Commons Registration Act 1965;

'telecommunications code' and 'telecommunications code system' have the same meaning as in Schedule 4 to the Telecommunications Act 1984.

(2)   In relation to any land which is subject to a farm business tenancy within the meaning of the Agricultural Tenancies Act 1995 or a tenancy to which the Agricultural Holdings Act 1986 applies, the definition of 'owner' in subsection (1) does not apply where it is excluded by section 2(5) or 21(4) or by paragraph 7(4) of Schedule 2.

(3) For the purposes of this Part, the Broads are to be treated as a National Park and the Broads Authority as a National Park authority.

(4) In subsection (3) 'the Broads' has the same meaning as in the Norfolk and Suffolk Broads Act 1988.

46 Repeal of previous legislation, and amendments relating to Part I

(1) The following provisions (which are superseded by the provisions of this Part) shall cease to have effect –

    (a) in section 193 of the Law of Property Act 1925, subsection (2) (power by deed to declare land subject to that section), and

    (b) sections 61 to 63 of the National Parks and Access to the Countryside Act 1949 (which relate to reviews of access requirements and the preparation of maps).

(2) No access agreement or access order under Part V of the National Parks and Access to the Countryside Act 1949 (access to open country) may be made after the commencement of this section in relation to land which is open country or registered common land for the purposes of this Part.

(3) Schedule 4 (which contains minor and consequential amendments relating to access to the countryside) has effect.

PART II

PUBLIC RIGHTS OF WAY AND ROAD TRAFFIC

. . .

Miscellaneous

. . .

68 Vehicular access across common land etc

(1) This section applies to a way which the owner or occupier (from time to time) of any premises has used as a means of access for vehicles to the premises, if that use of the way –

    (a) was an offence under an enactment applying to the land crossed by the way, but

    (b) would otherwise have been sufficient to create on or after the prescribed date, and to keep in existence, an easement giving a right of way for vehicles.

(2) Regulations may provide, as respects a way to which this section applies, for the creation in accordance with the regulations, on the application of the owner of the premises concerned and on compliance by him with prescribed requirements, of an easement subsisting at law for the benefit of the premises and giving a right of way for vehicles over that way.

(3)   An easement created in accordance with the regulations is subject to any enactment or rule of law which would apply to such an easement granted by the owner of the land.

(4)   The regulations may in particular –

    (a)   require that, where an application is made after the relevant use of the way has ceased, it is to be made within a specified time,

    (b)   specify grounds on which objections may be made and the procedure to apply to the making of objections,

    (c)   require any matter to be referred to and determined by the Lands Tribunal, and make provision as to procedure and costs,

    (d)   make provision as to the payment of any amount by the owner of the premises concerned to any person or into court and as to the time when any payment is to be made,

    (e)   provide for the determination of any such amount,

    (f)   make provision as to the date on which any easement is created,

    (g)   specify any limitation to which the easement is subject,

    (h)   provide for the easement to include any specified right incidental to the right of way,

    (i)   make different provision for different circumstances.

(5)   In this section –

'enactment' includes an enactment in a local or private Act and a byelaw, regulation or other provision having effect under an enactment;

'owner', in relation to any premises, means –

    (a)   a person, other than a mortgagee not in possession, who is for the time being entitled to dispose of the fee simple of the premises, whether in possession or in reversion, or

    (b)   a tenant under a long lease, within the meaning of the Landlord and Tenant Act 1987;

'prescribed' means prescribed by regulations;

'regulations' means regulations made, as respects England, by the Secretary of State and, as respects Wales, by the National Assembly for Wales.

(6)   Regulations under this section shall be made by statutory instrument, and no such regulations shall be made by the Secretary of State unless a draft has been laid before, and approved by a resolution of, each House of Parliament.

SCHEDULES

SCHEDULE 1

EXCEPTED LAND FOR PURPOSES OF PART I

PART I

EXCEPTED LAND

1   Land on which the soil is being, or has at any time within the previous twelve months been, disturbed by any ploughing or drilling undertaken for the purposes of planting or sowing crops or trees.

2   Land covered by buildings or the curtilage of such land.

3   Land within 20 metres of a dwelling.

4   Land used as a park or garden.

5   Land used for the getting of minerals by surface working (including quarrying).

6   Land used for the purposes of a railway (including a light railway) or tramway.

7   Land used for the purposes of a golf course, racecourse or aerodrome.

8   Land which does not fall within any of the preceding paragraphs and is covered by works used for the purposes of a statutory undertaking or a telecommunications code system [an electronic communications code network], or the curtilage of any such land.

9   Land as respects which development which will result in the land becoming land falling within any of paragraphs 2 to 8 is in the course of being carried out.

10   Land within 20 metres of a building which is used for housing livestock, not being a temporary or moveable structure.

11   Land covered by pens in use for the temporary reception or detention of livestock.

12   Land habitually used for the training of racehorses.

13   Land the use of which is regulated by byelaws under section 14 of the Military Lands Act 1892 or section 2 of the Military Lands Act 1900.

Amendment – Communications Act 2003, s 406(1), Sch 17.

PART II

SUPPLEMENTARY PROVISIONS

14   In this Schedule –

'building' includes any structure or erection and any part of a building as so defined, but does not include any fence or wall, or anything which is a means of access as defined by section 34; and for this purpose 'structure' includes any tent, caravan or other temporary or moveable structure;

'development' and 'minerals' have the same meaning as in the Town and Country Planning Act 1990;

'ploughing' and 'drilling' include respectively agricultural or forestry operations similar to ploughing and agricultural or forestry operations similar to drilling;

'statutory undertaker' means –

(a)   a person authorised by any enactment to carry on any railway, light railway, tramway, road transport, water transport, canal, inland navigation, dock, harbour, pier or lighthouse undertaking or any undertaking for the supply of hydraulic power,

(b)   any public gas transporter, within the meaning of Part I of the Gas Act 1986,

(c)   any water or sewerage undertaker,

(d)   any holder of a licence under section 6(1) of the Electricity Act 1989, or

(e)   the Environment Agency, [a universal service provider (within the meaning of the Postal Services Act 2000) in connection with the provision of a universal postal service (within the meaning of that Act)][, the Civil Aviation Authority or a person who holds a licence under Chapter I of Part I of the Transport Act 2000 (to the extent that the person is carrying out activities authorised by the licence)];

'statutory undertaking' means –

(a)   the undertaking of a statutory undertaker [(which, in the case of a universal service provider (within the meaning of the Postal Services Act 2000), means his undertaking so far as relating to the provision of a universal postal service (within the meaning of that Act) [and, in the case of a person who holds a licence under Chapter I of Part I of the Transport Act 2000, means that person's undertaking as licence holder])], or

(b)   an airport to which Part V of the Airports Act 1986 applies.

15   (1) Land is not to be treated as excepted land by reason of any development carried out on the land, if the carrying out of the development requires planning permission under Part III of the Town and Country Planning Act 1990 and that permission has not been granted.

        (2) Sub-paragraph (1) does not apply where the development is treated by section 191(2) of the Town and Country Planning Act 1990 as being lawful for the purposes of that Act.

16 The land which is excepted land by virtue of paragraph 10 does not include –

(a) any means of access, as defined by section 34, or

(b) any way leading to such a means of access,

if the means of access is necessary for giving the public reasonable access to access land.

17 Land which is habitually used for the training of racehorses is not to be treated by virtue of paragraph 11 as excepted land except –

(a) between dawn and midday on any day, and

(b) at any other time when it is in use for that purpose.

Amendment – SI 2001/1149; SI 2001/4050.

Modification – in relation to a public gas transporter: the Utilities Act 2000, s 76(7).

SCHEDULE 2

RESTRICTIONS TO BE OBSERVED BY PERSONS EXERCISING RIGHT OF

ACCESS

General restrictions

1 Section 2(1) does not entitle a person to be on any land if, in or on that land, he –

(a) drives or rides any vehicle other than an invalid carriage as defined by section 20(2) of the Chronically Sick and Disabled Persons Act 1970,

(b) uses a vessel or sailboard on any non-tidal water,

(c) has with him any animal other than a dog,

(d) commits any criminal offence,

(e) lights or tends a fire or does any act which is likely to cause a fire,

(f) intentionally or recklessly takes, kills, injures or disturbs any animal, bird or fish,

(g) intentionally or recklessly takes, damages or destroys any eggs or nests,

(h) feeds any livestock,

(i) bathes in any non-tidal water,

(j) engages in any operations of or connected with hunting, shooting, fishing, trapping, snaring, taking or destroying of animals, birds or fish or has with him any engine, instrument or apparatus used for hunting, shooting, fishing, trapping, snaring, taking or destroying animals, birds or fish,

(k) uses or has with him any metal detector,

(l) intentionally removes, damages or destroys any plant, shrub, tree or root or any part of a plant, shrub, tree or root,

(m) obstructs the flow of any drain or watercourse, or opens, shuts or otherwise interferes with any sluice-gate or other apparatus,

(n) without reasonable excuse, interferes with any fence, barrier or other device designed to prevent accidents to people or to enclose livestock,

(o)   neglects to shut any gate or to fasten it where any means of doing so is provided, except where it is reasonable to assume that a gate is intended to be left open,

(p)   affixes or writes any advertisement, bill, placard or notice,

(q)   in relation to any lawful activity which persons are engaging in or are about to engage in on that or adjoining land, does anything which is intended by him to have the effect –

    (i)   of intimidating those persons so as to deter them or any of them from engaging in that activity,

    (ii)   of obstructing that activity, or

    (iii) of disrupting that activity,

(r)   without reasonable excuse, does anything which (whether or not intended by him to have the effect mentioned in paragraph (q)) disturbs, annoys or obstructs any persons engaged in a lawful activity on the land,

(s)   engages in any organised games, or in camping, hang-gliding or para-gliding, or

(t)   engages in any activity which is organised or undertaken (whether by him or another) for any commercial purpose.

2   (1) In paragraph 1(k), 'metal detector' means any device designed or adapted for detecting or locating any metal or mineral in the ground.

    (2) For the purposes of paragraph 1(q) and (r), activity on any occasion on the part of a person or persons on land is 'lawful' if he or they may engage in the activity on the land on that occasion without committing an offence or trespassing on the land.

3   Regulations may amend paragraphs 1 and 2.

4   During the period beginning with 1st March and ending with 31st July in each year, section 2(1) does not entitle a person to be on any land if he takes, or allows to enter or remain, any dog which is not on a short lead.

5   Whatever the time of year, section 2(1) does not entitle a person to be on any land if he takes, or allows to enter or remain, any dog which is not on a short lead and which is in the vicinity of livestock.

6   In paragraphs 4 and 5, 'short lead' means a lead of fixed length and of not more than two metres.

Removal or relaxation of restrictions

7   (1) The relevant authority may by direction, with the consent of the owner of any land, remove or relax any of the restrictions imposed by paragraphs 1, 4 and 5 in relation to that land, either indefinitely or during a specified period.

    (2) In sub-paragraph (1), the reference to a specified period includes references –

(a) to a specified period in every calendar year, or

(b) to a period which is to be determined by the owner of the land in accordance with the direction and notified by him to the relevant authority in accordance with regulations.

(3) Regulations may make provision as to –

(a) the giving or revocation of directions under this paragraph,

(b) the variation of any direction given under this paragraph by a subsequent direction so given,

(c) the giving or revocation of consent for the purposes of sub-paragraph (1), and

(d) the steps to be taken by the relevant authority or the owner for informing the public about any direction under this paragraph or its revocation.

(4) In this paragraph –

'the relevant authority' has the meaning given by section 21;

'owner', in relation to any land which is subject to a farm business tenancy within the meaning of the Agricultural Tenancies Act 1995 or a tenancy to which the Agricultural Holdings Act 1986 applies, means the tenant under that tenancy.

Dedicated land

8   In relation to land to which a dedication under section 16 relates (whether or not it would be access land apart from the dedication), the provisions of this Schedule have effect subject to the terms of the dedication.

SCHEDULE 3

DELEGATION OF APPELLATE FUNCTIONS

Interpretation

1   In this Schedule –

'appointed person' means a person appointed under section 8(1)(a);

'the appointing authority' means –

(a) the Secretary of State, in relation to an appointment made by him, or

(b) the National Assembly for Wales, in relation to an appointment made by it;

'appointment', in the case of any appointed person, means appointment under section 8(1)(a).

Appointments

2   An appointment under section 8(1)(a) must be in writing and –

(a)   may relate to any particular appeal or matter specified in the appointment or to appeals or matters of a description so specified,

(b)   may provide for any function to which it relates to be exercisable by the appointed person either unconditionally or subject to the fulfilment of such conditions as may be specified in the appointment, and

(c)   may, by notice in writing given to the appointed person, be revoked at any time by the appointing authority in respect of any appeal or matter which has not been determined by the appointed person before that time.

Powers of appointed person

3   Subject to the provisions of this Schedule, an appointed person shall, in relation to any appeal or matter to which his appointment relates, have the same powers and duties as the appointing authority, other than –

(a)   any function of making regulations;

(b)   any function of holding an inquiry or other hearing or of causing an inquiry or other hearing to be held; or

(c)   any function of appointing a person for the purpose –

   (i)   of enabling persons to appear before and be heard by the person so appointed; or

   (ii)   of referring any question or matter to that person.

Holding of local inquiries and other hearings by appointed persons

4   (1) If either of the parties to an appeal or matter expresses a wish to appear before and be heard by the appointed person, the appointed person shall give both of them an opportunity of appearing and being heard.

(2) Whether or not a party to an appeal or matter has asked for an opportunity to appear and be heard, the appointed person –

   (a)   may hold a local inquiry or other hearing in connection with the appeal or matter, and

   (b)   shall, if the appointing authority so directs, hold a local inquiry in connection with the appeal or matter.

(3) Where an appointed person holds a local inquiry or other hearing by virtue of this Schedule, an assessor may be appointed by the appointing authority to sit with the appointed person at the inquiry or hearing and advise him on any matters arising, notwithstanding that the appointed person is to determine the appeal or matter.

(4) Subject to paragraph 5, the costs of a local inquiry held under this Schedule shall be defrayed by the appointing authority.

Local inquiries under this Schedule: evidence and costs

5   Subsections (2) to (5) of section 250 of the Local Government Act 1972 (local inquiries: evidence and costs) shall apply to local inquiries or other hearings held under this Schedule by an appointed person as they apply to inquiries caused to be held under that section by a Minister, but as if –

(a)   in subsection (2) (evidence) the reference to the person appointed to hold the inquiry were a reference to the appointed person,

(b)   in subsection (4) (recovery of costs of holding the inquiry) –

   (i)   references to the Minister causing the inquiry to be held were references to the appointing authority, and

   (ii)   references to a local authority included references to the appropriate countryside body, and

(c)   in subsection (5) (orders as to the costs of the parties) the reference to the Minister causing the inquiry to be held were a reference to the appointed person or the appointing authority.

Revocation of appointments and making of new appointments

6   (1) Where under paragraph 2(c) the appointment of the appointed person is revoked in respect of any appeal or matter, the appointing authority shall, unless he proposes to determine the appeal or matter himself, appoint another person under section 8(1)(a) to determine the appeal or matter instead.

   (2) Where such a new appointment is made, the consideration of the appeal or matter, or any hearing in connection with it, shall be begun afresh.

   (3) Nothing in sub-paragraph (2) shall require any person to be given an opportunity of making fresh representations or modifying or withdrawing any representations already made.

Certain acts and omissions of appointed person to be treated as those of appointing authority

7   (1) Anything done or omitted to be done by an appointed person in, or in connection with, the exercise or purported exercise of any function to which the appointment relates shall be treated for all purposes as done or omitted to be done by the appointing authority.

   (2) Sub-paragraph (1) does not apply –

   (a)   for the purposes of so much of any contract made between the appointing authority and the appointed person as relates to the exercise of the function, or

   (b)   for the purposes of any criminal proceedings brought in respect of anything done or omitted to be done as mentioned in that sub-paragraph.

SCHEDULE 4

MINOR AND CONSEQUENTIAL AMENDMENTS RELATING TO PART I

Law of Property Act 1925 (c 20)

1   In section 193(1) of the Law of Property Act 1925 (rights of public over commons and waste lands), in paragraph (b) of the proviso, after 'injuriously affected,' there is inserted 'for conserving flora, fauna or geological or physiographical features of the land,'.

Forestry Act 1967 (c 10)

2   In section 9 of the Forestry Act 1967 (requirement of licence for felling), in the definition of 'public open space' in subsection (6), after '1949' there is inserted 'or Part I of the Countryside and Rights of Way Act 2000)'.

Agriculture Act 1967 (c 22)

3   In section 52 of the Agriculture Act 1967 (control of afforestation), in the definition of 'public open space' in subsection (15), after '1949' there is inserted 'or Part I of the Countryside and Rights of Way Act 2000)'.

Countryside Act 1968 (c 41)

4   In section 2(6) of the Countryside Act 1968 (Countryside Agency and Countryside Council for Wales to make recommendations to public bodies in relation to byelaws) for 'and the Act of 1949' there is substituted ', the Act of 1949 and Part I of the Countryside and Rights of Way Act 2000'.

Local Government Act 1974 (c 7)

5   In section 9 of the Local Government Act 1974 (grants and loans by Countryside Agency and Countryside Council for Wales), for 'or the National Parks and Access to the Countryside Act 1949' there is substituted ', the National Parks and Access to the Countryside Act 1949 or the Countryside and Rights of Way Act 2000'.

Wildlife and Countryside Act 1981 (c 69)

6   In paragraph 13(1) of Schedule 13 to the Wildlife and Countryside Act 1981 (Countryside Agency's annual report on the discharge of their functions) after '1968 Act' there is inserted ', the Countryside and Rights of Way Act 2000'.

COMMONS REGISTRATION (GENERAL) REGULATIONS 1966

SI 1966 No 1471

PART I

PRELIMINARY

1 Title and commencement

These Regulations may be cited as the Commons Registration (General) Regulations 1966 and shall come into operation on 2nd January 1967.

2 Interpretation

(1) The Interpretation Act 1889 applies for the interpretation of these Regulations as it applies for the interpretation of an Act of Parliament.

(2) In these Regulations, unless the context otherwise requires –

'the Act' means the Commons Registration Act 1965;

'charity' bears the meaning assigned to that expression in section 45 of the Charities Act 1960, and 'charitable purposes' and 'charity trustees' bear the meanings assigned to those expressions in section 46 of that Act;

'concerned authority', in relation to a registration, means a local authority (other than the registration authority) in whose area any part of the land affected by the registration lies;

'Form' means one of the forms in Schedule 1 to these Regulations, or a form to substantially the same effect;

'Model Entry' means one of the specimen entries provided as examples in Part 1 of Schedule 2 to these Regulations, and 'Standard Entry' one of the specimen entries in Part 2 of that Schedule, or an entry to substantially the same effect;

'parcel of land', in relation to a search under Part VI of these Regulations, means a piece of land in separate occupation or separately rated at the time of the requisition for search; and for the purpose of this definition any land which is neither occupied nor rated shall be deemed to be occupied by the person who receives the rackrent therefor, whether on his own account or as agent or trustee for any other person, or who would so receive it if the land were let at a rackrent;

'provisional registration' means a registration under section 4 of the Act which has not become final;

'register map' means any map, other than a supplemental map, which, by virtue of any regulation made under the Act, for the time being forms part of a register;

'register unit' bears the meaning assigned to that expression in regulation 10 below;

'registration area' means the land in relation to which a local authority is the registration authority;

'supplemental map' bears the meaning assigned to that expression in regulation 20 below.

(3) A requirement or permission to publish a document in any area is a requirement or permission to cause it to be published in a newspaper circulating in that area, with, in the case of a requirement or permission to publish more than once, an interval of at least seven days between each publication.

(4) A requirement to display a document or copies thereof is a requirement to treat it, for the purposes of section 287 of the Local Government Act 1933 (public notices), as if it were a public notice within that section.

(5) Where the day or the last day on which anything is required or permitted by or in pursuance of these regulations to be done is a Sunday, Christmas Day, Good Friday, bank holiday or a day appointed for public thanksgiving or mourning, the requirement or permission shall be deemed to relate to the first day thereafter which is not one of the days before-mentioned.

3   Official stamp of registration authority

(1) Every registration authority shall have an official stamp for the purposes of the Act, as follows:–

COMMONS REGISTRATION ACT 1965

(Name of registration authority)

REGISTRATION AUTHORITY

(Date)

(2) A requirement upon a registration authority to stamp any document is a requirement to cause an impression of the said official stamp to be affixed to it, and that the impression shall bear the date mentioned in the requirement or (where no date is mentioned) the date when it was affixed.

(3) An indication in any form in Schedule 1 to these Regulations that the form shall bear the official stamp of a registration authority is a requirement upon the authority to stamp it.

PART II

THE REGISTERS AND PROVISIONAL REGISTRATION

4 The registers

(1) Every register, whether of common land or of town or village greens, shall consist of –

    (a) a general part,

    (b) a register map,

    (c) as many register units as there are registrations of land in the register, and

    (d) such supplemental maps (if any) as may be necessary.

(2) The general part of each register shall be in Form 1, and shall contain –

    (a) particulars of any agreement under section 2 of the Act to which the registration authority is a party;

    (b) particulars of any land situated in the area of the registration authority to which, by virtue of section 11 of the Act or of an order made thereunder, the registration provisions of the Act do not apply;

    (c) particulars of any transfer, to or from the registration authority, of responsibility for maintaining any register or register unit, otherwise than under section 2 of the Act;

    (d) such other information as may by any regulation made under the Act be required or authorized to be entered therein.

(3) Model Entries 1, 2 and 3 are provided for general guidance in complying with sub-paragraphs (a), (b) and (c) respectively of paragraph (2) above.

(4) The register map to be prepared under these Regulations shall be a provisional register map and shall be prepared in accordance with Part III thereof.

(5) The register units shall be prepared in accordance with regulation 10 below, and each register unit shall consist of three sections, called the land section, the rights section and the ownership section.

(6) The land section of each register unit shall be in Form 2, and shall contain the registrations of the common land, or of the town or village green, as the case may be, comprised therein, with a reference to the register map, and such other information as may by any regulation made under the Act be required or authorized to be entered therein.

(7) The rights section of each register unit shall be in Form 3, and shall contain the registrations of the rights of common registered as exercisable over the land comprised in the land section of the register unit, or any part thereof, particulars of the persons on whose applications the rights were registered and the capacities in which they applied, descriptions of the land (if any) to

which the rights are attached, and such other information as may by any regulation made under the Act be required or authorized to be entered therein.

(8) The ownership section of each register unit shall be in Form 4, and shall contain the registration of every person registered as owner of any part of the land comprised in the register unit, and such other information as may by any regulation made under the Act be required or authorized to be entered therein.

(9) Supplemental maps, where necessary, shall be prepared in accordance with Part III of these Regulations.

(10) Every register shall be bound, or otherwise held together and protected, in such manner as the Minister may approve.

5   Registration periods

(1) There shall be two periods during which applications for registration may be made, called the first registration period and the second registration period.

(2) The first registration period shall begin on 2nd January 1967 and end on 30th June 1968, and the second shall begin on 1st July 1968 and end on 2nd January 1970.

6   Notice of intention to make application

(1) Any person may, during the first registration period, give a registration authority notice in Form 5 of his intention to apply to the authority for registration during the second registration period, and the authority shall send him a written acknowledgment for that notice, and shall retain it until after the end of the second registration period.

(2) Form 6, if used for the purpose of an acknowledgment under this regulation, shall be sufficient.

[7   Applications in special cases]

[(1) Where a right of common is attached to any land, and is comprised in a tenancy of the land, an application for the registration of that right may be made by the landlord, the tenant, or both of them jointly.

(2) Where a right of common belongs to an ecclesiastical benefice of the Church of England which is vacant an application for the registration of that right may be made by the Church Commissioners.

(3) Where any land registered under the Act belongs to an ecclesiastical benefice of the Church of England which is vacant an application for the registration of a claim to the ownership of that land may be made by the Church Commissioners.

(4) The foregoing provisions of this regulation do not affect the right of any person entitled, apart from those provisions, to make any application under the Act.]

Amendment – SI 1968/658.

8 Applications, declarations and fees

(1) An application for registration must be –

   (a) in Form 7, 8, 9 or 10 as appropriate;
   (b) signed by [or on behalf of] every applicant who is an individual, and by the secretary or some other duly authorized officer of every applicant which is a body corporate or unincorporate; and
   (c) supported by a statutory declaration made by [every applicant].

(2) Every application for registration made during the second registration period must be accompanied by a fee of five pounds, unless either –

   (a) during the first registration period the applicant gave the registration authority notice in Form 5 of his intention to make that application; or
   (b) the application is for the registration of land as common land or as a town or village green, and the land did not become so registrable until after 30th April 1968; or
   (c) the application is for the registration of a right of common and the right did not become registrable until after 30th April 1968; or
   (d) the application is for the registration of a claim to ownership and the land to which it relates was not registered until after 30th April 1968.

[(3) An application for the registration of a right of common, or of a claim to the ownership of any land, made by a person who is not the owner of the right or, as the case may be, of the land, shall, unless that person is entitled by virtue of any provision of regulation 7 above to make the application, be supported by such further evidence (if any) of his right to make it as, after considering the application and the declaration in support, the registration authority may reasonably require.]

Amendment – SI 1968/658.

9 Disposal of applications

(1) On receiving an application for registration, a registration authority shall allot a distinguishing number to it, and shall mark the application form with that number. The number so allotted shall be from a single series, whatever the type of application.

(2) . . .

(3) The registration authority shall send to the applicant for registration a receipt for his application containing a statement of the number allotted thereto; and Form 6, if used for that purpose, shall be sufficient.

(4) Where a registration authority rejects an application for registration, it shall so inform the applicant in writing, giving the reasons for the rejection.

(5)   Where an application is made for the registration of a right of common attached to any land, but the right has already been registered in such manner that, if the application were acceded to, no conflict would arise between the two registrations, the registration authority shall not register the right again but (unless it determines to reject the application) shall note the application in the register.

(6)   Where a registration authority accepts an application for registration it shall make a registration in respect thereof, or as the case may require, shall note the application, in the appropriate register in accordance with regulation 10 below, and shall inform the applicant of the disposal of the application, using Form 11, 12 or 13, as appropriate, with such omissions and adaptations as may be necessary, and shall file the application form and any plan thereto which is not required for the purposes of regulation 20 below (supplemental maps).

(7)   References in this regulation to 'the applicant' shall, where two or more persons are concerned together in an application, be construed as references to that one of them whose name appears first in the application form.

Amendment – SI 1994/2567.

10   Method of registration

(1)   A registration authority shall, in making any registration, or in noting an application in a register pursuant either to section 4(4) of the Act or to regulation 9(5) above, follow as closely as possible such of the Model Entries 4 to 12 as may be applicable, with such variations and adaptations as the circumstances may require, and shall mark every registration as provisional.

(2)   The registration authority shall, when registering any land, enter the particulars on a fresh register sheet in Form 2, and shall place register sheets in Forms 3 and 4 immediately below that sheet in its place on the register.

(3)   The register sheets referred to in paragraphs (2) above and (6) below shall constitute a register unit, and shall be kept on the register in sequence with other register units.

(4)   Where a registration of land falls to be made in pursuance of an application which relates to two or more pieces of land, the registration authority may, if it thinks fit, prepare two or more register units, each comprising one or more of those pieces of land, and there shall then be deemed to be a separate registration in respect of the land comprised in each such unit; and in this paragraph 'piece of land' means an area of land comprised, with other land, in an application, and having no common boundary with any of that other land.

(5)   The registration authority shall allot a distinguishing number to each register unit from a separate series for each register. Every register unit number for the Register of Common Land shall bear the prefix CL, and every such number for the Register of Town or Village Greens shall bear the prefix VG.

(6)   The registration authority shall from time to time as necessary add fresh register sheets to a register unit, and every sheet forming part of a register unit shall be marked with the number of that unit.

(7)   Where a right of common affecting any minerals is registered, there shall be included in, or, as the case may require, added to, the registration of the land over which the right is exercised an entry in accordance with Standard Entry 1.

(8)   Every entry relating to any land, to rights thereover or to ownership thereof, which is required or authorized by the Act or any regulation made thereunder to be made in any section of a register shall be made in the appropriate section of the register unit relating to that land, and no entry forming part of a registration or of an amendment made pursuant to section 13 of the Act shall be made in the general part of a register or in any space on a register sheet headed 'Notes'.

11   Information to public about registrations

(1)   Not later than four weeks after the date of any registration the registration authority shall send a copy thereof to every concerned authority.

(2)   Where a registration is of land, or, being of rights or ownership, has necessitated the preparation of a supplemental map or the insertion of fresh particulars on the provisional register map, every copy of the registration sent out under this regulation shall be accompanied by a plan showing the relevant particulars.

(3)   Every authority to whom such a copy or plan is sent under this regulation shall keep it available for public inspection at all reasonable times.

12   Conflicting registrations

(1)   A registration authority shall, on making any registration (in this regulation referred to as the new registration) ascertain whether the new registration conflicts with any other registration in its registers (in this regulation referred to as the old registration) and, where it appears to the authority to do so, the following provisions of this regulation shall apply.

(2)   After making the new registration the registration authority shall add to each registration a note about the conflict in accordance with Standard Entry 2.

(3)   The registration authority shall, where the new registration was made on the application of any person, give that person notice of the conflict by means of Form 11, 12 or 13, as appropriate, and shall give the person (if any) on whose application the old registration was made, and any person whose application is noted (whether under section 4(4) of the Act or under regulation 9(5) above) notice thereof in Form 14.

(4)   Every copy of the entry of the new registration prepared in accordance with regulation 11 above shall include the note added under paragraph (2) above, and where regulation 14 below applies, the note added under that regulation.

(5)   The registration authority shall prepare fresh copies of the entry of the old registration, including the note added under paragraph (2) above, and, where regulation 14 below applies, the note added under that regulation, and shall

send one such copy, marked 'Replacement Copy', to every concerned authority.

(6)   Every authority receiving a replacement copy under paragraph (5) above shall destroy any earlier copy of the old registration in its possession and shall keep the replacement copy available for public inspection at all reasonable times.

(7)   A registration authority may, if it thinks fit, cancel or modify a registration to which this regulation applies if either –

(a)   the person (if any) on whose application it was made, or any person whose application is noted (whether under section 4(4) of the Act or under regulation 9(5) above) so requests, and the persons, or, as the case may be, the other persons (if any) whose applications have been noted under regulation 9(5) above consent in writing, or

(b)   the registration was made otherwise than on the application of any person;

and, where the authority cancels any registration under this paragraph, it shall also cancel any note under paragraph (2) above.

(8)   Where the registration of any land as common land or as a town or village green is cancelled under this regulation the registration authority shall also cancel the registration of any person as the owner thereof.

Amendment – SI 1994/256.

14   Double registration of land

(1)   Where any land is registered both as common land and as a town or village green, entries relating to that land of the classes mentioned in paragraph (2) below made in one register shall be deemed also to be made in the other, adapted, where applicable, as in paragraph 4(b) below, and the registration authority shall note the land, rights and ownership section of each register as indicated in Standard Entry 3.

(2)   The entries referred to in paragraph (1) above are –

(a)   in the land section, an entry under regulation 10(7) (as to inclusion of minerals);

(b)   in the rights and ownership sections, every entry.

(3)   The cancellation in one register, under regulation 12(8) above, of the registration of any person as owner of the land consequent upon the cancellation of the registration of the land in that register shall not affect the registration of the ownership of that person deemed, under this regulation, to have been made in the other register.

(4)   Where the registration in one register of any land registered in both registers is cancelled ... the registration authority shall cancel in each register the note made under paragraph (1) above, and shall transfer from the register wherein the registration of that land has been cancelled to the other register every entry deemed, under this regulation, to have been made therein, in the following manner:–

(a) every entry shall be allotted a fresh number and shall be dated as of the date when so transferred, but in the left-hand column of the register sheet, below such number and date, shall appear '(Formerly No .. .. dated .... in Register Unit No ......)';

(b) references to land in column 4 of the rights and ownership sections of the original register containing expressions valid only in relation to that register shall be adapted as necessary; and

(c) the register map shall be amended as necessary.

Amendment – SI 1968/989.

15 Interpretation of regulations 5 to 14

In regulations 5 to 14 above 'registration' means registration under section 4 of the Act and 'registered' shall be construed accordingly.

PART III

MAPS

16 Provisional register map

(1) Every registration authority shall prepare and keep up to date a provisional register map for each of its registers.

(2) Every such map shall be based on the ordnance map and shall be on a scale of not less, or not substantially less, than six inches to one mile, but where the registration authority considers it expedient to show any particulars on a larger scale, it may insert an inset map for that purpose.

(3) A provisional register map may consist of one sheet or of more than one, and further sheets may be added from time to time as necessary.

(4) Where such a map consists of more than one sheet, each sheet shall bear a distinguishing number, and the sheets shall be bound together bookwise, but so that sheets can be added or removed without damage.

(5) Every provisional register map shall show:–

(a) by black lines verged yellow inside the boundary, and the word EXEMPTED, the boundaries of any land situated in the area of the registration authority to which, by virtue of an order under section 11 of the Act, the provisions of sections 1 to 10 thereof do not apply;

(b) by black lines verged green inside the boundary, and the appropriate register unit number, the boundaries of the land comprised in each register unit;

(c) by red line suitably lettered, or by lettering alone, the limits of any land over which a registered right of common is exercisable, or to which a registration of ownership applies, so far as those limits do not coincide with the boundaries of the land comprised in a register unit, and cannot conveniently be described by reference to any feature appearing on the said map;

(d) by black hatching, and if necessary by lettering as well, land which has been removed from the register under section 13 of the Act [or by virtue of the Common Land (Rectification of Registers) Act 1989], or of which the registration has been cancelled;

(e) by black interrupted lines, any boundaries of the registration area falling within the said map;

(f) by such other colours and symbols as the registration authority may think fit, other particulars mentioned in the general part of the register, or in any registration (not being particulars of land to which rights of common are attached), which it is necessary or convenient to show on the said map.

(6) There shall be kept annexed to every provisional register map a table headed 'Key to Colouring and Symbols' containing a description or representation of every colour or symbol used in the said map (except such of those used under paragraph (5)(f) above as are not of general application) with a statement of the meaning of each such colour or symbol.

17 Overlays

(1) Where it appears to a registration authority that the inclusion on one surface of all the particulars required to be shown on a provisional register map or any sheet thereof would be impracticable or confusing, the authority may prepare one or more transparent overlays for the map or sheet, and may show thereon, instead of on the map or sheet itself, the particulars, or some of the particulars, required to be shown by virtue of sub-paragraphs (c), (d) and (f) of regulation 16(5) above.

(2) Every such overlay shall be fastened to the original map or sheet so that the details thereon coincide with those on the original, but so that it may be lifted away to enable either the original alone, or the original and any other overlay fastened thereto, to be inspected.

(3) Every overlay prepared under this regulation shall form part of the provisional register map.

18 Fresh editions

A registration authority may, whenever it deems it expedient to do so, prepare a fresh edition of a provisional register map or of any sheet thereof, showing only particulars of subsisting entries in the register. A fresh edition of a sheet forming part of a provisional register map shall bear the same number as the sheet it is to replace.

19 Indorsement

Every provisional register map consisting of one sheet, and every sheet of such a map consisting of more than one sheet, shall be indorsed as follows:–

'Provisional Register Map of (Common Land) (Town or Village Greens). (Sheet No ......). This is the .... edition of this (map) (sheet)' and shall be stamped by, and signed on behalf of, the registration authority, and shall then form part of the register and (in the case of a fresh edition) the map or sheet which is replaced shall be marked on its face 'This (map) (sheet) was replaced by a fresh edition on (date)', but shall not cease to be part of the register.

20 Supplemental maps

(1) Where a right of common attached to any land falls to be registered, and that land or any part thereof is described in the application for registration by means of a plan, the registration authority shall describe that land or part in the register by means of a map to be called a supplemental map in accordance with this regulation.

(2) The registration authority may adopt as the supplemental map the plan referred to in paragraph (1) above, or may itself prepare a map showing the necessary particulars; and where the authority so adopts a plan it shall not mark it otherwise than as mentioned in paragraph (4) below.

(3) The land to be described by means of a supplemental map (not being an adopted plan) shall be coloured, tinted, verged or hatched thereon in such manner as may seem to the registration authority most convenient for identifying it, and the means of identification used in any supplemental map shall be referred to in column 5 of the rights section of the register, as in the following example:–

'The land at &c as shown verged red within the boundary on the supplemental map bearing the number of this registration.'

(4) The supplemental map shall be stamped by the registration authority as of the date of the entry of registration, and shall be indorsed as follows:–

'Supplemental map referred to in column 5 of entry No ..... in the rights section of register unit No ..... in the Register of (Common Land) (Town or Village Greens)'

and shall then form part of the register.

(5) Supplemental maps shall be kept separately for each register, in register unit order, and within that order in entry number order.

PART IV

OTHER ENTRIES IN THE REGISTERS

21 Registration under Land Registration Acts 1925 and 1936

Where any land is registered under the Act, and the registration authority is notified by the Chief Land Registrar that the land has been registered under the Land Registration Acts 1925 and 1936, then –

(a) if the ownership of the land has not been registered under the Act, the authority shall note the ownership section of the register in accordance with Standard Entry 4;

(b) if the ownership of the land has been so registered, the authority shall, after deleting the registration of the ownership pursuant to section 12(b) of the Act, note the ownership section of the register in accordance with Standard Entry 5.

22   Matters affecting the public

(1) Where any of the matters to which this regulation applies affects land registered under the Act, the registration authority may enter a note thereof in the land section of the register notwithstanding that no application in that behalf has been made, and, where it has not done so, it shall do so upon application made in accordance with the following provisions of this regulation.

(2) This regulation applies to the following matters:–

   (a) schemes under Part I of the Commons Act 1899 or under the Metropolitan Commons Acts 1866 to 1898;
   (b) local Acts regulating the land;
   (c) Acts confirming provisional orders made under the Commons Act 1876;
   (d) limitations and conditions imposed under proviso (b) to section 193(1) of the Law of Property Act 1925.

(3) Applications under this regulation must be in writing and may be made by any local authority in whose area any part of the land lies, by any person charged by law with the management or regulation of the land or (in the case of the said limitations and conditions) by –

   (a) the owner of any part of the land;
   (b) any person appearing from the register to be interested in a right of common registered as exercisable thereover; or
   (c) where any part of the land, or any such right, belongs to an ecclesiastical benefice of the Church of England which is vacant, by the Church Commissioners.

(4) Any note entered in a register under this regulation shall be in accordance with Model Entry 13 or 14 as applicable, and, where the entry is made pursuant to an application, the registration authority shall send the applicant a copy of the entry.

23   Charitable interests

Where any land registered under the Act is held for charitable purposes, the registration authority shall, on the application in writing of the owner or the charity trustees, enter a note to that effect in the land section of the register, in accordance with Model Entry 15, and shall send the applicant a copy of the entry.

Amendment – SI 1990/311.

24 Private rights and interests

(1) Where any land is registered under the Act, the registration authority shall, upon application made in accordance with the following provisions of this regulation, enter a note in the land section of the register of the existence, in relation to that land, of a claim to any right or interest to which this regulation applies, unless it appears to the authority that the right or interest is of a trivial, obvious or transitory nature, or that an entry relating to it would be likely to cause confusion or inconvenience or unlikely to add substantially to the information obtainable from an inspection of the land.

(2) This regulation applies to the following rights and interests:–

   (a) easements;
   (b) profits à prendre other than rights of common;
   (c) franchises;
   (d) rights and interests of the lord of the manor (in that capacity) other than the ownership of the land;
   (e) where the ownership of any minerals in or under the land is severed from the ownership of the surface, the ownership of those minerals and all rights incident thereto;
   (f) rights of the lessee or licensee under any mineral lease or licence;
   (g) rights acquired by statutory undertakers for the purposes of their undertakings.

(3) Every application under this regulation must be in Form 16 and be made by the person claiming to be entitled to the right or interest, or, where the right or interest belongs to an ecclesiastical benefice of the Church of England which is vacant, by the Church Commissioners.

(4) Where a registration authority accepts an application under this regulation, it shall make a note in the register in accordance with Model Entries 16 to 19 as applicable, and shall send written notice to the applicant of the making of the note together with a copy of the note as entered.

(5) No marking shall be made on the register map or any supplemental map in connexion with any note under this regulation.

(6) Where a registration authority rejects an application under this regulation it shall so inform the applicant in writing, giving the reasons for the rejection.

25 Cancellation of certain entries

A registration authority may cancel an entry under regulation 22, 23 or 24 above if it is satisfied on reasonable grounds that the matter to which the entry relates is no longer subsisting.

26 New addresses

(1) Any person to whom this regulation applies, having changed his address, may apply in writing to the registration authority to note the new address on the

register, and the registration authority shall note the appropriate section of the register accordingly.

(2) This regulation applies to the following persons:–

    (a) where land is registered under the Act, any person registered as owner thereof and, where the registration of the land is provisional, the person (if any) on whose application it was made, and any person whose application has been noted under section 4(4) of the Act;

    (b) where a right of common is so registered, any person appearing from the register to be interested therein, and, where the registration is provisional, the person on whose application it was made and any person whose application is noted under regulation 9(5) above.

27 Land ceasing to be common land or a town or village green

(1) Where any land registered under the Act has ceased to be common land or a town or village green, application may be made to the registration authority, in accordance with the following provisions of this regulation, for the amendment of the register.

[(2) An application under this regulation may be made by the person who, at the date of the application, would have been entitled (whether or not by virtue of any provision of these Regulations) to apply under section 4 of the Act for the registration of a claim to the ownership of the land if at that date such an application could have been made.]

(3) Every such application must be –

    (a) in Form 17;

    (b) signed by [or on behalf of] every applicant who is an individual, and by the secretary or other duly authorized officer of every applicant which is a body corporate; and

    (c) supported by a statutory declaration made by every person who has signed the application, and by such further evidence (if any) as, after considering the application and declaration, the registration authority may reasonably require.

(4) Applications under this regulation shall be numbered in order of receipt by the registration authority, and shall be entitled, unless rejected, to be given effect to on the register in that order.

(5) The registration authority shall, on receipt of any application under this regulation which it does not, after preliminary consideration, determine to reject, publish in the concerned area, and shall display, a notice in Form 18, and shall send the notice to –

    (a) every concerned authority;

    (b) any person other than the applicant who is registered as owner of the land;

    (c) where a right of common is registered as exercisable over the land, any person appearing from the register to be interested therein, and, where the registration is provisional, the person on whose application it was made and any person whose application is noted under regulation 9(5) above.

(6) Every authority receiving a Form 18 notice under this regulation shall display copies thereof.

(7) Upon the expiration of forty days from the date on which paragraph (5) above is complied with, the registration authority shall further consider the application and shall consider any written representations which it has received, and, if it deems the application well-founded, shall amend the register as shown in Standard Entry 6.

(8) In this regulation 'concerned area' means, in the case of a registration authority which is the council of a county borough, an area including the area of the county borough and the areas of every concerned authority, and, in any other case, an area including the areas of every concerned authority.

Amendment – SI 1968/658.

PART V

AMENDMENT OF REGISTERS UNDER SECTION 13 OF ACT

28 Substituted land

(1) Where –

   (a) application is made to a registration authority under regulation 27 above with respect to any land registered under the Act, and
   (b) it appears to the authority that, under or by virtue of any of the enactments mentioned in paragraph (2) below, the said land (in this regulation referred to as the taken land) has ceased to be common land or a town or village green, and that certain other land not registered under the Act (in this regulation referred to as the substituted land) has become common land or a town or village green in substitution therefor,

the authority shall not give effect to the application until the substituted land has been registered under the Act, unless it is exempt from registration under section 11 thereof.

(2) The enactments referred to in paragraph (1) above are the following:–

   (a) sections 147 and 148 of the Inclosure Act 1845;
   (b) paragraph 11 of the First Schedule to the Acquisition of Land (Authorisation Procedure) Act 1946;
   (c) any other enactment providing, on the exchange of land, for the transfer of rights trusts or incidents attaching to the land given in exchange from that land to the land taken in exchange and vice versa.

(3) Substituted land in the same registration area as the taken land shall be registered in the register unit containing the registration of the taken land, with a statement as in Standard Entry 7, and both the taken and the

substituted land shall be identified by lettering in the register unit and on the register map.

29   Amendment in regard to registered rights

(1)   Where a right of common registered under the Act has been apportioned, varied, extinguished or released, or, being or having become a right in gross, has been transferred, application may be made to the registration authority, in accordance with the following provisions of this regulation, for the amendment of the register.

[(2)   (a)   An application under this regulation may be made by any person having an interest under the apportionment, variation, extinguishment, release or transfer.

(b)   For the purposes of this regulation the following are included in the expression 'person having an interest', but without prejudice to the generality of that expression:–

(i)   in the case of an apportionment, variation or transfer, any person who, at the date of the application under this regulation, would have been entitled (whether or not by virtue of any provision of these Regulations) to apply under section 4 of the Act for the registration of the right as apportioned, varied or transferred, if at that date such an application could have been made;

(ii)   in the case of an extinguishment or release, any person who, at the date of the application under this regulation, would have been entitled (whether or not by virtue of any provision of these Regulations) to apply under the said section 4 for the registration of a claim to the ownership of any part of the land over which the right extinguished or released was formerly exercisable, if at that date such an application could have been made.]

(3)   Every such application must be –

(a)   in Form 19;
(b)   signed by [or on behalf of] every applicant who is an individual, and by the secretary or other duly authorized officer of every applicant which is a body corporate; and
(c)   supported by a statutory declaration made by every person who has signed the application, and by such further evidence (if any) as, after considering the application and declaration, the registration authority may reasonably require.

(4)   Applications under this regulation shall be numbered in order of receipt by the registration authority and shall be entitled, unless rejected, to be given effect to on the register in that order.

(5)   The registration authority shall, on receipt of any application under this regulation which it does not after preliminary consideration determine to reject, serve notice in Form 20 upon every person (other than the applicant) appearing, either from the register or from any prior pending application under this regulation, to be interested in the right of common referred to in the

application, and, where the registration is provisional, upon the person on whose application it was made and any person whose application is noted under regulation 9(5) above.

(6) Upon the expiration of forty days from the date on which paragraph (5) above is complied with, the registration authority shall further consider the application and shall consider any written representations which it has

received, and, if it deems the application well-founded, shall make the necessary amendment to the register in accordance with Model Entry 20 or 21 as appropriate.

(7) Where an assurance entitled to be registered under the Yorkshire Registries Act 1884 effects any such apportionment, variation, extinguishment, release or transfer as is mentioned in paragraph (1) above, section 14 of that Act shall not apply to that assurance so far as it relates to that apportionment, variation, extinguishment, release or transfer.

Amendment – SI 1968/658.

30 Information about disposal of applications

(1) Where a registration authority has accepted an application under regulation 27 or 29 above, and has made the necessary amendment in the register, it shall give written notice thereof, with particulars of the amendment, to every concerned authority, to the applicant and to every person served with notice of the application, and, where the authority has rejected such an application, it shall give written notice of the rejection to the applicant and to every such person as aforesaid, giving the reasons for the rejection.

(2) An authority to whom a notice is sent under paragraph (1) above shall annex it to the copy of the registration to which it relates and keep it available for public inspection at all reasonable times.

PART VI

MISCELLANEOUS

31 Land descriptions

(1) Land must be described for the purposes of any application, other than an application under Part IV of these Regulations –

(a) by a plan accompanying the application and referred to therein; or
(b) in the case of land already registered under the Act, by a reference to the register sufficient to enable the land to be identified; or
(c) in the case of land to which rights of common are attached, by reference to the numbered parcels on the most recent edition of the ordnance map (quoting the edition).

(2) Any plan accompanying an application must –

(a)   be drawn to scale;
(b)   be in ink or other permanent medium;
(c)   be on a scale of not less, or not substantially less, than six inches to one mile;
(d)   show the land to be described by means of distinctive colouring; and
(e)   be marked as an exhibit to the statutory declaration in support of the application.

[31A   Applications signed by agents]

[Any application signed by an agent on behalf of an individual applicant shall be supported by such evidence (if any) of the agent's authority as, after considering the application, the registration authority may reasonably require.]

Amendment – 1968/658.

32   Official searches and certificates

(1)   Where any person requires a search to be made in [the registers], he may on payment of the prescribed fee lodge with the registration authority a requisition in that behalf.

(2)   A requisition for a search must be in Form 21, signed by the person making the same or by his solicitor, and must define the land in respect of which the search is to be made by means of a plan drawn to scale and (except where the applicant does not require a plan to be returned) furnished in duplicate.

(3)   The registration authority shall thereupon make the search required, and shall issue a certificate setting forth the results of the search by completing the appropriate portion of Form 21 and returning one copy of the form to the person who required the search or his solicitor.

(4)   A separate requisition for search shall be made in respect of each parcel of land against which a search is requested, except where for the purpose of a single registration or of a single transaction a certificate is required in respect of two or more parcels of land which have a common boundary or are separated only by a road, railway, river, stream or canal.

(5)   Every registration authority shall close its registers for entries at a fixed time each working day, and shall make no entries therein after that time until the next working day.

(6)   An official certificate of the result of the search shall extend to registrations effected during the day of the date of the certificate and shall be issued only when the registers have been closed for entries on that day.

Amendment – SI 1980/1195.
Modification – SI 1991/2684.

33   Certified copies and extracts

Any person may, on payment of the prescribed fee, bespeak from a registration authority, and the registration authority shall thereupon issue, a copy of, or extract from, the general part of any register maintained by it under the Act, or any map or register unit forming part of such a register, certified on behalf of the registration authority as a true copy or extract as at the date of issue thereof.

34 Fees for searches, etc

(1) The fees payable for searches and official certificates of search, and for certified copies and extracts, shall be those specified in Schedule 3 to these regulations.

(2) All fees payable by virtue of this regulation shall be paid in advance.

35 Supply of certain forms

Forms 1 to 4, 7 to 10, 16, 17, 19 and 21 shall be supplied to registration authorities under arrangements to be made by HM Stationery Office . . .

Amendment – SI 1982/210.

36 Errors and omissions

Where any clerical error or omission, or error or omission of a like nature, is discovered in a register, and can be corrected without either –

(a) increasing or diminishing the area of any land registered therein, or
(b) increasing the burden on any such land of any right of common so registered, or
(c) increasing the area of any land subject to any such right, or
(d) causing any registration to conflict with another registration, or
(e) affecting any provisional registration which falls to be referred to a Commons Commissioner, or any registration under section 4 of the Act which has become final,

the registration authority shall make the necessary correction, and, where the correction affects any provisional registration, shall inform every concerned authority in writing, and every such authority shall make a corresponding correction in the copy of the registration held by it.

[SCHEDULES 1, 2 and 3 ARE NOT REPRODUCED IN THIS BOOK]

COMMONS REGISTRATION (NEW LAND) REGULATIONS 1969

SI 1969 No 1843

1   Title and commencement

These Regulations may be cited as the Commons Registration (New Land) Regulations 1969, and shall come into operation on 3rd January 1970.

2   Interpretation

(1)   The Interpretation Act 1889 applies for the interpretation of these Regulations as it applies for the interpretation of an Act of Parliament.

(2)   In these Regulations, unless the context otherwise requires –

'the Act' means the Commons Registration Act 1965;

'application' means an application under these Regulations;

'concerned authority', in relation to an application to a registration authority, means a local authority (other than the registration authority) in whose area any part of the land affected by the application lies;

'Form 6' means the form so numbered in the General Regulations or a form to substantially the same effect, and 'Form' followed by a number above 28 means the form so numbered in the Schedule to these Regulations, or a form to substantially the same effect;

'the General Regulations' means the Commons Registration (General) Regulations 1966 as amended, and 'General Regulation' followed by a number means the regulation so numbered in the General Regulations;

'Model Entry' followed by a number means the specimen entry so numbered in Part I of Schedule 2 to the General Regulations, and 'Standard Entry' followed by a number means the specimen entry so numbered in Part 2 of that Schedule, or an entry to substantially the same effect;

'provisional registration' means a registration under section 4 of the Act which has not become final;

'substituted land' and, in relation to any substituted land, 'the taken land', bear the same meanings as in General Regulation 28.

(3)   A requirement upon a registration authority to publish a document in any area is a requirement to cause the document to be published in such one or more newspapers circulating in that area as shall appear to the authority sufficient to secure adequate publicity for it.

(4)   A requirement to display a document or copies thereof is a requirement to treat it, for the purposes of section 287 of the Local Government Act 1933 (public notices), as if it were a public notice within that section.

(5)   Where the day or the last day on which anything is required or permitted by or in pursuance of these Regulations to be done is a Sunday, Christmas Day, Good Friday, bank holiday or a day appointed for public thanksgiving or mourning, the requirement or permission shall be deemed to relate to the first day thereafter which is not one of the days before-mentioned.

(6)   Any requirement (however expressed) that a registration authority shall send anything to 'the applicant' shall, where a solicitor has been instructed for the purposes of an application, be deemed to be satisfied by sending it to the solicitor, or, where two or more persons are concerned together in an application and no solicitor has been instructed, to that one of them whose name appears first in the application form.

(7)   A requirement upon a registration authority to stamp any document is a requirement to cause an impression of its official stamp as described in General Regulation 3 to be affixed to it, and that the impression shall bear the date mentioned in the requirement or (where no date is mentioned) the date when it was affixed.

(8)   An indication in any form in the Schedule to these Regulations that the form shall bear the official stamp of a registration authority is a requirement upon the authority to stamp it.

Modification – in relation to solicitors: SI 1991/2684.

3   Land becoming common land or a town or village green

(1)   Where, after 2nd January 1970, any land becomes common land or a town or village green, application may be made subject to and in accordance with the provisions of these Regulations for the inclusion of that land in the appropriate register and for the registration of rights of common thereover and of persons claiming to be owners thereof.

(2)   Where any land is for the time being registered under the Act, no application shall be entertained for its registration under these Regulations, and, where any land is for the time being registered under section 4 of the Act (whether or not the registration has become final) no application shall be entertained for the registration of rights of common over it.

(3)   No person shall be registered under these Regulations as the owner of any land which is registered under the Land Registration Acts 1925 to 1966 and no person shall be registered under these Regulations as the owner of any other land unless the land itself is registered under these Regulations.

(4)   An application for the registration of any land as common land or as a town or village green may be made by any person, and a registration authority shall so register any land in any case where it registers rights over it under these Regulations.

(5)   An application for the registration of a right of common over land which is registered, or which is capable of being registered, under these Regulations, may be made by the owner of the right, or by any person entitled by law to act, in relation to the right, on the owner's behalf or in his stead, or, where the right belongs to an ecclesiastical benefice of the Church of England which is vacant, by the Church Commissioners.

(6)   An application for the registration of a claim to the ownership of any land registered under these Regulations may be made by the owner of the land, or by any person entitled by law to act, in relation to the land, on the owner's behalf or in his stead, or, where the land belongs to an ecclesiastical benefice of the Church of England which is vacant, by the Church Commissioners.

(7)   An application must be –

     (a)   in Form 29, 30, 31 or 32 as appropriate;

     (b)   signed by or on behalf of every applicant who is an individual, and by the secretary or some other duly authorised officer of every applicant which is a body corporate or unincorporate;

     (c)   accompanied by such documents (if any) as may be requisite under regulation 4 below;

     (d)   supported –

         (i)   by a statutory declaration as set out in the appropriate form of application, with such adaptations as the case may require, to be made by the applicant, or by one of the applicants if there is more than one, or by his or their solicitor, or, if the applicant is a body corporate or unincorporate, or charity trustees, by its or their solicitor or by the person who signed the application; and

         (ii)   by such further evidence, if any, as, at any time before finally disposing of the application, the registration authority may reasonably require.

Modification – in relation to solicitors: SI 1991/2684.

4   Documents to accompany applications

(1)   Subject to paragraph (2) below, every application must be accompanied by, or by a copy or sufficient abstract of, every document relating to the matter which the applicant has in his possession or under his control, or of which he has a right to the production.

(2)   In the case of an application for the registration of any rights of common, or of a claim to the ownership of any land, the applicant shall not be obliged to furnish to the registration authority, or to disclose the existence of, any document which he would not be obliged to abstract or produce to a purchaser under a contract for the sale by the applicant of the rights or the land made otherwise than by correspondence and containing no stipulations as to title.

Modification – in relation to solicitors: SI 1991/2684.

5   Disposal of applications

(1)   On receiving an application, the registration authority shall allot a distinguishing number to it, and shall mark the application form with that number.

(2)   Where a registration authority receives an application for the registration of a right of common affecting any coal or anthracite it shall, before entertaining the application, serve notice in writing to that effect upon [the Coal Authority], giving the name and address of the applicant and particulars of the right of common, of the land over which it is exercisable and of the land (if any) to which it is attached.

(3)   the registration authority shall send the applicant a receipt for his application containing a statement of the number allotted thereto; and Form 6, if used for that purpose, shall be sufficient.

(4)   Subject to paragraph (7) below, a registration authority shall, on receipt of an application –

   (a)   send a notice in Form 33, 34 or 35, as appropriate, to every person (other than the applicant) whom the registration authority has reason to believe (whether from information supplied by the applicant or otherwise) to be an owner, lessee, tenant or occupier of any part of the land affected by the application, or to be likely to wish to object to the application;

   (b)   publish in the concerned area, and display, such a notice as aforesaid, and send the notice and a copy of the application to every concerned authority;

   (c)   affix such a notice to some conspicuous object on any part of the land which is open, unenclosed and unoccupied, unless it appears to the registration authority that such a course would not be reasonably practicable.

(5)   The date to be inserted in any notice under paragraph (4) above by which statements in objection to an application must be submitted to the registration authority shall be such as to allow an interval of not less than six weeks from the latest of the following dates, that is to say, the date on which the notice is displayed by the registration authority, or is published, or may reasonably be expected to be delivered in due course of post or to be displayed under paragraph (6) below.

(6)   Every concerned authority receiving, under this regulation, a notice and a copy of an application shall forthwith display copies of the notice, and shall keep the copy of the application available for public inspection at all reasonable times until informed by the registration authority of the disposal of the application.

(7)   Where an application appears to a registration authority after preliminary consideration not to be duly made, the authority may reject it without complying with paragraph (4) above, but where it appears to the authority that any action by the applicant might put the application in order, the authority shall not reject the application under this paragraph without first giving the applicant a reasonable opportunity of taking that action.

(8)   In this regulation 'concerned area' means, in the case of a registration authority which is the council of a county borough, an area including the area of the county borough and the area of every concerned authority, and in any other case, an area including the area of every concerned authority.

Amendment – SI 1994/2567.

6   Consideration of objections

(1)   As soon as possible after the date by which statements in objection to an application have been required to be submitted, the registration authority shall proceed to the further consideration of the application, and the consideration of statements (if any) in objection thereto, in accordance with the following provisions of this regulation.

(2)   The registration authority shall not consider any statement in objection to an application unless it is in writing and signed by or on behalf of the person making it, but, subject as aforesaid, the authority shall consider every statement in objection to an application which it receives before the date on which it proceeds to the further consideration of the application under paragraph (1) above, and may consider any such statement which it receives on or after that date and before the authority finally disposes of the application.

(3)   The registration authority shall send the applicant a copy of every statement which it is required under paragraph (2) above to consider, and of every statement which it is permitted under that paragraph to consider and intends to consider, and shall not reject the application without giving the applicant a reasonable opportunity of dealing with the matters contained in the statement of which copies are sent to him under this paragraph and with any other matter in relation to the application which appears to the authority to afford prima facie grounds for rejecting the application.

Amendment – SI 1994/2567.

7   Method of registration

(1)   Where a registration authority accepts an application, it shall make the necessary registration, following as closely as possible whichever of the Model Entries 4 and 7 to 12 may be applicable, with such variations and adaptations as the circumstances may require, but with the substitution, for the words '(Registration provisional.)', of the words '(Registration under section 13 of the Act.)'.

(2)   The provisions of paragraphs (2) to (7) of General Regulation 10 shall apply to registrations under these Regulations as they apply to provisional registrations.

(3)   The provisions of regulation 9 of the Commons Registration (Objections and Maps) Regulations 1968 (Changes as to provisional maps) shall apply for the purposes of section 13 of the Act as they apply for the purposes of section 4 thereof ...

(4) Where a registration authority has made a registration under this regulation, it shall file the application form and any plan thereto which is not required for the purpose of General Regulation 20 (supplemental maps) and shall return all other documents which accompanied the application form to the applicant.

Amendment – Words omitted amend SI 1968/989.

8 Information about disposal of applications, and procedure on rejection

(1) When a registration authority has disposed of an application and, if it has accepted the application, has made the necessary registration, it shall give written notice of the fact to every concerned authority, to the applicant and to every person whose address is known to the registration authority and who objected to the application, and such notice shall include, where the registration authority has accepted the application, details of the registration, and, where it has rejected the application, the reasons for the rejection.

(2) A person shall be taken to have objected to an application for the purposes of paragraph (1) above if he submitted a statement in objection to the application which the registration authority was required to consider under paragraph (2) of regulation 6 above or which it did consider under that paragraph.

(3) Where a registration authority has rejected an application, it shall return the application form and all accompanying documents to the applicant.

9 Substituted land

(1) Where under these Regulations a registration authority registers any substituted land in a register, and the taken land is registered in that register, then –

(a) if no application has been duly made under General Regulation 27 for the removal of the taken land from the register, the authority shall nevertheless amend the register in relation to the taken land as shown in Standard Entry 6;

(b) if such an application has been duly made, the registration authority shall not be required to comply with paragraphs (5) to (8) of General Regulation 27 (except so much of paragraph (7) thereof as requires the register to be amended in accordance with Standard Entry 6).

(2) In General Regulation 28(1) (which prohibits the removal of any taken land from a register until the substituted land has been registered under the Act, unless the substituted land is exempt from registration under section 11 of the Act) the words 'unless it is exempt from registration under section 11 thereof' are hereby revoked, but without prejudice to their effect in relation to applications and registrations under section 4 of the Act.

10 Land descriptions

(1) Land must be described for the purposes of any application –

(a) by a plan accompanying the application and referred to therein; or

(b) in the case of land already registered under the Act, by a reference to the register sufficient to enable the land to be identified; or

(c) in the case of land to which rights of common are attached, by reference to the numbered parcels on the most recent edition of the ordnance map (quoting the edition).

(2) Any plan accompanying an application must –

(a) be drawn to scale;

(b) be in ink or other permanent medium;

(c) be on a scale of not less, or not substantially less, than six inches to one mile;

(d) show the land to be described by means of distinctive colouring; and

(e) be marked as an exhibit to the statutory declaration in support of the application.

SCHEDULE

FORMS

Form 29

This section for official use only
Official stamp of registration authority indicating date of receipt

Application No

Register unit No(s):

CL

CL

COMMONS REGISTRATION ACT 1965, SECTION 13

APPLICATION FOR THE REGISTRATION OF LAND WHICH BECAME COMMON LAND AFTER 2nd JANUARY 1970 IMPORTANT NOTE:– Before filling in this form, read carefully the notes at the end. An incorrectly completed application form may have to be rejected.

To the (1)

(1) Insert name of registration authority

Application is hereby made for the registration as common land of the land described below, which became so registrable after 2nd January 1970.

Part 1.

Name and address of the applicant or (if more than one) of every applicant.

(Give Christian names or forenames and surnames or, in the case of a body corporate or unincorporate, the full title of the body. If part 2 is not completed all correspondence and notices will be sent to the first-named applicant.)

Part 2.

Name and address of solicitor, if any.

(This part should be completed only if a solicitor has been instructed for the purposes of the application. If it is completed, all correspondence and notices will be sent to the solicitor.)

Part 3.

Particulars of the land to be registered, i.e. the land claimed to have become common land.

Name by which usually known

Locality

Colour on plan herewith

Part 4.

On what date did the land become common land?

Part 5.

How did the land become common land?

Part 6.

Name and address of every person whom the applicant believes to be an owner, lessee, tenant or occupier of any part of the land claimed to have become common land. (If none are known, write 'none'.)

Part 7.

Applications to register substituted land (see Note 5); to be disregarded in other cases.

Particulars of the 'taken land', ie the land which ceased to be common land when the land described in part 3 became common land.

Name by which usually known

Locality

Colour on plan herewith (if any)

If registered under the 1965 Act, register unit No(s).

Part 8.

List of supporting documents sent herewith, if any. (If none are sent, write 'none'.)

Part 9.

If there are any other facts relating to the application which ought to be brought to the attention of the registration authority (in particular if any person interested in the land is believed to dispute the claim that it has become common land) full particulars should be given here.

Date ....19 .....

Signatures (2) ....

> (2) The application must be signed by or on behalf of each individual applicant, and by the secretary of some other duly authorised officer of any applicant which is a body corporate or unincorporate.

STATUTORY DECLARATION IN SUPPORT

(See Note 10) To be made by the applicant, or by one of the applicants, or by his or their solicitor, or, if the applicant is a body corporate or unincorporate, by its solicitor or by the person who signed the application.

I   .... solemnly and sincerely declare as follows:–

1.   I am ((the person) (one of the persons) who (has) (have) signed the foregoing application)) ((the solicitor to (the applicant) ((3) .... one of the applicants)).

2.   I have read the Notes to the application form.

3.   The facts set out in the application form are to be the best of my knowledge and belief fully and truly stated and I am not aware of any other fact which should be brought to the attention of the registration authority as likely to affect its decision on this application, nor of any document relating to the matter other than those (if any) mentioned in parts 8 and 9 of the application.

4.   The plan now produced and shown to me marked(4) ' ' is the plan referred to in part 3 of the application.

5.   The plan now produced and shown to me marked (4) ' ' is the plan referred to in part 7 of the application.

And I make this solemn declaration, conscientiously believing the same to be true, and by virtue of the Statutory Declarations Act 1835.

(1)   Insert full name (and address if not given in application form).

(2)   Delete and adapt as necessary.

(3)   Insert name if applicable.

(4)   Insert 'marking' as on plan.

(5)   Delete this paragraph if there is no plan referred to in part 7.

Declared by the said .... at .... in the ....
of .... this .... day of .... 19 .....

Signature of Declarant

Before me,

Signature ....

Address ....

Qualification ....

REMINDER TO OFFICER TAKING DECLARATION: Please initial all alterations and mark any plan as an exhibit.

NOTES

1   Registration authorities

The applicant should take care to submit his application to the correct registration authority. This depends on the situation of the land which is claimed to have become common land. The registration authority for land in an administrative county is the county council; for land in a county borough, it is the county borough council, and for land in Greater London, it is the Greater London Council. However, if the land in question is partly in the area of one registration authority and partly in that of another, the authorities may by agreement have provided for one of them to be the registration authority for the whole of the land. An applicant concerned with the land lying close to the boundary of an administrative area, or partly in one area and partly in another, should therefore enquire whether such an agreement has been made and, if so, which authority is responsible for the land.

2   Who may apply for registration

An application for the registration of any land which has become common land after 2nd January 1970 may be made by any person, but a person who wishes to apply for the registration of rights of common over land which became common land after 2nd January 1970 should use C.R. Form 31 and not this form, whether or not the land itself has been registered under the Act.

3   No double registration

If the land is already registered under the Act, whether in the Register of Common Land or in the separate Register of Town or Village Greens, and whether the registration is provisional, final, or under section 13 of the Act (which relates to land becoming common land or a town or village green after2nd January 1970), an application for registration cannot be entertained, but this does not prevent the submission of an application later on, should the existing registration cease for any reason to be effective (as, for example, by the land being removed from the register under section 13 or by a provisional registration being cancelled or failing to achieve finality). If an earlier registration is believed to exist a search of the register may be obtained by means of C.R. Form 21 (a separate form must be used for each register).

4   Meaning of 'common land'

For the purpose of an application after 2nd January 1970, common land may be taken to mean either –

(a)   land which, after 2nd January 1970, became subject to rights of common (see Note 6 below) whether those rights are exercisable at all times or only during limited periods; or

(b)   land which, after 2nd January 1970, became 'substituted land', whether or not subject to rights of common (this category is explained in Note 5 below).

It does not include a town or village green or any land forming part of a highway. (There is a separate form available for applying for the registration under the Act of land which became a town or village green after 2nd January 1970). 'Land' includes land covered with water, so that common land can, for instance, include ponds and lakes.

5 How land can become common land

Land can become common land after 2nd January 1970 in any of the following ways:–

(1) By or under an Act of Parliament otherwise than as substituted land (as to substituted land, see category (4) below).

(2) By a grant by the owner of the land of rights of common over it.

(3) By rights of common being acquired over it by prescription.

(4) By substitution or exchange for other land which has ceased to be common land under –

    (a) sections 147 and 148 of the Inclosure Act 1845; or

    (b) paragraph 11 of Schedule 1 to the Acquisition of Land (Authorisation Procedure) Act 1946; or

    (c) any other enactment providing, on the exchange of land, for the transfer of rights, trusts or incidents attaching to the land given in exchange from that land to the land taken in exchange and vice versa.

Land in category (4) is referred to in this form as 'substituted land', and the land for which it is substituted, and which has ceased to be common land, is referred to as 'the taken land'. If this application is accepted for registration, and the taken land is registered in the Register of Common Land maintained by the same registration authority, the taken land will be removed from the register automatically provided the registration authority is satisfied as to the exact areas of both the substituted and the taken land. No separate application in regard to the latter is necessary in such a case.

6 Meaning of 'rights of common'

There are many different kinds of rights of common, some existing only in particular areas. This is why there is no exhaustive list or definition of rights of common in the Act. However, it may be said that a right of common is a right which a person has (generally in common with others including the owner of the soil) to take part of the natural produce of another man's land. Examples are: a right to turn out sheep or other animals to graze (common of pasture, called in the Act a right to graze animals); a right to turn out pigs to eat acorns and beechmast (pannage); a right to take tree loppings, gorse, furze, bushes or underwood (estovers); a right to take turf or peat (turbary); a right to take fish (piscary). There is also a right of common in the soil, as it is called, which consists of the right of taking sand, gravel, etc. from another man's land. These are only a few of the most frequently encountered rights of common; there are many others, and any person in doubt should seek legal advice. On the other hand, many rights connected with land are not rights of common and are not subject to the Act; for example, rights of way (public or private), and rights to water cattle, horses or other animals on the land of another.

The Act provides that cattlegates or beastgates (by whatever name known) and rights of sole or several vesture or herbage or of sole or several pasture are to be considered as rights of common. These are in essence various kinds of rights of pasture normally enjoyed to the exclusion of the owner of the land.

Rights held for a term of years or from year to year are not registrable under the Act, and, accordingly, land subject to such rights does not qualify for registration on that account, although it may do so in some other way, e.g. as substituted land.

7   Land descriptions

In addition to the particulars asked for at part 3 of the form, a plan of the land claimed to have become common land must accompany the application. The particulars in part 3 are necessary to enable the registration authority to identify the land concerned, but the main description of the land will be by means of the plan. This must be drawn to scale, in ink or other permanent medium, and be on a scale of not less, or not substantially less, than six inches to one mile. It must show the land by means of distinctive colouring (a coloured edging inside the boundary will usually suffice) and it must be marked as an exhibit to the statutory declaration (see Note 10 below). If the land to be registered is substituted land (see Note 5 above), then a description of the taken land must be given in part 7, and a plan of this area, too, may have to be provided. If the taken land has already been registered under the Act (as it will have been in most cases) and comprises the whole of the land in one or more register units, a plan is unnecessary provided the register unit number(s) are quoted. If the taken land comprises only part of the land in a register unit a plan may be dispensed with if the land can be described by reference to some physical feature such as a road, river or railway; the description might, for example, read: 'The land in register unit No ..... lying to the south of the road from A to B'. Where this method is not practicable, or the taken land is not registered under the Act, it must be described by a plan which must conform to the requirements mentioned above. Where two plans accompany the application, a different colour should be used in each.

8   Grounds of application: evidence

In part 5 should be set out, as concisely as possible, a statement of the facts relied on to show that the land became common land on the date stated in part 4; this date must be after 2nd January 1970, otherwise the application cannot be entertained. The statement should include particulars of every Act of Parliament, statutory order, order of court, deed or other instrument, and of every act or event, which is material for the purpose. The registration authority has power to call for such further evidence in support of the application as it may reasonably require. If the land is substituted land (see Note 5 above) there should be included in part 5 particulars of the enactment and of the compulsory purchase order, order of exchange or other instrument authorising the exchange or substitution, and of the instrument (if any) under which the exchange or substitution actually took place.

9 Supporting documents

The application must be accompanied by the original or (preferably) by a copy or sufficient abstract of every document relating to the matter which the applicant has in his possession or under his control, or of which he has a right to the production. The following are examples of documents which, under this rule, may normally be expected to be among the documents accompanying applications in the particular cases mentioned:–

(1) Where the land is stated to have become common land by virtue of a private or local Act or of a statutory instrument, the award or other instrument of allotment (if any) made thereunder.

(2) Where the land is stated to have become common land by a grant of rights of common, a copy of the deed of grant.

(3) Where the land is stated to have become common land by the acquisition of rights of common over it by prescription, and there is a declaration by a court of competent jurisdiction to that effect, an office copy of the order embodying that declaration. (In the absence of such a declaration, a claim based solely on the Prescription Act 1832 cannot be admitted, and the claim based on prescription otherwise than under that Act is unlikely to be admitted if any objection is received by the registration authority.)

(4) Where the land is stated to be substituted land (see Note 5 above), the original or a duly authenticated copy (a) of the compulsory purchase order, order of exchange or other instrument authorising the exchange or substitution, and (b) of the instrument (if any) under which the exchange or substitution actually took place.

The foregoing list is not exhaustive and in special cases the applicant may need to consult the registration authority. Applicants are strongly recommended NOT to forward the original of any deed or other private document. Instead, a copy should be supplied, preferably indorsed with a certificate signed by a solicitor that it has been examined against the original. The applicant should indicate, either on the copy itself or in part 8 of the application, as convenient, who has the original and where it maybe inspected. If any document relating to the matter is believed to exist, but neither the original nor a copy can be produced, the fact should be mentioned in part 9 of the application, where particulars of the missing document should be given and its non-production accounted for.

The registration authority has power to call for such further evidence as it may reasonably require.

10 Statutory Declaration

The statutory declaration must be made before a justice of the peace, commissioner for oaths or notary public. The plan (or each plan) accompanying the application and referred to in the statutory declaration must be marked as an exhibit and signed by the officer taking the declaration (initialling is insufficient). A plan is marked by writing on the face in ink an identifying symbol such as the letter 'A'. If there is more than one plan a different identifying letter must be used for each. On the back of the plan should appear these words:

This is the exhibit marked 'A' referred to in the statutory declaration of (name of declarant) made this (date) .... 19 ..... before me,

(Signature and qualification)

11   Action by registration authority

The registration authority will on receipt of the application send an acknowledgement. If this is not received within 10 days the applicant should communicate with the authority. Unless the application has to be rejected after preliminary consideration, the registration authority will give publicity to it and will consider it further in the light of any objections which may be received. The applicant will be supplied with copies of all objections which fall to be considered and will have an opportunity of answering them. Later, the applicant will be informed whether the application has been accepted or rejected. If it is accepted, the land will be registered as common land, and the applicant will be supplied with particulars of the registration. If it is rejected, the applicant will be notified of the reasons for the rejection.

12   False statements

The making of a false statement for the purposes of this application may render the maker liable to prosecution.

Form 30

This section for official use only

Official stamp of registration authority indicating date of receipt

Application No

Register unit No(s):

VG

VG

COMMONS REGISTRATION ACT 1965, SECTION 13

APPLICATION FOR THE REGISTRATION OF LAND WHICH BECAME A TOWN OR VILLAGE GREEN AFTER 2nd JANUARY 1970I

IMPORTANT NOTE:– Before filling in this form, read carefully the notes at the end. An incorrectly completed application form may have to be rejected.

To the(1)

(1) Insert name of registration authority

Application is hereby made for the registration as a town or village green of the land described below, which became so registrable after 2nd January 1970.

Part 1

Name and address of the applicant or (if more than one) of every applicant.

(Give Christian names or forenames and surname or, in the case of a body corporate or unincorporate, the full title of the body. If part 2 is not completed all correspondence and notices will be sent to the first named applicant.)

Part 2

Name and address of solicitor, if any.

(This part should be completed only if a solicitor has been instructed for the purposes of the application. If it is completed, all correspondence and notices will be sent to the solicitor.)

Part 3

Particulars of the land to be registered, ie the land claimed to have become a town or village green.

Name by which usually known

Locality

Colour on plan herewith

Part 4

On what date did the land become a town or village green?

Part 5

How did the land become a town or village green?

Part 6

Name and address of every person whom the applicant believes to bean owner, lessee, tenant or occupier of any part of the land claimed to have become a town or village green. (If none are known, write 'none'.)

Part 7

For applications to register substituted land (see Note 5); to be disregarded in other cases.

Particulars of the 'taken land', ie the land which ceased to be a town or village green (or part thereof) when the land described in part 3 became a town or village green (or part).

Name by which usually known

Locality

Colour on plan herewith (if any)

If registered under the 1965 Act, register unit No(s).

Part 8

List of supporting documents sent herewith, if any. (If none are sent, write 'none'.)

Part 9

If there are any other facts relating to the application which ought to be brought to the attention of the registration authority (in particular if any person interested in the land is believed to dispute the claim that it has become a town or village green) full particulars should be given here.

Date .... 19 .....

Signatures(2) ....

(2) The application must be signed by or on behalf of each individual applicant, and by the secretary or some other duly authorised officer of any applicant which is a body corporate or unincorporate.

STATUTORY DECLARATION IN SUPPORT

(See Note 9) To be made by the applicant, or by one of the applicants, or by his or their solicitor, or, if the applicant is a body corporate or unincorporate, by its solicitor or by the person who signed the application.

I solemnly and sincerely declare as follows:–

1.   I am ((the person) (one of the persons) who (has) (have) signed the foregoing application)) ((the solicitor to (the applicant) ((3) .... one of the applicants)).

2.   I have read the Notes to the application form.

3.   The facts set out in the application form are to the best of my knowledge and belief fully and truly stated and I am not aware of any other fact which should be brought to the attention of the registration authority as likely to affect its decision on this application, nor of any document relating to the matter other than those (if any) mentioned in parts 8 and 9 of the application.

4.   The plan now produced and shown to me marked (4) ' ' is the plan referred to in part 3 of the application.

5.   The plan now produced and shown to me marked(4) ' ' is the plan referred to in part 7 of the application.

And I make this solemn declaration, conscientiously believing the same to be true, and by virtue of the Statutory Declarations Act 1835.

(1)   Insert full name (and address if not given in the application form).
(2)   Delete and adapt as necessary.
(3)   Insert name if applicable.
(4)   Insert 'marking' as on plan
(5)   Delete this paragraph if there is no plan referred to in part 7

Declared by the said .... at .... in the .... of
.... this .... day of .... 19 .....

Signature of Declarant

Before me,

Signature ....

Address ....

Qualification ....

REMINDER TO OFFICER TAKING DECLARATION: Please initial all alterations and mark any plan as an exhibit.

NOTES

1   Registration authorities

The applicant should take care to submit his application to the correct registration authority. This depends on the situation of the land which is claimed to have become a town or village green. The registration authority for land in an administrative county is the county council; for land in a county borough, it is the county borough council, and for land in Greater London, it is the Greater London Council. However if the land in question is partly in the area of one registration authority and partly in that of another, the authorities may by agreement have provided for one of them to be the registration authority for the whole of the land. An applicant concerned with land lying close to the boundary of an administrative area, or partly in one area and partly in another, should therefore enquire whether such an agreement has been made and, if so, which authority is responsible for the land.

2   Who may apply for registration

An application for the registration of any land which has become a town or village green after 2nd January 1970 may be made by any person.

3   No double registration

If the land is already registered under the Act, whether in the Register of Town or Village Greens or in the separate Register of Common Land, and whether the registration is provisional, final, or under section 13 of the Act (which relates to land becoming common land or a town or village green after 2nd January 1970), an application for registration cannot be entertained, but this does not prevent the submission of an application later on, should the existing registration cease for any reason to be effective (as, for example, by the land being removed from the register under section 13 or by a provisional registration being cancelled or failing to achieve finality). If an earlier registration is believed to exist a search of the register may be obtained by means of C.R. Form 21 (a separate form must be used for each register).

4   Meaning of 'town or village green'

'Town or village green' is defined in the Commons Registration Act 1965 as land –

(a)   which has been allotted by or under any Act for the exercise or recreation of the inhabitants of any locality, or

(b)   on which the inhabitants of any locality have a customary right to indulge in lawful sports and pastimes, or

(c)   on which the inhabitants of any locality have indulged in such sports and pastimes as of right for not less than twenty years.

While a town or village green can be subject to rights of common, it does not include land which is registered as common land in the separate Register of Common Land maintained under the Act. (There is a separate form available for applying for the registration under the Act of land which became common land after 2nd January 1970.) 'Land' includes land covered with water so that a town or village green can, for instance, include a pond.

5   How land can become a town or village green

Land can become a town or village green after 2nd January 1970 in one of the following ways:–

(1)   By or under an Act of Parliament otherwise than as substituted land (as to substituted land, see category (4) below).

(2)   By customary right established by judicial decision.

(3)   By the actual use of the land by the local inhabitants for lawful sports and pastimes as of right for not less than 20 years.

(4)   By substitution or exchange for other land which has ceased to be a town or village green under –

>   (a)   sections 147 and 148 of the Inclosure Act 1845; or
>   (b)   paragraph 11 or Schedule 1 to the Acquisition of Land (Authorisation Procedure) Act 1946; or
>   (c)   any other enactment providing, on the exchange of land, for the transfer of rights, trusts or incidents attaching to the land given in exchange from that land to the land taken in exchange and vice versa.

Land in category (4) is referred to in this form as 'substituted land', and the land for which it is substituted, and which has ceased to be a town or village green, is referred to as 'the taken land'. If this application is accepted for registration, and the taken land is registered in the Register of Town or Village Greens maintained by the same registration authority, the taken land will be removed from the register automatically provided the registration authority is satisfied as to the exact areas of both the substituted and the taken land. No separate application in regard to the latter is necessary in such a case.

6   Land descriptions

In addition to the particulars asked for at part 3 of the form, a plan of the land claimed to have become a town or village green must accompany the application. The particulars in part 3 are necessary to enable the registration authority to identify the land concerned, but the main description of the land will be by means of the plan. This must be drawn to scale, in ink or other permanent medium, and be on a scale of not less, or not substantially less, than six inches to one mile. It must show the land by means of distinctive colouring (a coloured edging inside the boundary will usually suffice) and it must be marked as an exhibit to the statutory declaration (see Note 9 below). If the land to be registered is substituted land (see Note 5 above), then a description of the taken land must be given in part 7, and a plan of this area, too, may have to be provided. If the taken land has already been registered under the Act (as it will have been in most cases) and comprises the whole of the land in one or more register units, a plan is unnecessary provided the register unit number(s) are quoted. If the taken land comprises only part of the land in a register unit a plan may be dispensed with if the land can be described by reference to some physical feature such as a road, river or railway; the description might, for example, read 'The land in register unit No ..... lying to the south of the road from A to B'. Where this method is not practicable, or the taken land is not registered under the Act, it must be described by a plan which must conform to the requirements mentioned above. Where two plans accompany the application, a different colour should be used in each.

7   Grounds of application: evidence

In part 5 should be set out, as concisely as possible, a statement of the facts relied on to show that the land became a town or village green on the date stated in part 4; this date must be after 2nd January 1970, otherwise the application cannot be entertained. The statement should include particulars of every Act of Parliament, statutory order, order of court, deed or other instrument, and of every act or event, which is material for the purpose. The registration authority has power to call for such further evidence in support of the application as it may reasonably require. If the land is substituted land (see Note 5 above) there should be included in part 5 particulars of the enactment and of the compulsory purchase order, order of exchange or other instrument authorising the exchange or substitution, and of the instrument (if any) under which the exchange or substitution actually took place.

8   Supporting documents

The application must be accompanied by the original or (preferably) by a copy or sufficient abstract of every document relating to the matter which the applicant has in his possession or under his control, or of which he has a right to the production. The following are examples of documents which, under this rule, may normally be expected to be among the documents accompanying applications in the particular cases mentioned:–

(1)   Where the land is stated to have become a town or village green by virtue of a private or local Act or of a statutory instrument, the award or other instrument of allotment (if any) made thereunder.

(2)   Where the land is stated to have become a town or village green by customary right, an office copy of an order of a court of competent jurisdiction embodying a declaration to that effect.

(3)   Where the land is stated to have become a town or village green by the actual use of the land by the local inhabitants for lawful sports and pastimes as of right for not less than 20 years, and there is a declaration by a court of competent jurisdiction to that effect, an office copy of the order embodying that declaration.

(4)   Where the land is stated to be substituted land (see Note 5 above), the original or a duly authenticated copy (a) of the compulsory purchase order, order of exchange or other instrument authorising the exchange or substitution, and (b) of the instrument (if any) under which the exchange or substitution actually took place.

The foregoing list is not exhaustive and in special cases the applicant may need to consult the registration authority. Applicants are strongly recommended NOT to forward the original of any deed or other private document. Instead, a copy should be supplied, preferably indorsed with a certificate signed by a solicitor that it has been examined against the original. The applicant should indicate, either on the copy itself or in part 8 of the application, as convenient, who has the original and where it may be inspected. If any document relating to the matter is believed to exist but, neither the original nor a copy can be produced, the fact should be mentioned in part 9 of the application, where particulars of the missing document should be given and its non-production accounted for.

The registration authority has power to call for such further evidence as it may reasonably require.

9   Statutory Declaration

The statutory declaration must be made before a justice of the peace, commissioner for oaths or notary public. The plan (or each plan) accompanying the application and referred to in the statutory declaration must be marked as an exhibit and signed by the officer taking the declaration (initialling is insufficient). A plan is marked by writing on the face in ink an identifying symbol such as the letter 'A'. If there is more than one plan a different identifying letter must be used for each. On the back of the plan should appear these words:

This is the exhibit marked 'A' referred to in the statutory declaration of (name of declarant) made this (date) .... 19..... before me,

....

(Signature and qualification)

10   Action by registration authority

The registration authority will on receipt of the application send an acknowledgement. If this is not received within 10 days the applicant should communicate with the authority. Unless the application has to be rejected after preliminary consideration, the registration authority will give publicity to it and will consider it further in the light of any objections which may be received. The applicant will be supplied with copies of all objections which fall to be considered and will have an opportunity of answering them. Later, the applicant will be informed whether the application has been accepted or rejected. If it is accepted, the land will be registered as a town or village green, and the applicant will be supplied with particulars of the registration. If it is rejected, the applicant will be notified of the reasons for the rejection.

11   False statements

The making of a false statement for the purposes of this application may render the maker liable to prosecution.

Form 31

This section for official use only

Official stamp of registration authority indicating date of receipt

Application No'

Register Unit No(s):

COMMONS REGISTRATION ACT 1965, SECTION 13

APPLICATION FOR THE REGISTRATION OF A RIGHT OF COMMON OVER LAND, WHERE BOTH THE RIGHT AND THE LAND BECAME REGISTRABLE AFTER 2nd JANUARY 1970. IMPORTANT NOTE:– Before filling in this form, read carefully the notes at the end. An incorrectly completed application may have to be rejected.

To the(1)

(1) Insert name of registration authority.

Application is hereby made for the registration of the right of common of which particulars are set out below.

Part 1.

Name and address of the applicant or (if more than one) of every applicant, and the capacity in which he applies.

(Give Christian names or forenames and surname or, in the case of a body corporate, the full title of the body. If part 2 is not completed all correspondence and notices will be sent to the first-named applicant.)

Part 2.

Name and address of solicitor, if any.

(This part should be completed only if a solicitor has been instructed for the purposes of the application. If it is completed, all correspondence and notices will be sent to the solicitor.)

Part 3.

Particulars of the land over which the right of common is exercisable.

(a)   Name by which usually known

(b)   Locality

(c)   Colour on plan herewith (if any)

If the land is registered under the 1965 Act, registration particulars –

(d)   Register(2)

(2) Insert 'Common Land' or 'Town or Village Greens'.

(e)   Register unit No(s).

Part 4.

Description of the right of common, including, if it is exercisable only during limited periods, full particulars of the periods, and, if it is a right to graze animals, details of the number(s) and kind(s) of animals.

Part 5.

Description of the farm, holding or other land to which the right is attached, if any. (If the right is not attached to any land, the fact should be stated here.)

Name by which usually known

Locality, OS Nos and reference to ordnance map (if given), and any further description

Colour on plan herewith (if any)

Part 6.

On what date did the right first become exercisable over the land described in part 3 above?

Part 7.

How did the right first become exercisable over the land described in part 3 above?

Part 8.

Name and address of every person whom the applicant believes to be an owner, lessee, tenant or occupier of any part of the land described in part 3 above. (If none are known, write 'none'.)

Part 9.

List of supporting documents sent herewith, if any. (If none are sent, write 'none'.)

Part 10.

If there are any other facts relating to the application which ought to be brought to the attention of the registration authority (in particular if any person interested in the land described in part 3 above is believed to dispute the claim that it is subject to rights of common) full particulars should be given here.

Date .... 19 .....

Signatures (3) ....

(3) The application must be signed by or on behalf of each individual applicant, and by the secretary or some other duly authorised officer of any applicant which is a body corporate or charity trustees. STATUTORY DECLARATION IN SUPPORT

(See Note 12) To be made by the applicant, or by one of the applicants, or by his or their solicitor, or, if the applicant is a body corporate or charity trustees, by its or their solicitor or by the person who signed the application.

I solemnly and sincerely declare as follows:–

1. I am ((the person) (one of the persons) who (has) (have) signed the foregoing application)) ((the solicitor to (the applicant) ((3) .... one of the applicants)).

2. I have read the Notes to the application form.

3. The facts set out in the application form are to the best of my knowledge and belief fully and truly stated and I am not aware of any other fact which should be brought to the attention of the registration authority as likely to affect its decision on this application, nor of any document which ought to be submitted or disclosed to the authority other than those (if any) mentioned in parts 9 and 10 of the application.

4. The plan now produced and shown to me marked(4) ' ' is the plan referred to in part 3 of the application.

5. The plan now produced and shown to me marked (4) ' ' is the plan referred to in part 5 of the application.

And I make this solemn declaration, conscientiously believing the same to be true, and by virtue of the Statutory Declarations Act 1835.

(1) Insert full name (and address if not given in the application form).

(2) Delete and adapt as necessary.

(3) Insert name if applicable.

(4) Insert 'marking' as on plan.

(5) Delete this paragraph if there is no plan referred to in part 5.

Declared by the said .... at .... in the .... of............ this .... day of .... 19 ..... Signature of Declarant

Before me,

Signature ....

Address ....

Qualification ....

REMINDER TO OFFICER TAKING DECLARATION: Please initial all alterations and mark any plan as an exhibit.

NOTES

1   Registration authorities

The applicant should take care to submit his application to the correct registration authority. This depends on the situation of the land over which the right of common is claimed. The registration authority for land in an administrative county is the county council; for land in a county borough, it is the county borough council, and for land in Greater London, it is the Greater London Council. However, if the land over which the right is claimed is partly in the area of one registration authority and partly in that of another, the authorities may by agreement have provided for one of them to be the registration authority for the whole of the land. An applicant concerned with land lying close to the boundary of an administrative area, or partly in one area and partly in another, should therefore enquire whether an agreement has been made and, if so, which authority is responsible for the land.

2   When to use this form

This form should not be used in cases where a right of common has been shifted from one piece of land to another in the circumstances mentioned in category (4) of Note 5 below, and both pieces of land are in the area of one registration authority. In such cases, re-registration of the right of common is automatic on registration of the substituted land. The matter is fully explained in Note 5. Nor should it be used where a right of common which has already been registered has been apportioned or varied, or, in the case of a registered right in gross (that is, not attached to any land), has been transferred. In such cases amendment of the register should be applied for on CR Form 19. In all other cases within Note 9 below this form should be used to apply to register a right of common whether or not the land over which the right is claimed to be exercisable has itself been registered, since it is not necessary for the land over which a right of common is exercisable to be registered before an application for the registration of the right itself is made: see Note 13 below.

3   Who may apply for registration

An application for the registration of a right of common may be made by the owner of the right or, where the right belongs to an ecclesiastical benefice of the Church of England which is vacant, by the Church Commissioners.

In certain cases a person may be entitled by law to apply on behalf of the owner of the right or in his stead. Examples are:

(a)   a receiver appointed under section 105 of the Mental Health Act 1959;

(b)   charity trustees where the right of common is vested in the Official Custodian for Charities;

(c)   trustees for the purposes of the Settled Land Act 1925 authorised by order under section 24 of that Act.

In all cases the applicant should state in part 1 the capacity in which he applies (e.g. as owner of the right). If he applies on behalf of, or instead of, another person he should also state in part I:–

(a)   the Act of Parliament, statutory instrument, order of court or other authority under which he claims to be entitled to apply;

(b)   the name and address of the person on whose behalf or in whose stead the application is made; and

(c)   the capacity of that person (who will normally be the owner of the right).

Where the Church Commissioners apply with respect to a right of common belonging to a vacant benefice, the fact should be stated, and the name of the benefice given, in part 1. Where charity trustees apply the fact should be stated, and the name of the charity given, in part 1.

4   Meaning of 'rights of common'

There are many different kinds of rights of common, some existing only in particular areas. This is why there is no exhaustive list or definition of rights of common in the Act. However, it may be said that a right of common is a right which a person has (generally in common with others including the owner of the soil) to take part of the natural produce of another man's land. Examples are: a right to turn out sheep or other animals to graze (common of pasture, called in the Act a right to graze animals); a right to turn out pigs to eat acorns and beechmast (pannage); a right to take tree loppings, gorse, furze, bushes or underwood (estovers); a right to take turf or peat (turbary); a right to take fish (piscary). There is also a right of common in the soil, as it is called, which consists of the right of taking sand, gravel, stone, etc from another man's land. These are only a few of the most frequently encountered rights of common; there are many others, and any person in doubt should seek legal advice. On the other hand, many rights connected with land are not rights of common and are not subject to the Act; for example, rights of way (public or private), and rights to water cattle, horses or other animals on the land of another.

The Act provides that cattlegates or beastgates (by whatever name known) and rights of sole or several vesture or herbage or of sole or several pasture are to be considered as rights of common. These are in essence various kinds of rights of pasture normally enjoyed to the exclusion of the owner of the land.

Rights held for a term of years or from year to year are not registrable under the Act.

5   How land can become subject to rights of common

Land can become subject to rights of common after 2nd January 1970 in one of the following ways:–

(1)   By or under an Act of Parliament, otherwise than as substituted land (as to substituted land, see category (4) below).

(2)   By a grant by the owner of the land of rights of common over it.

(3)   By rights of common being acquired over it by prescription.

(4)   By substitution or exchange for other land which has ceased to be common land under –

   (a)   sections 147 and 148 of the Inclosure Act 1845; or
   (b)   paragraph 11 of Schedule 1 to the Acquisition of Land (Authorisation Procedure) Act 1946; or
   (c)   any other enactment providing, on the exchange of land, for the transfer of rights trusts or incidents attaching to the land given in exchange from that land to the land taken in exchange and vice versa.

Land in category (4) is referred to in this form as 'substituted land', and the land for which it is substituted, and which has ceased to be subject to rights of common, is referred to as 'the taken land'. If both the taken and the substituted land are in the area of one registration authority, then when the substituted land is registered under the Act, a note will appear in the register to the effect that rights of common (if any) which subsisted over the taken land at the date of the substitution or exchange have shifted over to the substituted land, and no application for the re-registration of these rights will be necessary. Inquiry should be made of the registration authority whether the substituted land has been registered, and whether a note about the shifting of the rights appears in the register.

6   Land descriptions

(a)   For purposes of part 3. Except where the land has already been registered under the Act (see Note 7 below), the particulars asked for at (a), (b) and (c) of part 3 of the form must be given, and a plan must accompany the application. The particulars at (a) and (b) of part 3 are necessary to enable the registration authority to identify the land concerned, but the main description of the land will be by means of the plan. This must be drawn to scale, in ink or other permanent medium, and be on a scale of not less, or not substantially less, than six inches to one mile. It must show the land to be described by means of distinctive colouring (a coloured edging inside the boundary will usually suffice), and it must be marked as an exhibit to the statutory declaration (see Note 12 below).

Where the land has already been registered (see Note 7 below) and comprises the whole of the land in one or more register units, a plan is unnecessary provided the register and register unit number(s) are quoted at (d) and (e) of part 3 of the form. If the application concerns only part of the land in a register unit a plan may be dispensed with if the land can be described by reference to some physical feature such as a road, river or railway; the description might, for example, read 'The land in register unit No ..... lying to the south of the road from A to B'. Where this method is not practicable the land must be described by a plan prepared as mentioned above. Where the procedure of reference to an existing register unit is adopted, part 3 of the form should be adapted accordingly.

(b) For purposes of part 5. If the right is attached to any farm, holding or other land, that land must be described in part 5. This may be done either by a plan prepared as explained in (a) above, or, alternatively, by reference to the numbered parcels on the most recent edition of the ordnance map (quoting the edition), supplemented, where necessary to describe part of a parcel, or any land not numbered on the ordnance map, by a plan prepared in accordance with (a) above. Sufficient particulars of the locality must in any case be given to enable the land to be identified on the ordnance map. Where two plans accompany the application, a different colour should be used in each.

If the right is held in gross, that is, not attached to any land, that fact should be stated in part 5.

7   Inspection and search of registers

To ascertain whether land has been registered under the Act, anyone may inspect the registers free of charge at the office of the registration authority. Alternatively, an official certificate of search may be obtained from the registration authority. A requisition for such search must be made in writing on CR Form No 21, a separate requisition being required for each register. If the land is registered, the certificate will reveal the register unit number(s) and whether any rights of common and claims to ownership are registered.

8   Rights for limited periods: grazing rights

Certain rights of common (usually grazing rights) are not exercisable at all times but only during limited periods. In the case of a right of common to which this applies, full particulars must be given in part 4 of the period or periods during which the right is exercisable. Further, if the right (by whatever name it may be known) consists of or includes a right to graze animals, or animals of any class, the applicant must state at part 4 the number of animals, or the numbers of animals of different classes, to be entered in the register.

9   Date for part 6

The date to be entered in part 6 is the date on which the right of common first came into existence and became registrable as exercisable over the land described in part 3. If this date is before 3rd January 1970 the application cannot be entertained by the registration authority. Moreover, the land over which the right is exercisable must have become registrable under the Act after 2nd January 1970, whether it has in fact been so registered or not. If either the right or the land was registrable under the Act before 3rd January 1970 it is now too late to apply for the registration of either.

10   Grounds of application: evidence

In part 7 should beset out, as concisely as possible, a statement of the facts relied on to show that the right of common came into existence and became registrable on the date stated in part 6 (as to this date, see Note 9 above). The statement should include particulars of every Act of Parliament, statutory order, order of court, deed or other instrument, and of every act or event, which is material for the purpose. The registration authority has power to call for such further evidence in support of the application as it may reasonably require.

11   Supporting documents

The application must be accompanied by the original or (preferably) by a copy or sufficient abstract of every document relating to the matter which the applicant has in his possession or under his control, or of which he has a right to the production, with the exception of documents which he would not be obliged to abstract or produce to a purchaser under a contract for the sale of the right of common made otherwise than by correspondence and containing no stipulations as to title. The following are examples of documents which, under this rule, may normally be expected to be among the documents accompanying applications in the particular cases mentioned:–

(1)   Where the right is stated to have become exercisable by virtue of a private or local Act or of a statutory instrument, the award or other instrument of allotment (if any) made thereunder.

(2)   Where the right is stated to have become exercisable by a grant of rights of common, a copy of the deed of grant.

(3)   Where the right is stated to have become exercisable by prescription, and there is a declaration by a court of competent jurisdiction to that effect, an office copy of the order embodying that declaration. (In the absence of such a declaration, a claim based solely on the Prescription Act 1832 cannot be admitted, and a claim based on prescription otherwise than under that Act is unlikely to be admitted if any objection is received by the registration authority.

The foregoing list is not exhaustive and in special cases the applicant may need to consult the registration authority. Applicants are strongly recommended NOT to forward the original of any deed or other private document. Instead, a copy should be supplied, preferably indorsed with certificate signed by a solicitor that it has been examined against the original. The applicant should indicate, either on the copy itself or in part 9 of the application, as convenient, who has the original and where it may be inspected.

If for any reason a document cannot be produced, the fact should be mentioned in part 10 of the application, where particulars of the missing document should be given and its non-production accounted for.

The registration authority has power to call for such further evidence as it may reasonably require.

12   Statutory declaration

The statutory declaration must be made before a justice of the peace, commissioner for oaths or notary public. Any plan referred to in the statutory declaration must be marked as an exhibit and signed by the officer taking the declaration (initialling is insufficient). A plan is marked by writing on the face in ink an identifying symbol such as the letter 'A'. On the back of the plan should appear these words:–

This is the exhibit marked 'A' referred to in the statutory declaration of (name of declarant) made this (date) ………………….. 19 ….. before me,

(Signature and qualification)

If there is more than one plan care should be taken to choose a different letter for each.

13   Action by registration authority

The registration authority will on receipt of the application send an acknowledgement. If this is not received within 10 days the applicant should communicate with the authority. Unless the application has to be rejected after preliminary consideration, the registration authority will give publicity to it and will consider it further in the right of any objections which may be received. The applicant will be supplied with copies of all objections which fall to be considered and will have an opportunity of answering them. Later, the applicant will be informed whether the application has been accepted or rejected. If the application is accepted, and the land over which the right is exercisable is not already registered under the Act, this will be done, and, whether or not the land is already registered, the right of common will be registered and the applicant will be supplied with particulars of the registration. If the application is rejected, the applicant will be notified of the reasons for the rejection.

14   False statements

The making of a false statement for the purposes of this application may render the maker liable to prosecution.

Form 33

(Name of registration authority)

COMMONS REGISTRATION ACT 1965

Notice of application for registration of land claimed to have become

(common land) (a town or village green)(1) after 2nd January 1970

To every reputed owner, lessee, tenant or occupier of any part of the land described below, and to all others whom it may concern.

Application has been made to the registration authority, the (name and address of registration authority) by (name and address of applicant) under section 13 of the Commons Registration Act 1965 for the inclusion in the Register of (Common Land) (Town or Village Greens)(1) of the land described (at Annex A)(2) below, which it is claimed became (common land) (a town or village green)(1) on (date given in part 4 of Form 29 or 30) (in substitution for the land described at Annex B below, which, it is claimed, ceased to be (common land) (a town or village green)(1) on that date)(2), under and by virtue of (account of circumstances, etc., summarised from part 5 of Form 29 or 30).

The application, which includes a plan of ( ),(3) may be inspected at (address where application available) (and copies of the application and plan(s) may be inspected at the following local authority offices (insert names and addresses of concerned local authorities, if any)).(1)

If the registration authority is satisfied that the land described (at Annex A)(2) below has become (common land) (a town or village green)(1) as claimed, it will so register the land, and such registration will be conclusive evidence of the status of the land as at the date of registration. (The land described at Annex B below will then be removed from the register).(2)

Any person wishing to object to the registration of the land as (common land) (a town or village green)(1) (or to the removal from the register of the land described at Annex B below)(2) should send a written and signed statement of the facts on which he bases his objection to (name and address of registration authority) so as to arrive not later than(4)

Dated .... 19 .....

(Signature on behalf of registration authority) .

(ANNEX A)(2)

Description of the land claimed to have become (common land) (a town or village .... green)(1)

(ANNEX B)(2)

(Description of the land claimed to have ceased to be (common land) (a town or village green) (1) including a reference to the register unit number if the land is registered)(2)

> (1) Delete as necessary.
> (2) For substituted land cases only.
> (3) Insert 'the land proposed for registration' or, in a substituted land case where a plan of the taken land is also provided, 'both areas'.
> (4) Insert date in accordance with regulation 5(5).

Form 34

(Name of registration authority)

COMMONS REGISTRATION ACT 1965 Notice of application for registration of rights of common over land (registered) (claimed to be registrable) (under section 13 of the Act

To every reputed owner, lessee, tenant or occupier of any part of the land lastly described below, and to all others whom it may concern.

Application has been made to the registration authority, the (name of registration authority) for the registration under section 13 of the Commons Registration Act 1965 of the right(s) of common specified in Annex A below which (is)(are)(1) claimed by the (person) (persons respectively)(1named in the said Annex to be exercisable over the land described in Annex B below. The alleged origin of the right(s) is as stated in Annex A.

The application, (which includes a plan of) (and register unit No ….. in the Register of (Common Land) (Town or Village Greens) (1) which (comprises) (includes)(1)) (1) the land over which the right(s) (is)(are) claimed to be exercisable (and a plan or other description of the land to which they are attached)(1) may be inspected at (insert address where application etc. available) (and copies of the application and plan(s) may be inspected at the following local authority offices (insert names and addresses of concerned local authorities, if any))(1).

If the registration under the Act of (any of)(1) the said right(s) of common is effected, it will be conclusive evidence of the matters registered as at the date of registration.

(If any of the said rights are registered, the land over which the rights are exercisable will be registered also, and such registration will be conclusive evidence of the matters registered as at the date of registration.)(2)

Any person wishing to object to the registration of (any of)(2) the said right(s) of common (or to the registration of the said land)(1) should send a written and signed statement of the facts on which he bases his objection to (name and address of registration authority) so as to arrive not later than(3)

Dated ………………….. 19 …..

(Signature on behalf of registration authority)

ANNEX A

Description of the claimed right(s) of common

Name and address of claimant	Particulars of the claimed right of common	**Particulars of the land (if any) to which the right is alleged to be attached**	Alleged origin of the right

(1) Delete or adapt as necessary.
(2) For use only where the land has not yet been registered under section 13.
(3) Insert date in accordance with regulation 5(5).

ANNEX B

Description of the land over which the claimed rights are alleged to be exercisable

Form 35

(Name of registration authority)

COMMONS REGISTRATION ACT 1965

Notice of application for registration of a claim to the ownership of land registered under section 13 of the Act

To every reputed owner, lessee, tenant or occupier of any part of the land described below, and to all others whom it may concern.

Application has been made to the registration authority, the (name of registration authority) for the registration in the Register of (Common Land) (Town or Village Greens)(1) of (name and address) as owner of the land described below, which was registered as (common land) (a town or village green)(1) under Register unit No ..... on (date of registration) under section 13 of the Act.

The application, and the register unit affected, may be inspected at (insert address where register maintained) (and copies of the application alone may be inspected at the following local authority offices (insert names and addresses of concerned local authorities, if any))(1).

Any person wishing to object to the application should send a written and signed statement of the facts upon which he bases his objection to (name and address of registration authority) so as to arrive not later than(2)

Dated .... 19 ......

(Signature on behalf of registration authority)

DESCRIPTION OF THE LAND referred to above

(1)   Delete as necessary.
(2)   Insert date in accordance with regulation 5(5).

VEHICULAR ACCESS ACROSS COMMON AND OTHER LAND (ENGLAND) REGULATIONS 2002

SI 2002 No 1711

1 Title, commencement and extent

(1) These Regulations may be cited as the Vehicular Access Across Common and Other Land (England) Regulations 2002 and shall come into force on the day after the date on which they are made.

(2) These Regulations shall apply to land in England only.

(3) For the purposes of paragraph (2), 'land' means any land which is crossed by a way used as a means of access for vehicles to premises.

2 Interpretation

(1) In these Regulations –

'the Act' means the Countryside and Rights of Way Act 2000;

'the applicant', 'the land' and 'the land owner' have the meanings given in regulation 3(2);

'compensation sum' means the amount of compensation payable by the applicant;

'easement' means an easement subsisting at law for the benefit of the premises and giving a right of way for vehicles;

'the parties' means the applicant and the land owner and 'party' shall be construed accordingly;

'the premises' means the premises served by the way in respect of which an application for an easement is made;

'the value of the premises' has the meaning given in regulation 11(4).

(2) Any reference in these Regulations to a numbered regulation shall be construed as a reference to the regulation so numbered in these Regulations.

3 Entitlement to make an application

(1) An owner of any premises may, as respects a way to which section 68 of the Act applies, apply for the creation of an easement in accordance with these Regulations.

(2) For the purposes of these Regulations, the owner who makes an application shall be referred to as 'the applicant', the land crossed by the way shall be referred to as 'the land' and the person who, for the time being, has the freehold title to the land, shall be referred to as 'the land owner'.

4   Prescribed date

The prescribed date for the purpose of section 68(1)(b) of the Act is 5th May 1993.

5   Nature of easement

An easement created in accordance with these Regulations shall –

(a)   be subject to any limitation agreed by the parties or determined by the Lands Tribunal;

(b)   include any right incidental to the right of way agreed by the parties or determined by the Lands Tribunal; and

(c)   be subject to any rule of law which would apply to the easement had it been acquired by prescription.

6   Procedure for making an application

(1)   An application for the easement shall be made by the applicant serving a notice on the land owner.

(2)   The application must be served within 12 months of the date on which these Regulations come into force or, if later, the date on which the relevant use of the way has ceased.

(3)   The application shall contain the information specified in paragraph 1, and be accompanied by the information specified in paragraph 2, of the Schedule to these Regulations.

7   Unopposed applications

(1)   Where the land owner does not object to the application he shall, within three months of receipt of the application, serve a notice on the applicant, agreeing to the application.

(2)   The notice shall contain the following information –

(a)   the name and address of the land owner and a description of his interest in the land; and

(b)   a statement confirming that upon payment of the compensation sum he will provide a written receipt.

(3)   The notice shall be accompanied by evidence of the land owner's title to the land.

8   Opposed applications

(1)   Where the land owner has objections to the application, he shall, within three months of receipt of the application, serve a notice (a 'counter notice') on the applicant, objecting to the application.

(2)   Objections to the application may be made on the following grounds –

(a)   the applicant has served the application after the expiry of the period for service;

(b)   the applicant has not provided the information required by regulation 6(3);

(c)   information provided by the applicant is not correct;

(d)   the easement should be subject to limitations other than those (if any) described in the application;

(e)   any rights incidental to the right of way, which are described in the application as being rights which should be included in the easement, are not agreed;

(f)   the value of the premises is not agreed.

(3)   The counter notice shall contain the following information–

(a)   the name and address of the land owner and a description of his interest in the land;

(b)   the objections to the application; and

(c)   any alternative proposals.

(4)   The counter notice shall be accompanied by –

(a)   any evidence relevant to the objections and alternative proposals; and

(b)   evidence of the land owner's title to the land.

9   Amended application and amended counter notice

(1)   Within two months of receipt of a counter notice, the applicant may serve on the land owner an amended application addressing the objections and any alternative proposals set out in the counter notice.

(2)   An amended application shall contain the information specified in paragraph 1 of the Schedule to these Regulations and shall be accompanied by any evidence relevant to the applicant's response to the objections and any alternative proposals set out in the counter notice.

(3)   Where the applicant has served an amended application on the land owner, the land owner shall, within two months of receipt of the amended application –

(a)   serve a notice on the applicant agreeing to the amended application and confirming that upon payment of the compensation sum he will provide a written receipt, or

(b)   serve an amended counter notice on the applicant objecting to the amended application.

(4)   An amended counter notice shall comply with regulation 8(2), (3) and (4)(a) and, for this purpose –

(a)   references in regulation 8(2) and (3) to the application, except for the reference in sub-paragraph (a) of regulation 8(2), shall be treated as references to the amended application; and

(b)   an objection may also be made on the ground that the applicant has served the amended application after the expiry of the period for service or has not provided the information required by paragraph (2) of this regulation.

(5)   Where the land owner has served an amended counter notice on the applicant, the applicant may, within two months of receipt of the amended counter notice, serve a notice on the land owner agreeing to the amended counter notice.

10   Lands Tribunal

(1)   Where a counter notice has been served, either party may, where there is a dispute relating to any matter other than the value of the premises, request the Lands Tribunal to determine the matter in dispute by sending a notice of reference to the Lands Tribunal in accordance with the Lands Tribunal Rules 1996.

(2)   The notice of reference shall have annexed to it –

(a)   the application;
(b)   the counter notice; and
(c)   if applicable, the amended application and amended counter notice.

11   Calculation of the compensation sum

(1)   Subject to paragraph (2), the compensation sum shall be 2 per cent of the value of the premises.

(2)   Where the premises were in existence on –

(a)   31st December 1905; or
(b)   30th November 1930,

the compensation sum shall be 0.25 per cent. or 0.5 per cent. of the value of the premises respectively.

(3)   Where the premises are in residential use and replaced other premises on the same site which were also in residential use ('the former premises'), the compensation sum shall be calculated in accordance with paragraph (2) by reference to the date on which the former premises were in existence.

(4)   For the purposes of these Regulations, the value of the premises shall be calculated as at the valuation date on the basis of the open market value of the premises with the benefit of the easement.

(5)   In paragraph (4), the 'valuation date' means the date as at which the premises are valued for the purposes of the application, being a date no more than 3 months before the date on which the application is served.

12 Determination of the compensation sum in default of agreement

(1) Where no agreement can be reached on the value of the premises, either party may serve on the other a notice (the 'valuation notice') requiring the amount to be determined by a chartered surveyor.

(2) Where a valuation notice has been served, the appointment of a chartered surveyor shall be agreed by the parties within one month of the service of the valuation notice and, where agreement on such appointment cannot be reached, either party may request the President of the Royal Institution of Chartered Surveyors to appoint a chartered surveyor.

(3) Where a chartered surveyor has been appointed in accordance with paragraph (2), the following provisions shall apply as appropriate –

   (a) where the appointment has been made by the President of the Royal Institution of Chartered Surveyors, the parties shall be equally liable for the costs of that appointment;

   (b) unless the parties agree that the chartered surveyor shall act as an independent expert, he shall act as an arbitrator and the provisions of the Arbitration Act 1996 shall apply; and

   (c) where the chartered surveyor acts as an independent expert, the parties shall –

      (i) be bound by his final decision; and

      (ii) each party shall bear their own costs and shall be equally liable for the fees and costs of the chartered surveyor.

13 Payment of the compensation sum

(1) Where –

   (a) the land owner has notified the applicant in accordance with regulation 7 or 9(3)(a);

   (b) the applicant has notified the land owner in accordance with regulation 9(5); or

   (c) any matters in dispute have been determined in accordance with regulation 10 or 12,

the applicant shall pay the compensation sum to the land owner.

(2) The compensation sum shall be paid within two months of –

   (a) the date of notification under regulation 7 or paragraph (3)(a) or (5) of regulation 9, as the case may be; or

   (b) where a determination is made under regulation 10 or 12, the date of the determination or, if more than one such determination is made, the date of the last determination.

(3) The land owner shall, within one month from the date of receipt of the compensation sum, provide the applicant with a written receipt for that sum.

14   Payment into court

Where –

(a)   the land owner does not serve a notice in accordance with either regulation 7 or 8; or

(b)   the applicant has served an amended application on the land owner and the land owner fails to act in accordance with regulation 9(3),

the applicant may, within two months of the expiry of the period for service of a notice under regulation 7, 8 or 9(3), as the case may be, pay the compensation sum into a county court in accordance with the Court Funds Rules 1987.

15   Creation of the easement

Upon payment of the compensation sum either –

(a)   to the land owner in accordance with regulation 13; or

(b)   into court in accordance with regulation 14,

the easement shall be created.

16   Notices

(1)   A notice under these Regulations shall be in writing and may be served by sending it by post.

(2)   Where any notice is required by these Regulations to be served within a specified period, the parties may, except in the case of an application, agree in writing to extend or further extend that period.

17   Abandonment etc by applicant

Where the applicant withdraws or otherwise fails to continue with the application at any stage, he shall be liable for the reasonable costs incurred by the land owner.

SCHEDULE

INFORMATION TO BE PROVIDED BY THE APPLICANT

1   The application shall contain the following information –

(a)   the name and address of the applicant;

(b)   a description of the premises;

(c)   a description of the applicant's interest in the premises;

(d)   details of the current use of the premises and the use during the period giving rise to the entitlement to apply for the easement;

(e)   where the relevant use of the way has ceased, the date of the cessation;

(f) where the premises, or, where regulation 11(3) applies, the former premises, were in existence on 31st December 1905 or 30th November 1930, a statement confirming those facts;

(g) the nature of the use of the access, including any limitation or incidental right to which the easement should be subject or which should be included in the easement;

(h) the dimensions of the width of the way; and

(i) the proposed compensation sum to be paid to the land owner in respect of the easement, together with the basis on which it is calculated.

2 The application shall be accompanied by –

(a) a map of an appropriate scale (1:1250 or 1:2500) showing the premises (marked in blue), the way (marked in red) and sufficient other land to establish the exact location of the premises and the way in relation to the surrounding area;

(b) evidence (which may include a statutory declaration) that –

(i) the way is a way to which section 68 of the Act applies; and
(ii) where the application is served after 12 months of the date on which these Regulations come into force, either that the relevant use of the way has not ceased or that such use ceased no more than 12 months before the date on which the application is served; and

(c) an estimate prepared by a chartered surveyor of the value of the premises as at the valuation date, and 'valuation date' has the same meaning for this purpose as in regulation 11(4).

INDEX

References are to paragraph numbers.

Abandonment of rights 7.2.2
  presumption, when arises
    7.2.2
Abatement 5.3.4, 6.6.3(*c*), 6.6.4
  self-help, limitations 6.6.4
'Access land' 10.3–10.3.3, *see also*
  Access rights
Access rights 10.1 *et seq*
  common land, overview 1.2,
    11.2
  common law 10.2
    customary rights 9.4, 10.2.2
    easement of recreation
      10.2.1
    see also Custom/customary
      rights
  fencing, etc, impeding 6.6.3(*c*)
    consent for 1.8.2, 11.9.2
  local Acts 10.6
  National Parks 10.5.4, 11.2
  open country 10.3.1, 10.5.3
  payment to owner for 11.2
  public, on foot (CROW) 1.2,
    1.6, 8.5.2, 10.3, 11.8
    access land 10.3–10.3.3
    bylaws to regulate 10.3.5
    dogs 10.3.3, 11.8
    exceptions 10.3.2
    exclusion 10.3.3, 11.8
    general right 10.3.1
    land not being access land
      10.3.4
    mapping, duties and rights
      relating to, *see* Mapping
    repeal of LPA provision
      10.4
    restrictions, grounds for
      10.3.3, 11.8
  public, on foot (LPA 1925) 5.5,
    10.4–10.4.6

    borough or urban commons
      10.4.3
    'common' 10.4.1, 10.4.2
    driving vehicle, offence
      11.10
    'manorial waste' 10.4.1
    metropolitan commons
      10.4, 10.4.2, 12.4.1(*c*)
    registration of commons,
      effect of 10.4.6
    repeal of provision by
      CROW 10.4
    riding not included 10.4.5
    right of access, extent and
      limitations 10.4, 10.4.5
    rural common, deed of
      dedication 10.4.4,
      12.4.1(*c*)
  recreational use, for 10.5.1,
    10.5.2, 11.2
  'registered common land'
    10.3.1
  regulation, additional statutory
    10.5
  vehicular, *see* Vehicular access
  views, for 10.5.1
Acquisition of right 6.1 *et seq*
  custom, *see* Custom/customary
    rights
  grant, *see* Grant of right of
    common
  operation of law 4.2.3(*a*),
    4.3.1(*b*), 6.2.4, 6.4
  prescription, *see* Prescription
  reservation, *see* Reservation of
    right
  statute, under 6.1, 6.5, 8.6.1,
    8.7.2
Agricultural use
  see also Animals; Grazing right;
    Pasturage; Shack

Agricultural use – *cont*
  importance, historical   2.2.1
  management associations,
    proposals for   1.8.3(*b*)
Allotted land, *see* Green, town or
  village
Amendment of register, *see*
  Registration
Ancient monument site, access
  10.3.4
Animal(s)
  see Drive the common (animals);
    Pannage; Piscary;
    Shooting/game; Warren
  common of pasture appendant,
    types   4.3.1(*d*)
  cows, *see* Cattle
  fencing of, *see* Fencing
  husbandry, *see* Grazing right;
    Pasturage
  number of
    common of pasture
      appendant, limit for
      4.3.1(*c*)
    common of pasture in gross,
      for   4.3.4
    over-grazing problems
      11.7.3, 11.7.4
    registration of   4.1.1,
      4.3.2(*b*), 8.1, 8.4.6
    shack, for   3.3.3
    stints, *see* Stinted pasture
    too many, remedy   6.6.3(*b*)
    vicinage, limitation for
      4.2.2(*d*)
  protection of, *see* Site of Special
    Scientific Interest
  regulation of turning out right
    1.8.3(*b*), 11.5.1
  sheep, *see* Sheep
Appeal, *see* Mapping: Judicial
  Review: Registration
Appendant right, *see* Right of
  common
Approach of book   1.1
Approvement, right of   5.3.10,
  7.4.1

consent of Secretary of State
  7.4.1
  private Acts   7.4.1
Appurtenant right, *see* Right of
  common
Ashdown Forest   3.4
  see also Forest
  fencing   11.9.2
  local Act regulates   11.6

Beastgate   4.9.1, 4.9.6, 6.4, 8.2.2(*b*)
Bote
  meaning and types   1.3, 4.5
Box Hill Common   8.2.4
Bridleway   10.1
Building(s)
  compulsory acquisition, control
    after   7.3.1
  consent of Secretary of State to
    11.9.2
  land covered with/livestock
    pens, etc, CROW access
    exception   10.3.2
  obstruction, as   6.6.3(*c*)
  restrictions on   6.6.3(*c*), 11.9.2,
    11.11
  village/town green   9.6.4
Bylaws
  CROW, power in   10.3.5
  commons, as to   10.5.1, 10.5.2,
    11.5
  greens, as to   9.6.3(*a*)–(*c*)
  metropolitan commons, power
    11.4
  non-metropolitan commons,
    power   11.3

Car, *see* Vehicular access
Cattle   4.3.1(*d*), 4.5, *see also*
  Pasturage
Cattlegate   3.3.4, 4.9.1, 4.9.6, 6.4,
  8.2.2(*b*)
Church warden
  see also Parish council
  allotment of land to, on
    inclosure   7.4.2(*a*), 9.3, 9.6.1

Cliff/foreshore, *see* Sea

Common field system (historical)
2.2.3

Common land
background, *see* Historical
background
definition 1.2, 5.1, 6.1
compulsory acquisition, for
12.2.1
metropolitan common, *see*
Metropolitan commons
registration purposes 1.7,
3.2, 3.3.6, 8.2.2–8.2.4, 8.3
lease of, *see* Lease
new/land becoming,
registration of 6.1, 8.7.2,
8.7.4
ownership, and powers with
5.1 *et seq*
registration, *see* Registration
registration failure, ceasing to
be on 8.6.1
statistics and facts 1.5, 1.7
types 3.1 *et seq*

Common Land Policy Statement
(2002) 1.8.1, 1.8.3

Common law
enforceability of customary
law 6.2.1(*b*)
prescription at 6.2.4(*a*)

Commonable land
'commonable' 3.3.1
fencing 11.9.2
historical background 1.2
lands within 5.4
meaning 3.3.1
registration 1.2, 3.3.6
rights of common, owner
having 1.3

Commoners 1.3, *see also* Right of
common

Commons, *see* Common land

Commons association, *see*
Management

Commons Commissioners 8.6.2,
8.8
aggrieved person's right 8.8

Compensation

compulsory acquisition, on, for
commoners 12.5
disagreement settlement
12.5.4
effect of payment 12.5.1,
12.5.5
exchange land, relevance to
12.5.2
meeting/committee to
determine 12.5.1
owners of soil, commoners
are 12.5
public rights unaffected
12.5.5
valuation of rights 12.5.3
compulsory acquisition, on, for
freehold 12.4.1–12.4.3
owner of soil 12.4.1, 12.4.3
severance or injurious
affection 12.4.2
valuation of freehold 12.4.1
extinguishment of rights, on
7.3.1
inclosure, for 7.4.2(*a*)
management scheme, under
11.5
vehicular access easement 5.5

Compulsory acquisition 6.5, 7.1,
7.3.1, 12.1 *et seq*
building or works after,
controls 7.3.1
common land, procedure 12.2
'common' 12.2.1
compensation for freeholder
and commoners, *see*
Compensation
discharge of previous rights
12.2.2
exchange of land 8.7.2,
8.7.5, 12.2.1, 12.2.2, 12.5.2
exclusion of special
Parliamentary procedure
12.2.1
notice, public inquiry and
objections 12.2.1, 12.2.2
special Parliamentary
procedure 12.2, 12.2.3

Compulsory acquisition – *cont*
    improvement of management,
        for   12.2.1, 12.3
    local authority powers   7.3.1,
        12.1 *et seq*
    order for   12.1
    principles and purposes   12.1
    rights over commons, of   12.1,
        12.3
        additional land to
            compensate   12.3
        exclusion of special
            Parliamentary procedure
            12.3
        public inquiry, etc   12.2.1,
            12.3
    valuation for   12.4.1, 12.5.3
    'waste land of the manor', of
        8.2.4
Coney-burrow   5.3.6
Consent, ministerial, *see* Secretary
    of State
Conservation issues   1.8.3(*b*),
    11.7.3, 11.7.4
    compulsory purchase for
        preservation   12.2.1, 12.2.2
Copyholds, *see* Historical
    background
Couchancy   3.3.3, 4.3.2, 8.1
Council
    borough or urban council
        commons, access rights
            10.4.3
    district, model form of access
        scheme   10.5.2
    ownership of land
        commons, trustee status
            5.5
        greens   9.6.1
    parish, *see* Parish council
    registration authority   8.4.1
    urban district
        management powers, *see*
            Management
        nuisance prevention
            9.6.3(b)
Countryside Agency, *see* Mapping
Countryside Council, *see* Wales

Creation of rights   6.1, 6.2
    see also Acquisition of right
    methods of   8.7.2
    new right   8.7.2
Custom/customary rights   10.2.2
    access   9.4, 10.2.2
    acquisition of right by   4.2,
        4.2.1, 4.7, 6.1, 6.2.1
        conversion of customary
            rights of   6.2.1(*b*)
        copyholders and manorial
            courts   6.2.1(*a*)
        village green   9.4–9.4.4, *see*
            also Green, town or
            village
    enforceability
        common law   6.2.1(*b*),
            10.2.2
        customary court   6.2.1(*a*)
    existence date   6.2.1(*a*), 6.2.1(*b*)
    limitation of right by   5.3.9
    new, restriction on   6.2.1(*a*)
    requirements to establish
        9.4.1–9.4.3, 10.2.2
    time in existence (immemorial)
        9.4.2, 10.2.2, *see also* Time
    town or village green, as to use
        of, *see* Green, town or village
Customary freehold, *see* Historical
    background
Customary rights/court, *see*
    Custom/customary rights

Damage
    right of common, to   6.6.3–6.6.5
    soil, to, by commoner   6.6.2
Damages
    nuisance, for   6.6.3(*c*)
    surcharging to recover   6.6.3(*b*)
Dartmoor   4.3.2(*c*), 10.6
    local Act regulates   11.6
Deed
    grant of right by   6.2.2(*a*)
    transfer of right by   6.4
Deed of dedication   10.4.4, 10.5.3
Demesne land   3.2, 4.2

Dog
 restriction on, access land
  10.3.3, 11.8
Drainage 11.3, 11.5
 highway, compulsory purchase
  for 12.2.1, 12.3
Drive, right to/prohibition, *see*
 Vehicular access
Drive the common (animals) 5.3.8,
 5.3.9, 6.6.3(*b*)
Duck 5.3.6
Dwelling-house/ancillary land
 objection to registration 8.7.7

Easement 5.5
 claim for (vehicular access),
  CROW provision 5.5
   notices by landowner 5.5
   time-limits 5.5
 grant of 5.3.11
  express grant, restrictions on
   5.3.11
  implied 5.3.11
 overriding of 7.3.1
 preventing a wrong becoming
  6.6.3(*c*)
 profit à prendre compared 4.2.2
 recreation, of 10.2.1
 vehicular access, for 1.8.3(*b*)
English Nature, *see* Site of Special
 Scientific Interest
Epping Forest 3.3.4, 3.4, 8.4.5, 10.6
 local Act regulates 11.6
Estovers 4.5
 extent 6.6.1
 scope 4.5
Exchange of land 8.7.2, 8.7.5,
 12.2.1, 12.2.2
 amendment of register 8.7.5
 certificate 12.2.1, 12.2.2, 12.5.2
 compensation to commoners,
  and 12.5.2
 'equally advantageous' 12.2.1
 vesting and rights in 12.2.2
Extinguishment of rights 7.1 *et seq*
 amendment of register 8.7.5
 express 7.2.3

non-registration, and 7.3.2
non-use or abandonment 7.2.2

statute, by 7.3, *see also*
 Compulsory acquisition
unity of ownership 7.2.1

Fencing 11.9
 consent requirement 11.9.2
  extension proposal 1.8.2
 duty to fence 11.9.1
 obstruction, as 6.6.3(*c*)
 right 11.9.2
 village green 9.6.4, 10.2.2
Feudal system, *see* Historical
 background
Fish 4.6
Flora and fauna, protection of
 11.7–11.7.4
Foldage 4.3.5
Footpath, public 10.1
Forest
 meaning and background 3.4
 pannage, time of 4.8
 registration exemptions 8.4.5
 Royal 3.4
  rights of common over land
   in 3.4
Forest of Dean 3.4, 8.4.5, *see also*
 Forest
Fraud 8.7.6
Free fold 4.3.5
Freehold 1.3

Game, *see* Shooting/game; Warren
Garden, public 12.2, 12.2.1
Gated
 meaning 3.3.4
Gated pasture
 inclosure of 7.4.2(a)
Grant of right of common 4.2,
 4.2.1, 4.2.3(a)–(c)
 contract or agreement to grant
  6.2.2(*a*)
 express 6.2.2
  formalities for 6.2.2(*a*)

Grant of right of common – *cont*
  express – *cont*
    grantor, competence
      required   6.2.2(*b*)
    land not registered as
      commons, over   6.3.2
    new grant (after 1970)
      8.7.2
    registered commons, over,
      position as to   6.3.1
  implied, *see* Prescription
  registered commons, over
    6.3.1
Grazing right
  see also Pasturage
  background   2.5, 4.1
  exclusive   6.2.2(*c*)
  grant, right to   5.3.2, 5.3.9, 5.5
  interference with   6.6.3(*a*)
  management associations
    proposed   1.8.3(*b*)
  owner of commons   11.2
  registration of, and number of
    animals   4.1, 8.4.6
  right in gross   1.8.3(*b*), 4.2.3(*c*)
  SSSI designation, effect on
    11.7.3
  severance   11.7.3
  unregistered right   4.1
  vicinage, by reason of   4.2.3(*d*),
    6.6.3(*b*)
Green, town or village   9.1 *et seq*
  allotment of/allotted land
    7.4.2(*a*), 9.3, 9.6
    effect of allotment   9.3
    nuisances and offences
      9.6.3(*d*), 9.6.4
  buildings and works on   9.6.4
  compulsory acquisition,
    procedure   12.2.1, *see also*
    Compulsory acquisition
  customary rights   8.3, 9.1, 9.4
    allotted land having   9.3
    characteristics of   9.4
    deficiencies in requirement
      for   9.4.4, 9.5.1
    enforcement   6.2.1(*b*), 9.4

  establishing, requirements
    for   9.4.1–9.4.3
  immemorial, reasonable and
    continuous existence
    9.4, 9.4.2
  local community, exercise
    in relation to 'locality' by
    9.4, 9.4.1
  recognition at common law
    9.4
  recreational activities within
    9.4.3
  registration basis   8.7.3,
    9.2.1, 9.2.2
  sports and pastimes, to
    indulge in   9.4
  driving vehicle on, offence
    9.6.5
  fences   9.6.4, 10.2.2
  historical background   9.1
  inclosure exclusion   7.4.2(*a*)
  land becoming, after 1970   8.7.2
  meaning   1.4
  management provisions
    applicable   9.6.3(*a*)–(*d*)
  manorial waste, part of   9.1, 9.4
  new   9.2.3
  not common land   8.3
  unclaimed land   8.6.2
  ownership
    local authority   8.6.2, 9.6.1
    parish council/church
      warden   7.4.2(*a*), 9.3,
      9.6.1
    registration of   9.6.1
  parking on   1.8.3(*a*), 9.6.4, 9.6.5
  proposals as to   1.8.3
  public rights, whether exist
    8.5.2, 8.7.2, 10.2
  recreational activities, range
    1.4, 9.4.3, 9.5.6
  registration   1.4, 8.1, 8.2.1, 8.3,
    9.2.1, 9.6.1
    amendments, non-statutory
      inquiry or hearing prior
      to   9.2.3
    bases for   9.2.1
    challenge to decision   9.2.3

Green, town or village – *cont*
  registration – *cont*
    classification for....9.2.1
    custom, based on, *see*
      'customary rights' *above*
    definition for 8.3, 9.2.1
    non-registration, effect on
      status 9.2.2
    separate register, duty to
      maintain 8.4.2, 9.2.1
    twenty year user basis, *see*
      'sports and pastimes, use
      for' *below*
  rights of common, subject to
    9.1, 9.4, 9.6.2
    conflict of rights/rights
      prevailing 9.6.2
  sports and pastimes, use for
    9.2.1, 9.4.4, 9.5
    activities within scope
      9.5.6
    'as of right' 9.5.4
    'composite class' 9.5.6
    continuing use 9.5.5
    effect of registration on basis
      of 8.5.2, 8.7.2, 9.2.2,
      9.5.7
    implied permission,
      effect of 9.5.4
    'locality', or neighbourhood
      within 9.5.3
    obstruction 9.6.4
    period of use 9.2.1, 9.5
    predominant use 9.5.3
    reason for amending
      provision 9.5.1
    significant number of
      inhabitants, by 9.5.2
    toleration of 9.5.4
Gross, rights in 1.8.3(*b*), 4.2.3(*c*),
  4.3.4, 6.1
  appurtenant rights becoming
    6.4

Half-year lands 3.3.2
Hare 5.3.6
Hay-bote 4.5

Herbage, *see* Sole, rights of
Hereditament, *see* Incorporeal
  hereditament
High Court
  case stated for, where error of
    law 8.8
  judicial review 8.7.4
  rectification of register, order
    for 8.7.4, 8.7.6
Highway 8.3, 10.1
  creating, widening, etc,
    compulsory purchase for
      12.1, 12.2.1, 12.3, *see also*
      Compulsory acquisition
Historical background 1.6, 2.1
  et seq, 3.1
  copyholds 4.2.1, 4.3.2(*a*), 5.1,
    6.1
    abolition, effect of 6.2.1(*b*)
    custom, rights by 6.2.1(*a*)
    part of land within manor
      8.2.4
  customary freeholds 4.2.1,
    4.3.2(*a*), 5.1, 6.1
  forests, *see* Forest
  freeholds 4.2.1
  inclosure, *see* Inclosure
  management 11.1
  manors, *see* Manor(s); Manorial
    waste
  post-Conquest 2.3
    approvement of common
      land 2.3.2
    feudal system 2.3
    manorial courts, regulation
      by 2.3.1, 6.2.1(*a*), 11.1
    private commons ownership
      2.3
  pre-Conquest 2.2
    agricultural practices,
      significance 2.2.1,
      2.2.1(a)
    Anglo-Saxon period 2.2.3
    Celtic times, crop rotation in
      2.2.2
    co-operation, necessity of
      2.2.1(a), 2.2.2
    inter-commoning 2.2.1(c)

Historical background – *cont*
  pre-Conquest – *cont*
    limitation of common rights
      2.2.3
    open-field system   2.2.1(b),
      2.2.3, 3.3.1, 5.4
    Roman invasion, effect of
      2.2.2
    restriction on customary
    rights/rights of common
      2.4.1, 2.5
    towns, nineteenth century
      growth of   2.5
    village/town greens   9.1
Horse–riding
  see also Bridleway
  not allowed   10.4.5
House-bote   4.5
Hunting
  Royal rights   3.4

Improvement
  compulsory purchase for
    improvement of
      management   12.2.1,
        12.2.2, 12.3
  provision or scheme for   11.3,
    11.4, 11.5
Inclosure   2.4, 3.3.5, 6.5, 7.1, 7.4
  see also Approvement, right of
  allotment of land   7.4.2(*a*),
    9.3, 9.6
  application   7.4.2(*a*)
  approval   7.4.2
  benefit of neighbourhood,
    provisions for   7.4.2(*b*)
  compensation   7.4.2(*a*)
  consequences   2.4.1
  excluded land   7.4.2(*a*)
  horse and sheep, effects of rise
    of   2.4.1
  land capable of   7.4.2(*a*)
  post-1845   7.4.2
  pre-1845   7.4.1
  present climate   7.4.2(*c*)
  regulated pasture provisions,
    See Regulated pasture

restrictions on   2.5, 7.4.2(*b*)
Incorporeal hereditament   1.3,
  4.2.2, 5.2, 6.4
Injurious affection
  compulsory acquisition,
    compensation for   12.4.2
Interference, *see* Damages;
  Obstruction; Right of common

Judicial review   8.7.4

Lammas lands   3.3.2, 5.4
  meaning and rights over   3.3.2
  registration   8.2.3
Land Registry, registration with
  no duplication with Commons
    registration   8.4.7, 8.7.4
  overriding interests   8.7.4
Lease
  grant of *profit à prendre* by
    leaseholder   6.2.2(*b*)
  land to which rights of common
    attached, over   7.2.1
  leasehold estate   1.3
  power   5.3.1, 5.3.9
  rights attached, exclusion from
    registration   8.2.2(*b*)
Legal estates   1.3
Legal interest
  right of common as   1.3, 4.2.2,
    6.2.2(*a*)
    formal requirements
      6.2.2(*a*)
Legal memory   6.2.1(*a*), 6.2.1(*b*),
  6.2.4(*a*), 9.4, 9.4.2, 10.2.2
Levancy   3.3.3, 4.3.2, 8.1
Licence   5.3
Local authority
  see also Council; Parish council
  compulsory purchase
    powers, *see* Compulsory
      acquisition
  open spaces management
    powers   9.6.3(*c*)

Local authority – *cont*
  owner
    commons, of, and
      management policies
      11.2
    unclaimed green,
      registration as 8.6.2,
      9.6.1
  protective powers over
    unclaimed commons 8.6.3
London
  council, registration as green
    owner 8.6.2, 9.6.1
  land near, inclosure exclusion
    7.4.2(*a*)
  registration authority in 8.4.1
Lord of the manor
  management through steward
    and courts 11.1
  meaning 5.3
  ownership of soil of common
    5.3
    compensation on
      compulsory acquisition
      12.4.1–12.4.3
    rights and powers incidental
      to 5.3.1–5.3.11
  Lost modern grant 6.2.4(*b*)

Management 9.6.3, 11.1 *et seq*
  see also Regulated pasture
  access exclusion or restriction
    for period 11.8
  commons association 1.8.3(*b*),
    11.7.4
    model constitution 11.7.4
  greens, town or village 9.6.3
  local authority policies and
    powers 11.2
  local regulation 11.4, 11.6
  metropolitan commons
    9.6.3(*a*), 11.4
  non-metropolitan commons
    regulation procedure 11.3
  'open spaces' 9.6.3(*c*)
  owner's interest in 11.2
  proposals 1.8.3(*b*)

  urban district council regulation
    powers 9.6.3(*b*), 11.5
    improvement schemes 11.5
    turning out of animals
      11.5.1
Manor(s) 1.2
  courts 2.3.1, 6.2.1(*a*)
  creation of 2.3
  land within 3.2, 4.2, 8.2.4
  landownership
    forms 4.2.1
    lord's ownership and
      incidental rights 5.2
  see also Lord of the manor
Manorial court 2.3.1, 6.2.1(*a*), 11.1
Manorial waste 3.2, 4.2
  'common land' 8.2.2, 8.2.4
  inclosure of, *see* Inclosure
  lease, and effect of 5.3.1, 5.3.9
  meaning 8.2.4
  not subject to rights of common
    8.2.4
  public access, LPA provision
    10.4, 10.4.1, *see also* Access
    rights
  registration 3.2, 8.2.4
    background 3.2
  rights over 3.2
    shooting/game, grant of
      5.3.5, 5.3.9
  'waste land of the manor' 8.2.4
Manuring 4.2.3(*a*), 4.3.1(*d*), 11.3
Mapping
  duty under CROW 10.3,
    10.3.2, 10.3.6
    'access land', of 10.3.1
    appeal right and procedure
      10.3.10
    conclusive form 10.3.11
    confirmation of map 10.3.9
    consultations 10.3.8
    provisional form, issue in
      10.3.6, 10.3.9
    representations 10.3.7
    review, periodic 10.3.11
Marl 4.7, 4.9.5
Mast 4.8

Metropolitan commons 7.4.2(*a*)
　　7.4.2(*c*)
　　management of, provisions for
　　　9.6.3(*a*)
　　meaning 9.6.3(*a*), 11.4
　　public access 12.4.1(*c*)
　　　LPA provision 10.4, 10.4.2
　　　see also Access rights
　　regulation of 11.4
Military, land used by 10.3.2
Minerals 4.7, 5.3.7
　　extraction 5.3.7, 5.3.9
　　land used for getting up 10.3.2
Moor 10.5.3, *see also* Dartmoor;
　　Uplands

National Park 10.5.3, 11.2
National Trust
　　duty as to commons 11.11
Nature reserve 11.7, *see also* Site of
　　Special Scientific Interest
New Forest 8.4.5
　　local Act regulates 11.6
Non-user of rights 7.2.2
Nuisance
　　abatement action 5.3.4, 6.6.3(*c*)
　　allotted land, on, offence
　　　9.6.3(*d*)
　　prevention, UDC powers
　　　9.6.3(*b*)
　　self-abatement 5.3.4, 6.6.4
　　　cases for use 6.6.4
　　　limitations as to use 6.6.4

Obstruction 6.6.3(*c*), 9.6.4, *see also*
　　Nuisance
Open country
　　access on foot to 10.3.1, 10.5.3,
　　　11.2, *see also* Access rights
　　mapping 10.3.6
　　　appeal 10.3.10
　　　see also Mapping
Open-field system 2.2.1(b), 2.2.3,
　　3.3.1, 5.4
　　modern day examples 5.4
Open spaces

compulsory acquisition, and
　　definition for 12.2, 12.2.1
management powers 9.6.3(*c*),
　　see also Management
Operation of law, *see* Acquisition of
　　rights
Ownership issues 4.2.1, 5.2 *et seq*
　　compulsory acquisition
　　　compensation 12.4.1–12.4.3
　　dwelling-house/ancillary land,
　　　objection to registration
　　　8.7.7
　　easements, grant of, *see*
　　　Easement fencing duty,
　　　land adjoining common
　　　11.9.1
　　grazing for animals of owner
　　　5.3.3, 5.3.9
　　greens, *see* Green, town or
　　　village land adjacent to
　　　commons
　　　fencing duty 11.9.1
　　　vehicular access 1.8.3(*b*),
　　　　5.5
　　local authority as owner 11.2
　　management scheme, objections
　　　to 11.5
　　merging of rights on single
　　　ownership 7.2.1, 8.7.5
　　public use, and 10.1
　　reference to Commons
　　　Commissioner, unclaimed
　　　land 8.6.2
　　registration, *see* Registration
　　removal of rights from register,
　　　owner's application 8.7.5
　　rights incidental to
　　　5.3.1–5.3.11, 5.5
　　soil of common, owner of 5.3
　　　management powers 11.2

Pannage 1.3, 4.8
　　time of 4.8
Parish council
　　open spaces/greens,
　　　management powers
　　　9.6.3(*c*)

Parish council – *cont*
  ownership
    common, trustee status   5.5
    green   9.6.1
Parking
  village green, on, *see* Green,
    town or village
Partridge   5.3.6
Pastimes (customary right), *see*
Green, town or village
Pasturage   4.3
  abandonment   7.2.2
  appendant   4.2.3(*a*), 4.3.1, 4.3
    background and
      characteristics
      4.3.1(*b*)–(*e*)
    number of animals,
      limitation   4.3.1(*c*)
    registration, effect of
      4.3.1(*a*)
    type of animals, limitation
      4.3.1(*d*)
  appurtenant   4.2.3(*b*), 4.3.2
    creation   4.3.2(*b*)
    number of animals   4.3.2(*b*)
    registration   4.3.2(*b*)
    severance   11.7.3
    who could exercise   4.3.2(*a*)
  extent   6.6.1
  foldcourse, right of   4.3.5
  forests, rights in   3.4
  forms   4.3
  herbage contrasted   4.9.3
  in gross   4.2.3(*c*), 4.3, 4.3.4
    number of animals
      4.3.4
  meaning   4.3
  regulated   3.3.5, 3.3.6
  shepherding by vehicle,
    incidental   4.3
  sole right distinguished
    4.9.1
  stinted, *see* Stinted pasture
  vicinage, by reason of
    4.2.3(*d*), 4.3, 4.3.3
    nature of   4.2.3(*d*), 4.3.3
    registration   4.3.3
    termination of   4.3.3

Pasture
  consumption of   6.6.3(*c*)
  ownership of soil, and right
    to/right to licence   5.3, 11.2
  regulated, *see* Regulated pasture
  right of common, *see* Pasturage
  sole right in   4.9.1, 4.9.4–4.9.6
  stint/stinted, *see* Stinted pasture
Pavilion, sports   9.6.4
Peat   4.4
Pheasant   5.3.6
Pigs, *see* Pannage
Pipes and cables, *see* Wayleave
Piscary   1.3, 4.6
  nature of/creation of   4.6
Planning
  appropriation by authority, and
    consent to   7.3.1
  compulsory purchase by
    authority, *see* Compulsory
    acquisition
  permission, mineral extraction
    5.3.7
Plough or cart-bote   4.5
Prescription   6.2.4
  acquisition of right by   4.2,
    4.2.2, 4.2.3(*a*)–(*c*), 4.3.4,
    6.2.4
    appendant rights not so
      acquirable   6.2.4
    common in the soil   4.7
    common law, claim at and
      defeat of   6.2.4(*a*)
    Commons Registration Act,
      effect   6.3.3
    customary right acquisition
      distinguished   6.2.4
    land not registered as
      commons   6.3.2(*b*)
    lost modern grant
      doctrine   6.2.4(*b*)
    periods for   6.2.4(*a*), (*b*), (*c*)
    piscary, common of   4.6
    Prescription Act, claim
      under   6.2.4(*c*)
    registered common, over
      6.3.3(*a*)
    requirements, general   6.2.4

Prescription – *cont*
   acquisition of right by – *cont*
      unlawful acts, no acquisition
         from   6.2.4(*b*), 9.6.5
      vehicular right of way   5.5
   limitation of right by   5.3.9
   new right arising by,
      registration of   8.7.2
Profit à prendre
   contract to grant   6.2.2(*a*)
   equitable interest   6.2.2(*a*)
   legal interest, formalities for
      6.2.2(*a*)
   meaning   4.2.2, 4.9.5, 5.5
   right of common as   1.3, 4.2,
      4.2.2, 6.2.2(*a*)
      sole profit not   4.9.5, 6.2.2(*a*)
   shooting right is   5.3.5, 5.5
Public rights
   access, *see* Access rights;
   Highway town or village green
      8.5.2, 8.7.2

Quarry, *see* Minerals

Rabbit   5.3.6
Recreation
   easement of   10.2.1
   historical background   2.5
   neighbourhood schemes
      10.5.1, 10.5.2, *see also*
      Green, town or village
   public, *see* Access rights
Rectification of register, *see*
   Registration
Reform proposals   1.8
Registers
   commons, *see* Registration
   land, *see* Land Registry,
      registration with
   'Registered common land'
      access rights (CROW), for
      10.3.1
Registration   8.1 *et seq*
   amendment or variation   6.3.1,
      7.1

circumstances for   8.7–8.7.5,
      9.2.3
fraud or error, on   8.7.6
non-statutory inquiry or
      hearing   8.8, 9.2.3
order of High Court for
      rectification   8.7.4, 8.7.6
appeal   8.6.1, 8.8
application   8.4.3
   notification of   8.4.4
authorities   8.4.1
background   1.7, 6.1
common land   8.1, 8.2.1, 8.4.2
   definition   8.2.2
Commons Commissioners
      8.6.2, 8.8
   error of law, aggrieved
      person's right   8.8
continuing obligation   8.2.1
definitions for   1.7, 6.4,
      8.2.2–8.2.4, 8.3
deletion of entry on Land
      Registry registration   8.4.7
de-registration grounds   1.8.1
   restriction proposed   1.8.1
effects of   8.5
   conclusive evidence   8.5.2
excluded rights   8.2.2(*b*)
exempted land   8.4.5
failure, effect of   6.1, 6.2.1(*a*),
      7.3.2, 8.2.1, 8.6
failure to appeal, effect of
      6.2.4(*b*)
'final'   8.4.3, 8.5.2
inaccuracy of registers   11.7.4
introduction of   1.6, 1.7
land ceasing to be common land
      8.7.5
Land Registry, *see* Land
      Registry, registration with
land subject to rights of
      common   3.1 *et seq*, 6.1,
      8.2.2, 8.2.3
lost modern grant doctrine, and
      6.2.4(*b*)
new land or rights, position as
      to   6.3.1–6.3.3, 8.1, 8.2.1,
      8.7.2

Registration – *cont*
  new land or rights, position as
    to – *cont*
    acceptance of application
      8.7.4
    notification and objections
      period 8.7.4
    previously registered land
      8.7.2
    rejection of application,
      remedy 8.7.4
  numbers of animals 4.1.1,
    4.3.2(*b*), 8.1, 8.4.6
  objections to 8.4.3, 8.4.4, 8.5.1,
    8.5.2, 8.6.1
    Commissioners dealt with
      8.8
    fraud inducing objector to
      withdraw 8.7.6
  ownership 8.1, 8.2.1
    changes in 11.7.4
  procedure 8.4
  'provisional' 8.4.3, 8.5.1
    extinguishment on objection
      8.6.1
    notification of owner 8.7.7
  rectification, *see* 'amendment or
    variation' *above*
  regulated pasture 11.3
  removal of entry 8.7.5, *see also*
    'amendment or variation'
    above
  rights of common 8.1, 8.2.1
    definition 8.2.2(*b*)
    new common land, over
      8.7.2
    over registered commons, of
      6.3.1
    variation of 8.7.5
  town or village green, *see* Green,
    town or village
  transfer of registered right 6.4
  waste land of manor, *see*
    Manorial waste
Registration (Land Registry), *see*
  Land Registry, registration with
Regulated pasture 3.3.5, 3.3.6, 11.3
  effect of award of 11.3

fencing 11.9.2
ownership 11.3
registration, position as to 11.3
Regulation, *see* Management
Reservation of right 6.1, 6.2.3,
  6.2.3
  circumstances 6.2.3
  deed of conveyance, in 6.2.3
  new right 8.7.2
Right of common
  abandonment 7.2.2
  acquisition, *see* Acquisition of
    rights; Prescription
  adjustment, order providing for
    11.3
  appendant 4.2.3, 4.2.3(*a*), 4.3.1,
    6.1
    transfer 6.4
  appurtenant 4.2.3, 4.2.3(*b*),
    4.3.2, 6.1
    exclusive grazing right
      cannot be 6.2.2(*c*)
    severance 6.4
    transfer 6.4
  background 4.1.1, 4.2.1
  classification and types 4.1
    et seq
  conservation issues,
    reconciliation with 1.8.3(*b*),
    11.7.3, 11.7.4
  creation 6.1, 6.2
    effect of Commons
      Registration Act 6.3
    see also Acquisition of rights
  customary, *see*
    Custom/customary rights
  definition 1.7, 8.2.2
  examples 1.3
  extent 6.6.1
  extinguishment, *see*
    Extinguishment of rights
  forests 3.4
  holder
    historical 1.3
    'occupier' 11.7.3
  in gross 4.2.3, 4.2.3(*c*), 6.1
    appurtenant rights
      becoming 6.4

Right of common – *cont*
  incorporeal hereditament, as
      4.2.2, 5.2, 6.4
  interference with, remedies
      6.6.3–6.6.5
    abatement, *see* Abatement
    obstructions 6.6.3(*c*), *see*
        also Nuisance
  statutory offences 6.6.5
  too many animals, surcharging
      right 6.6.3(*b*)
    types of interference
        6.6.3(*a*)
  land subject to, as 'common
      land' 3.1 *et seq*, 6.1, 8.2.2,
      8.2.3
  legal interest, as 1.3, 4.2.2,
      6.2.2(*a*), 6.6
    formalities for 6.2.2(*a*)
  limitations 6.6.1
  limited periods, exercisable for
      8.2.3
  meaning, background 1.3
  new, express grant of 6.1,
      6.3.1, 6.3.2
    land not registered as
        commons 6.3.2
    registered commons, over,
        whether possible 6.3.1
  new, implied grant of
      (prescription) 6.3.3
  overriding, statutory powers
      7.3.1
  owner's rights 5.3.3, 5.3.9
  protection/remedies 6.1, 6.6
  registration, *see* Registration
  registration failure, not
      exercisable after 8.6.1
  subject matter of 4.3–4.9
    removal of/consumption of
        6.6.3(*c*)
    see also Estovers; Pannage;
        Pasturage; Piscary; Soil;
        Turbary
  suspension 7.2.1
  termination, *see* Extinguishment
      of rights
  transfer, *see* Transfer of right

  unregistered 4.1, 4.2.3
  vicinage, by reason of 4.2.3,
      4.2.3(*d*), 6.1
    limitation of number of
        animals 4.2.3(*d*)
Right of way
  grant over common land,
      difficulties 5.5
  non-user 7.2.2
  vehicular
    CROW provision for
        easement 1.8.3(*b*), 5.5
    offence 5.5
River
  fishing rights 4.6
Road 5.5, *see also* Highway
Royal Commission Report 1.6, 2.1,
    2.2.1(c), 2.2.3, 2.3, 2.4.1, 8.1
Royal forests 3.4, 4.8, 8.4.5
  rights of common over 3.4
Rural White Paper (2000) 1.8.1

Sand 4.7, 4.9.5
Sea
  foreshore/cliff 10.5.3
  waste lands adjoining,
      boundary 3.2
Secretary of State
  compulsory acquisition,
      certificate excluding special
      procedure 12.2.1
  consent of, circumstances for
      1.8.2, 7.3.1, 7.4.1, 11.9.2
Self-help, *see* Abatement
Several owner 5.4, 6.2.2(*a*), *see also*
    Sole, rights of
Severance compensation
  compulsory acquisition, on
      12.4.2
Severance of grazing/pasture
    rights 11.7.3
Shack 3.3.3, 5.4
Sheep
  see also Fencing; Grazing right;
      Pasturage
  common of pasture appendant
      4.3.1(*d*)

Sheep – *cont*
   rise in sheep farming (historical)
      2.4.1
   sheep heaves   3.3.4
   sheepwalk   4.3.5
Shooting/game
   owner's rights/grant of rights
      4.9.1, 5.3, 5.3.5, 5.3.9, 5.5
Site of Special Scientific Interest
   11.7
   English Nature, powers   11.7.1,
      11.7.3
   grazing rights, effect of
      designation on   11.7.3
   notification of intended
      operations   11.7
      effect of   11.7.1
      'occupier', scope   11.7.3
   severed grazing rights,
      problems with   11.7.3
   special order for specific plant
      or animal   11.7.2
Soil
   common in   1.3, 4.7, 10.1
      nature of/creation of   4.7
   damage to, during exercise of
      rights   6.6.2
   ownership of, common land
      5.3, *see also* Ownership
         issues
   sole profit, effect of grant of
      4.9.1
   sole rights   4.9.5, 5.3
      vesture   4.9.2
Sole profit, *see* Sole, rights of
Sole, rights of   4.9, 6.2.2(*a*)
   herbage   4.9.3, 4.9.5, 4.9.6, 5.3
   land exercised over   4.9.6
   lease of   8.2.2(*b*)
   meaning and grant of   4.9.1
   pasture   4.9.1, 4.9.4–4.9.6, 5.3
   profit à prendre sole   4.9.5,
      6.2.2(*a*)
   registration   4.9.6, 6.4, 8.2.2(*b*)
   right of common, as   8.2.2(*b*)
   vesture   4.9.2, 4.9.5, 4.9.6
Sports or pastimes, land used for,
   see Green, town or village

Statute
   creation of rights by   6.1, 6.5,
      8.6.1, 8.7.2
   extinguishment of rights by
      7.3, *see also* Compulsory
         acquisition
Statutory undertaking   10.3.2
Stinted pasture   3.3.4
   fencing   11.9.2
   inclosure of   7.4.2(*a*)
   stint   4.9.1, 4.9.4, 8.2.2(*b*)
Stone   4.7
Substitution of land, *see* Exchange
   of land

Telecommunications apparatus
   10.3.2
Tenancy, *see* Lease
Termination of rights, *see*
   Extinguishment of rights
Timber, *see* Bote; Estovers; Tree
Time
   immemorial, *see* Legal memory
   rights of common at certain
      times of year   3.3, 8.2.3
   prescription, minimum for
      6.2.4(*a*), (*b*), (*c*)
   recreational use of green, for
      registration purposes   9.2.1
Town green, *see* Green, town or
   village
Transfer of right   6.1, 6.4
   appendant or appurtenant
      rights   6.4
Tree
   felling   5.3.4, 5.3.9
   nuisance   5.3.4
   planting   5.3.4, 5.3.9, 11.3
Turbary   1.3, 4.4
   extent   6.6.1
Turf   4.4

Unclaimed land
   common land, protective
      powers   8.6.3

Unclaimed land – *cont*
town or village green   8.6.2,
9.6.1
Unitary authority   8.4.1
Unity of ownership   7.2.1, 8.7.5
Uplands   10.3.1, 10.5.3, *see also*
Grazing right; Pasture

Vehicular access
CROW provision for, common
land   1.8.3(*b*), 5.5
compensation and disputes
procedure   5.5
time-limits   5.5
prohibition/offences   5.5, 9.6.5,
11.10
right of way acquired by user,
CA case   5.5
village/town green, parking on
9.6.4, 9.6.5
Vesture, *see* Sole, rights of
Vicinage, *see* Right of common

Village green, *see* Green, town or
village

Wales
access to district council
common, model form
10.5.2
mapping duty (Countryside
Council)   10.3.6, 10.3.11
appeals   10.3.10
Site of Special Scientific
Interest(Countryside
Council)   11.7.1
Warren   5.3.6
grant of free warren   5.3.6, 5.3.9
Waste land
see also Manorial waste
meaning   8.2.4, 10.4.1
Wayleave
grant of   5.3.11
Wood, *see* Estovers; Tree
Woodland
exchange land   12.2.1